STATISTICS FOR SIX SIGMA GREEN BELTS
WITH MINITAB® AND JMP™

STATISTICS FOR SIX SIGMA GREEN BELTS

WITH MINITAB® AND JMP™

David M. Levine

PEARSON PRENTICE HALL
AN IMPRINT OF PEARSON EDUCATION

Upper Saddle River, NJ • Boston • Indianapolis • New York • London
San Francisco • Toronto • Sydney • Tokyo • Singapore • Hong Kong
Cape Town • Madrid • Paris • Milan • Munich • Amsterdam

Publisher: Tim Moore
Executive Editor: Jim Boyd
Editorial Assistant: Susan Abraham
Director of Marketing and Associate Editor-in-Chief: Amy Neidlinger
International Marketing Manager: Tim Galligan
Cover Designer: Chuti Prasertsith
Managing Editor: Gina Kanouse
Project Editor: Kayla Dugger
Copy Editor: Sarah Kearns
Indexer: David Levine
Proofreader: Sheri Cain
Compositor: Jake McFarland
Manufacturing Buyer: Dan Uhrig

© 2006 by Pearson Education, Inc.
Publishing as Prentice Hall
Upper Saddle River, New Jersey 07458

Prentice Hall offers excellent discounts on this book when ordered in quantity for bulk purchases or special sales. For more information, please contact U.S. Corporate and Government Sales, 1-800-382-3419, corpsales@pearson-techgroup.com. For sales outside the U.S., please contact International Sales, 1-317-581-3793, international@pearsontechgroup.com.

Company and product names mentioned herein are the trademarks or registered trademarks of their respective owners.

Printed in the United States of America

First Printing

ISBN 0-13-229195-9

Pearson Education LTD.
Pearson Education Australia PTY, Limited.
Pearson Education Singapore, Pte. Ltd.
Pearson Education North Asia, Ltd.
Pearson Education Canada, Ltd.
Pearson Educatión de Mexico, S.A. de C.V.
Pearson Education—Japan
Pearson Education Malaysia, Pte. Ltd.

Library of Congress Cataloging-in-Publication Data

Levine, David M., 1946-
  Statistics for Six Sigma green belts / David M. Levine.
    p. cm.
  ISBN 0-13-229195-9 (hardback : alk. paper) 1. Six sigma (Quality control standard) 2. Quality control—Statistical methods. I. Title.
  TS156.L48 2006
  519.5—dc22
                              2005034090

To my wife Marilyn
and
my daughter Sharyn

CONTENTS

Acknowledgments   xvii

About the Author   xix

Preface   xxi

1   FUNDAMENTALS OF SIX SIGMA   1

     Introduction   2

     1.1   What Is Six Sigma?   2

         The DMAIC Model   2

     1.2   Roles in a Six Sigma Organization   3

         Master Black Belt   3

         Black Belt   4

         Green Belt   4

     1.3   Statistics and Six Sigma   4

     1.4   Learning Statistics for Six Sigma Using This Book   5

     Summary   6

     References   6

2   INTRODUCTION TO STATISTICS   7

     Introduction   8

     2.1   Enumerative and Analytic Studies   8

         Distinguishing Between Enumerative and Analytic Studies   9

     2.2   Types of Sampling   9

         Simple Random Sample   11

         Stratified Sample   11

         Systematic Sample   12

         Cluster Sample   12

     2.3   Types of Variables   13

     2.4   Operational Definitions   14

     Summary   14

     References   15

     A2.1   Introduction to Minitab Version 14   16

         Minitab Overview   16

         Using Minitab Worksheets   16

Opening and Saving Worksheets and Other Components   17

Printing Worksheets, Graphs, and Sessions   18

Selecting a Random Sample   19

A2.2   Introduction to JMP Version 6   **20**

JMP Overview   20

Using JMP Data Tables   20

Selecting a Random Sample   21

3   PRESENTING DATA IN CHARTS AND TABLES   **23**

Introduction   **24**

3.1   Graphing Attribute Data   **24**

The Bar Chart   24

The Pareto Diagram   25

3.2   Graphing Measurement Data   **27**

Histogram   27

The Dot Plot   28

The Run Chart   28

Summary   **30**

References   **30**

A3.1   Using Minitab to Construct Charts   **31**

Generating a Bar Chart   31

Generating a Pareto Diagram   32

Generating a Histogram   32

Generating a Dot Plot   33

Generating a Run Chart   34

A3.2   Using JMP to Construct Charts   **35**

Generating a Bar Chart   35

Generating a Pareto Diagram   35

Generating a Histogram   36

Generating a Run Chart   36

4   DESCRIPTIVE STATISTICS   **39**

Introduction   **40**

4.1   Measures of Central Tendency   **40**

The Arithmetic Mean   40

The Median   42

The Mode   43

Quartiles   44

4.2	**Measures of Variation**	**46**
	The Range	46
	The Variance and the Standard Deviation	47
4.3	**The Shape of Distributions**	**50**
	Shape	50
	The Five-Number Summary	52
	The Box-and-Whisker Plot	53
	Summary	**56**
	References	**56**
A4.1	**Using Minitab for Descriptive Statistics**	**57**
	Calculating Descriptive Statistics	57
	Generating a Box-and-Whisker Plot	57
A4.2	**Using JMP for Descriptive Statistics**	**58**
	Generating Descriptive Statistics and a Box-and-Whisker Plot	58

5   PROBABILITY AND PROBABILITY DISTRIBUTIONS   59

5.1	**What Is Probability?**	**60**
5.2	**Some Rules of Probability**	**62**
5.3	**The Probability Distribution**	**66**
	The Average or Expected Value of a Random Variable	68
	Standard Deviation of a Random Variable (σ)	69
5.4	**The Binomial Distribution**	**72**
	Characteristics of the Binomial Distribution	75
5.5	**The Poisson Distribution**	**76**
	Characteristics of the Poisson Distribution	78
5.6	**The Normal Distribution**	**78**
	Characteristics of the Normal Distribution	79
5.7	**The Normal Probability Plot**	**85**
	Summary	**86**
	References	**87**
A5.1	**Using Minitab for Probability Distributions and Plots**	**88**
	Computing Binomial Probabilities	88
	Computing Poisson Probabilities	88
	Computing Normal Probabilities	89
	Constructing a Normal Probability Plot	89
A5.2	**Using JMP for Probability Distributions and Plots**	**91**
	Computing Binomial Probabilities	91
	Computing Poisson Probabilities	92
	Computing Normal Probabilities	92
	Constructing a Normal Probability Plot	93

6	**SAMPLING DISTRIBUTIONS AND CONFIDENCE INTERVALS**	**95**
6.1	**Sampling Distributions**	**96**
	Basic Concepts	96
	Sampling Distribution of the Mean	97
	Sampling Distribution of the Proportion	99
6.2	**Basic Concepts of Confidence Intervals**	**99**
6.3	**Confidence Interval Estimate for the Mean (σ Unknown)**	**102**
6.4	**Prediction Interval Estimate for a Future Individual Value**	**105**
6.5	**Confidence Interval Estimate for the Proportion**	**106**
	Summary	**108**
	References	**108**
A6.1	**Using Minitab to Construct Confidence Intervals**	**109**
	Constructing the Confidence Interval Estimate for the Mean	109
	Constructing the Confidence Interval Estimate for the Proportion	110
A6.2	**Using JMP to Construct Confidence Intervals**	**111**
	Constructing the Confidence Interval Estimate for the Mean	111
	Constructing the Confidence Interval Estimate for the Proportion	111
7	**HYPOTHESIS TESTING**	**113**
	Introduction	**114**
7.1	**Fundamental Concepts of Hypothesis Testing**	**114**
	The Critical Value of the Test Statistic	116
	Regions of Rejection and Nonrejection	117
	Risks in Decision Making Using Hypothesis-Testing Methodology	118
	Level of Significance	118
	The Confidence Coefficient	118
	The β Risk	119
	The Power of a Test	119
	The p-Value Approach to Hypothesis Testing	121
7.2	**Testing for the Difference Between Two Proportions**	**122**
7.3	**Testing for the Difference Between the Means of Two Independent Groups**	**126**
	Pooled-Variance t Test for the Difference in Two Means	126
	Separate-Variance t Test for Differences in Two Means	131

7.4	**Testing for the Difference Between Two Variances**	**131**
	The F Test for the Ratio of Two Variances	132
	The Levene Test for the Difference Between Variances	134
7.5	**One-Way ANOVA: Testing for Differences Among the Means of Three or More Groups**	**134**
	F Test for Differences in Three or More Means	134
	Multiple Comparisons: The Tukey Procedure	138
	ANOVA Assumptions	140
	Levene's Test for Homogeneity of Variance	142
7.6	**Wilcoxon Rank Sum Test for the Difference Between Two Medians**	**143**
7.7	**Kruskal-Wallis Rank Test: Nonparametric Analysis for the One-Way ANOVA**	**145**
	Summary	**147**
	References	**149**
A7.1	**Using Minitab for Hypothesis Testing**	**150**
	Testing for the Difference Between Two Proportions	150
	Testing for the Difference Between the Means of Two Independent Samples	150
	Testing for the Difference Between Two Variances	152
	Generating a One-Way ANOVA with Multiple Comparisons	152
	Testing for Equal Variances in the Analysis of Variance	153
	The Wilcoxon Rank Sum Test	154
	The Kruskal-Wallis Rank Test	154
A7.2	**Using JMP for Hypothesis Testing**	**155**
	Stacking Data	155
	Tests for the Difference Between Two Means, Tests for the Difference Between Two Variances, and the Wilcoxon Rank Sum Test	155
	The One-Way ANOVA, Tukey Multiple Comparisons, Tests for Variances, and the Kruskal-Wallis Rank Test	156
8	**DESIGN OF EXPERIMENTS**	**157**
	Introduction	**158**
8.1	**Design of Experiments: Background and Rationale**	**158**
8.2	**Two-Factor Factorial Designs**	**159**
8.3	**2^k Factorial Designs**	**171**
8.4	**Fractional Factorial Designs**	**189**
	Choosing the Treatment Combinations	190
	Summary	**203**
	References	**203**

A8.1	**Using Minitab for the Design of Experiments**		**205**
	Two-Way ANOVA		205
	Main Effects Plot		205
	Interaction Plot		205
	Factorial Design		206
	Fractional Factorial Design		208
A8.2	**Using JMP for the Design of Experiments**		**209**
	Two-Way ANOVA		209
	Factorial Design		210
	Fractional Factorial Design		210

9   SIMPLE LINEAR REGRESSION   211

	Introduction		**212**
9.1	**Types of Regression Models**		**212**
9.2	**Determining the Simple Linear Regression Equation**		**213**
	The Y Intercept and the Slope		213
	Least-Squares Method		214
	Regression Model Prediction		218
9.3	**Measures of Variation**		**221**
	The Coefficient of Determination		224
	The Coefficient of Correlation		224
	Standard Error of the Estimate		225
9.4	**Assumptions**		**226**
9.5	**Residual Analysis**		**226**
	Evaluating the Assumptions		227
9.6	**Inferences About the Slope**		**229**
	t Test for the Slope		229
	F Test for the Slope		230
	Confidence Interval Estimate of the Slope (β_1)		231
9.7	**Estimation of Predicted Values**		**232**
	The Prediction Interval		232
9.8	**Pitfalls in Regression Analysis**		**232**
	Summary		**236**
	References		**236**
A9.1	**Using Minitab for Simple Linear Regression**		**237**
	Scatter Plot		237
	Simple Linear Regression		237
A9.2	**Using JMP for Simple Linear Regression**		**239**

10 **MULTIPLE REGRESSION** **241**

    Introduction **242**

10.1 **Developing the Multiple Regression Model** **242**

    Interpreting the Regression Coefficients 243

    Predicting the Dependent Variable Y 245

10.2 **Coefficient of Multiple Determination and the Overall F Test** **246**

    Coefficients of Multiple Determination 246

    Test for the Significance of the Overall Multiple
Regression Model 246

10.3 **Residual Analysis for the Multiple Regression Model** **247**

10.4 **Inferences Concerning the Population Regression Coefficients** **249**

    Tests of Hypothesis 249

    Confidence Interval Estimation 249

10.5 **Using Dummy Variables and Interaction Terms in
Regression Models** **250**

10.6 **Collinearity** **255**

10.7 **Model Building** **257**

    The Stepwise Regression Approach to Model Building 259

    The Best-Subsets Approach to Model Building 261

    Model Validation 266

10.8 **Logistic Regression** **266**

    Summary **272**

    References **272**

A10.1 **Using Minitab for Multiple Regression** **273**

    Generating a Multiple Regression Equation 273

    Using Minitab for a Three-Dimensional Plot 273

    Using Minitab for Dummy Variables and Interactions 274

    Using Minitab for Stepwise Regression and Best-Subsets
Regression 274

    Using Minitab for Logistic Regression 275

A10.2 **Using JMP for Multiple Regression** **276**

    Generating a Multiple Regression Equation 276

    Using JMP for Dummy Variables 277

    Using JMP for Interactions 277

    Using JMP for Stepwise Regression and All Possible
Regressions 278

    Using JMP for Logistic Regression 278

11 CONTROL CHARTS FOR SIX SIGMA MANAGEMENT   279

11.1	Basic Concepts of Control Charts	280
11.2	Control Limits and Patterns	282
11.3	Rules for Determining Out-of-Control Points	283
11.4	The p-Chart	285
11.5	The c-Chart	290
11.6	The u-Chart	293
11.7	Control Charts for the Mean and Range	296
11.8	Control Charts for the Mean and the Standard Deviation	301
11.9	Individual Value and Moving Range Charts	306
	Summary	310
	References	311
A11.1	Using Minitab for Control Charts	312
	Generating Zone Limits	312
	The p-Chart	312
	The c-Chart	313
	The u-Chart	313
	R and $\bar{X}$ Charts	314
	S and $\bar{X}$ Charts	315
	Individual Value and Moving Range Charts	316
A11.2	Using JMP for Control Charts	318
	The p-Chart	318
	The c-Chart	318
	The u-Chart	319
	$\bar{X}$ and R-Charts	319
	$\bar{X}$ and S-Charts	320
	Individual Value and Moving Range Charts	320

A REVIEW OF ARITHMETIC AND ALGEBRA   321

Part 1	Fill in the Correct Answer	321
Part 2	Select the Correct Answer	322
	Symbols	323
	Exponents and Square Roots	325
	Equations	326
	Answers to Quiz	327

B SUMMATION NOTATION   329

| | References | 332 |

C   STATISTICAL TABLES   **333**

D   DOCUMENTATION OF DATA FILES   **347**

Glossary   349

Index   359

Acknowledgments

I would like to thank The American Society for Quality, The American Society for Testing and Materials, and the American Statistical Association for allowing us to use their data and statistical tables in this book. I would like to thank Professor Howard Gitlow (University of Miami), Roger Hoerl (General Electric Corp.), and Edward Popovich (Boca Raton Community Hospital and Sterling Enterprises International) for their comments and suggestions.

I would especially like to thank my editor, Jim Boyd, of Financial Times Prentice Hall, for his insights and encouragement. I would also like to thank Sarah Kearns for her copy editing, Sheri Cain for her proofreading, and Kayla Dugger for her work in the production of the book.

ABOUT THE AUTHOR

David M. Levine is Professor Emeritus of Statistics and Computer Information Systems at Bernard M. Baruch College (City University of New York). He received B.B.A. and M.B.A. degrees in Statistics from City College of New York and a Ph.D. from New York University in Industrial Engineering and Operations Research. He is nationally recognized as a leading innovator in business statistics education and is the co-author of such best-selling statistics textbooks as *Statistics for Managers Using Microsoft Excel*, *Basic Business Statistics: Concepts and Applications*, *Business Statistics: A First Course*, and *Applied Statistics for Engineers and Scientists Using Microsoft Excel and Minitab*. He also recently wrote *Even You Can Learn Statistics*, published by Financial Times Prentice Hall. He is co-author of *Six Sigma for Green Belts and Champions*, Financial Times Prentice Hall (2005), *Design for Six Sigma for Green Belts and Champions*, Financial Times Prentice Hall (2006), and *Quality Management*, Third Edition, McGraw-Hill-Irwin (2005). He has published articles in various journals, including *Psychometrika*, *The American Statistician*, *Communications in Statistics*, *Multivariate Behavioral Research*, *Journal of Systems Management*, *Quality Progress*, and *The American Anthropologist*. While at Baruch College, Dr. Levine received numerous awards for outstanding teaching.

PREFACE

Green belts working in a Six Sigma organization need to be familiar with statistics because statistical tools are an essential part of each phase of the Six Sigma DMAIC model. This book focuses on those statistical tools that are most important for Six Sigma green belts. The objective of this book is to familiarize readers with these tools, so that they will be able to use either the Minitab or JMP software to analyze their data. Among the important features of this book are the following:

- **Provides a simple nonmathematical presentation of topics.** Every concept is explained in plain English with a minimum of mathematical symbols. Most of the equations are separated into optional boxes that complement the main material.
- **Covers the statistical topics that are most important for Six Sigma green belts.** After beginning with the use of tables and charts and descriptive statistics, the book includes coverage of those statistical topics that are most important for Six Sigma green belts; i.e., statistical process control charts, design of experiments, and regression. This book minimizes emphasis on probability, probability distributions, and sampling distributions.
- **Covers statistical topics by focusing on the interpretation of output generated by the Minitab and JMP software.**
- **Includes chapter-ending appendices that provide step-by-step instructions (with screenshots of dialog boxes) for using Minitab Version 14 and JMP Version 6 for the statistical topics covered in the chapter.**
- **Provides step-by-step instructions using worked-out examples for each statistical method covered.**
- **Includes service industry applications.** This book focuses on applications of Six Sigma in service industries. These service applications enable those who work in service industries to understand the role of Six Sigma in their industries, something that is difficult for them to see when examples from manufacturing industries are used.

CONTACTING THE AUTHOR

I have gone to great lengths to make this book both pedagogically sound and error-free. If you have any suggestions or require clarification about any of the material, or if you find any errors, contact me at

DAVID_LEVINE@BARUCH.CUNY.EDU
David M. Levine

CHAPTER 1

Fundamentals of Six Sigma

INTRODUCTION

1.1 **WHAT IS SIX SIGMA?**

1.2 **ROLES IN A SIX SIGMA ORGANIZATION**

1.3 **STATISTICS AND SIX SIGMA**

1.4 **LEARNING STATISTICS FOR SIX SIGMA USING THIS BOOK**

SUMMARY

REFERENCES

LEARNING OBJECTIVES

After reading this chapter, you will be able to

- Know what the acronym DMAIC stands for.
- Understand the difference between the role of a Six Sigma green belt, black belt, and master black belt.
- Understand the role of statistics in Six Sigma management.

INTRODUCTION

Six Sigma management is a quality improvement system originally developed by Motorola in the mid-1980s. Six Sigma offers a prescriptive and systematic approach to quality improvement and places a great deal of emphasis on accountability and bottom-line results. Many companies all over the world use Six Sigma management to improve efficiency, cut costs, eliminate defects, and reduce product variation.

1.1   WHAT IS SIX SIGMA?

The name Six Sigma comes from the fact that it is a managerial approach designed to create processes that result in no more than 3.4 defects per million. One of the aspects that distinguishes Six Sigma from other approaches is a clear focus on achieving bottom-line results in a relatively short three- to six-month period of time. After seeing the huge financial successes at Motorola, GE, and other early adopters of Six Sigma management, many companies worldwide have now instituted Six Sigma management programs [see References 1, 2, 3, and 5].

The DMAIC Model

To guide managers in their task of improving short- and long-term results, Six Sigma uses a five-step process known as the **DMAIC model**, named for the five steps in the process: **D**efine, **M**easure, **A**nalyze, **I**mprove, and **C**ontrol.

- **Define.** The problem is defined along with the costs, benefits, and impact on the customer.
- **Measure.** Operational definitions for each **critical-to-quality** (**CTQ**) characteristic are developed. In addition, the measurement procedure is verified so that it is consistent over repeated measurements.
- **Analyze.** The root causes of *why* defects occur are determined, and variables in the process causing the defects are identified. Data are collected to determine benchmark values for each process variable.
- **Improve.** The importance of each process variable on the CTQ characteristic are studied using designed experiments (see Chapter 8, "Design of Experiments"). The objective is to determine the best level for each variable.
- **Control.** The objective is to maintain the benefits for the long term by avoiding potential problems that can occur when a process is changed.

1.2   ROLES IN A SIX SIGMA ORGANIZATION

The roles of senior executive (CEO or president), executive committee, champion, process owner, master black belt, black belt, and green belt are critical to the Six Sigma management process.

The **senior executive** provides the impetus, direction, and alignment necessary for Six Sigma's ultimate success. The most successful, highly publicized Six Sigma efforts have all had unwavering, clear, and committed leadership from top management. Although it may be possible to initiate Six Sigma concepts and processes at lower levels, dramatic success will not be possible until the senior executive becomes engaged and takes a leadership role.

The members of the **executive committee** are the top management of an organization. They should operate at the same level of commitment for Six Sigma management as the senior executive.

Champions take a very active sponsorship and leadership role in conducting and implementing Six Sigma projects. They work closely with the executive committee, the black belt assigned to their project, and the master black belt overseeing their project. A champion should be a member of the executive committee or at least a trusted direct report of a member of the executive committee. He or she should have enough influence to remove obstacles or provide resources without having to go higher in the organization.

A **process owner** is the manager of a process. He or she has responsibility for the process and has the authority to change the process on his or her signature. The process owner should be identified and involved immediately in all Six Sigma projects relating to his or her own area.

Master Black Belt

A **master black belt** takes on a leadership role as keeper of the Six Sigma process and advisor to senior executives or business unit managers. He or she must leverage his or her skills with projects that are led by black belts and green belts. Frequently, master black belts report directly to senior executives or business unit managers. A master black belt has successfully led many teams through complex Six Sigma projects. He or she is a proven change agent, leader, facilitator, and technical expert in Six Sigma management. It is always best for an organization to develop its own master black belts. However, sometimes it is impossible for an organization to develop its own master black belts because of the lead time required to become a master black belt. Thus, circumstances sometimes require hiring master black belts from outside the organization.

Black Belt

A **black belt** is a full-time change agent and improvement leader who may not be an expert in the process under study [see Reference 4]. A black belt is a quality professional who is mentored by a master black belt, but who may report to a manager for his or her tour of duty as a black belt.

Green Belt

A **green belt** is an individual who works on projects part-time (25%), either as a team member for complex projects or as a project leader for simpler projects. Most managers in a mature Six Sigma organization are green belts. Green belt certification is a critical prerequisite for advancement into upper management in a Six Sigma organization.

Green belts leading simpler projects have the following responsibilities:

- Refine a project charter for the project.
- Review the project charter with the project's champion.
- Select the team members for the project.
- Communicate with the champion, master black belt, black belt, and process owner throughout all stages of the project.
- Facilitate the team through all phases of the project.
- Schedule meetings and coordinate logistics.
- Analyze data through all phases of the project.
- Train team members in the basic tools and methods through all phases of the project.

In complicated Six Sigma projects, green belts work closely with the team leader (black belt) to keep the team functioning and progressing through the various stages of the Six Sigma project.

1.3   STATISTICS AND SIX SIGMA

Many Six Sigma tools and methods involve *statistics*. What exactly is meant by statistics, and why is statistics such an integral part of Six Sigma management? To understand the importance of statistics for improving quality, you can go back to a famous 1925 quote of Walter Shewhart, widely considered to be the father of quality control:

> The long-range contribution of statistics depends not so much upon getting a lot of highly trained statisticians into industry as it does in creating a statistically minded generation of physicists, chemists, engineers, and others who will in any way have a hand in developing and directing the production processes of tomorrow.

This quote is just as valid today as it was more than 75 years ago. The goal of this book is *not* to make you a statistician. The goal is to enable you to learn enough so that you will be able to use the statistical methods that are involved in each phase of the DMAIC model. Using Minitab and/or JMP statistical software will help you achieve this goal while at the same time minimize your need for formulas and computations.

Table 1.1 summarizes the statistical methods that are commonly used in the various phases of the DMAIC model.

TABLE 1.1 Phases of the DMAIC Model, Statistical Methods Used, and Chapters in This Book

Phase of DMAIC Model	Statistical Methods	Chapters
Define	Tables and Charts	3
	Descriptive Statistics	4
	Statistical Process Control Charts	11
Measure	Tables and Charts	3
	Descriptive Statistics	4
	Normal Distribution	5
	Analysis of Variance	6, 7, 8
	Statistical Process Control Charts	11
Analyze	Tables and Charts	3
	Descriptive Statistics	4
	Analysis of Variance	6, 7, 8
	Regression Analysis	9, 10
	Statistical Process Control Charts	11
Improve	Tables and Charts	3
	Descriptive Statistics	4
	Analysis of Variance	6, 7, 8
	Regression Analysis	9, 10
	Design of Experiments	8
Control	Statistical Process Control Charts	11

1.4 LEARNING STATISTICS FOR SIX SIGMA USING THIS BOOK

This book assumes no previous knowledge of statistics. Perhaps you may have taken a previous course in statistics. Most likely, such a course focused on computing results using statistical formulas. If that was the case, you will find the approach in this book very different. This book provides the following approach:

- **Provides a simple nonmathematical presentation of topics.** Every concept is explained in plain English with a minimum of mathematical symbols. Most of the equations are separated into optional boxes that complement the main material.

- **Covers statistical topics by focusing on the interpretation of output generated by the Minitab and JMP software.**
- **Includes chapter-ending appendices that provide step-by-step instructions (with screenshots of dialog boxes) for using Minitab Version 14 and JMP Version 6 for the statistical topics covered in the chapter.**
- **Provides step-by-step instructions using worked-out examples for each statistical method covered.**

SUMMARY

Six Sigma management is used by many companies around the world. Six Sigma uses the DMAIC model that contains five phases: Define, Measure, Analyze, Improve, and Control. Many different roles are important in a Six Sigma organization. Statistics is an important ingredient in such an organization. The purpose of this book is to enable you to learn enough so that you will be able to use statistical methods as an integral part of Six Sigma management.

REFERENCES

1. Arndt, M., "Quality Isn't Just for Widgets," *Business Week*, July 22, 2002, 72–73.

2. Gitlow, H. S., and D. M. Levine, *Six Sigma for Green Belts and Champions*, (Upper Saddle River, NJ: Financial Times Prentice Hall, 2005).

3. Hahn, G. J., N. Doganaksoy, and R. Hoerl, "The Evolution of Six Sigma," *Quality Engineering*, 2000, 12, 317–326.

4. Hoerl, R., "Six Sigma Black Belts: What Do They Need to Know?" *Journal of Quality Technology*, 33, 4, October 2001, 391–406.

5. Snee, R. D., "Impact of Six Sigma on Quality," *Quality Engineering*, 2000, 12, ix–xiv.

CHAPTER 2

Introduction to Statistics

INTRODUCTION

2.1 ENUMERATIVE AND ANALYTIC STUDIES

2.2 TYPES OF SAMPLING

2.3 TYPES OF VARIABLES

2.4 OPERATIONAL DEFINITIONS

SUMMARY

REFERENCES

APPENDIX 2.1
   INTRODUCTION TO MINITAB VERSION 14

APPENDIX 2.2
   INTRODUCTION TO JMP VERSION 6

LEARNING OBJECTIVES

After reading this chapter, you will be able to

- Distinguish between enumerative and analytic studies.
- Distinguish between different sampling methods.
- Understand the importance of operational definitions.
- Use the Minitab Version 14 and JMP Version 6 statistical software packages to select samples.

INTRODUCTION

The definition of *statistics*, according to Deming [see References 4 and 5], is to study and understand variation in processes and populations, interactions among the variables in processes and populations, operational definitions (definitions of process and population variables that promote effective communication between people), and ultimately, to take action to reduce variation in a process or population. Hence, statistics is broadly defined as the study of data to provide a basis for action on a population or process. Statistics is often divided into two branches: descriptive statistics and inferential statistics.

Descriptive statistics focus on the collection, analysis, presentation, and description of a set of data. For example, the United States Census Bureau collects data every 10 years (and has done so since 1790) concerning many characteristics of residents of the United States. Another example of descriptive statistics is the employee benefits used by the employees of an organization in fiscal year 2005. These benefits might include healthcare costs, dental costs, sick leave, and the specific healthcare provider chosen by the employee.

Inferential statistics focus on making decisions about a large set of data, called the **population**, from a subset of the data, called the **sample**. The invention of the computer eased the computational burden of statistical methods and opened up access to these methods to a wide audience. Today, the preferred approach is to use statistical software such as Minitab or JMP (as we will do in this book) to perform the computations involved in using various statistical methods.

2.1   ENUMERATIVE AND ANALYTIC STUDIES

There are two types of statistical studies: enumerative and analytic. The two types of studies have different purposes, so you need to understand the distinction between them.

Enumerative studies are used to draw conclusions about a population fixed in place and time. A common example of an enumerative study is a political poll in which you select a sample of registered voters from a list of all registered voters in a particular geographical area as of a certain time such as October 2005. Based on the results of the sample, you make statistical inferences about the entire voter registration list in the geographical area as of October 2005. Another example of an enumerative study is a study of the waiting time at a bank branch during lunch hours in 2005. Based on a sample of customers selected, inferences can be made about the average waiting time in 2005. Dynamic questions, such as why the people come to the bank during the lunch hour or why the waiting time varies, are not considered in an enumerative study. Each of these examples is time-specific and static. There is no reference to the past or the future.

Analytic studies are used to study the cause-and-effect systems of a process to improve the future functioning of a process. An example of an analytic study related to the waiting time at the bank during lunch hours is to study why there was variation in the average waiting time and what factors could be causing this variation to improve the future waiting time at the bank. Another example of an analytical study is determining why there is variation in the time it takes to fulfill orders that are received at a web site. Another example of an analytic study is comparing ways of marketing a financial service to increase market share. Each of these examples focuses on the future, not on the past or present. You use the information to make dynamic decisions to improve the future functioning of a process.

Distinguishing Between Enumerative and Analytic Studies

A simple rule for distinguishing between an enumerative study and an analytic study is as follows:

> If a 100% sample answers the question under investigation, the study is enumerative; if not, the study is analytic.

2.2   TYPES OF SAMPLING

Now, in order to become familiar with sampling, you need to become familiar with some terms.

A **population**, also called a *universe*, is the entire group of units, items, services, people, etc., under investigation for a fixed period of time and a fixed location.

A **frame** is a physical list of the units in the population.

The **gap** is the difference between the units in the population and the units in the frame.

If the units in the gap are distributed like the units in the frame, no problems should occur due to the gap. However, if the units in the gap are not distributed like the units in the frame, a systematic bias could result from the analysis of the frame. For example, if the frame of New York City residents over 18 years of age is the voter registration list, then a statistical analysis of the people on the list may contain bias if the distribution of people 18 and older is different for people on the list (frame) and people not on the list (gap). An example of where this difference might have an impact is if a survey was conducted to determine attitudes toward immigration because the voter registration list would not include residents who were not citizens.

A **sample** is the portion of a population that is selected to gather information to provide a basis for action on the population. Rather than taking a complete census of the whole population, statistical sampling procedures focus on collecting a small portion of the larger population. For example, 50 accounts receivable drawn from a list, or frame, of 10,000 accounts receivable constitute a sample. The resulting sample provides information that can be used to estimate characteristics of the entire frame.

There are four main reasons for drawing a sample. These are depicted in Exhibit 2.1.

EXHIBIT 2.1   REASONS FOR DRAWING A SAMPLE

1. A sample is less time-consuming than a census.
2. A sample is less costly to administer than a census.
3. A sample is less cumbersome and more practical to administer than a census.
4. A sample provides higher-quality data than a census.

There are two kinds of samples: nonprobability samples and probability samples.

> In a **nonprobability sample**, items or individuals are chosen without the benefit of a frame. Because nonprobability samples choose units without the benefit of a frame, there is an unknown probability of selection (and in some cases, participants have self-selected).

For a nonprobability sample, the theory of statistical inference should not be applied to the sample data. For example, many companies conduct surveys by giving visitors to their web site the opportunity to complete survey forms and submit them electronically. The response to these surveys can provide large amounts of data, but because the sample consists of self-selected web users, there is no frame. Nonprobability samples are selected for convenience (**convenience sample**) based on the opinion of an expert (**judgment sample**) or on a desired proportional representation of certain classes of items, units, or people in the sample (**quota sample**). Nonprobability samples are all subject to an unknown degree of bias. Bias is caused by the absence of a frame and the ensuing classes of items or people that may be systematically denied representation in the sample (the gap).

Nonprobability samples have the potential advantages of convenience, speed, and lower cost. However, they have two major disadvantages: potential selection bias and the ensuing lack of generalizability of the results. These disadvantages more than offset the advantages. Therefore, you should only use nonprobability sampling methods when you want to develop rough approximations at low cost or when small-scale initial or pilot studies will be followed by more rigorous investigations.

You should use probability sampling whenever possible, because valid statistical inferences can be made from a probability sample.

> In a **probability sample**, the items or individuals are chosen from a frame, and hence, the individual units in the population have a known probability of selection from the frame.

The four types of probability samples most commonly used are simple random, stratified, systematic, and cluster. These sampling methods vary from one another in their cost, accuracy, and complexity.

Simple Random Sample

In a **simple random sample**, every sample of a fixed size has the same chance of selection as every other sample of that size. Simple random sampling is the most elementary random sampling technique. It forms the basis for the other random sampling techniques. With simple random sampling, n represents the sample size, and N represents the frame size, not the population size. Every item or person in the frame is numbered from 1 to N. The chance of selecting any particular member of the frame on the first draw is $1/N$.

You use random numbers to select items from the frame to eliminate bias and hold uncertainty within known limits. For example, in Appendix 2.1 on page 19, Minitab is used to select a simple random sample of items from a frame of items. (Appendix 2.2 on page 21 uses JMP to select a random sample.)

Two important points to remember are that different samples of size n will yield different sample statistics, and different methods of measurement will yield different sample statistics. Random samples, however, do not have bias on average, and the sampling error can be held to known limits by increasing the sample size. These are the advantages of probability sampling over nonprobability sampling.

Stratified Sample

In a **stratified sample**, the N items in the frame are divided into subpopulations, or strata, according to some common characteristic. A simple random sample is selected within each of the strata, and you combine the results from the separate simple random samples. Stratified sampling can decrease the overall sample size, and, consequently, lower the cost of a sample. A stratified sample will have a smaller sample size than a simple random sample if the items are similar within a stratum (called *homogeneity*) and the strata are different from each other (called *heterogeneity*). As an example of stratified sampling, suppose that a company has workers located at several facilities in a geographical area. The workers within each location are similar to each other with respect to the characteristic being studied, but the workers at the different locations are different from each other with respect to the characteristic being studied. Rather than take a simple random sample of all workers, it is cost efficient to sample the workers by location, and then combine the results into a single estimate of a characteristic being studied.

Systematic Sample

In a **systematic sample**, the N individuals or items in the frame are placed into k groups by dividing the size of the frame N by the desired sample size n. To select a systematic sample, you choose the first individual or item at random from the k individuals or items in the first group in the frame. You select the rest of the sample by taking every kth individual or item thereafter from the entire frame.

If the frame consists of a listing of prenumbered checks, sales receipts, or invoices, or a preset number of consecutive items coming off an assembly line, a systematic sample is faster and easier to select than a simple random sample. A shortcoming of a systematic sample occurs if the frame has a pattern. For example, if homes are being assessed, and every fifth home is a corner house, and the random number selected is 5, then the entire sample will consist of corner houses. Corner houses are known to have higher assessed values than other houses. Consequently, the average assessed value of the homes in the sample will be inflated due to the corner house phenomenon.

Cluster Sample

In a **cluster sample**, you divide the N individuals or items in the frame into many *clusters*. Clusters are naturally occurring subdivisions of a frame, such as counties, election districts, city blocks, apartment buildings, factories, or families. You take a random sampling of clusters and study all individuals or items in each selected cluster. This is called single-stage cluster sampling.

Cluster sampling methods are more cost effective than simple random sampling methods if the population is spread over a wide geographic region. Cluster samples are very useful in reducing travel time. However, cluster sampling methods tend to be less efficient than either simple random sampling methods or stratified sampling methods. In addition, cluster sampling methods are useful in cutting the cost of developing a frame because first, a frame is made of the clusters, and second, a frame is made only of the individual units in the selected clusters. Cluster sampling often requires a larger overall sample size to produce results as precise as those from more efficient procedures. A detailed discussion of systematic sampling, stratified sampling, and cluster sampling procedures can be found in Reference 5.

2.3 TYPES OF VARIABLES

Numerical information collected about a product, service, process, individual, or item is called **data**. Because no two things are exactly alike, data inherently varies. Each characteristic of interest is referred to as a **variable**. In Six Sigma, the term **CTQ** is used as an acronym for critical-to-quality characteristics for a product, service, or process. In addition, the term **CTP** is used as an acronym for a critical-to-process characteristic in the design of a product or service. Data are classified into two types: attribute data and measurement data.

Attribute data (also referred to as *categorical* or *count data*) occurs when a variable is either classified into categories or used to count occurrences of a phenomenon. Attribute data places an item or person into one of two or more categories. For example, gender has only two categories. In other cases, there are many possible categories into which the variable can be classified. For example, there could be many reasons for a defective product or service. Regardless of the number of categories, the data consists of the number or frequency of items in a particular category, whether it is the number of voters in a sample who prefer a particular candidate in an election or the number of occurrences of each reason for a defective product or service. Count data consists of the number of occurrences of a phenomenon in an item or person. Examples of count data are the number of blemishes in a yard of fabric or the number of cars entering a highway at a certain location during a specific time period.

Measurement data (also referred to as *continuous* or *variables data*) results from a measurement taken on an item or person. Any value can theoretically occur, limited only by the precision of the measuring process. For example, height, weight, temperature, and cycle time are examples of measurement data.

Variables can also be described according to the level of measurement scale. There are four scales of measurement: nominal, ordinal, interval, and ratio. Attribute data classified into categories is **nominal scale** data—for example, conforming versus non-conforming, on versus off, male versus female. No ranking of the data is implied. Nominal scale data is the weakest form of measurement. An **ordinal scale** is used for data that can be ranked, but cannot be measured—for example, ranking attitudes on a 1 to 5 scale, where 1 = very dissatisfied, 2 = dissatisfied, 3 = neutral, 4 = satisfied, and 5 = very satisfied. Ordinal scale data involves a stronger form of measurement than attribute data. However, differences between categories cannot be measured.

Measurement data can be classified into interval- and ratio-scaled data. In an **interval scale**, differences between measurements are a meaningful amount, but there is no true zero point. In a **ratio scale**, not only are differences between measurements a meaningful amount, but there is a true zero point. Temperature in degrees Fahrenheit or Celsius is interval scaled because the difference between 30 and 32 degrees is the same as the difference between 38 and 40 degrees, but there is no true zero point ($0°$ F is not the same as $0°$ C). Weight and time are ratio-scaled variables that have a true zero point; zero pounds are the same as zero grams, which are the same as zero stones. Twenty minutes is twice as long as ten minutes, and ten minutes is twice as long as five minutes.

2.4   OPERATIONAL DEFINITIONS

All variables need to have an operational definition. Major problems occur when the measurement definitions for CTQs and CTPs are inconsistent over time or vary from individual to individual. Ambiguous definitions, such as defective, safe, round, and hot, have no meaning that can be communicated unless they are operationally defined.

> An **operational definition** is a definition that provides communicable meaning to the users of the definition.

An example [see Reference 3] that illustrates the importance of operational definitions involved the 2000 U. S. Presidential election and the disputed ballots in the state of Florida. A review of 175,010 Florida ballots that were rejected for either no presidential vote or votes for two or more candidates was conducted with the help of the National Opinion Research Center of the University of Chicago. Nine operational definitions were used to evaluate the ballots to determine whether they should be counted. The nine operational definitions led to different results. Three of the operational definitions (including one pursued by Al Gore) led to margins of victory for George Bush that ranged from 225 to 493 votes. Six of the operational definitions (including one pursued by George Bush) led to margins of victory for Al Gore that ranged from 42 to 171 votes.

SUMMARY

This chapter provided an introduction to the field of statistics and why statistics is such a vital tool in Six Sigma management. Some basic principles were defined, and different types of sampling methods were discussed.

REFERENCES

1. Beninger, J. M., and D. L. Robyn, "Quantitative Graphics in Statistics," *The American Statistician*, 32, 1978, 1–11.

2. Berenson, M. L., D. M. Levine, and T. C. Krehbiel, *Basic Business Statistics: Concepts and Applications*, 10th ed. (Upper Saddle River, NJ: Prentice Hall, 2006).

3. Calmes, J. and E. P. Foldessy, "In Election Review, Bush Wins with No Supreme Court Help," *Wall Street Journal*, November 12, 2001, A1, A14.

4. Deming, W. E., *Out of the Crisis* (Cambridge, MA: MIT Center for Advanced Engineering Study, 1986).

5. Deming, W. E., *Some Theory of Sampling*, (New York: John Wiley, 1950).

6. Hahn, G. J. and W. Q. Meeker, "Assumptions for Statistical Inference," *The American Statistician*, 1993, 47, 1–11.

7. JMP Version 6 (Cary, NC: SAS Institute, 2005).

8. Minitab Version 14 (State College, PA: Minitab, 2004).

Appendix 2.1
Introduction to Minitab Version 14

Minitab Overview

Minitab is an example of a statistical package, a set of programs designed to perform statistical analysis to a high degree of numerical accuracy. Minitab initially evolved from efforts at Pennsylvania State University to improve the teaching of statistics and quickly spread to many other colleges and universities. Today, while maintaining its academic base, Minitab has become a commercial product that is used in many large corporations and is widely used by companies involved in Six Sigma management.

In Minitab, you create and open **projects** to store all of your data and results. A **session**, or log of activities, a **project manager** that summarizes the project contents, and any worksheets or graphs used are the components that form a project. Project components are displayed in separate windows inside the Minitab application window. By default, you will see only the session and one worksheet window when you begin a new project in Minitab. (You can bring any window to the front by selecting the window in the Minitab Windows menu.) You can open and save an entire project or, as is done in this text, open and save worksheets. Minitab's statistical rigor, availability for many different types of computer systems, and commercial acceptance make this program a great tool for using statistics in Six Sigma management.

Using Minitab Worksheets

You enter data in a Minitab worksheet so that each variable is assigned to a column. Minitab worksheets are organized as numbered rows and columns numbered in the form Cn, in which C1 is the first column. You enter variable labels in a special unnumbered row that precedes row 1 (see Figure A2.1). Unlike worksheets in program such as Microsoft Excel, currently, Minitab worksheets do not accept formulas and do not automatically recalculate themselves when you change the values of the supporting data.

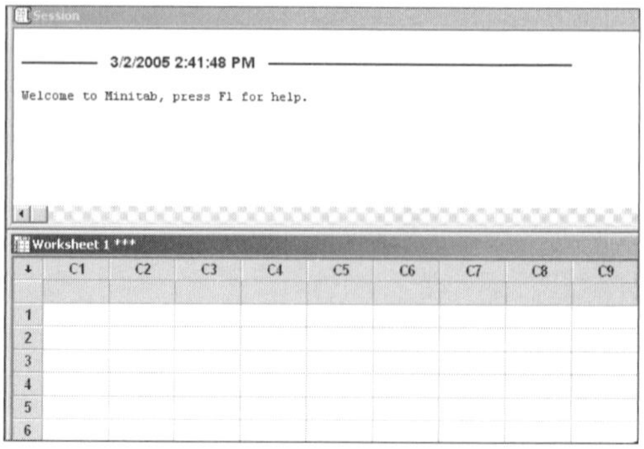

FIGURE A2.1   Minitab Application Window

By default, Minitab names opened worksheets serially in the form of Worksheet1, Worksheet2, and so on. Better names are ones that reflect the content of the worksheets, such as **ORDER** for a worksheet that contains data for the order fulfillment times (see Chapter 3, "Presenting Data in Charts and Tables"). To give a sheet a descriptive name, open the Project Manager window, right-click the icon for the worksheet, select **Rename** from the shortcut menu, and type in the new name.

Opening and Saving Worksheets and Other Components

You open worksheets to use data that have been created by you or others at an earlier time. To open a Minitab worksheet, first select **File → Open Worksheet**.

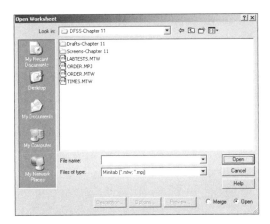

FIGURE A2.2 Minitab Open Worksheet Dialog Box

In the Open Worksheet dialog box that appears (see Figure A2.2):

1. Select the appropriate folder (also known as a directory) from the Look in: drop-down list box.

2. Check (and select, if necessary) the proper Files of type: value from the drop-down list at the bottom of the dialog box. Typically, you will not need to make this selection because the default choice, Minitab, will list all Minitab worksheets and projects. However, to list all Microsoft Excel files, select Excel (*.xls); to list every file in the folder, select All.

3. If necessary, change the display of files in the central files list box by clicking the rightmost (View menu) button on the top row of buttons and selecting the appropriate view from the drop-down list.

4. Select the file to be opened from the files list box. If the file does not appear, verify that steps 1, 2, and 3 were done correctly.

5. Click the **Open** button.

To open a Minitab project that can include the session, worksheets, and graphs, select Minitab project in step 2 or select the similar **File → Open Project**. Individual graphs can be opened as well by selecting **File → Open Graph**.

You can save a worksheet individually to ensure its future availability, to protect yourself against a system failure, or to later import it into another project. To save a worksheet, select the worksheet's window, and then select **File → Save Current Worksheet As**. In the Save Worksheet As dialog box that appears (see Figure A2.3):

1. Select the appropriate folder from the Save in: drop-down list box.

2. Check (and select, if necessary) the proper Save as: type value from the drop-down list at the bottom of the dialog box. Typically, you will

want to accept the default choice, Minitab, but select Minitab Portable to use the data on a different type of computer system or select an earlier version, such as Minitab 13, to use the data in that earlier version.

3. Enter (or edit) the name of the file in the File name: edit box.

4. Optionally, click the Description button, and in the Worksheet Description dialog box (not shown), enter documentary information and click the OK button.

5. Click the **Save** button (in the Save Worksheet As dialog box).

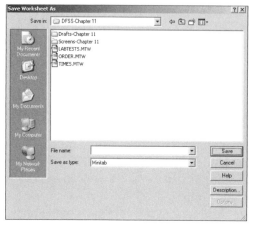

FIGURE A2.3   Minitab Save Worksheet As Dialog Box

To save a Minitab project, select the similar **File → Save Project As**. The Save Project As dialog box (not shown) contains an Options button that displays the Save Project–Options dialog box in which you can indicate which project components other than worksheets (session, dialog settings, graphs, and Project Manager content) will be saved.

You can save individual graphs and the session separately by first selecting their windows, and then selecting the similar **File → Save Graph As** or **File → Save Session As**, as appropriate. Minitab graphs can be saved in either a Minitab graph format or any one of several common graphics formats, and session files can be saved as simple or formatted text files.

You can repeat a save procedure and save a worksheet, project, or other component using a second name as an easy way to create a backup copy that can be used should some problem make your original file unusable.

Printing Worksheets, Graphs, and Sessions

Printing components gives you the means to study and review data and results away from the computer screen. To print a specific worksheet, graph, or session:

1. Select the window of the worksheet, graph, or session to be printed.

2. Select **File → Print** *object,* where *object* is either Worksheet, Graph, or Session Window, depending on the component window you selected.

3. If you are printing a worksheet, select **Formatting Options** and add a title in the Data Window Print Options dialog box that appears. Then, click the **OK** button in that dialog box (see Figure A2.4).

4. In the Print dialog box that appears, select the printer to be used, set the Number of copies to the proper value, and click the **OK** button.

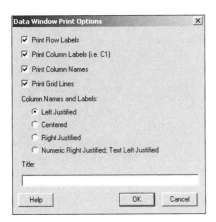

FIGURE A2.4 Minitab Data Window Print Options Dialog Box

After printing, verify the contents of your printout. Most printing problems or failures will trigger the display of an informational dialog box. Click the **OK** button of any such dialog box and correct the problem noted before attempting a second print operation.

Selecting a Random Sample

To select a random sample from a population using Minitab, open the 🖭 **ORDER.MTW** worksheet. Select **Calc → Random Data → Sample from Columns**, then do the following:

1. In the Sample From Columns dialog box (see Figure A2.5), enter **10** in the Sample rows from column(s): edit box.
2. Enter **C1** or **Time** in the edit box. Enter **C2** in the Store samples in: edit box. Click the **OK** button.

Column C2 of Figure A2.6 illustrates the sample results. If these instructions are repeated, a different sample of 10 data values would be selected.

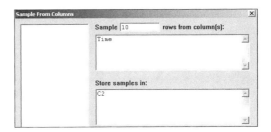

FIGURE A2.5 Minitab Sample From Columns Dialog Box

↓	C1	C2
	Time	Samples
1	63.6	64.6
2	66.3	77.2
3	86.1	74.5
4	66.0	85.4
5	56.2	63.0
6	83.7	63.6
7	83.2	71.9
8	62.0	67.4
9	81.8	61.1
10	73.2	88.9
11	82.5	
12	86.2	
13	83.1	

FIGURE A2.6 Minitab Sample of 10 Order Fulfillment Times Selected from a Population of 200 Order Fulfillment Times

Appendix 2.2
Introduction to JMP Version 6

JMP Overview

JMP is an example of a statistical package, a set of programs designed to perform statistical analysis to a high degree of numerical accuracy. JMP was developed by the SAS Institute, Inc. JMP's statistical rigor, availability for different types of computer systems, and commercial acceptance make this program a great tool for using statistics in Six Sigma management.

Using JMP Data Tables

You start JMP by double-clicking the JMP application icon. A JMP session begins by displaying a menu bar and a JMP Starter window (see Figure A2.7).

You use a JMP data table to enter data for variables by column. If you are creating a new set of data, select **File → New** or the **New Data Table** button. If you are opening an existing JMP file, select **File → Open** or the **Open Data Table** button.

Opening a file creates a JMP data table. Figure A2.8 illustrates the data table window for the time-to-get-ready data (**TIMES.JMP**) that will be discussed in Chapter 4, "Descriptive Statistics." Each row is identified with a row number and each column has a column label. In JMP, the blue triangle to the left of the column name in the panel on the left side of the data table window indicates that this variable is continuous (or you can click the triangle to get a pop-up menu that also

FIGURE A2.7
JMP Menu Bar and Starter Window

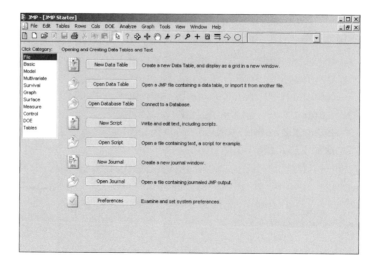

indicates that the variable in the column is continuous). A set of red vertical bars indicates a nominal scale variable, while a set of green vertical bars indicates an ordinal scale variable.

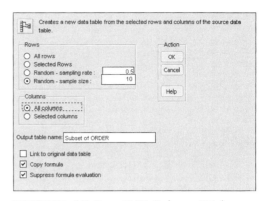

FIGURE A2.9   JMP Subset Dialog Box

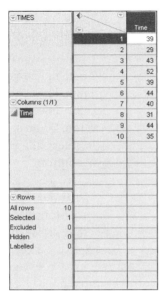

FIGURE A2.8   JMP Data Table Window

Selecting a Random Sample

To select a random sample from a population using JMP, open the ⬛ **ORDER.JMP** data table. Select **Tables → Subset**:

1. In the JMP: Subset dialog box (see Figure A2.9), select the Random – sample size: option button and enter **10** in the edit box.

2. Click the **OK** button.

Figure A2.10 illustrates the sample results. If these instructions are repeated, a different sample of 10 data values would be selected.

FIGURE A2.10   JMP Sample of 10 Order Fulfillment Times Selected from a Population of 200 Order Fulfillment Times

CHAPTER 3

Presenting Data in Charts and Tables

INTRODUCTION

3.1 GRAPHING ATTRIBUTE DATA

3.2 GRAPHING MEASUREMENT DATA

SUMMARY

REFERENCES

**APPENDIX 3.1
USING MINITAB TO CONSTRUCT CHARTS**

**APPENDIX 3.2
USING JMP TO CONSTRUCT CHARTS**

LEARNING OBJECTIVES

After reading this chapter, you will be able to

- Construct charts for attribute data.
- Construct charts for measurement data.
- Use the Minitab 14 and JMP statistical software packages to construct charts.

INTRODUCTION

Graphics refers to the visual representation of data. Graphics have been used by civilizations throughout recorded history. The following 1801 quote by Playfair [see Reference 1] summarizes the importance of graphics:

> I have succeeded in proposing and putting into practice a new and useful mode of stating accounts…as much information may be obtained in five minutes as would require whole days to imprint on the memory, in a lasting manner, by a table of figures.

More recently, the widespread availability of statistical and spreadsheet software for personal computers has enabled users to quickly produce many different graphs, even for large data sets. In this book, the Minitab and JMP statistical software packages will be used to construct many different graphs.

3.1   GRAPHING ATTRIBUTE DATA

When you have attribute data, you tally responses into categories and determine the frequency or percentage in each category. Two widely used graphs, the bar chart and the Pareto diagram, will be discussed.

The Bar Chart

A **bar chart** presents each category of an attribute type variable as a bar whose length is the frequency or percentage of values falling into a category. The data in Table 3.1 represent a summary table of the number of errors and the type of error for laboratory tests.

TABLE 3.1   Summary Table for Causes of Defects in Laboratory Tests

Cause	Frequency	Percentage
Social Security Number	226	49.8
Name	71	15.6
Date of Birth	58	12.8
Test	44	9.7
Doctor	39	8.6
Others	16	3.5
Total	454	100.0

 LABTESTS
Source: Extracted from N. B. Riebling, S. Condon, and D. Gopen, "Toward Error-Free Lab Work," *Six Sigma Forum Magazine*, Vol. 4, November 2004, p. 23–29. Reprinted with permission from the *Six Sigma Forum Magazine* © 2004 American Society for Quality.

Figure 3.1 is a Minitab bar chart of the causes of defects in the lab tests. Figure 3.2 is a JMP bar chart.

FIGURE 3.1
Minitab Bar Chart of the Causes of Defects in Lab Tests

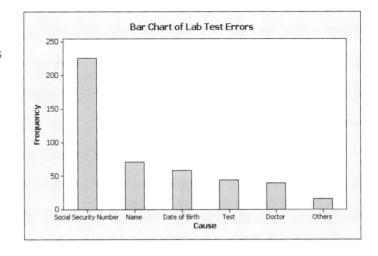

FIGURE 3.2
JMP Bar Chart of the Causes of Defects in Lab Tests

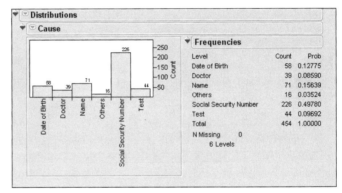

The bar for the defects due to social security number in Figure 3.1 or 3.2 stands out because there are 226 defective lab tests due to social security number. In addition, you can see that there are a large number of defects due to name (71) and date of birth (58).

The Pareto Diagram

A **Pareto diagram** is a special type of bar chart in which the categories of an attribute type variable are listed on the X-axis, the frequencies in each category (listed from largest to smallest frequency) are shown on the left side Y-axis, and the cumulative percentage of frequencies are shown on the right side Y-axis. Regardless of frequency, the "Other" category is always placed at the right side of the X-axis.

The main principle behind the Pareto diagram is to separate the "vital few response categories" from the "trivial many response categories," enabling you to focus on the critical categories. The Pareto diagram promotes prioritization of effort, which discourages micromanagement. Figure 3.3 is a Minitab Pareto diagram of the causes of defects in the lab tests, and Figure 3.4 is a JMP Pareto diagram.

FIGURE 3.3
Minitab Pareto Diagram of the Causes of Defects in Lab Tests

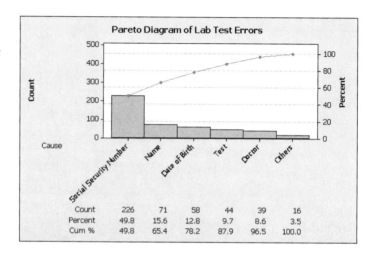

FIGURE 3.4
JMP Pareto Diagram of the Causes of Defects in Lab Tests

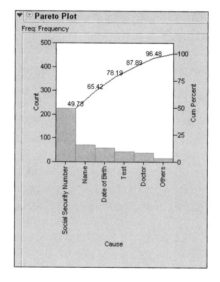

From Figures 3.3 or 3.4, you see that social security number is the first category listed (with 49.8% of the defects), followed by name (with 15.6%), followed by date of birth (with 12.8%). The two most frequently occurring categories, social security number and name, account for 65.4% of the defects; the three most frequently occurring categories—social security number, name, and date of birth—account for

78.2% of the defects, and so on. 49.8% of the defects are accounted for by only one category. Thus, the priority problem is social security number.

3.2 GRAPHING MEASUREMENT DATA

Histogram

A **histogram** is a special bar chart for measurement data. In the histogram, the data are grouped into adjacent numerical categories; for example, 100 to less than 200, 200 to less than 300, 300 to less than 400, and so on. You can use Minitab or JMP to organize the data into groups and plot the histogram. The difference between a bar chart and a histogram is that the X-axis on a bar chart is a listing of categories, while the X-axis on a histogram is a measurement scale. In addition, in the histogram, there are no gaps between adjacent bars.

To illustrate the histogram, you can examine the order fulfillment process at a web site. Order fulfillment consists of several steps, including receiving an order, picking the parts of the order, checking the order, packing, and shipping the order. The data in the file 🌐 **ORDER** consist of the time in minutes to fulfill a sample of 200 orders. Figure 3.5 presents the Minitab histogram of the time to fulfill the orders. Figure 3.6 illustrates a JMP histogram.

FIGURE 3.5
Minitab Histogram of the Time to Fulfill Orders

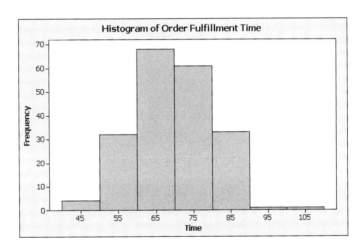

FIGURE 3.6
JMP Histogram of the Time to Fulfill Orders

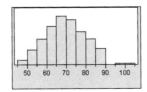

Minitab and JMP group the data into numerical classes. For these data, in Figure 3.5, notice tick marks at 45, 55, 65, 75, 85, 95, and 105. These tick marks are located at the midpoint of the class interval, so the first class whose midpoint is 45 contains values between 40 to less than 50 minutes, the second class contains values between 50 to less than 60 minutes, and so on. In Figure 3.6, the data are grouped into classes of five minutes, 45 to 50, 50 to 55, and so on, up to 100 to 105. Most of the order fulfillment times shown in Figures 3.5 and 3.6 are in the center of the distribution, with very few values either below 50 minutes or above 90 minutes. The distribution appears to be approximately bell-shaped with a heavy concentration of order fulfillment times between 60 and 80 minutes.

The Dot Plot

A **dot plot** is a graph of measurement data in which dots are stacked vertically on the horizontal axis for each value of the variable of interest. Figure 3.7 is a Minitab dot plot of the order fulfillment time.

FIGURE 3.7
Minitab Dot Plot of
Fulfillment Times

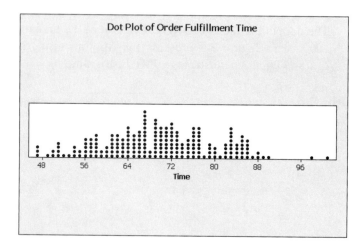

Notice that the dot plot for these data looks different from the histogram. This occurs because the histogram groups the data into class intervals, while the dot plot shows each data value, with the height representing the frequency at each horizontal (time) value. However, the dot plot also shows a concentration of values in the center of the distribution between 55 and 85 minutes and shows the order fulfillment times that are very low and very high.

The Run Chart

When data are collected over time, you should plot the variable of interest in sequential order of their collection before you plot any other graph, calculate descriptive statistics, or perform any statistical analyses. You need to do this because of the possible existence of a **lurking variable**, one that has an important effect on the CTQ or CTP being studied, but has not been considered in the statistical study. A **run chart** is a type of chart in which you plot all of the measurements at a particular time for a CTQ or CTP on the *Y*-axis at that time period, and time on the *X*-axis. Referring to the data concerning the order fulfillment process, Figure 3.8 illustrates the Minitab run chart for the fulfillment times plotted in the sequence in which they were received. Figure 3.9 displays the JMP run chart.

FIGURE 3.8
Minitab Run Chart of
Fulfillment Times

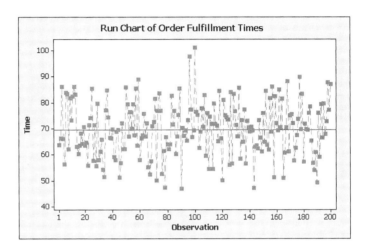

FIGURE 3.9
JMP Run Chart of
Fulfillment Times

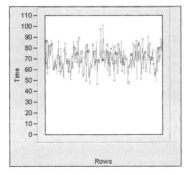

From Figure 3.8 or 3.9, observe that although there is a great deal of variation in the fulfillment times, there does not appear to be a pattern in the sequential order of the fulfillment times. In Chapter 11, "Control Charts for Six Sigma Managment," you will learn how to determine if only common causes are present in the fulfillment times. If so, then you can use the histogram and the dot plot previously shown to study the distribution of the fulfillment times.

SUMMARY

In this chapter, you learned about various graphical presentations. If you have a categorical (attribute) variable, you can construct a bar chart and a Pareto diagram. If you have a continuous (measurement) variable, you can construct a histogram, a dot chart, and a run chart.

REFERENCES

1. Beninger, J. M., and D. L. Robyn, "Quantitative Graphics in Statistics," *The American Statistician*, 32, 1978, 1–11.

2. Berenson, M. L., D. M. Levine, and T. C. Krehbiel, *Basic Business Statistics: Concepts and Applications*, 10th ed. (Upper Saddle River, NJ: Prentice Hall, 2006).

3. JMP Version 6 (Cary, NC: SAS Institute, 2005).

4. Minitab Version 14 (State College, PA: Minitab, 2004).

Appendix 3.1
Using Minitab to Construct Charts

You can use Minitab to create the charts presented in this chapter. If you have not already read Appendix 2.1, "Introduction to Minitab Version 14," you should do so now.

Generating a Bar Chart

To produce the bar chart in Figure 3.1 on page 25, open the ⊕ **LABTESTS** worksheet. Select **Graph → Bar Chart**. Then, do the following:

1. In the Bar Charts dialog box (see Figure A3.1), in the Bars represent: drop-down list box, select **Values from a table** because the frequencies in each category are provided (if you are using raw data, select Counts of unique values in the Bars represent: edit box). Select the **Simple** graph box. Click the **OK** button.

2. In the Bar Chart—Values from a table, One column of values, Simple dialog box (see Figure A3.2), enter **C2** or **Frequency** in the Categorical Variable: edit box. Enter **C1** or **Cause** in the Categorical variable: edit box. Click the **OK** button.

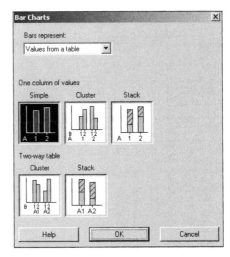

FIGURE A3.1
Minitab Bar Charts Dialog Box

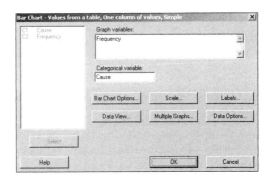

FIGURE A3.2
Minitab Bar Chart—Values from a Table, One Column of Values, Simple Dialog Box

To select colors for the bars and borders in the bar chart,

1. Right-click on any of the bars of the bar chart.
2. Select **Edit Bars**.
3. In the Attributes tab of the Edit Bars dialog box (see Figure A3.3), enter selections for Fill Pattern and Border and Fill Lines.

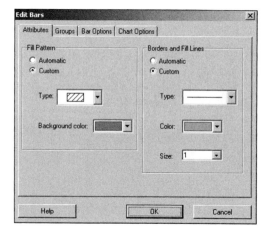

FIGURE A3.3
Minitab Edit Bars Dialog Box

Generating a Pareto Diagram

To produce the Pareto diagram of Figure 3.3 on page 26, open the ⊞ **LABTESTS** worksheet. This data set contains the causes of the defects in column C1 and the frequency of defects in column C2. Select **Stat → Quality Tools → Pareto Chart**. In the Pareto Chart dialog box (see Figure A3.4),

1. Select the **Chart defects table** option button.
2. In the Labels in: edit box, enter **C1** or **Cause**.

3. In the Frequencies in: edit box, enter **C2** or **Frequency**.
4. In the Combine defects after the first edit box, enter **99.9**.
5. Click the **OK** button.

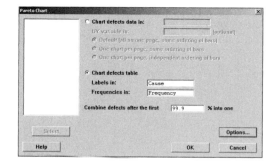

FIGURE A3.4
Minitab Pareto Chart Dialog Box

If the variable of interest is located in a single column and is in raw form with each row indicating a type of error, you select the Charts defects data in: option button and enter the appropriate column number or variable name in the Chart defects data in: edit box.

To select colors for the bars and borders in the Pareto diagram:

1. Right-click on any of the bars of the Pareto diagram.
2. Select **Edit Bars**.
3. In the Attributes tab of the Edit Bars dialog box, enter selections for Fill Pattern and Border and Fill Lines (see Figure A3.3).

Generating a Histogram

To produce the histogram in Figure 3.5 on page 27, open the ⊞ **ORDER.MTW** worksheet. Select **Graph → Histogram**.

1. In the Histograms dialog box (see Figure A3.5), select **Simple**. Click the **OK** button.

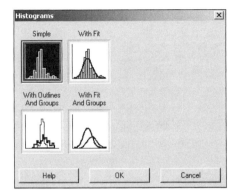

FIGURE A3.5
Minitab Histograms Dialog Box

2. In the Histogram—Simple dialog box (see Figure A3.6), enter **C1** or **Time** in the Graph variables: edit box. Click the **OK** button to produce the histogram.

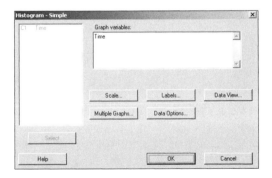

FIGURE A3.6
Minitab Histogram—Simple Dialog Box

To select colors for the bars and borders in the histogram and to define your own class groupings,

1. Right-click on any of the bars of the histogram.

2. Select **Edit Bars**.

3. In the Attributes tab of the Edit Bars dialog box, enter selections for Fill Pattern and Border and Fill Lines.

4. To define your own class groupings, select the **Binning** tab (see Figure A3.7). Select the **Midpoint** option button to specify midpoints (as in Figure 3.5) or the **Cutpoint** option button to specify class limits. Select the **Midpoint/Cutpoint** option button. Enter the set of values (such as 45 55 65 75 85 95 105) in the edit box. Click the **OK** button.

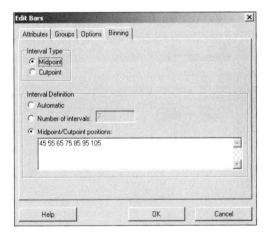

FIGURE A3.7
Minitab Edit Bars Binning Tab

Generating a Dot Plot

To produce a dot plot using Minitab, open the ⬛ **ORDER.MTW** worksheet. Select **Graph → Dotplot**, and then do the following:

1. In the Dotplots dialog box (see Figure A3.8), select the **One Y Simple** box. (If dot plots of more than one group are desired, select the **One Y With Groups** box.)

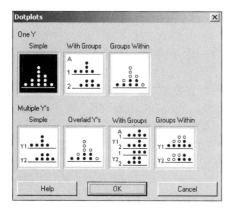

FIGURE A3.8
Minitab Dotplots Dialog Box

2. In the Dotplot—One Y, Simple dialog box (see Figure A3.9), in the Graph variables: edit box, enter **C1** or **Time**. Click the **OK** button.

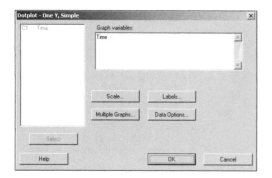

FIGURE A3.9
Minitab Dotplot—One Y, Simple Dialog Box

Generating a Run Chart

To produce the run chart in Figure 3.8 on page 29, open the ▤ **ORDER** worksheet. To generate a run chart of the order times, do the following:

1. Select **Stat → Quality Tools → Run Chart**.

2. In the Run Chart dialog box (see Figure A3.10), select the **Single column:** option button. Enter **C1** or **Time** in the edit box. Enter **1** in the Subgroup size: edit box. Click the **OK** button.

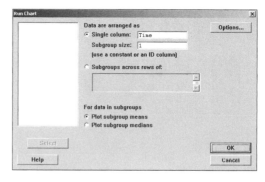

FIGURE A3.10
Minitab Run Chart Dialog Box

Appendix 3.2
Using JMP to Construct Charts

You can use JMP to create the charts presented in this chapter. If you have not already read Appendix 2.2 on page 20, "Introduction to JMP Version 6," you should do so now.

Generating a Bar Chart

To produce the bar chart in Figure 3.2 on page 25, open the 🌐 **LABTESTS.JMP** data table. Select **Analyze → Distribution**. Then do the following:

1. Select **Cause** and click the **Y, Columns** button. Select **Frequency** and click the **Freq** button. Click the **OK** button (see Figure A3.11).

FIGURE A3.11
JMP Distribution Dialog Box for Generating a Bar Chart

2. Click the red triangle next to Cause. Select **Histogram Options → Count Axis**.

3. Click the red triangle next to Cause. Select **Histogram Options → Show Counts**.

4. Click the red triangle next to Cause. Select **Histogram Options** and deselect **Vertical**.

To select colors for the bars and background,

1. Right-click on any one of the bars of the bar chart.

2. Select **Histogram Color** and choose a color for the bar. Continue by selecting colors for the other bars.

3. Right-click on any one of the bars of the bar chart. Select **Background Color** and select a color.

Generating a Pareto Diagram

To produce the Pareto diagram of Figure 3.4 on page 26, open the 🌐 **LABTESTS. JMP** data table. Select **Graph → Pareto Plot**. Then, do the following:

1. Select **Cause**. Click the **Y, Cause** button. Select **Frequency**. Click the **Freq** button. Click the **OK** button (see Figure A3.12).

FIGURE A3.12
JMP Pareto Plot Dialog Box

2. Click the red triangle next to the Pareto Plot. Select **Label Cum Percent Points**.

   To select colors for the bars and background,

1. Right-click on any one of the bars of the bar chart.

2. Select **Causes → Colors**. Select a color for the bar. Continue by selecting colors for other bars.

Generating a Histogram

To produce a histogram, open the  **ORDER.JMP** data table. Select **Analyze → Distribution**. Then do the following:

1. Select **Time**. Click the **Y, Columns** button. Click the **OK** button (see Figure A3.13). You will get a vertical histogram, a vertical outlier box-and-whisker plot (see Section 4.3), and descriptive statistics (see Sections 4.1 and 4.2).

2. Click the down arrow next to the Time variable. Select **Display Options → Horizontal Layout** to reorganize the output horizontally.

3. To adjust the histogram bars, select **Tools → Grabber**. Position the hand on one of the bars of the histogram, and hold down the mouse. Move the

hand to the left to increase the bar width and combine intervals. Move the hand to the right to decrease the bar width showing more bars.

FIGURE A3.13
JMP Distribution Dialog Box for Generating a Histogram

To select colors for the bars and background,

1. Right-click on any one of the bars of the bar chart.

2. Select **Histogram Color** and choose a color for the bar. Continue by selecting colors for the other bars.

3. Right-click on any one of the bars of the bar chart. Select **Background Color** and select a color.

Generating a Run Chart

To produce the run chart in Figure 3.9 on page 29, open the ORDER.JMP data table. To generate a run chart of the order times, do the following:

1. Select **Graph → Chart**.

2. In the Report: Chart dialog box (see Figure A3.14), deselect the **Overlay** check box. Select **Vertical**. Select **Line Chart**. Select the **Show Points** and **Connect Points** check boxes.

3. Select **Time**. Click the **Statistics** button. Select the **OK** button.

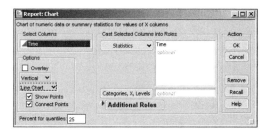

FIGURE A3.14
JMP Chart Dialog Box for a Run Chart

4. Click the red triangle next to Chart.
   Deselect **Thick Connect Line**.

CHAPTER 4

Descriptive Statistics

INTRODUCTION

4.1 MEASURES OF CENTRAL TENDENCY

4.2 MEASURES OF VARIATION

4.3 THE SHAPE OF DISTRIBUTIONS

SUMMARY

REFERENCES

APPENDIX 4.1
USING MINITAB FOR DESCRIPTIVE STATISTICS

APPENDIX 4.2
USING JMP FOR DESCRIPTIVE STATISTICS

LEARNING OBJECTIVES

After reading this chapter, you will be able to

- Describe the properties of central tendency, variation, and shape in measurement data.
- Use the Minitab and JMP statistical software to compute descriptive statistics.

INTRODUCTION

Among the most important summarizing activities of descriptive statistics are those statistical methods that help measure properties of a numerical variable. Reading this chapter will allow you to learn about some of the methods used to identify the properties of central tendency, variation, and shape.

4.1   MEASURES OF CENTRAL TENDENCY

Although the graphs discussed in Chapter 3, "Presenting Data in Charts and Tables," are extremely useful for getting a visual picture of what the distribution of a CTQ or CTP looks like, you need to compute measures of central tendency or location. Three measures of central tendency will be developed: the arithmetic mean (often called the *mean* or *average*), the median, and the mode. If you compute these measures from a sample, they are **statistics**. If you compute these measures from a population, they are **parameters**. (To distinguish sample statistics and population parameters, Roman letters are used for sample statistics, and Greek letters are used for population parameters.)

The Arithmetic Mean

The arithmetic mean (also called the *mean* or *average*) is the most commonly used measure of central tendency. You calculate the arithmetic mean by summing the numerical values of the variable, and then you divide this sum by the number of values.

For a sample containing a set of n values, $X_1, X_2, \ldots, X_n$, the arithmetic mean of a sample (given by the symbol $\bar{X}$ called X *bar*) is written as:

$$\bar{X} = \frac{\text{sum of the values}}{\text{number of values}}$$

To illustrate the computation of the sample mean, consider the following example related to your personal life: the time it takes to get ready to go to work in the morning. Many people wonder why it seems to take longer than they anticipate getting ready to leave for work, but very few people have actually measured the time it takes them to get ready in the morning. Suppose you operationally define the time to get ready as the time in minutes (rounded to the nearest minute) from when you get out of bed to when you leave your home. You decide to measure these data for a period of 10 consecutive working days, with the following results:

Day	1	2	3	4	5	6	7	8	9	10
Time (minutes)	39	29	43	52	39	44	40	31	44	35

 TIMES

To compute the mean time, first compute the sum of all the data values, 39 + 29 + 43 + 52 + 39 + 44 + 40 + 31 + 44 + 35, which is 396. Then, take this sum of 396 and divide by 10, the number of data values. The result, 39.6, is the mean time to get ready.

Although the mean time to get ready is 39.6 minutes, not one individual day in the sample actually had that value. In addition, the calculation of the mean is based on all the values in the set of data. No other commonly used measure of central tendency possesses this characteristic.

CAUTION: WHEN TO USE THE ARITHMETIC MEAN

Because its computation is based on every value, the mean is greatly affected by any extreme value or values. When there are extreme values, the mean presents a distorted representation of the data. Thus, the mean is not the best measure of central tendency to use for describing or summarizing a set of data that has extreme values.

To demonstrate the effect that extreme values have when summarizing and describing the property of central tendency, suppose that the highest value of 52 minutes was actually 98 minutes. In this case, the mean is equal to:

$$\overline{X} = \frac{\text{sum of the values}}{\text{number of values}}$$

$$\overline{X} = \frac{442}{10} = 44.2$$

You see how one extreme value has dramatically changed the mean? Instead of being a number "somewhere" in the middle of the 10 get-ready times, the new mean of 44.2 minutes is greater than 9 of the ten get-ready times. Thus, the mean is not a very good measure of central tendency for the revised time to get ready data.

USING SUMMATION NOTATION IN EQUATIONS {OPTIONAL}

Although you can represent the formula for the mean with just a few words, for most every other statistic, this is not practical. In statistics, formulas are represented using a notation called **summation notation** (see Appendix B, "Summation Notation," for further discussion). Instead of using the formula with words, such as the following:

$$\text{arithmetic mean} = \frac{\text{sum of the values}}{\text{number of values}}$$

Continues

You use the following three symbols to develop the equation for the arithmetic mean:

1. An uppercase italic X with a horizontal line above it, $\bar{X}$, pronounced as "X bar," which is the arithmetic mean of the sample.
2. The lowercase italic n, which represents the number of values that were summed in the sample. This is also known as the *sample size*.
3. A subscripted uppercase italic X (for example, X_1) that represents one of the data values being summed. When there are n values in the sample, the last value is X_n.

Using these three symbols, you can write the following equation:

$$\bar{X} = \frac{X_1 + X_2 + \cdots + X_n}{n}$$

In this equation, the ellipsis ($\cdots$) is used instead of writing out all the values of X. You use the Greek letter sigma as a symbol that represents the sum of all the values, so that the formula simplifies to the following:

$$\bar{X} = \frac{\sum_{i=1}^{n} X_i}{n} \qquad (4.1)$$

The Median

The **median** is the value that splits a ranked set of data into two equal parts. If there are no ties, half the values will be smaller than the median, and half will be larger. The median is not affected by any extreme values in a set of data. Whenever an extreme value is present, the median is preferred instead of the mean in describing the central tendency of a set of data.

To calculate the median from a set of data, you must first rank the data values from smallest to largest. Then, the median is computed, as described next.

MEDIAN

The median is the value such that 50% of the values are smaller and 50% of the values are larger.

$$\text{Median} = \frac{n+1}{2} \text{ ranked value} \qquad (4.2)$$

where n = the number of values

You use Equation (4.2) to compute the median by following one of two rules:

Rule 1   If there is an *odd* number of values in the data set, the median is the middle ranked value.

Rule 2   If there is an *even* number of values in the data set, then the median is the average of the two values in the middle of the data set.

To compute the median for the sample of 10 times to get ready in the morning, you place the raw data in order as follows:

| 29 | 31 | 35 | 39 | 39 | 40 | 43 | 44 | 44 | 52 |

Ranks:

| 1 | 2 | 3 | 4 | 5 | 6 | 7 | 8 | 9 | 10 |

↑

Median = 39.5

Using rule 2 for the even-sized sample of 10 days, the median corresponds to the $(10 + 1)/2 = 5.5$ ranked value, halfway between the fifth-ranked value and the sixth-ranked value. Because the fifth-ranked value is 39 and the sixth-ranked value is 40, the median is the average of 39 and 40, or 39.5. The median of 39.5 means that for half of the days, the time to get ready is less than or equal to 39.5 minutes, and for half of the days, the time to get ready is greater than or equal to 39.5 minutes.

To illustrate the computation of the median when there is odd number of values, you can compute the median for the second week (5 days) of the study (days 6 through 10). The times for these days were:

| 44 | 40 | 31 | 44 | 35 |

Placing these values in order results in the following:

| 31 | 35 | 40 | 44 | 44 |

Ranks:

| 1 | 2 | 3 | 4 | 5 |

↑

Median = 40

Using rule 1 for the odd number of 5 days, the median corresponds to the $(5 + 1)/2 =$ third-ranked value. The third-ranked value is 40 minutes.

The Mode

The **mode** is the value in a set of data that appears most frequently. Like the median and unlike the mean, extreme values do not affect the mode. You should use the mode only for descriptive purposes, because it is more variable from sample to sample than either the mean or the median. For measurement variables, often there is no mode or there are several modes. For the get-ready times for the 10 days, there are two modes, 39 minutes and 44 minutes, because each of these values occurs twice.

Quartiles

Quartiles split a set of data into four equal parts. 25.0% of the values are smaller than the first quartile, Q_1, and 75.0% are larger. The second quartile, Q_2, is the median. 50.0% of the values are smaller than the median and 50.0% are larger. 75.0% of the values are smaller than the third quartile, Q_3, and 25.0% are larger.

The quartiles are defined in Equations (4.3) and (4.4).

FIRST QUARTILE Q_1

The **first quartile Q_1**, is the value such that 25.0% of the values are smaller and 75.0% are larger.

$$Q_1 = \frac{n+1}{4} \text{ ranked value} \qquad (4.3)$$

where n = sample size

THIRD QUARTILE Q_3

The **third quartile Q_3**, is the value such that 75.0% of the values are smaller and 25.0% are larger.

$$Q_3 = \frac{3(n+1)}{4} \text{ ranked value} \qquad (4.4)$$

where n = sample size

Using the sample of 10 times to get ready in the morning, you place the raw data in order as follows:

| 29 | 31 | 35 | 39 | 39 | 40 | 43 | 44 | 44 | 52 |

Ranks:

| 1 | 2 | 3 | 4 | 5 | 6 | 7 | 8 | 9 | 10 |

The first quartile is the $(n + 1)/4$ or $(10 + 1)/4 = 2.75$ ranked value, 75% past the second-ranked value. Because the second-ranked value is 31 and the third-ranked value is 35 (and their difference is $35 - 31 = 4$), the first quartile is 34 [because $31 + (3/4)(4) = 31 + 3 = 34$]. This means that on 25% of the days, the time to get ready is less than or equal to 34 minutes, and on 75% of the days, the time to get ready is greater than or equal to 34 minutes.

The third quartile is the $3(n + 1)/4$ or $3(10 + 1)/4 = 8.25$ ranked value, 25% past the eighth-ranked value. Because the eighth-ranked value is 44 and the ninth-ranked value is also 44, the third quartile is 44 $[44 + (\frac{1}{4})(0)]$. This means that on 75% of the days, the time to get ready is less than or equal to 44 minutes, and on 25% of the days, the time to get ready is greater than or equal to 44 minutes.

When you have a large number of data values, it is impractical to manually compute descriptive statistics, such as the mean, median, and quartiles. You should use statistical software such as Minitab or JMP. Figure 4.1 illustrates Minitab descriptive statistics while Figure 4.2 represents JMP descriptive statistics for the time to get ready in the morning data. Additional descriptive statistics included in Figures 4.1 and 4.2 will be discussed in Sections 4.2 and 4.3.

Descriptive Statistics: Time

Variable	Total Count	Mean	Standard Deviation	Variance	Sum	Minimum	Q1	Median	Q3
Time	10	39.60	6.77	45.82	396.00	29.00	34.00	39.50	44.00

Variable	Maximum	Range	Skewness
Time	52.00	23.00	0.09

FIGURE 4.1   Minitab Descriptive Statistics for the Time to Get Ready in the Morning Data

FIGURE 4.2
JMP Descriptive
Statistics for the Time
to Get Ready in the
Morning Data

Now that you have examined the descriptive statistics for the time to get ready data, you can return to the fulfillment time data previously discussed in Chapter 3. Figure 4.3 illustrates Minitab descriptive statistics for the fulfillment time data. Figure 4.4 is JMP output.

From Figures 4.3 and 4.4, you see that the mean of 69.637 minutes is very close to the median of 69.5 minutes. The median of 69.5 minutes tells you that half the orders take 69.5 minutes or less to fill, and half the orders take 69.5 minutes or more. The first quartile of 62.35 minutes tells you that 25 percent of the orders take 62.35 minutes or less to fill (and 75 percent take 62.35 minutes or more). The third quartile of 76.75 minutes tells you that 75 percent of the orders take 76.75 minutes or less to fill (and 25 percent take 76.75 minutes or more). The fastest fulfillment time was 46.8 minutes and the slowest fulfillment time was 101.1 minutes.

FIGURE 4.3
Minitab Descriptive
Statistics for the Ful-
fillment Time Data

```
Descriptive Statistics: Time

            Total
Variable  Count    Mean   StDev  Variance  Minimum      Q1  Median      Q3
Time        200  69.637  10.411  108.383   46.800  62.350  69.500  76.750


Variable  Maximum   Range  Skewness
Time      101.100  54.300      0.10
```

FIGURE 4.4
JMP Descriptive
Statistics for the Ful-
fillment Time Data

Quantiles			Moments	
100.0%	maximum	101.10	Mean	69.6365
99.5%		101.08	Std Dev	10.410693
97.5%		88.09	Std Err Mean	0.7361472
90.0%		83.97	upper 95% Mean	71.08815
75.0%	quartile	76.75	lower 95% Mean	68.18485
50.0%	median	69.50	N	200
25.0%	quartile	62.35		
10.0%		56.11		
2.5%		50.10		
0.5%		46.80		
0.0%	minimum	46.80		

4.2   MEASURES OF VARIATION

A second important property that describes a set of numerical data is variation. **Variation** is the amount of **dispersion**, or spread, in a set of data, be it a sample or a population. Three frequently used measures of variation are the range, the variance, and the standard deviation.

The Range

The range is the simplest measure of variation in a set of data.

> RANGE
>
> The **range** is equal to the largest value minus the smallest value:
>
> $$\text{Range} = \text{largest value} - \text{smallest value} \qquad (4.5)$$

Using the data pertaining to the time to get ready in the morning on page 43:

$$\text{Range} = \text{largest value} - \text{smallest value}$$
$$\text{Range} = 52 - 29 = 23 \text{ minutes}$$

This means that the largest difference between any two days in the time to get ready in the morning is 23 minutes.

Referring to the data concerning the fulfillment time of orders, in Figure 4.3 or 4.4 on page 46, observe that the range is 54.3 minutes. This means that the largest difference in the fulfillment time of any two orders is 54.3 minutes.

The Variance and the Standard Deviation

Although the range is a measure of the total spread, it does not consider *how* the values distribute around the mean. Two commonly used measures of variation that take into account how all the values in the data are distributed around the mean are the variance and the standard deviation. These statistics measure how the values fluctuate around the mean.

A simple measure around the mean might just take the difference between each value and the mean, and then sum these differences. However, if you did that, you would find that because the mean is the balance point in a set of data, for every set of data, these differences would sum to zero. One measure of variation that would differ from data set to data set would square the difference between each value and the mean and then sum these squared differences. In statistics, this quantity is called a **sum of squares** (or **SS**) and will be encountered again in Chapters 5–10. This sum of squares is then divided by the number of values minus 1 (for sample data) to get the sample **variance**. The square root of the sample variance (S^2) is the sample **standard deviation** (S). This statistic is the most widely used measure of variation. The steps for computing the variance and the standard deviation of a sample of data are presented in Exhibit 4.1.

EXHIBIT 4.1   COMPUTING S^2 AND S

To compute S^2, the sample variance, do the following:

1. Compute the difference between each value and the mean.
2. Square each difference.
3. Add the squared differences.
4. Divide this total by $n - 1$.

To compute S, the sample standard deviation, take the square root of the variance.

Table 4.1 illustrates the computation of the variance and standard deviation using the steps of Exhibit 4.2 for the time to get ready in the morning data. You can see that the sum of the differences between the individual values and the mean is equal to zero.

TABLE 4.1   Computing the Sample Variance and Sample Standard Deviation for the Time to Get Ready in the Morning Data

Time (X)	Difference Between X and the Mean	Squared Differences Around the Mean
39	-0.6	0.36
29	-10.6	112.36
43	3.4	11.56
52	12.4	153.76
39	-0.6	0.36
44	4.4	19.36
40	0.4	0.16
31	-8.6	73.96
44	4.4	19.36
35	-4.6	21.16
Mean = 39.6	Sum of Differences = 0	Sum of Squared Differences = 412.4

You calculate the sample variance S^2 by dividing the sum of the squared differences computed in step 3 (412.4) by the sample size (10) minus 1:

$$\text{Sample variance } (S^2) = \frac{412.4}{9} = 45.82$$

Because the variance is in squared units (in squared minutes for these data), to compute the standard deviation, you take the squared root of the variance. Thus:

$$\text{Sample standard deviation } (S) = \sqrt{45.82} = 6.77$$

For the order fulfillment times data summarized in Figures 4.3 and 4.4 on page 46, the standard deviation is 10.411 minutes. (Minitab labels the standard deviation as "StDev," while JMP labels the standard deviation as "Std Dev.") How can you interpret this value? The standard deviation helps you to know how a set of data clusters or distributes around its mean. For almost all sets of data that have a single mode, most of the values lie within an interval of plus or minus 3 standard deviations above and below the mean. Therefore, knowing the mean and the standard deviation usually helps define the range in which most of the data values are clustering. Thus, for the order fulfillment times, it is reasonable to state that most of the fulfillment times will be between the mean of 69.637 ± (3) × 10.411) or 38.404 minutes and 100.87 minutes.

As summarized in Exhibit 4.2, you can make the following statements about the range, variance, and standard deviation.

EXHIBIT 4.2   CHARACTERISTICS OF THE RANGE, VARIANCE, AND STANDARD DEVIATION

1. The more spread out or dispersed the data are, the larger will be the range, the variance, and the standard deviation.

2. The more concentrated or homogeneous the data are, the smaller will be the range, the variance, and the standard deviation.

3. If the values are all the same (so that there is no variation in the data), the range, variance, and standard deviation will all be zero.

4. The range, variance, or standard deviation will always be greater than or equal to zero.

These three measures of variation will be used extensively in Chapters 5–11.

EQUATIONS FOR THE VARIANCE AND STANDARD DEVIATION {OPTIONAL}

$$S^2 = \frac{\sum\limits_{i=1}^{n}(X_i - \bar{X})^2}{n-1} \qquad (4.6)$$

$$S = \sqrt{\frac{\sum\limits_{i=1}^{n}(X_i - \bar{X})^2}{n-1}} \qquad (4.7)$$

where

$\bar{X}$ = sample mean

n = sample size

$X_i = i^{th}$ value of the variable X

$\sum\limits_{i=1}^{n}(X_i - \bar{X})^2$ = summation of all the squared differences between the X values and $\bar{X}$

Using the results of Table 4.1 and Equations (4.6) and (4.7):

$$S^2 = \frac{\sum\limits_{i=1}^{n}(X_i - \bar{X})^2}{n-1}$$

$$S^2 = \frac{412.4}{10-1} = 45.82$$

$$S = \sqrt{45.82} = 6.77$$

4.3   THE SHAPE OF DISTRIBUTIONS

Shape

Shape is a third important property of a set of measurement data. Shape is the pattern of distribution of the data. You can use either a histogram or a dot plot to study the shape of a distribution of data.

A distribution will either be **symmetrical**, when low and high values balance each other out, or **skewed**, not symmetrical and showing an imbalance of low values and high values. To determine the shape of a data set, you compare the mean with the median. If these two measures are equal, the CTQ or X is considered to be symmetrical (or zero-skewed). If the mean is less than the median, the variable is called *negative*, or **left-skewed**. If the mean is greater than the median, the variable is described as *positive*, or **right-skewed**. Thus:

Mean > median: positive, or right-skewness
Mean < median: negative, or left-skewness
Mean = median: symmetry, or zero-skewness

Positive skewness occurs when the mean is increased by some unusually high values. Negative skewness occurs when the mean is reduced by some extremely low values. The distribution of a CTQ or CTP is symmetrical when there are no really extreme values in a particular direction so that low and high values balance each other out. Figure 4.5 depicts the shapes of three data sets.

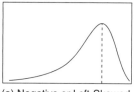
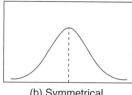
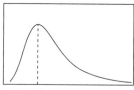

(a) Negative or Left-Skewed   (b) Symmetrical   (c) Positive or Right-Skewed

FIGURE 4.5   A Comparison of Three Data Sets Differing in Shape

The data in panel A are negative, or left-skewed. In this panel, there is a long tail and distortion to the left that is caused by some extremely small values. These extremely small values pull the mean downward so that the mean is less than the median. The data in panel B are symmetrical; each half of the curve is a mirror image of the other half of the curve. The low and high values on the scale balance, and the mean equals the median. The data in panel C are positive, or right-skewed. In this panel, there is a long tail on the right of the distribution and a distortion to the right that is caused by some extremely large values. These extremely large values pull the mean upward so that the mean is greater than the median.

Referring to the fulfillment time of orders illustrated in the histograms of Figures 3.5 and 3.6 on page 27 and the dot plot of Figure 3.7 on page 28, the distribution appears to be approximately symmetric. In Figure 4.3 on page 46, Minitab displays a skewness statistic (that is based on the cubed differences around the mean) equal to 0.10. Since this value is close to zero, you conclude that the order fulfillment times are approximately symmetric.

In addition to determining whether a set of data is symmetric or skewed, you are often concerned with whether there is more than one concentration of data in the distribution of values. A distribution with two concentrations of data is called **bimodal**. The existence of a bimodal distribution is often a signal that data from two groups have been inappropriately combined into a single group.

As an illustration of a bimodal distribution, a bank collected data on a sample of 200 customers who arrived during peak times to determine the waiting time (in minutes) to conduct a transaction. Figure 4.6 presents a Minitab histogram of the waiting times.

FIGURE 4.6

Minitab Histogram of the Waiting Times at a Bank

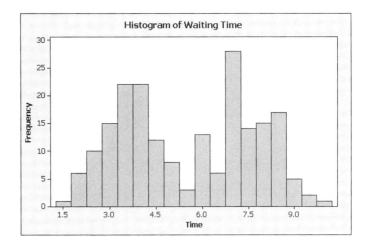

There appear to be two peaks in the distribution of waiting times. One peak is between 3.5 and 4.5, and the other peak is between 6 and 7.5. In fact, the data are from a sample of 100 customers at two different branches of the bank. The peak time for the first branch from which the data was collected was Friday from 12 noon until 2 p.m. (The branch was located in the central business district of a city.) The peak time for the second branch from which the data was collected was Friday from 5 p.m. until 7 p.m. (The branch was located in a residential neighborhood.)

Figure 4.7 is a Minitab dot plot of the waiting times for each of the banks.

From Figure 4.7, observe that the distribution of the waiting times is different for the two banks. The distribution for bank 1 (located in the business district) is concentrated between 3 and 4 minutes, and the distribution for bank 2 (located in a residential neighborhood) is concentrated between 7 and 8 minutes.

FIGURE 4.7
Minitab Dot Plot of
the Waiting Times for
Two Banks

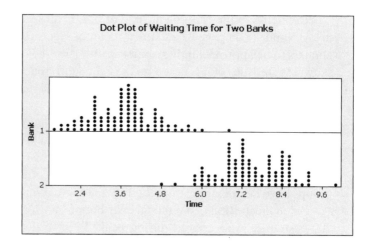

The Five-Number Summary

The five-number summary provides another way to determine the shape of the distribution.

A five-number summary consists of the following:

Smallest value Q_1 Median Q_3 largest value

Table 4.2 explains how the relationship among the "five numbers" allows you to recognize the shape of a data set.

TABLE 4.2   Relationships Among the Five Number Summary and the Type of Distribution

	Type of Distribution		
	Symmetric	**Right-Skewed**	**Left-Skewed**
Distance from the *smallest value* to the median versus the distance from the median to the *largest value*.	Both distances are the same.	The distance from the *smallest value* to the median is less than the distance from the median to the *largest value*.	The distance from the *smallest value* to the median is greater than the distance from the median to the *largest value*.
Distance from the *smallest value* to Q_1 versus the distance from Q_3 to the *largest value*.	Both distances are the same.	The distance from the *smallest value* to Q_1 is less than the distance from Q_3 to the *largest value*.	The distance from the *smallest value* to Q_1 is greater than the distance from Q_3 to the *largest value*.

	Type of Distribution		
	Symmetric	**Right-Skewed**	**Left-Skewed**
Distance from Q_1 to the median versus the distance from the median to Q_3.	Both distances are the same.	The distance from Q_1 to the median is less than the distance from the median to Q_3.	The distance from Q_1 to the median is greater than the distance from the median to Q_3.

For the sample of 10 get-ready times, the smallest value is 29 and the largest value is 52. Calculations done previously show that the median = 39.5, the first quartile = 34, and the third quartile = 44 (see pages 43 – 45). Therefore, the five-number summary is as follows:

    29   34   39.5   44   52

The distance from the median to the *largest value* (52 – 39.5 = 12.5) is slightly greater than the distance from the *smallest value* to the median (39.5 – 29 = 10.5). The distance from Q_3 to the *largest value* (52 – 44 = 8) is more the distance from the *smallest value* to Q_1 (34 – 29 = 5). Therefore, the get-ready times are slightly right-skewed.

The Box-and-Whisker Plot

The **box-and-whisker plot** provides a graphical representation of the data based on the five-number summary. The line drawn within the box represents the location of the median value in the data. The line at the lower end of the box represents the location of Q_1, and the line at the upper end of the box represents the location of Q_3. Thus, the box contains the middle 50% of the values in the distribution. The lower 25% of the data are represented by a line (i.e., a *whisker*) connecting the lower end of the box to the location of the smallest value. Similarly, the upper 25% of the data are represented by a line connecting the upper end of the box to the largest value. Figure 4.8 demonstrates the relationship between the box-and-whisker plot and the polygon. Four different types of distributions are depicted with their box-and-whisker plot.

When a data set is perfectly symmetrical, as is the case in Figure 4.8(A) and (D), the mean and median are the same. In addition, the length of the left (or lower) whisker will equal the length of the right (or upper) whisker, and the median line will divide the box in half.

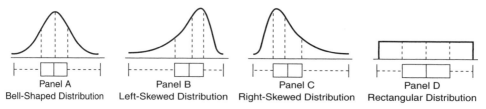

Panel A	Panel B	Panel C	Panel D
Bell-Shaped Distribution	Left-Skewed Distribution	Right-Skewed Distribution	Rectangular Distribution

FIGURE 4.8   Four Hypothetical Distributions Examined Through Their Box-and-Whisker Plots and Corresponding Distributions

Note: Area under each distribution is split into quartiles corresponding to the five-number summary for the respective box-and-whisker plot.

When a data set is left-skewed, as in Figure 4.8(B), the few small values distort the mean toward the left tail. For this hypothetical left-skewed distribution, 75% of all data values are found between the left (or lower) edge of the box (Q_1) and the end of the right (or upper) whisker. Therefore, the long left (or lower) whisker contains the distribution of only the smallest 25% of the values, demonstrating the distortion from symmetry in this data set.

For the right-skewed data set in Figure 4.8(C), the concentration of values is on the low end of the scale (i.e., the left side of the box-and-whisker plot). Here, 75% of all data values are found between the beginning of the left (or lower) whisker (smallest value) and the right (or upper) edge of the box (Q_3) and the remaining 25% of the values are dispersed along the long right (or upper) whisker at the upper end of the scale.

Figure 4.9 represents the Minitab box-and-whisker plot of the time to get ready in the morning.

FIGURE 4.9
Minitab Box-and-Whisker Plot of the Time to Get Ready in the Morning

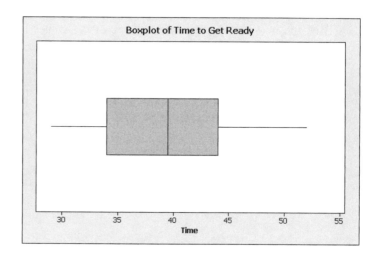

The box-and-whisker plot seems to indicate an approximately symmetric distribution of the time to get ready. The median line in the middle of the box is

approximately equidistant from the ends of the box, and the length of the whiskers does not appear to be very different.

Figure 4.10 presents the Minitab box-and-whisker plot of the order fulfillment times. Figure 4.11 presents the JMP box-and-whisker plot of the order fulfillment times.

Notice that in Figure 4.10, an asterisk appears at the right side of the box-and-whisker plot. This represents an extreme value, or *outlier*, in the data. Other than the extreme value, the remainder of the distribution appears approximately symmetric. In Figure 4.11, JMP provides two different box-and-whisker plots, along with a histogram. The top box-and-whisker plot is an outlier plot that also identifies points with extreme values. The box-and-whisker plot closest to the histogram is a quantile plot that shows the five-number summary and also additional quantiles such as the 10th percentage point and the 90th percentage point.

The box-and-whisker plot is particularly useful when you are comparing two or more groups. In such a situation, separate box-and-whisker plots are shown side by side so you can directly compare the different groups in terms of central tendency, variation, and shape.

FIGURE 4.10
Minitab Box-and-Whisker Plot of the Order Fulfillment Times

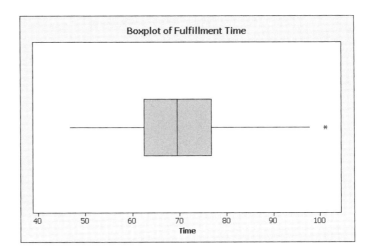

FIGURE 4.11
JMP Box-and-Whisker Plot of the Order Fulfillment Times

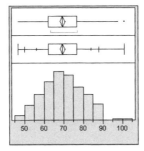

SUMMARY

This chapter explained the properties of central tendency, variation, and shape that allow you to describe a set of data values for measurement data.

REFERENCES

1. Berenson, M. L., D. M. Levine, and T. C. Krehbiel. *Basic Business Statistics: Concepts and Applications,* 10th Ed. (Upper Saddle River, NJ: Prentice Hall, 2006).

2. JMP Version 6 (Cary, NC: SAS Institute, 2005).

3. Minitab Version 14 (State College, PA: Minitab, 2004).

Appendix 4.1
Using Minitab for Descriptive Statistics

Calculating Descriptive Statistics

To compute descriptive statistics for the order fulfillment times shown in Figure 4.3 on page 46, open the ⊕ **ORDER.MTW** worksheet. Select **Stat → Basic Statistics → Display Descriptive Statistics**:

1. In the Display Descriptive Statistics dialog box (see Figure A4.1), enter **C1** or **Time** in the Variables: edit box.

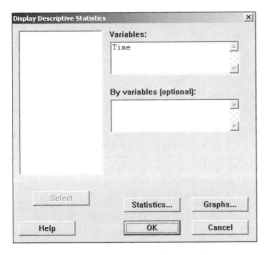

FIGURE A4.1   Minitab Display Descriptive Statistics Dialog Box

2. Select the **Statistics** button. In the Descriptive Statistics—Statistics dialog box (see Figure A4.2), select the **Mean, Standard deviation,**

Variance, First quartile, Median, Third quartile, Minimum, Maximum, Range, Skewness, and **N total** (the sample size) check boxes. Click the **OK** button to return to the Display Descriptive Statistics dialog box. Click the **OK** button again to compute the descriptive statistics.

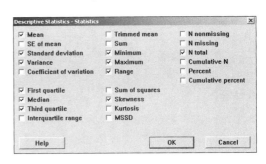

FIGURE A4.2   Minitab Descriptive Statistics—Statistics Dialog Box

Generating a Box-and-Whisker Plot

To produce a box-and-whisker plot using Minitab, open the ⊕ **ORDER.MTW** worksheet. Select **Graph → Boxplot**:

1. In the Boxplots dialog box (see Figure A4.3), select the **One Y Simple** choice. (If you want to generate a side-by-side box-and-whisker plot for two or more groups, select the **One Y With Groups** choice.)

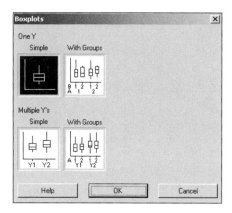

FIGURE A4.3 Minitab Boxplots Dialog Box

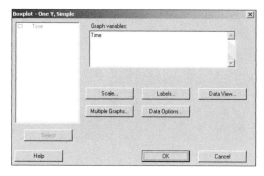

FIGURE A4.4 Minitab Boxplots— One Y, Simple Dialog Box

2. In the Boxplot—One Y, Simple dialog box (see Figure A4.4), enter **C1** or **Time** in the Graph variables: edit box.

3. Select the **Scale** button. In the Axis and Ticks tab, select the **Transpose value and category scales** check box to produce a horizontal box-and-whisker plot. Click the **OK** button.

Appendix 4.2
Using JMP for Descriptive Statistics

Generating Descriptive Statistics and a Box-and-Whisker Plot

To compute descriptive statistics and produce a histogram and a box-and-whisker plot, open the ⬤ **ORDER.JMP** data table. Select **Analyze → Distribution**. Then do the following:

1. Select **Time**. Click the **Y, Columns** button. Click the **OK** button. You will get a vertical histogram, a vertical outlier box-and-whisker plot, and descriptive statistics.

2. Click the red triangle next to the Time variable. Select **Display Options → Horizontal Layout** to reorganize the output horizontally. Click **Display Options → More Moments** to compute additional statistics.

3. Click the red triangle next to the Time variable again. Select **Quantile Box Plot**.

CHAPTER 5

Probability and Probability Distributions

5.1 **WHAT IS PROBABILITY?**

5.2 **SOME RULES OF PROBABILITY**

5.3 **THE PROBABILITY DISTRIBUTION**

5.4 **THE BINOMIAL DISTRIBUTION**

5.5 **THE POISSON DISTRIBUTION**

5.6 **THE NORMAL DISTRIBUTION**

5.7 **THE NORMAL PROBABILITY PLOT**

SUMMARY

REFERENCES

APPENDIX 5.1
  USING MINITAB FOR PROBABILITY DISTRIBUTIONS AND PLOTS

APPENDIX 5.2
  USING JMP FOR PROBABILITY DISTRIBUTIONS AND PLOTS

LEARNING OBJECTIVES

After reading this chapter, you will be able to

- Understand basic probability concepts.
- Understand the basic properties of a probability distribution.
- Compute the mean and standard deviation of a probability distribution.
- Understand when to use the binomial, Poisson, and normal distributions and how to compute probabilities using these distributions.
- Use a normal probability plot to evaluate whether a set of data is normally distributed.

5.1   WHAT IS PROBABILITY?

The word *probability* is often used as a synonym for *chance, likelihood,* or *possibility.* These are words that you hear all the time with respect to the behavior of cycle times, safety performance (accidents), or quality of products or services. A **probability** is just the numeric value representing the chance, likelihood, or possibility that a particular event will occur, such as a defective customer transaction, a cycle time greater than 20 minutes, or an OSHA (Occupational Safety and Health Administration) reportable accident. In all these instances, the probability attached is a proportion or fraction whose values range *between 0 and 1, inclusively.*

The basic elements of probability theory are the individual outcomes of a particular process, such as an experimental trial or natural phenomenon. Each possible type of occurrence is referred to as an **event**. Each individual or distinct outcome is referred to as an **elementary event**. For example, when filling an order, the two possible outcomes are filled correctly and filled incorrectly. Each of these outcomes represents an elementary event. When rolling a standard six-sided die in which the six faces of the die contain either one, two, three, four, five, or six dots, there are six possible elementary events (see Figure 5.1). An event can be any one of these elementary events, a set of them, or a subset of all of them. For example, the event of an *even number of dots* is represented by three elementary events—two dots, four dots, or six dots.

FIGURE 5.1

Six Sides of a Pair of Dice

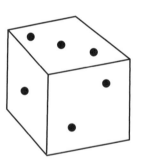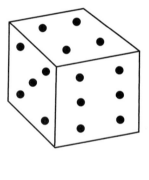

There are three distinct approaches for assigning a probability to an event occurring: the classical approach, the empirical (relative frequency) approach, and the subjective approach.

The **classical approach** for assigning probability is based on prior knowledge of the population involved. Classical probability often assumes that all elementary events are equally likely to occur. When this is true, $P(A)$, the probability that a particular event A will occur, is defined by:

$$\text{Probability of Event } A = \frac{\text{number of ways } A \text{ can occur}}{\text{total number of elementary events}}$$

EQUATION FOR THE PROBABILITY OF EVENT A USING THE CLASSICAL APPROACH {OPTIONAL}

$$P(A) = \frac{X_A}{T} \qquad (5.1)$$

where

X_A = number of ways A can occur

T = total number of elementary events

Figure 5.1 illustrates the classical probability approach. If the die is rolled a single time, the probability of getting the face with three dots is 1/6. There is only one face out of a total of six possible faces (i.e., elementary events) that contains exactly three dots. In the classical approach, you assume that the rolling process is totally random and has no memory, so that each of the six faces is equally likely to occur on each and every roll of the die. Thus, on any roll, the probability the face with three dots will occur remains 1/6. In the long run, assuming the process is working properly, you would theoretically expect 1,000 ($1/6 \times 6,000$) out of 6,000 rolls to result in a face with three dots.

The **empirical (relative frequency) approach to probability** states that if an experiment is conducted a large number of times (say M times), then the probability of event A occurring is the number of times A occurred during the experiments divided by M, the maximum number of times that A could have occurred during these experiments.

EQUATION FOR THE PROBABILITY OF EVENT A USING THE EMPIRICAL APPROACH {OPTIONAL}

$$P(A) = \frac{k}{M} \qquad (5.2)$$

where

k = number of times A occurred during these experiments

M = maximum number of times that event A could have occurred during these experiments

For example, suppose that in processing bank loans, a study of the most recent 500 loan applications indicated that the type of loan requested was omitted 12 times.

Consequently, the relative frequency probability of omitting the type of loan requested is:

$$P(\text{Omit type of loan selected}) = \frac{12}{500} = 0.024$$

Analytic studies are conducted to determine process characteristics. However, process characteristics have a past and present, and they will have a future. Thus, there is no frame from which classical probabilities can be calculated. Probabilities concerning process characteristics must be determined empirically, through experimentation; they must be relative frequency probabilities. For example, a newly hired worker is expected to perform an administrative operation, entering data from sales slips into a computer terminal. Is it possible to predict the percentage of entries per hour that will be in error? Unfortunately not; the best you can do is to train workers properly, then observe them performing their jobs over a long period of time. If a worker's efforts represent a stable system (see Chapter 11, "Control Charts for Six Sigma Management"), you can compute the relative frequency of sales slips entered with errors per hour as an estimate of the probability of a sales slip being entered with errors. You can use this relative frequency probability to predict the percentage of sales slips entered with errors per hour.

It is not always possible to use the classical approach or the empirical approach when assigning probabilities. In many circumstances, where either the number of elementary events or actual data are not available for the calculation of relative frequencies, the **subjective approach** is often used. Subjective probabilities can be based on expert opinion, or even gut feelings or hunches. While the process knowledge-based classical approach and the observed data-based empirical approach to probability assignment are considered *objective*, a subjective approach to probability assessment is used when individuals use different ways to judge the likely outcome of an event. Different individuals might provide differing assessments as to what future traffic patterns will be, what the weather will be like tomorrow, or what future economic conditions will be.

5.2   SOME RULES OF PROBABILITY

Several basic rules govern the theory of probability.

Rule 1: A **probability** is a number between 0 and 1 that is assigned to an event or outcome of some process or experiment.

The smallest possible probability value is 0. An event or outcome that has a probability of 0 is called a **null event** and has no chance of occurring. In the case of the die, the event of a face of seven has a probability of 0 because such an event cannot occur. In addition, no event can possibly have a probability that is below 0.

The largest possible probability value is 1.0. An event or outcome that has a probability of 1.0 is called a **certain event** and must occur. When rolling a single die, the event of a face with fewer than seven dots has a probability of 1.0 because it is certain that one of the six possible elementary events of one, two, three, four, five, or six dots must occur. This set of elementary events is also considered to be **collectively exhaustive** because one of them must occur. No event can have a probability that is above 1.0.

> **Rule 2**: The event that A does not occur is called "A complement" or simply "not A" and is given the symbol A'. If P(A) represents the probability of event A occurring, then 1 − P(A) represents the probability of event A not occurring, or P(A').

For example, in the case of the bank loan application, the complement of observing that the type of loan requested was omitted is observing that the type of loan requested is checked. Because the probability of omitting the type of loan request is 12/500, the probability of not omitting the type of loan request is 1 − (12/500) = 488/500 or:

$$P \text{ (Not omitting loan request)} = 1 - P \text{ (Omitting loan request)}$$
$$= 1 - 12/500$$
$$= 488/500$$
$$= 0.976$$

> **Rule 3**: If two events A and B are **mutually exclusive**, then the probability of both events A and B occurring simultaneously is 0.

If two events are *mutually exclusive*, they both *cannot* occur at the same time. When rolling a standard six-sided die in which the six faces of the die contain either one, two, three, four, five, or six dots, there are six possible elementary events. On one roll of a single die, the face of the die cannot have three dots *and* also have four dots. It can have one or the other, but not both.

> **Rule 4**: If two events A and B are *mutually exclusive*, then the probability of either event A *or* event B occurring is the sum of their separate probabilities.

In the example concerning the single die, if you want to determine the probability that a face that has two dots *or* three dots will occur, then:

$$P \text{ (Face 2 } or \text{ Face 3)} = P \text{ (Face 2)} + P \text{ (Face 3)}$$
$$= \frac{1}{6} + \frac{1}{6}$$

$$P \text{ (Face 2 } or \text{ Face 3)} = \frac{2}{6} = \frac{1}{3} = 0.333$$

You can extend this addition rule for *mutually exclusive* events to consider cases in which there are more than two events. In the case of the die, suppose you wanted to know the probability of an even-numbered outcome (i.e., two, four, or six dots). Then:

$$P \text{ (Even)} = P \text{ (Face 2 } or \text{ 4 } or \text{ 6)} = P \text{ (Face 2)} + P \text{ (Face 4)} + P \text{ (Face 6)}$$

$$= \frac{1}{6} + \frac{1}{6} + \frac{1}{6}$$

$$= \frac{3}{6} = \frac{1}{2}$$

$$P \text{ (Even)} = P \text{ (Face 2 } or \text{ 4 } or \text{ 6)} = 0.50$$

Rule 5: If events in a set are mutually exclusive and collectively exhaustive, the sum of their probabilities must add to 1.0.

In the example of the single die, the events of a face with an even number of dots and a face with an odd number of dots are mutually exclusive and collectively exhaustive. They are mutually exclusive because even and odd cannot occur simultaneously on the roll of a single die. They are also collectively exhaustive because either even or odd must occur on a particular roll. Therefore, the probability of a face with an even *or* odd number of dots is:

$$P \text{ (even } or \text{ odd)} = P \text{ (face 2 } or \text{ 4 } or \text{ 6)} + P \text{ (face 1 } or \text{ 3 } or \text{ 5)}$$

$$= \frac{3}{6} + \frac{3}{6}$$

$$P \text{ (even } or \text{ odd)} = \frac{6}{6} = 1.0$$

Rule 6: If two events *A* and *B* are *not* mutually exclusive, then the probability of either event *A or* event *B* occurring is the sum of their separate probabilities minus the probability of their simultaneous occurrence (called **joint probability**).

To illustrate this rule, consider the example concerning the die. The events of a face with an even number of dots and a face with fewer than 5 dots are not mutually exclusive, because the results of two dots and four dots each satisfy the criteria of having an even number of dots and also having fewer than five dots. Thus, to determine the probability of having a face with an even number of dots or having a face with fewer than five dots, you add the probability of having a face with an even number of dots to the probability of having a face with fewer than five dots, then subtract the joint probability of simultaneously having a face with an even number of dots and a face with fewer than five dots. The reason that this joint probability must be subtracted is that it has already been included twice in computing the probability of having a face with an even number of dots and having a face with fewer than five dots.

Therefore, since it has been "double counted," it must be subtracted to provide the correct result. Thus:

P (having a face with an even number of dots
or having a face with fewer than five dots)

= [*P* (having a face with an even number of dots
+ *P* (having a face with fewer than five dots)]

– *P* (having a face with an even number of dots
and having a face with fewer than five dots)

$$= \frac{3}{6} + \frac{4}{6} - \frac{2}{6}$$

$$= \frac{5}{6}$$

$$= 0.833$$

Rule 7: If two events *A* and *B* are *independent*, then the probability of both events *A and B* occurring is equal to the product of their respective probabilities. Two events are **independent** if the occurrence of one event in no way affects the occurrence of the second event.

In the case of rolling a "fair" single die twice, you can assume that the result of the first roll is independent of the result of the second roll. Thus, to determine the probability that the face that contains five dots would occur on *each* of two rolls, you have:

P (5 dots on roll 1 *and* 5 dots on roll 2) = *P* (5 dots on roll 1) × *P* (5 dots on roll 2)

$$= \frac{1}{6} \times \frac{1}{6}$$

$$= \frac{1}{36}$$

Rule 8: If two events *A and B* are *not independent*, then the probability of both events *A and B* occurring is the product of the probability of event *A* times the conditional probability of event *B* occurring, given that event *A* has occurred.

To show an example of events that are not independent, consider a standard deck of 52 cards that contains four suits (hearts, diamonds, clubs, and spades) with each suit having 13 cards (Ace, 2, 3, 4, 5, 6, 7, 8, 9, 10, Jack, Queen, and King). If the deck was thoroughly shuffled and you selected two cards from the deck, what is the probability that both cards are hearts?

The probability that the first card selected is a heart is 13/52 or $\frac{1}{4}$, because 13 of the 52 cards are hearts. However, since the second card is selected without returning the first card to the deck, the number of cards remaining after the first selection is 51. If the first card is a heart, the probability that the second card is a heart is 12/51, since 12 hearts remain in the deck. Therefore:

$$P \text{ (Heart on first } and \text{ heart on second)} = \left(\left(\frac{13}{52} \right) \left(\frac{12}{51} \right) \right)$$

$$= \frac{156}{2,652}$$

$$= 0.0588$$

Thus, there is a 5.88% chance that both cards selected will be hearts.

5.3   THE PROBABILITY DISTRIBUTION

Now that probability has been defined and some rules of probability have been illustrated, a variable of interest that has many different outcomes can be studied. Consider the number of defective transactions that can occur in three independent transactions, where the probability of a defective transaction is 0.5. This example assumes that, based on past history, you know that each time a transaction takes place, the result (defective or not defective) is independent of any other transaction, and the probability of defective transaction on any randomly selected transaction is 0.50.

The possible outcomes that can occur in terms of the number of defective transactions are shown in Table 5.1.

TABLE 5.1   Outcomes of Three Transactions

Outcomes	First Transaction	Second Transaction	Third Transaction
1	Defective	Defective	Defective
2	Defective	Defective	Not Defective
3	Defective	Not Defective	Defective
4	Defective	Not Defective	Not Defective
5	Not Defective	Defective	Defective
6	Not Defective	Defective	Not Defective
7	Not Defective	Not Defective	Defective
8	Not Defective	Not Defective	Not Defective

The probability of occurrence of a particular outcome [for example, first transaction is defective (D_1), second transaction is defective (D_2), and third transaction is defective (D_3)] is calculated by extending Rule 7 of probability (see page 65) to the case of three events. Thus:

$$P(D_1 \text{ and } D_2 \text{ and } D_3) = P(D_1) \times P(D_2) \times P(D_3)$$

Because each transaction has a probability of being defective of 0.5:

$$P(D_1 \text{ and } D_2 \text{ and } D_3) = (0.5)(0.5)(0.5) = 0.125$$

Another way of looking at this example is to consider each of the rows in Table 5.1 as a distinct elementary event. Because the event D_1 and D_2 and D_3 can only occur one way, and there are eight elementary events:

$$\text{Probability of event } D_1 \text{ and } D_2 \text{ and } D_3 = \frac{\text{number of ways event can occur}}{\text{total number of elementary events}}$$

$$P(D_1 \text{ and } D_2 \text{ and } D_3) = \frac{1}{8} \, 0.125$$

You can make similar calculations for each of the other seven possible outcomes. In this instance, the probability that the transaction is defective is 0.5. Therefore, the probability of a defective transaction is the same as the probability of a transaction that is not defective. The results are organized in terms of the probability of particular number of defective transactions in three independent transactions. The results for all the possible outcomes are summarized in Table 5.2.

TABLE 5.2 Distribution of the Number of Defective Transactions in Three Independent Transactions in Which the Probability of a Defective Transaction is 0.50

Number of Defective Transactions	Frequency	Probability
0	1	0.125
1	3	0.375
2	3	0.375
3	1	0.125
	8	1.000

Table 5.2 is an example of a probability distribution for a discrete variable. A **discrete variable** is based on a count of the number of occurrences of an attribute, such as number of defective items or number of blemishes in a yard of wallpaper.

A **probability distribution** for a discrete random variable is a listing of all possible distinct outcomes and their probabilities of occurring. Because all possible outcomes are listed, the sum of the probabilities must add to 1.0.

Table 5.2 satisfies this definition of the probability distribution since all outcomes (0, 1, 2, and 3 defective transactions) are listed, and the sum of the probabilities adds to 1.0.

The Average or Expected Value of a Random Variable

The mean (μ) of a probability distribution is also called the **expected value** of the distribution. The mean (μ) of a probability distribution is computed by multiplying each possible outcome X by its corresponding probability, then summing the resulting products:

Mean = sum of [each value × the probability of each value]

If there are three transactions per day (refer to Table 5.2), you compute the mean or expected value of the number of defective transactions, as shown in Table 5.3.

TABLE 5.3   Computing the Expected Value of a Probability Distribution

Number of Defective Transactions	Probability	(Number of Defective Transactions) × (Probability)
0	0.125	$(0) \times (0.125) = 0$
1	0.375	$(1) \times (0.375) = 0.375$
2	0.375	$(2) \times (0.375) = 0.75$
3	0.125	$(3) \times (0.125) = \underline{0.375}$
		Mean = 1.50

Mean = sum of [each value × the probability of each value]
Mean = (0)(0.125) + (1)(0.375) + (2)(0.375) + (3)(0.125)
      = 0 + 0.375 + 0.750 + 0.375
      = 1.50

Notice that in this example, the mean or expected value of the number of defective transactions is 1.5, a value that is impossible. The mean of 1.5 defective transactions tells you that, in the long run, if you have 3 transactions per day for many days, the mean number of defective transactions you can expect is 1.5.

EQUATION FOR THE MEAN OF A PROBABILITY DISTRIBUTION {OPTIONAL}

$$\mu = \sum_{i=1}^{N} X_i P(X_i) \qquad (5.3)$$

where

X = random variable of interest

X_i = ith outcome of X

$P(X_i)$ = probability of occurrence of the ith outcome of X

$i = 1, 2, \ldots, N$

N = the number of outcomes for X

Standard Deviation of a Random Variable (σ)

As was the case with sample data, the **standard deviation** of a probability distribution is a measure of variation around the mean or expected value. You compute this summary measure by multiplying the squared difference between each possible value and the mean by its corresponding probability, summing the resulting products, and then taking the square root of this result.

σ = standard deviation = square root of [sum of (squared differences between a value and the mean) × (probability of the value)]

If there are three transactions per day (refer to Table 5.2 on page 67), you calculate the standard deviation of the number of defective transactions, as shown in Table 5.4.

TABLE 5.4 Computing the Standard Deviation of a Probability Distribution

Number of Defective Transactions	Probability	(Number of Defective Transactions – Mean Number of Defective Transactions)^2 × (Probability)
0	0.125	$(0-1.5)^2 \times (0.125) = 2.25 \times (0.125) = 0.28125$
1	0.375	$(1-1.5)^2 \times (0.375) = 0.25 \times (0.375) = 0.09375$
2	0.375	$(2-1.5)^2 \times (0.375) = 0.25 \times (0.375) = 0.09375$
3	0.125	$(3-1.5)^2 \times (0.125) = 2.25 \times (0.125) = 0.28125$
		Total = 0.75

$\sigma = \sqrt{0.75} = 0.866$

σ = standard deviation = square root of [sum of (squared differences between a value and the mean) $\times$ (probability of the value)]

$\sigma^2 = (0 - 1.5)^2(0.125) + (1 - 1.5)^2(0.375) + (2 - 1.5)^2(0.375) + (3 - 1.5)^2(0.125)$
$= 2.25(0.125) + 0.25(0.375) + 0.25(0.375) + 2.25(0.125)$
$= 0.75$

and

$\sigma = \sqrt{0.75} = 0.866$

EQUATION FOR THE STANDARD DEVIATION OF A PROBABILITY DISTRIBUTION {OPTIONAL}

$$\sigma = \sqrt{\sum_{i=1}^{N}(X_i - \mu)^2 P(X_i)} \qquad (5.4)$$

where

X = random variable of interest

X_i = ith outcome of X

$P(X_i)$ = probability of occurrence of the ith outcome of X

$i = 1, 2, ... , N$

N = number of outcomes for X

One common application for the mean and standard deviation of a probability distribution is in finance. Suppose that you are deciding between two alternative investments. Investment A is a mutual fund whose portfolio consists of a combination of stocks that make up the Dow Jones Industrial Average. Investment B consists of shares of a growth stock. You estimate the returns (per $1,000 investment) for each investment alternative and the three economic conditions (recession, stable economy, and expanding economy). You also provide your subjective probability of the occurrence of each economic condition. The results are summarized in Table 5.5.

The mean return for the two investments is computed as follows:

Mean for the Dow Jones Fund = (-100)(0.2) + (100)(0.5) + (250)(0.3) = $105
Mean for the Growth Stock = (-200)(0.2) + (50)(0.5) + (350)(0.3) = $90

You can calculate the standard deviation for the two investments as is done in Tables 5.6 and 5.7.

TABLE 5.5 Estimated Return for Two Investments Under Three Economic Conditions

		Investment	
Probability	Economic Condition	Dow Jones Fund (A)	Growth Stock (B)
0.2	Recession	-$100	-$200
0.5	Stable economy	+ 100	+50
0.3	Expanding economy	+ 250	+ 350

TABLE 5.6 Computing the Standard Deviation for Dow Jones Fund (A)

Probability	Economic Event	Dow Jones Fund (A)	(Return – Mean Return)^2 × Probability
0.2	Recession	-$100	$(-100 - 105)^2 \times (0.2) = (42,025)$ × (0.2) = 8,405
0.5	Stable economy	+ 100	$(100 - 105)^2 \times (0.5) = (25)$ × (0.5) = 12.5
0.3	Expanding economy	+ 250	$(250 - 105)^2 \times (0.3)$ = (21,025) × (0.3) = 6,307.5
			$\sigma = \sqrt{14,725} = \$121.35$

TABLE 5.7 Computing the Standard Deviation for Growth Stock (B)

Probability	Economic Event	Growth Stock (B)	(Return – Mean Return)^2 × Probability
0.2	Recession	-$200	$(-200 - 90)^2 \times (0.2) = (84,100)$ × (0.2) = 16,820
0.5	Stable economy	+ 50	$(50 - 90)^2 \times (0.5) = (1,600) \times$ (0.5) = 800
0.3	Expanding economy	+ 350	$(350 - 90)^2 \times (0.3) = (67,600) \times$ (0.3) = 20,280
			$\sigma = \sqrt{37,900} = \$194.68$

σ = standard deviation = square root of [sum of (squared differences between a value and the mean) × (probability of the value)]

$$\sigma_A = \sqrt{(0.2)(-100 - 105)^2 + (0.5)(100 - 105)^2 + (0.3)(250 - 105)^2}$$
$$= \sqrt{14,725}$$
$$= \$121.35$$

$$\sigma_B = \sqrt{(0.2)(-200-90)^2 + (0.5)(50-90)^2 + (0.3)(350-90)^2}$$
$$= \sqrt{37,900}$$
$$= \$194.68$$

Thus, the Dow Jones Fund has a higher mean return and a lower standard deviation than the growth fund, indicating less variation (more stability) in the return under the different economic conditions.

In this section, the concepts of a probability distribution, the mean or expected value of a discrete probability distribution, and the standard deviation of a discrete probability distribution were defined. In the remainder of the chapter, two specific discrete probability distributions (binomial distribution and Poisson distribution) that are important in statistics and Six Sigma management will be developed, along with a very important distribution that is frequently appropriate for measurement or continuous data (normal distribution).

5.4   THE BINOMIAL DISTRIBUTION

Many studies involve probability distributions that are based on attribute data in which the outcomes of a variable (CTQ or CTP) are in only two categories, arbitrarily called *success* or *failure*, *defect* or *conforming*, or *on-time* or *late*. When classifying each event studied as either a success or a failure, which outcome is classified as a success and which one is classified as a failure is not important. For example, in the context of statistical process control (see Chapter 11), an item that has failed inspection could be classified as a success since the goal in process control is usually to study nonconformance. In such circumstances, you can use the binomial probability distribution to analyze the number of nonconforming items in a sample of n units.

The **binomial distribution** has four properties, shown in Exhibit 5.1.

EXHIBIT 5.1   PROPERTIES OF THE BINOMIAL DISTRIBUTION

1. The sample consists of a fixed number of observations, called n.
2. Each observation is classified into one of two mutually exclusive and collectively exhaustive categories, usually called *success* or *failure*.
3. The probability of an observation being classified as success, p, is constant from observation to observation, and the probability of an observation being classified as failure, $1 - p$, is constant from observation to observation.
4. The outcome (success or failure) of any observation is independent of the outcome of any other observation.

Accuracy in taking orders at the drive-thru window is an important quality feature for fast food chains. Each month, *QSR Magazine* (www.qsrmagazine.com) publishes the results of its surveys. Accuracy is measured as the percentage of orders consisting of a main item, side item, and drink (but omitting one standard item, such as a pickle) that are filled correctly. In a recent month, suppose that the percentage of correct orders of this type filled at McDonald's is approximately 90%. Suppose that you and two friends go to the drive-thru window at McDonald's and each of you place an order of the type just mentioned. The fast food order-filling data fits the binomial distribution if:

1. There are a fixed number of observations (three fast food orders from you and your friends).
2. Each observation is classified into one of two categories (correct fast food order or incorrect fast food order).
3. The probability of a correct fast food order is the same for all fast food orders filled.
4. The outcome on one fast food order is independent of the outcome of any other fast food order.

To determine the probability of two correct fast food orders in three fast food orders, from Table 5.1 on page 66, observe that of the eight possible outcomes, there are three ways of having two successes (in this case, two correct fast food orders):

Correct (C_1)	Correct (C_2)	Incorrect (I_3)
Correct (C_1)	Incorrect (I_2)	Correct (C_3)
Incorrect (I_1)	Correct (C_2)	Correct (C_3)

You can develop the equation for determining the probability of a particular number of successes (X) for a given number of observations n by multiplying the number of ways of getting two correct fast food orders (one incorrect fast food order) in three fast food orders by the probability of two correct fast food orders in three fast food orders *in a specific order.*

From above, there are three ways of having two correct fast food orders in three fast food orders. The probability of two correct fast food orders in three fast food orders in a specific order (such as Correct—Correct—Incorrect) is:

$$P\,(C_1 \text{ and } C_2 \text{ and } I_3) = P\,(C_1) \times P\,(C_2) \times P\,(I_3)$$

If p = the probability of a correct fast food order = 0.90, then $(1 - p)$ equals the probability of an incorrect fast food order = 0.10. Then:

$$
\begin{aligned}
P\,(C_1) \times P\,(C_2) \times P\,(I_3) &= p \times p \times (1 - p) \\
&= p^2 \times (1 - p) \\
&= (0.9)^2 \times 0.1 \\
&= 0.081
\end{aligned}
$$

Multiplying $3 \times 0.081 = 0.243$. This is the probability that two of the three fast food orders will be correct. A similar derivation can be done for any value of p and any sample size n. Optional Equation (5.5) presents the general formula for determining any binomial probability. However, such computations become complicated as the sample size increases. Instead, you can use Minitab or JMP. Figure 5.2 illustrates Minitab calculations for the fast food orders.

FIGURE 5.2

Minitab Binomial Distribution Calculations for $n = 3$ and $p = 0.9$

```
Binomial with n = 3 and p = 0.9

x   P( X = x )
0        0.001
1        0.027
2        0.243
3        0.729
```

From Figure 5.2, observe that the probability of zero correct fast food orders is 0.001, one correct fast food order is 0.027, two correct fast food orders is 0.243, and three correct fast food orders is 0.729.

EQUATION FOR THE BINOMIAL DISTRIBUTION {OPTIONAL}

$$P(X = x \mid n, p) = \frac{n!}{x!(n-x)!} p^x (1-p)^{n-x} \qquad (5.5)$$

where

$P(X = x \mid n, p)$ = the probability that $X = x$, given a knowledge of n and p

n = sample size

p = probability of success

$1 - p$ = probability of failure

x = number of successes in the sample $(X = 0, 1, 2, ..., n)$

$n! = (n)(n-1)(n-2)...(1)$

0! is defined as equal to 1

To determine the probability of two correct fast food orders in three fast food orders, with $n = 3$, $p = 0.9$, and $x = 2$, use Equation (5.5), as follows:

$$P(X = 2 \mid n = 3, p = 0.9) = \frac{3!}{2!(3-2)!}(0.9)^2(1-(0.9)^{(3-2)}$$

$$= \frac{3!}{2!(1)!}(0.9)^2(1-(0.9))^1$$

$$= (3)(0.81)(0.10)$$

$$= (3)(0.081) = 0.243$$

Characteristics of the Binomial Distribution

Each time you specify a set of parameters n and p, a particular binomial probability distribution can be generated.

Shape. Binomial distributions can be symmetrical or skewed. Whenever $p = 0.5$, the binomial distribution will be symmetrical, regardless of how large or small the value of n. However, when $p \neq 0.5$, the distribution will be skewed. If $p < 0.5$, the distribution will be positive or right skewed. If $p > 0.5$, the distribution will be negative or left skewed. The closer p is to 0.5 and the larger the number of observations in the sample, n, the more symmetrical the distribution will be.

Mean. The mean of a binomial distribution is the product of the sample size, n, and the probability of success, p.

Mean = sample size × probability of success

EQUATION FOR THE MEAN OF THE BINOMIAL DISTRIBUTION {OPTIONAL}

$$\mu = np \qquad (5.6)$$

For example, when dealing with three fast food orders and $p = 0.9$, the mean is 2.7 correct orders, the product of the sample size $n = 3$, and the probability of a correct fast food order $p = 0.9$.

Mean = 3 × 0.9 = 2.7

Standard Deviation. The standard deviation of a binomial distribution is equal to the square root of the product of the sample size, n, the probability of success, p, and the probability of failure, $(1 - p)$.

Standard deviation = square root [(sample size × probability of success)
× (1 – probability of success)]

EQUATION FOR THE STANDARD DEVIATION OF THE BINOMIAL DISTRIBUTION {OPTIONAL}

$$\sigma_x = \sqrt{np(1-p)} \qquad (5.7)$$

For example, when there are three fast food orders, with the probability of a correct fast food order $p = 0.9$, the standard deviation is 0.52 [the square root of the product of the sample size $n = 3$ and the probability of success $p = 0.9$ times the probability of failure $(1 - 0.9)$].

$$\text{Standard deviation} = \text{square root } [3 \times (0.9) \times (1 - 0.9)] = 0.52$$

5.5   THE POISSON DISTRIBUTION

Many studies are based on counts of the number of nonconformities or defects per *area of opportunity*. An **area of opportunity** is a continuous unit of time, volume, or other such area in which more than one occurrence of an event can occur. Examples are the surface defects on a new refrigerator, number of complaints in a hotel in a week, or number of accidents in a factory in a month. In such circumstances, you can use the **Poisson probability distribution** to calculate probabilities. This includes applications to the theory of area of opportunity control charts that will be discussed in Section 11.6. Exhibit 5.2 describes the properties that must be true about a specific situation to use the Poisson distribution.

EXHIBIT 5.2   THE POISSON DISTRIBUTION

The Poisson distribution is used in situations that have the following properties:

1. You are counting the number of times a particular event occurs in a given area of opportunity. The area of opportunity is defined by time, length, geography, surface area, etc.
2. The probability that an event occurs in a given area of opportunity is the same for all areas of opportunity.
3. The number of events that occur in one area of opportunity is independent of the number of events that occur in other areas of opportunity.
4. The probability that two or more events will occur in an area of opportunity approaches zero as the area of opportunity becomes smaller.

Consider the number of customers arriving during the lunch hour at a bank located in the central business district in a large city. Of interest to you is the number of customers that arrive each minute. Does this situation match the four properties of the Poisson distribution given in Exhibit 5.2? First, the *event* of interest is a customer arriving and the *given area of opportunity* is defined as a 1-minute interval at the bank during lunch hour. Will zero customers arrive, one customer, two customers, etc.? Second, it is reasonable to assume that the probability that a customer arrives during a randomly selected 1-minute interval is the same for all 1-minute intervals. Third, the arrival of one customer in any 1-minute interval has no effect on (i.e., is statistically independent of) the arrival of any other customer in any other 1-minute interval. Finally, the probability that two or more customers will arrive in a given time period approaches zero as the time interval becomes small. For example, there is virtually no probability that two customers will arrive in a time interval with a width of 1/100th of a second. Thus, you can use the Poisson distribution (see Equation 5.8) to compute probabilities concerning the number of customers arriving at the bank in a 1-minute time interval during the lunch hour.

To demonstrate the application of the Poisson probability distribution, suppose that past data indicates that the mean number of arrivals of customers during the lunch hour is three per minute. To compute the probability of the arrival of a particular number of customers in the next minute, you can use Minitab or JMP.

Figure 5.3 illustrates the probability of the number of arrivals, from zero arrivals up to 12 arrivals. For example, observe that with a mean of three arrivals per minute, the probability of zero arrivals is 0.049787, the probability of one arrival is 0.149361, and the probability of two arrivals is 0.224042, while the probability of 12 arrivals is only 0.000055. Thus, to compute the probability of two or fewer arrivals, you would add the probability of zero arrivals (0.049787), one arrival (0.149361), and two arrivals (0.224042).

Probability of two or fewer arrivals = 0.049787 + 0.149361 + 0.224042 = 0.42319

FIGURE 5.3

Minitab Poisson Distribution Calculations for a Mean of Three Arrivals per Minute

```
Poisson with mu = 3

x    P( X = x )
0     0.049787
1     0.149361
2     0.224042
3     0.224042
4     0.168031
5     0.100819
6     0.050409
7     0.021604
8     0.008102
9     0.002701
10    0.000810
11    0.000221
12    0.000055
```

Thus, there is a 42.319% chance that two or fewer customers will arrive in the next minute if the mean number of arrivals is three per minute.

EQUATION FOR THE POISSON DISTRIBUTION {OPTIONAL}

$$P(X = x \mid \lambda) = \frac{e^{-\lambda}\lambda^x}{x!} \qquad (5.8)$$

where

$P(X = x \mid \lambda)$ = probability that $X = x$, given a knowledge of λ

λ = mean number of nonconformities per area of opportunity

e = mathematical constant approximated by 2.71828

x = number of successes per area of opportunity in the sample ($X = 0, 1, 2, ..., \infty$)

Continues

To determine the probability of exactly two arrivals in the next minute given a mean of three arrivals per minute in the bank during lunch hour, use Equation 5.8 as follows:

$$P(X = 2 \mid \lambda = 3) = \frac{e^{-3}(3)^2}{2!}$$

$$= \frac{(2.71828)^{-3}(3)^2}{2!}$$

$$= \frac{9}{(2.71828)^2(2)}$$

$$= 0.224042$$

Characteristics of the Poisson Distribution

Each time you specify the mean, a particular Poisson probability distribution is generated. A Poisson distribution will be right skewed, but will approach symmetry, with a peak in the center as the mean gets large. An important property of the Poisson distribution is that the mean and variance are equal. In the example concerning the number of arrivals at a bank, the mean or expected number of arrivals is three per minute, and the standard deviation is the square root of 3, or 1.732 arrivals per minute.

5.6   THE NORMAL DISTRIBUTION

The **normal distribution** is a continuous bell-shaped distribution used for measurement data. Continuous distributions differ from discrete distributions such as the binomial and Poisson distributions in the following ways:

1. Any value within the range of the variable can occur, rather than just specific (i.e., integer) values. For example, cycle time can be measured to as many decimal places as are appropriate.

2. The probability of occurrence of a specific value of X is zero. For example, the probability of a cycle time being measured at exactly 3.0000000000 seconds approaches zero as the number of digits to the right of the decimal point gets larger.

3. Probabilities can be computed by cumulating an area under a curve. For example, the probability that a cycle time is between 2.00 and 3.00 minutes can be determined if the form of the curve is known and stable.

The normal distribution is used to represent a wide variety of continuous measurement data (variables, or CTQs, and CTPs). Many natural phenomena, such as cycle time to complete an activity, measurement errors, the dimension of industrial parts, and voltage output, have been found to follow a normal distribution. An example of a normal distribution is depicted in Figure 5.4. Additionally, statistical inference utilizes the normal distribution (see Chapters 6–10).

FIGURE 5.4
The Normal
Distribution

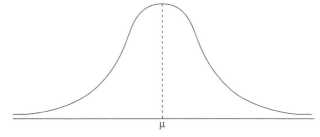

Characteristics of the Normal Distribution

Exhibit 5.3 illustrates several important theoretical properties of the normal distribution.

EXHIBIT 5.3   PROPERTIES OF THE NORMAL DISTRIBUTION

1. The normal distribution is bell-shaped and symmetrical in appearance.
2. The normal distribution measures of central tendency (mean, median, and mode) are all identical.
3. The normal distribution probabilities are determined by two characteristics: its mean, μ, and its standard deviation, σ.
4. The normal distribution has a theoretically infinite range.

Probability under the normal curve can be found either by using a table of the normal distribution (see Table C.1 in Appendix C) or by having Minitab or JMP compute the probability. Table C.1 provides the area or probability *less than* a specific number of standard deviation units (called **Z** or **standardized normal units**) from the mean.

$$\text{Standardized normal units} = Z = \frac{\text{individual value - mean}}{\text{standard deviation}}$$

Table C.1 provides this probability for standard deviation units (or Z) ranging from -3.99 to +6.0. To illustrate how to find a probability or area under the normal curve, examine Figure 5.5.

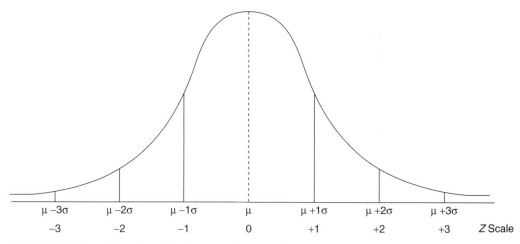

μ −3σ	μ −2σ	μ −1σ	μ	μ +1σ	μ +2σ	μ +3σ	
−3	−2	−1	0	+1	+2	+3	Z Scale

FIGURE 5.5   The Standard Normal Distribution

First, you can find the probability of a value that is *less* than three standard deviations below the mean (-3σ) by using Table 5.8, which is extracted from the complete table of the normal distribution shown in Table C.1.

TABLE 5.8   Finding a Cumulative Area Below -3 Standard Deviations

Z	.00	.01	.02	.03	.04	.05	.06	.07	.08	.09
.	.	.	.	.	.	.	.	.	.	.
.	.	.	.	.	.	.	.	.	.	.
.	.	.	.	.	.	.	.	.	.	.
-3.0 →	0.00135	0.00131	0.00126	0.00122	0.00118	0.00114	0.00111	0.00107	0.00103	0.00100

Source: Extracted from Table C.1.

From Table 5.8, the probability that a value will be below -3.00 standard deviation (or Z) units is 0.00135 or 0.135%.

Next, you can compute the probability that a value will be less than three standard deviations *above* the mean (+3σ). Table 5.9, extracted from the complete normal table shown in Table C.1, shows the area below +3.00 standard deviation (or Z) units.

From Table 5.9, the probability that a value is below +3 standard deviation (or Z) units is 0.99865 or 99.865%. The complement of the probability that a value is below +3 standard deviation (or Z) units is the probability that a value is above 3 standard deviation (or Z) units. This is illustrated in Figure 5.6.

TABLE 5.9   Finding a Cumulative Area Below +3 Standard Deviations

Z	.00	.01	.02	.03	.04	.05	.06	.07	.08	.09
+3.0 →	0.99865	0.99869	0.99874	0.99878	0.99882	0.99886	0.99889	0.99893	0.99897	0.99900

Source: Extracted from Table C.1.

FIGURE 5.6   Computing the Probability or Area Under the Normal Curve

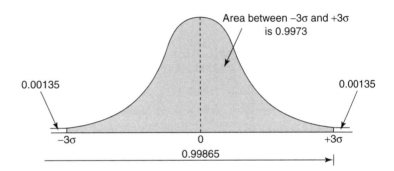

Thus, the probability that a value is above 3 standard deviation (or Z) units is equal to $1.0 - 0.99865 = 0.00135$. Observe that the area above $+3\sigma$ is the same as the area below -3σ. This occurs because the normal distribution is symmetric, so that each half of the curve is a mirror image of the other half of the curve. The area that is more than 3 standard deviations from the mean is equal to the sum of the area below -3σ (0.00135) and the area above $+3\sigma$ (0.00135). This is equal to $0.00135 + 0.00135 = 0.0027$, or 0.27%. Stated another way, there is a 27 out of ten thousand chance that a value will be more than 3 standard deviations from the mean. The complement of this statement is that there is a $1 - 0.0027 = 0.9973$, or 99.73%, chance that a value will be *within* 3 standard deviations of the mean. Table 5.10 summarizes this information for several different standard deviation units.

TABLE 5.10   Normal Probabilities for Selected Number of Standard Deviation Units

Number of Standard Deviation Units	Probability or Area Outside These Units	Probability or Area Within These Units
-1σ to $+1\sigma$	0.3174	0.6826
-2σ to $+2\sigma$	0.0456	0.9544
-3σ to $+3\sigma$	0.0027	0.9973
-6σ to $+6\sigma$	0.000000002	0.999999998

The previous examples involved using the normal tables to find an area under the normal curve that corresponded to a specific Z value. There are many circumstances when you want to do the opposite of this; that is, you want to find the Z value that corresponds to a specific area. For example, you might want to find the Z value that corresponds to a cumulative area of 1%, 5%, 95%, or 99%. You might also want to find lower and upper Z values between which 95% of the area under the curve is contained.

In order to find the Z value that corresponds to a specific area, instead of starting with the Z value and looking up the cumulative area less than Z in the table, you locate the cumulative area in the body of the standard normal table, and then determine the Z value that corresponds to this cumulative area. Suppose that you want to find the Z values such that 95% of the normal curve is contained between a lower Z value and an upper Z value with 2.5% below the lower Z value, and 2.5% above the upper Z value. Using Figure 5.7, you determine that you need to find the Z value that corresponds to a cumulative area of 0.025 and the Z value that corresponds to a cumulative area of 0.975.

FIGURE 5.7
Finding the Z Value
Corresponding to a
Given Area

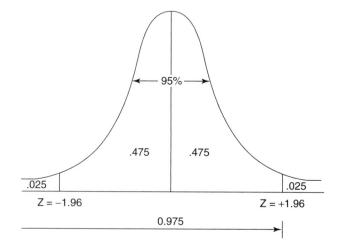

Table 5.11 contains a portion of Table C.1 that is needed to find the Z value that corresponds to a cumulative area of 0.025. To find the Z value that corresponds to a cumulative area of 0.025, you look in the body of Table 5.11 until you see the value of 0.025 (or the closest value to 0.025). Then, you determine the row and column that this value corresponds to. Locating the value of 0.025, you see that it is located in the -1.9 row and the .06 column. Thus, the Z value that corresponds to a cumulative area of 0.025 is -1.96.

TABLE 5.11 Partial Table C.1 for Finding Z Value that Corresponds to a
Cumulative Area of 0.025

Z	.00	.01	.02	.03	.04	.05	.06	.07	.08	.09
	.	.	.	.	.	.		.	.	.
	.	.	.	.	.	.		.	.	.
-2.0	0.0228	0.0222	0.0217	0.0212	0.0207	0.0202	0.0197	0.0192	0.0188	0.0183
-1.9	0.0287	0.0281	0.0274	0.0268	0.0262	0.0256	0.0250	0.0244	0.0239	0.0233

Table 5.12 contains a portion of Table C.1 that is needed to find the Z value that corresponds to a cumulative area of 0.975. To find the Z value that corresponds to a cumulative area of 0.975, you look in the body of Table 5.12 until you see the value of 0.975 (or the closest value to 0.975). Then you determine the row and column that this value corresponds to. Locating the value of 0.975, you see that it is located in the 1.9 row and the .06 column. Thus, the Z value that corresponds to a cumulative area of 0.975 is 1.96. Taking this result along with the Z value of -1.96 for a cumulative area of 0.025 means that 95% of all the values will be between $Z = -1.96$ and $Z = 1.96$.

TABLE 5.12 Partial Table C.1 for Finding Z Value that Corresponds to a
Cumulative Area of 0.975

Z	.00	.01	.02	.03	.04	.05	.06	.07	.08	.09
	.	.	.	.	.	.		.	.	.
	.	.	.	.	.	.		.	.	.
+1.9	0.9713	0.9719	0.9726	0.9732	0.9738	0.9744	0.9750	0.9756	0.9761	0.9767
+2.0	0.9772	0.9778	0.9783	0.9788	0.9793	0.9798	0.9803	0.9808	0.9812	0.9817

You can use Minitab to compute any probability or area under the normal curve. Figure 5.8 displays the probability that a value will be less than -3σ.

FIGURE 5.8
Minitab Normal
Probabilities

```
Cumulative Distribution Function

Normal with mean = 0 and standard deviation = 1

x   P( X <= x )
-3     0.0013499
```

In each of the previous examples concerning the normal distribution, the mean of the distribution was 0 and the standard deviation was 1.0. (This is called a **standardized normal distribution**.) To learn how to find a probability for a normal distribution that has a mean different from 0 and/or a standard deviation different from 1, you can examine the following example.

Suppose that a radiology facility at a hospital is studying the waiting time for patients scheduled to have X-rays. Past experience has indicated that the waiting time is stable (see Chapter 11) and approximately normally distributed, with a mean $\mu = 27$ minutes and a standard deviation $\sigma = 5$ minutes. Suppose that you want to determine the proportion of all patient waiting times between 20 and 30 minutes. (For our purposes, this is the same as determining the probability that a single waiting time will be between 20 and 30 minutes.) You can use Table C.1, the table of the probabilities of the cumulative standardized normal distribution, to find this probability.

First, you need to convert the waiting times to a standardized normal unit by subtracting the mean and then dividing by the standard deviation. Thus:

$$\text{Standardized normal units } = Z = \frac{\text{individual value - mean}}{\text{standard deviation}}$$

$$\text{Standardized normal units } = \frac{20 - 27}{5} = -1.4$$

$$\text{Standardized normal units } = \frac{30 - 27}{5} = 0.6$$

The waiting time of 20 minutes is 1.4 standard deviation (or Z) units below the mean of 27 minutes, and the waiting time of 30 minutes is 0.6 standard deviation (or Z) units above the mean of 27 minutes. You can find the area by using Table C.1 or by using Minitab or JMP. Figure 5.9 illustrates using Table C.1. Figure 5.10 illustrates Minitab.

FIGURE 5.9
Computing the Probability Between -1.4 and +0.6 Standard Deviation Units

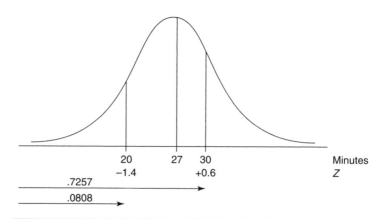

FIGURE 5.10
Minitab Normal Probabilities for the Area Below -1.4 (20 minutes) and +0.6 (30 minutes) Standard Deviation Units

```
Normal with mean = 27 and standard deviation = 5

  x   P( X <= x )
 20      0.080757
 30      0.725747
```

The area below 30 minutes ($Z = 0.60$) is 0.7257. The area below 20 minutes ($Z = -1.40$) is 0.0808. Therefore, the area or probability of a waiting time between 20 and 30 minutes is $0.7257 - 0.0808 = 0.6449$.

5.7 THE NORMAL PROBABILITY PLOT

The normal probability plot helps you evaluate whether a set of data follows a normal distribution. Minitab uses an approach to the normal probability plot that transforms the vertical Y axis in a special way so that if the data are normally distributed, a plot of the data from lowest to highest will follow a straight line. JMP uses a quantile-quantile plot (known as a Q-Q plot) that transforms each value in order from lowest to highest to a Z score and then plots the data values against the Z scores. With either method, if the data are left skewed, the curve will rise more rapidly at first and then level off. If the data are right skewed, the data will rise more slowly at first and then rise at a faster rate for higher values of the variable being plotted. Figure 5.11 illustrates the typical shape of normal probability plots for a left-skewed distribution, a normal distribution, and a right-skewed distribution.

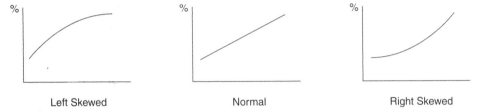

Left Skewed   Normal   Right Skewed

FIGURE 5.11 Normal Probability Plots for a Left-Skewed Distribution, a Normal Distribution, and a Right-Skewed Distribution

To illustrate the normal probability plot, you can use the order fulfillment data discussed in Section 3.2 on page 27. Figure 5.12 is a Minitab normal probability plot of the fulfillment times of 200 orders from a web site. Figure 5.13 is a JMP normal probability plot. Consistent with the results of the histogram on page 27, the straight line that the data approximately follow in this normal probability plot appears to indicate that the order fulfillment time is normally distributed.

FIGURE 5.12
Minitab Normal
Probability Plot of the
Fulfillment Times of
200 Orders from a
Web Site

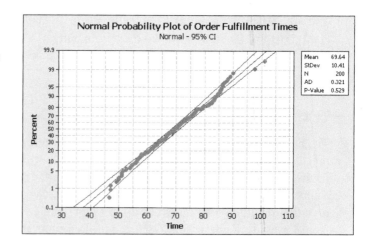

FIGURE 5.13
JMP Normal
Probability Plot of
the Fulfillment Times
of 200 Orders from a
Web Site

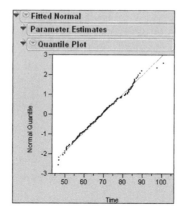

SUMMARY

This chapter covered the basic concepts of probability. First, some rules of probability were discussed, followed by the development and definition of the probability distribution. Next, the binomial, Poisson, and normal distributions were emphasized, along with how to compute probabilities for each of these distributions. Finally, the normal probability plot was introduced as a tool for evaluating whether a set of data approximately follows a normal distribution.

REFERENCES

1. Berenson, M. L., Levine, D. M., and Krehbiel, T. C. *Basic Business Statistics: Concepts and Applications*, 10ᵗʰ ed. (Upper Saddle River, NJ: Prentice Hall, 2006).

2. Levine, D. M., Ramsey, P. C., and Smidt, R. K. *Applied Statistics for Engineers and Scientists Using Microsoft Excel and Minitab* (Upper Saddle River, NJ: Prentice Hall, 2001).

3. *JMP Version 6* (Cary, NC: SAS Institute, 2005).

4. *Minitab Version 14* (State College, PA: Minitab, Inc., 2004).

Appendix 5.1
Using Minitab for Probability Distributions and Plots

Computing Binomial Probabilities

You can use Minitab to compute binomial probabilities. Referring to the example in Section 5.4 in which $n = 3$ and $p = 0.9$, you compute the binomial probabilities shown in Figure 5.2 on page 74 as follows:

1. Enter **0 1 2 3** in the first four rows of column C1. Label column C1 **Correct Orders**.
2. Select **Calc → Probability Distributions → Binomial**.
3. In the Binomial Distribution dialog box (see Figure A5.1), select the **Probability** option button. Enter **3** in the Number of trials: edit box and **.9** in the Probability of success: edit box. Enter **C1** or **Correct Orders** in the Input column: edit box. Click the **OK** button.

Computing Poisson Probabilities

You can use Minitab to compute Poisson probabilities. Referring to the example in Section 5.5 in which the mean = 3, you find the Poisson probabilities shown in Figure 5.3 on page 77 as follows:

1. Enter **0 1 2 3 4 5 6 7 8 9 10 11 12** in the first 13 rows of Column C1. Label Column C1 **Arrivals**.
2. Select **Calc → Probability Distributions → Poisson**.
3. In the Poisson Distribution dialog box (see Figure A5.2), select the **Probability** option button. Enter **3** in the Mean: edit box. Enter **C1** or **Arrivals** in the Input column: edit box. Click the **OK** button.

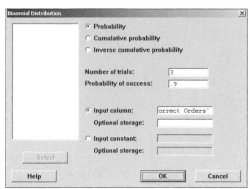

FIGURE A5.1   Binomial Distribution Dialog Box

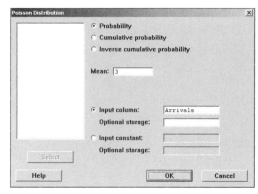

FIGURE A5.2   Poisson Distribution Dialog Box

Computing Normal Probabilities

You can use Minitab to compute normal probabilities. Referring to the example in Section 5.6 in which $\mu = 0$ and $\sigma = 1$, you find the probability below -3 standard deviations, as follows:

1. Enter **-3** in the first row of Column C1.
2. Select **Calc → Probability Distributions → Normal**.
3. In the Normal Distribution dialog box (see Figure A5.3), select the **Cumulative probability** option button. Enter **0** in the Mean: edit box and **1** in the Standard Deviation edit box. Enter **C1** in the Input column: edit box. Click the **OK** button.

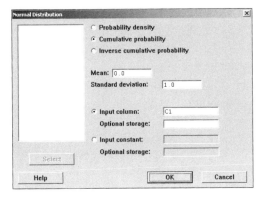

FIGURE A5.3 Normal Distribution Dialog Box

To find the Z value corresponding to a cumulative area of 0.975:

1. Enter **.975** in row 1 of column C2.
2. Select **Calc → Probability Distributions → Normal**.

3. Select the **Inverse cumulative probability** option button. Enter **0** in the Mean: edit box and **1** in the Standard Deviation: edit box.
4. Select the **Input Column** option button and enter **C2** in the edit box. Click the **OK** button.

You will get a value of 1.96.

Constructing a Normal Probability Plot

To use Minitab to generate a normal probability plot, open the **ORDER.MTW** worksheet. Select **Graph → Probability Plot**, and then do the following:

1. In the Probability Plots dialog box, select the **Single** choice.
2. In the Probability Plot—Single dialog box (see Figure A5.4), in the Graph variables: edit box, enter **C1** or **Time**.
3. Select the **Distribution** option button. In the Probability Plot—Distribution dialog box (see Figure A5.5), select the **Distribution** tab. In the Distribution: drop-down list box, select **Normal**. Click the **OK** button to return to the Probability Plot—Single dialog box.
4. Click the **OK** button to generate the normal probability plot.

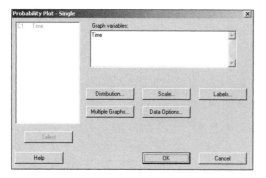

FIGURE A5.4   Probability Plot—
Single Dialog Box

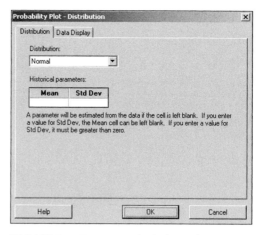

FIGURE A5.5   Probability Plot—
Distribution Dialog Box

Appendix 5.2
Using JMP for Probability Distributions and Plots

Computing Binomial Probabilities

You can use JMP to compute binomial probabilities. Referring to the example in Section 5.4 in which $n = 3$ and $p = 0.9$, you compute binomial probabilities as follows:

1. Open a new JMP data table.
2. Select **Cols → New Column**.
3. Select the **Column Properties** button. Select **Formula** from the pop-up menu.
4. In the dialog box that appears (see Figure A5.6), select **Probability → Binomial Probability**.

5. In the edit box that begins with Binomial Probability (see Figure A5.7): enter **.9** for p, the probability of success; **3** for n, the sample size; and **2** for k [defined in Equation 5.5) as x], the number of successes. Click the **OK** button. In the New Column dialog box, click the **OK** button.

Double-click on row 1 of the data table to add a row. JMP returns the probability of exactly two successes in a sample of $n = 3$ when $p = 0.9$. If you want to compute the cumulative probability of x or fewer successes, you should select **Binomial Distribution** instead of Binomial Probability.

FIGURE A5.6
Formula Dialog Box

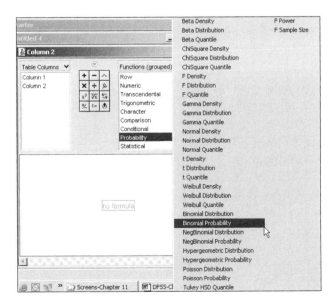

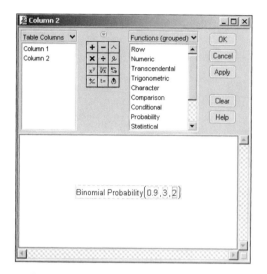

FIGURE A5.7   Binomial Probability Dialog Box

Computing Poisson Probabilities

You can use JMP to compute Poisson probabilities. Referring to the example in Section 5.5 in which the mean = 3, you find the Poisson probabilities of two or fewer successes as follows:

1. Open a new JMP data table.
2. Select **Cols → New Column**.
3. Select the **Column Properties** button. Select **Formula** from the pop-up menu.
4. In the dialog box that appears (see Figure A5.6), select **Probability → Poisson Distribution**.
5. In the edit box that begins with Poisson Distribution, enter 3 for *lambda*, the mean number of successes, and 2 for *k* [defined in Equation (5.6) as *x*], the number of successes. Click the **OK** button. In the New Column dialog box, click the **OK** button.

Double-click on row 1 of the data table to add a row. JMP returns the cumulative probability of two or fewer successes when the mean is 3. If you want to compute the probability of exactly *x* successes, select **Poisson Probability** instead of Poisson Distribution.

Computing Normal Probabilities

You can use JMP to compute normal probabilities. Referring to the example in Section 5.6 in which $\mu = 27$ and $\sigma = 5$, you find the probability of a waiting time less than 30 minutes by doing the following.

1. Open a new JMP data table.
2. Select **Cols → New Column**.
3. Select the **Column Properties** button. Select **Formula** from the pop-up menu.
4. In the dialog box that appears (see Figure A5.6), select **Probability → Normal Distribution**.
5. In the edit box that begins with Normal Distribution, click the ^ key in the upper-right corner of the first row of the Calculator keypad twice. Enter **30** for the value of *x*, **27** for the mean, and **5** for the standard deviation. Click the **OK** button. In the New Column dialog box, click the **OK** button.

Double-click on row 1 of the data table to add a row. JMP returns the probability of less than 30 minutes (a Z value of 0.6) equal to 0.7257.

To find the Z value corresponding to a cumulative area of 0.975:

1. Open a new JMP data table.
2. Select **Cols → New Column**.

3. Select the **Column Properties** button. Select **Formula** from the pop-up menu.

4. In the dialog box that appears (see Figure A5.6), select **Probability → Normal Quantile**.

5. In the edit box that begins with Normal Quantile, enter **0.975**. Click the **OK** button. In the New Column dialog box, click the **OK** button.

Double-click on row 1 of the data table to add a row. JMP returns the Z value of 1.96.

Constructing a Normal Probability Plot

To use JMP to generate a normal probability plot, open the **ORDER.JMP** data table. Select **Analyze → Distribution**. Then, do the following:

1. Select **Time**. Click the **Y, Columns** button. Click the **OK** button. You will get a vertical histogram, a vertical outlier box-and-whisker plot, and descriptive statistics.

2. Click the red triangle next to the Time variable. Select **Display Options → Horizontal Layout** to reorganize the output horizontally.

3. Click the red triangle next to the Time variable. Select **Fit Distribution → Normal**.

4. Click the red triangle next to Fitted Normal. Select **Quantile Plot**.

CHAPTER 6

Sampling Distributions and Confidence Intervals

6.1 **SAMPLING DISTRIBUTIONS**

6.2 **BASIC CONCEPTS OF CONFIDENCE INTERVALS**

6.3 **CONFIDENCE INTERVAL ESTIMATE FOR THE MEAN (σ UNKNOWN)**

6.4 **PREDICTION INTERVAL ESTIMATE FOR A FUTURE INDIVIDUAL VALUE**

6.5 **CONFIDENCE INTERVAL ESTIMATE FOR THE PROPORTION**

SUMMARY

REFERENCES

APPENDIX 6.1 USING MINITAB TO CONSTRUCT CONFIDENCE INTERVALS

APPENDIX 6.2 USING JMP TO CONSTRUCT CONFIDENCE INTERVALS

LEARNING OBJECTIVES

After reading this chapter, you will be able to

- Understand the concept of a sampling distribution.
- Understand the concept of a confidence interval.
- Construct confidence interval estimates for the mean and the proportion.
- Construct a prediction interval for an individual value.
- Understand the difference between a confidence interval and a prediction interval.

6.1   SAMPLING DISTRIBUTIONS

Basic Concepts

In Chapters 2–4, the basic concepts of statistics were introduced, and a variety of useful graphs and descriptive statistical measures were developed. In Chapter 5, "Probability and Probability Distributions," the rules of probability were discussed, the probability distribution was defined, and some specific probability distributions used in Six Sigma management, such as the binomial, Poisson, and normal distributions, were studied.

This chapter provides the foundation for using statistical inference. In Chapter 2, "Introduction to Statistics," **inferential statistics** were defined as those in which conclusions about a large set of data, called the *population*, are made from a subset of the data, called the *sample*. Enumerative studies frequently select a random sample from a frame, something that is at least theoretically possible in this type of study. In the case of analytical studies, although a population does not exist because it is not possible to develop a frame of future output, nevertheless the methods of statistical inference are considered to be useful (along with graphical methods) by most Six Sigma experts [see Reference 3]. In this and subsequent chapters, the term "population" is used instead of "frame" to provide consistency with other statistical texts.

In enumerative or analytical studies, the key focus is on using the sample statistic to draw conclusions about a population parameter. In practice, you usually select only one sample. However, statisticians have developed the theory necessary that allows you to draw conclusions about an entire population based only on a single sample. This is accomplished through the concept of the sampling distribution.

A **sampling distribution** is the distribution of a sample statistic (such as the mean) for all possible samples of size n.

For example, if a population (frame) contains 1,000 items, the sampling distribution of the mean for samples of 15 items would be developed by taking *every* different sample of 15 items from the population of 1,000 items, computing the mean, then arranging all the sample means in a distribution. Actually doing this selection of all the possible samples is an involved, time-consuming task that is not necessary in practice. You primarily need to understand the following principles:

- Every sample statistic has a sampling distribution.
- A specific sample statistic is used to estimate its corresponding population parameter.

Statisticians have extensively studied sampling distributions for many different statistics. Some of these well-known sampling distributions are used extensively in this chapter and in Chapters 7–10.

Sampling Distribution of the Mean

The mean is the most widely used measure in statistics. In Section 4.1, you learned that the mean is calculated by summing the observed numerical values, then dividing the sum by the number of values:

$$\text{arithmetic mean} = \frac{\text{sum of all the values}}{\text{number of values}}$$

Because the mean is based on the computation of all the values in the sample, it can vary from sample to sample, especially when extreme values, or outliers, are present. Statisticians developed the Central Limit Theorem to describe the behavior of the sampling distribution of the mean.

CENTRAL LIMIT THEOREM

Regardless of the shape of the distribution of the individual values in a population (frame), as the sample size gets *large*, the sampling distribution of the mean can be approximated by a normal distribution.

Figure 6.1 represents the sampling distribution of the mean for three different populations (frames). For each population, the sampling distribution of the sample mean is shown for all samples of $n = 2, n = 5$, and $n = 30$.

Panel A of Figure 6.1 illustrates the sampling distribution of the mean for a normally distributed population. When the population is normally distributed, the sampling distribution of the mean is normally distributed, regardless of the sample size. As the sample size increases, the variability of the sample mean from sample to sample decreases. This occurs because the influence of extreme values on an individual mean becomes smaller as the sample size gets larger.

Panel B of Figure 6.1 displays the sampling distribution from a population with a uniform (or rectangular) distribution. When samples of $n = 2$ are selected, there is a peaking, or *central limiting*, effect already working in which there are more sample means in the center than there are individual values in the population. For $n = 5$, the sampling distribution is bell-shaped and approximately normal. When $n = 30$, the sampling distribution appears to be very similar to a normal distribution. In general, the larger the sample size, the more closely the sampling distribution will follow a normal distribution. As with all cases, the mean of each sampling distribution is equal to the mean of the population, and the variability decreases as the sample size increases.

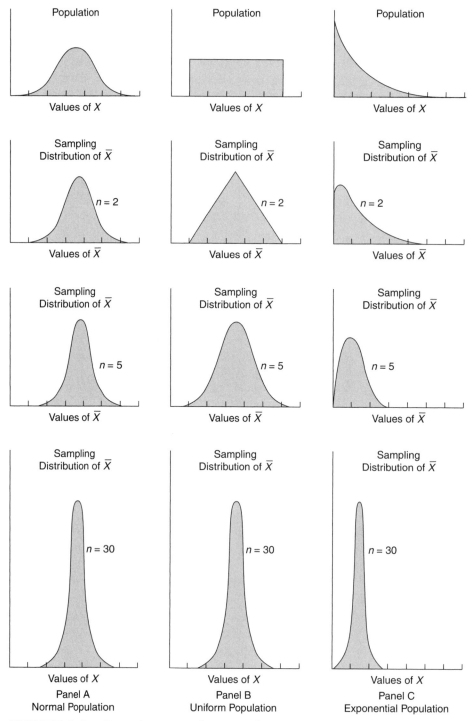

FIGURE 6.1   Sampling Distribution of the Mean for Different Populations for Samples of $n = 2$, 5, and 30

Panel C of Figure 6.1 presents a population from an exponential distribution that is very right skewed. When $n = 2$, the sampling distribution is still highly right skewed, but less so than the distribution of the population. For $n = 5$, the sampling distribution is approximately symmetric, with only a slight right skew. When $n = 30$, the sampling distribution appears to be approximately normally distributed. Again, the mean of each sampling distribution is equal to the mean of the population, and the variability decreases as the sample size increases.

The results displayed in these statistical distributions (normal, uniform, exponential) allow statisticians to state the following conclusions, as presented in Exhibit 6.1.

EXHIBIT 6.1   NORMALITY AND THE SAMPLING DISTRIBUTION OF THE MEAN

1. For most population distributions, regardless of shape, the sampling distribution of the mean is approximately normally distributed if samples of at least 30 are selected.
2. If the population distribution is fairly symmetrical, the sampling distribution of the mean is approximately normal for samples as small as five.
3. If the population is normally distributed, the sampling distribution of the mean is normally distributed, regardless of the sample size.

Sampling Distribution of the Proportion

In Chapter 2, the simplest form of attribute data was defined in which a variable was classified into one of only two categories. The proportion of successes in each category follows a binomial distribution, as discussed in Section 5.4. However, you can use the normal distribution to approximate the binomial distribution when the mean number of successes and the mean number of failures are *each* at least five. In most cases in which you are making inferences about the proportion, the sample size is more than sufficient to meet the conditions for using the normal approximation [see References 1 and 6].

6.2   BASIC CONCEPTS OF CONFIDENCE INTERVALS

The development of the sampling distribution of the statistic of interest is crucial for being able to use the sample statistic to draw a conclusion about a population parameter. However, the results of a sample statistic, such as the mean, computed from a single sample, provides only a **point estimate** of the population parameter. The point estimate is a single value and will almost certainly be different if you select a different sample. Thus, statisticians have developed an **interval estimate** in which you estimate the value of the characteristic for the entire population with a specific degree of certainty with a lower and upper limit.

To develop the concept of the interval estimate, return to the example concerning the fulfillment time of 200 orders from a web site, 🌐 **ORDER** first discussed in Chapter 3, "Presenting Data in Charts and Tables." For now, consider these 200 order fulfillment times to be the population. Although in an actual situation, the population characteristics are rarely known, for this population, the mean, μ = 69.637 minutes, and the standard deviation, σ = 10.411 minutes.

To examine the variation of the sample mean from sample to sample, 20 different samples of n = 10 were selected from this population of 200 orders. The results for these samples are summarized in Figure 6.2.

FIGURE 6.2

Minitab Sample Statistics for 20 Samples of n = 10 Selected from the Population of 200 Orders

Variable	Count	Mean	StDev	Minimum	Median	Maximum	Range
Sample 1	10	74.15	13.39	56.10	76.85	97.70	41.60
Sample 2	10	61.10	10.60	46.80	61.35	79.50	32.70
Sample 3	10	74.36	6.50	62.50	74.50	84.00	21.50
Sample 4	10	70.40	12.80	47.20	70.95	84.00	36.80
Sample 5	10	62.18	10.85	47.10	59.70	84.00	36.90
Sample 6	10	67.03	9.68	51.10	69.60	83.30	32.20
Sample 7	10	69.03	8.81	56.60	68.85	83.70	27.10
Sample 8	10	72.30	11.52	54.20	71.35	87.00	32.80
Sample 9	10	68.18	14.10	50.10	69.95	86.20	36.10
Sample 10	10	66.67	9.08	57.10	64.65	86.10	29.00
Sample 11	10	72.42	9.76	59.60	74.65	86.10	26.50
Sample 12	10	76.26	11.69	50.10	80.60	87.00	36.90
Sample 13	10	65.74	12.11	47.10	62.15	86.10	39.00
Sample 14	10	69.99	10.97	51.00	73.40	84.60	33.60
Sample 15	10	75.76	8.60	61.10	75.05	87.80	26.70
Sample 16	10	67.94	9.19	56.70	67.70	87.80	31.10
Sample 17	10	71.05	10.48	50.10	71.15	86.20	36.10
Sample 18	10	71.68	7.96	55.60	72.35	82.60	27.00
Sample 19	10	70.97	9.83	54.40	70.05	84.60	30.20
Sample 20	10	74.48	8.80	62.00	76.25	85.70	23.70

From Figure 6.2, you can see the following:

1. The sample statistics differ from sample to sample. The sample means vary from 61.10 to 76.26 minutes, the sample standard deviations vary from 6.50 to 14.10 minutes, the sample medians vary from 61.35 to 76.85 minutes, and the sample ranges vary from 21.50 to 41.60 minutes.

2. Some of the sample means are greater than the population mean of 69.637 minutes, and some of the sample means are less than the population mean.

3. Some of the sample standard deviations are greater than the population standard deviation of 10.411 minutes, and some of the sample standard deviations are less than the population standard deviation.

4. The variation in the sample range from sample to sample is much more than the variation in the sample standard deviation.

The fact that sample statistics vary from sample to sample is called **sampling error**. Sampling error is the variation that occurs due to selecting a single sample from the population. The size of the sampling error is primarily based on the amount of variation in the population and on the sample size. Larger samples have less sampling error than small samples, but will cost more.

Because *only one sample is actually selected in practice*, statisticians have developed methods for estimating the population parameter that consists of an interval with a lower and upper limit, rather than a single value. This interval is called a **confidence interval estimate**. Using the data concerning the order fulfillment times illustrated in Figure 6.2, 95% confidence interval estimates of the population mean order fulfillment time for each of the 20 samples of $n = 10$ previously selected are illustrated in Figure 6.3.

FIGURE 6.3

Minitab Confidence Interval Estimates of the Mean for 20 Samples of $n = 10$ Selected from the Population of 200 Orders

Variable	N	Mean	StDev	SE Mean	95% CI
Sample 1	10	74.1500	13.3876	3.2922	(67.6973, 80.6027)
Sample 2	10	61.1000	10.5991	3.2922	(54.6473, 67.5527)
Sample 3	10	74.3600	6.4958	3.2922	(67.9073, 80.8127)
Sample 4	10	70.4000	12.8044	3.2922	(63.9473, 76.8527)
Sample 5	10	62.1800	10.8490	3.2922	(55.7273, 68.6327)
Sample 6	10	67.0300	9.6768	3.2922	(60.5773, 73.4827)
Sample 7	10	69.0300	8.8121	3.2922	(62.5773, 75.4827)
Sample 8	10	72.3000	11.5247	3.2922	(65.8473, 78.7527)
Sample 9	10	68.1800	14.1025	3.2922	(61.7273, 74.6327)
Sample 10	10	66.6700	9.0809	3.2922	(60.2173, 73.1227)
Sample 11	10	72.4200	9.7626	3.2922	(65.9673, 78.8727)
Sample 12	10	76.2600	11.6860	3.2922	(69.8073, 82.7127)
Sample 13	10	65.7400	12.1050	3.2922	(59.2873, 72.1927)
Sample 14	10	69.9900	10.9749	3.2922	(63.5373, 76.4427)
Sample 15	10	75.7600	8.6040	3.2922	(69.3073, 82.2127)
Sample 16	10	67.9400	9.1918	3.2922	(61.4873, 74.3927)
Sample 17	10	71.0500	10.4810	3.2922	(64.5973, 77.5027)
Sample 18	10	71.6800	7.9567	3.2922	(65.2273, 78.1327)
Sample 19	10	70.9700	9.8270	3.2922	(64.5173, 77.4227)
Sample 20	10	74.4800	8.8028	3.2922	(68.0273, 80.9327)

Begin by examining the first sample selected. The sample mean is 74.15 minutes, the sample standard deviation is 13.3876 minutes, and the interval estimate for the population mean is 67.6973 – 80.6027 minutes. You do not know for sure whether this interval estimate is actually correct, because in an actual study, you rarely know the actual value of the population mean. However, *in the example concerning the order fulfillment times*, the population mean is known to be 69.637 minutes. If you examine the interval 67.6973 – 80.6027 minutes, you see that the population mean of 69.637 minutes is included *between* these lower and upper limits. Thus, the first sample provides a correct estimate of the population mean in the form of an interval estimate. Looking over the other 19 samples, you see that similar results occur for all the other samples *except* for samples 2 and 12. For each of the intervals generated (other than samples 2 and 12), the population mean of 69.637 minutes is located *somewhere* within the interval.

However, for sample 2, the sample mean is 61.10 minutes, and the interval is 54.6473 to 67.5527 minutes, while for sample 12, the interval is between 69.8073 and 82.7127 minutes. The population mean of 69.637 minutes is *not* located within the interval, and any estimate of the population mean made using either of these intervals is incorrect.

In practice, the dilemma concerning the interval estimate has two aspects. Only one sample is actually selected, and you have no way to be 100% certain that your interval correctly estimates the population characteristic of interest. However, by setting the level of certainty at a value below 100% and using an interval estimate of the population parameter of interest, you can develop an inference about the population with a given degree of certainty.

> In general, a **95% confidence interval estimate** can be interpreted to mean that if all possible samples of the same size n were selected, 95% of them would include the population parameter somewhere within the interval, and 5% would not.

Although 95% is the most common confidence level used, if more confidence is needed, 99% is typically used. If less confidence is needed, 90% is typically used. However, there is a trade-off between the level of confidence and the width of the interval. For a given sample size, if you want more confidence that your interval contains the population parameter, you will have a wider interval and, thus, more sampling error.

The fundamental concepts of confidence interval estimation remain the same, regardless of the population characteristics being estimated. To develop a confidence interval estimate, you need to know the sample statistic used to estimate the population parameter and the sampling distribution of the sample statistic.

6.3   CONFIDENCE INTERVAL ESTIMATE FOR THE MEAN (σ UNKNOWN)

The most common confidence interval estimate involves estimating the mean of a population. In virtually all cases, the population mean is estimated from sample data in which only the sample mean and sample standard deviation are available, not the standard deviation of the population. For this situation, statisticians [see Reference 1] have developed a sampling distribution called the t distribution to construct a confidence interval estimate of the mean. The confidence interval estimate for the mean is illustrated in the following example.

In New York State, savings banks are permitted to sell a form of life insurance called Savings Bank Life Insurance (SBLI). The approval process consists of underwriting, which includes a review of the application, a medical information bureau check, possible requests for additional medical information and medical exams, and a policy compilation stage where the policy pages are generated and sent to the bank for delivery. The ability to deliver approved policies to customers in a timely manner is critical to the profitability of this service to the bank. During a period of one month, a random sample of 24 approved policies was selected and the total processing time in days was recorded, with the results presented in Table 6.1.

TABLE 6.1   Processing Time in Days for a Sample of 24 Insurance Policies

73	19	26	64	28	28
31	60	56	31	56	22
43	45	48	27	37	37
63	50	51	69	46	47

INSURANCE-TIME

Figure 6.4 represents the Minitab confidence interval estimate of the population mean for the time to process 24 insurance applications. Figure 6.5 presents JMP output.

```
One-Sample T: Time

Variable    N     Mean    StDev   SE Mean        95% CI
Time       24  44.0417  15.5437   3.1728   (37.4781, 50.6052)
```

FIGURE 6.4   Minitab Confidence Interval Estimate of the Population Mean for the Processing Time of 24 Insurance Applications

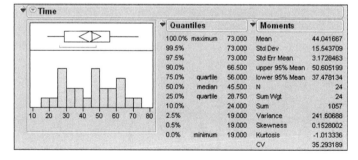

FIGURE 6.5   JMP Confidence Interval Estimate of the Population Mean for the Processing Time of 24 Insurance Applications

Thus, you conclude with 95% confidence that the population mean time to process insurance applications is between 37.478 and 50.605 days.

Figure 6.6 displays the Minitab normal probability plot of the time to process insurance applications.

You see that the points on the normal probability plot appear to be distributed across an approximately straight line from lowest to highest value. Thus, there is little reason to suspect a serious departure from the normality assumption that would affect the validity of the confidence interval estimate.

FIGURE 6.6
Minitab Normal
Probability Plot of
the Processing
Time of Insurance
Applications

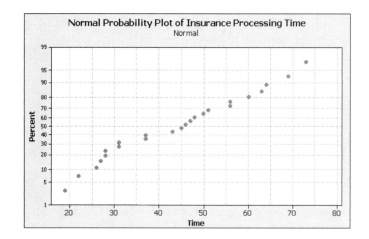

CAUTION: ASSUMPTIONS OF THE CONFIDENCE INTERVAL ESTIMATE
FOR THE MEAN

The t distribution assumes that the variable being studied is normally distributed.
In practice, however, as long as the sample size is large enough and the population is not very skewed, you can use the t distribution to estimate the population
mean when the population standard deviation (σ) is unknown. You should be
concerned about the validity of the confidence interval primarily when dealing
with a small sample size and a skewed population distribution. The assumption of
normality in the population can be assessed by evaluating the shape of the sample data using a histogram, box-and-whisker plot, or normal probability plot.

EQUATION FOR CONFIDENCE INTERVAL FOR A MEAN σ UNKNOWN {OPTIONAL}

$$\overline{X} \pm t_{n-1}\frac{S}{\sqrt{n}}$$

or   (6.1)

$$\overline{X} - t_{n-1}\frac{S}{\sqrt{n}} \leq \mu \leq \overline{X} + t_{n-1}\frac{S}{\sqrt{n}}$$

where t_{n-1} is the critical value of the t distribution with $n-1$ degrees of freedom for an
area of $\alpha/2$ in the upper tail.

Using the Minitab output shown in Figure 6.4, $\overline{X} = 44.0417$ and $S = 15.5437$.
Because $n = 24$, there are $24 - 1 = 23$ degrees of freedom. For 95% confidence, the area
in the upper tail of the t distribution is $0.05/2 = 0.025$. Using Table C.2 in Appendix C,

the critical value for the row with 23 degrees of freedom and the column with an area of 0.025 is 2.0687. Using Equation (6.1):

$$\overline{X} \pm t_{n-1} \frac{S}{\sqrt{n}}$$

$$= 44.0417 \pm (2.0687) \frac{15.5437}{\sqrt{24}}$$

$$= 44.0417 \pm 6.5637$$

$$37.478 \le \mu \le 50.605$$

6.4 PREDICTION INTERVAL ESTIMATE FOR A FUTURE INDIVIDUAL VALUE

In addition to a confidence interval estimate of the population mean, often you need to predict the outcome of a future individual value [see Reference 4]. Although the form of the prediction interval is similar to the confidence interval estimate of the mean shown in Equation (6.1), the interpretation of the prediction interval is different. The **prediction interval** is estimating an observable future individual value X_f, *not* an unknown population parameter μ. Because neither Minitab nor JMP currently computes a prediction interval, the prediction interval is shown in Equation (6.2).

$$\overline{X} \pm t_{n-1} S \sqrt{1 + \frac{1}{n}}$$

$$\overline{X} - t_{n-1} S \sqrt{1 + \frac{1}{n}} \le X_f \le \overline{X} + t_{n-1} S \sqrt{1 + \frac{1}{n}} \qquad (6.2)$$

where X_f is a future individual value of X.

Returning to the example concerning the processing time of insurance applications, suppose that you wanted to construct a 95% prediction interval estimate of the future processing time of an individual insurance application. Using Equation (6.2):

$$\overline{X} \pm t_{n-1} S \sqrt{1 + \frac{1}{n}}$$

$$= 44.0417 \pm (2.0687)(15.5437) \sqrt{1 + \frac{1}{24}}$$

$$= 44.0417 \pm 32.8183$$

$$11.2234 \le X_f \le 76.86$$

Thus, you predict with 95% assurance that a future individual insurance application will take between 11.22 and 76.86 days to process. This result differs markedly from the confidence interval estimate of the population mean. The prediction interval is substantially wider because you are estimating a *future individual value*, not the population mean.

6.5   CONFIDENCE INTERVAL ESTIMATE FOR THE PROPORTION

A confidence interval estimate for an attribute can be constructed to estimate the proportion of successes in a given category. Instead of using the sample mean to estimate the population mean, you use the sample proportion of successes (p):

$$\text{proportion of successes} = \frac{\text{number of successes}}{\text{sample size}}$$

to estimate the population proportion (π). The sample statistic p follows a binomial distribution that can be approximated by the normal distribution for most studies.

To demonstrate the confidence interval estimate of the proportion, you can examine the situation faced by the quality engineer for a large city newspaper. In the production of a newspaper, an important quality characteristic relates to the proportion of newspapers that are printed, even though a nonconforming attribute, such as excessive ruboff, improper page setup, missing pages, or duplicate pages, is present. Because it is impractical (and would be extremely time-consuming and expensive) to examine every newspaper printed, a random sample of 200 newspapers is selected for study. Suppose that, in a sample of 200, a total of 35 contain some type of nonconformance. Figure 6.7 consists of a Minitab 95% confidence interval estimate for the percentage of nonconforming newspapers.

```
Sample   X    N  Sample p          95% CI
1       35  200  0.175000   (0.122340, 0.227660)
```

FIGURE 6.7   Minitab 95% Confidence Interval Estimate for the Proportion of Nonconforming Newspapers

Therefore, 95% of all confidence intervals computed from a random sample of 200 newspapers will contain the population proportion. Because the population proportion is unknown, the interval 12.2% to 22.8% may be one of the 95% of the intervals containing the population proportion. There is a 5% chance of constructing an interval that does not include the population proportion.

For a given sample size, confidence intervals for proportions often seem to be wider than those for measurement variables. With continuous variables, the measurement on each respondent contributes more information than for a categorical variable. In other words, a categorical variable with only two possible values is a very crude measure, compared with a continuous variable, so each value contributes only a little information about the parameter being estimated.

EQUATION FOR THE CONFIDENCE INTERVAL ESTIMATE FOR THE PROPORTION {OPTIONAL}

$$p \pm Z\sqrt{\frac{p(1-p)}{n}}$$

or   (6.3)

$$p - Z\sqrt{\frac{p(1-p)}{n}} \leq \pi \leq p + Z\sqrt{\frac{p(1-p)}{n}}$$

where

$p = \dfrac{X}{n}$ = sample proportion

π = population proportion

Z = critical value from the normal distribution

n = sample size

For these data, $p = 35/200 = 0.175$. For a 95% level of confidence, the lower tail area of 0.025 provides a Z value from the normal distribution of -1.96, and the upper tail area of 0.025 provides a Z value from the normal distribution of +1.96.

Using Equation (6.3):

$$p \pm Z\sqrt{\frac{p(1-p)}{n}}$$

$$= 0.175 \pm (1.96)\sqrt{\frac{(0.175)(0.825)}{200}}$$

$$= 0.175 \pm (1.96)(0.0269)$$

$$= 0.175 \pm 0.053$$

$$0.122 \leq \pi \leq 0.228$$

ASSUMPTIONS OF THE CONFIDENCE INTERVAL ESTIMATE FOR THE PRO-
PORTION

In most studies, the number of successes and failures is sufficiently large that the
normal distribution provides an excellent approximation to the binomial distribution. If there are fewer than a mean of five successes or failures in the data, the
confidence intervals computed can be adjusted to provide more exact intervals
[see Reference 6].

SUMMARY

In this chapter, the concept of the sampling
distribution of a statistic served as the foundation for developing confidence interval
estimates of the mean and the proportion.
The assumption of each confidence interval
was stated, and methods for evaluating the
validity of the assumption were shown. In
addition, the distinction was made between
the confidence interval and the prediction
interval.

REFERENCES

1. Berenson, M. L., D. M. Levine, and T.
   C. Krehbiel. *Basic Business Statistics:
   Concepts and Applications*, 10th ed.
   (Upper Saddle River, NJ: Prentice
   Hall, 2006).

2. Cochran, W. G. *Sampling Techniques*,
   3rd Ed. (New York: John Wiley, 1977).

3. Hahn, G. J. and W. Q. Meeker.
   "Assumptions for Statistical
   Inference." *The American Statistician.*
   1993, 47, 1–11.

4. Hahn, G. J. and W. Nelson. "A Survey
   of Prediction Intervals and Their
   Applications." *Journal of Quality Technology.* 1973, 5, 178–188.

5. *JMP Version 6* (Cary, NC: SAS
   Institute, 2005).

6. Minitab Version 14 (State College,
   PA: Minitab, 2004).

Appendix 6.1
Using Minitab to Construct Confidence Intervals

Constructing the Confidence Interval Estimate for the Mean

To construct the confidence interval estimate of the mean time to process insurance applications illustrated in Figure 6.4 on page 103, open the **INSURANCE-TIME.MTW** worksheet. Select **Stat → Basic Statistics → 1-Sample t**:

1. In the 1-Sample t (Test and Confidence Interval) dialog box (see Figure A6.1), select the Samples in columns: edit box, and enter **C1** or **Time**. (If you have summarized data instead of the actual data, select the **Summarized data** option button and enter values for the sample size, mean, and standard deviation.)

2. Click the **Options** button. In the 1-Sample t—Options dialog box (see Figure A6.2), enter **95** in the Confidence level: edit box. Enter **not equal** in the Alternative drop-down list box. Click the **OK** button to return to the 1-Sample t (Test and Confidence Interval) dialog box. (Click the **Graphs** button to generate a histogram or box-and-whisker plot.) Click the **OK** button.

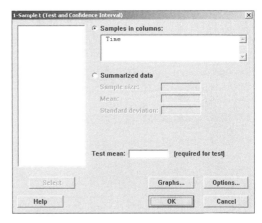

FIGURE A6.1 Minitab 1-Sample t (Test and Confidence Interval) Dialog Box

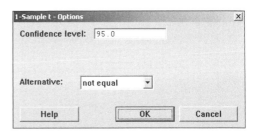

FIGURE A6.2 Minitab 1-Sample t—Options Dialog Box

Constructing the Confidence Interval Estimate for the Proportion

To construct the confidence interval estimate of the proportion of nonconforming newspapers illustrated in Figure 6.7 on page 106, select **Stat → Basic Statistics → 1 Proportion**:

1. In the 1 Proportion (Test and Confidence Interval) dialog box (see Figure A6.3), select the **Summarized data** option button. Enter **200** in the Number of trials: edit box. Enter **35** in the Number of events: edit box.

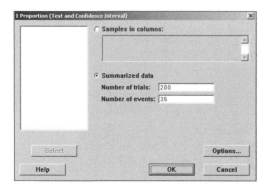

FIGURE A6.3   Minitab 1 Proportion (Test and Confidence Interval) Dialog Box

2. Click the **Options** button. In the 1 Proportion — Options dialog box (see Figure A6.4), enter **95** in the Confidence level: edit box. Enter **not equal** in the Alternative: drop-down list box. Select the **Use test and interval based on the normal distribution** check box (uncheck this if this selection is not desired). Click the **OK** button to return to the 1 Proportion (Test and Confidence Interval) dialog box. Click the **OK** button.

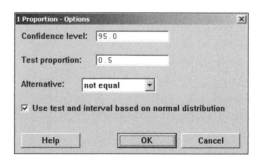

FIGURE A6.4   Minitab 1 Proportion—Options Dialog Box

Appendix 6.2
Using JMP to Construct Confidence Intervals

Constructing the Confidence Interval Estimate for the Mean

To construct the confidence interval estimate of the mean time to process insurance applications illustrated in Figure 6.5 on page 103, open the **INSURANCE-TIME.JMP** data table. Select **Analyze → Distribution**. Then do the following:

1. Select **Time**. Click the **Y, Columns** button. Click the **OK** button. You will get a vertical histogram, a vertical outlier box-and-whisker plot, and descriptive statistics including a 95% confidence interval. To generate a confidence interval different from 95%, click the red triangle next to the Time variable. Select **Confidence Interval** and then select the desired level of confidence.

2. Click the red triangle next to the Time variable. Select **Display Options → Horizontal Layout** to reorganize the output horizontally.

Constructing the Confidence Interval Estimate for the Proportion

You can use JMP to construct a confidence interval for a categorical variable when you have raw data. For an ordinal or nominal variable, select **Analyze → Distribution**. Then, select **Confidence Interval →** and select the desired level of confidence. JMP will construct a confidence interval for each category of the categorical variable.

CHAPTER 7

Hypothesis Testing

INTRODUCTION

7.1 FUNDAMENTAL CONCEPTS OF HYPOTHESIS TESTING

7.2 TESTING FOR THE DIFFERENCE BETWEEN TWO PROPORTIONS

7.3 TESTING FOR THE DIFFERENCE BETWEEN THE MEANS OF TWO INDEPENDENT GROUPS

7.4 TESTING FOR THE DIFFERENCE BETWEEN TWO VARIANCES

7.5 ONE-WAY ANOVA

7.6 WILCOXON RANK SUM TEST FOR THE DIFFERENCE BETWEEN TWO MEDIANS

7.7 KRUSKAL-WALLIS RANK TEST

SUMMARY

REFERENCES

APPENDIX 7.1 USING MINITAB FOR HYPOTHESIS TESTING

APPENDIX 7.2 USING JMP FOR HYPOTHESIS TESTING

LEARNING OBJECTIVES

After reading this chapter, you will be able to

- Understand the basic principles of hypothesis testing.
- Understand the assumptions of hypothesis testing and know what to do if they are violated.
- Test for differences between means, proportions, variances, and medians using hypothesis tests.
- Know how and when to use nonparametric tests.

INTRODUCTION

In Chapter 6, "Sampling Distributions and Confidence Intervals," the concept of a sampling distribution was developed, and confidence intervals were used to estimate population parameters. This chapter focuses on making inferences about the hypothesized values of two or more population parameters using sample statistics and hypothesis testing procedures. The variable of interest is the CTQ, and the populations of interest are the different levels of a CTP (X). For example, the CTQ could be the order fulfillment times at a web site, and the populations of interest might be the different ways of filling the orders. These methods are referred to as **hypothesis testing** or **tests of statistical significance**. These procedures are used for enumerative studies and for guidance in designed experiments.

7.1   FUNDAMENTAL CONCEPTS OF HYPOTHESIS TESTING

Hypothesis testing typically begins with some theory, claim, or assertion about a particular population parameter (CTQ) of one or more populations (levels of a CTP or X). For example, a study may be designed to determine whether the waiting time (CTQ) was higher in bank 1 ($X = 1$) or bank 2 ($X = 2$). To state this quantitatively, CTQ = $f(X)$, where CTQ = waiting time, and $X = 1$ if bank 1 and $X = 2$ if bank 2. X either is or is not a statistically significant predictor of CTQ. A sample of waiting time is selected from each bank. If the waiting times are similar in both banks, the means and the standard deviations should be similar in both banks.

The hypothesis that the mean waiting times are equal in the two banks (no statistically significant difference in the mean waiting times between the banks) is referred to as the **null hypothesis**. A null hypothesis is always a statement containing no difference between a parameter and a hypothesized value for that parameter, or no difference between the parameters for two or more populations. The symbol H_0 is commonly used to identify the null hypothesis. Because you want to compare the mean value of a CTQ for the low and high levels of an X, the null hypothesis is stated as either:

$$H_{0A}: \mu_1 = \mu_2 \text{ or } \mu_1 - \mu_2 = 0$$
$$H_{0B}: \mu_1 \leq \mu_2 \text{ or } \mu_1 - \mu_2 \leq 0$$
$$H_{0C}: \mu_1 \geq \mu_2 \text{ or } \mu_1 - \mu_2 \geq 0$$

H_{0A} is used to test the null hypothesis of no difference between two population means when there is no information about which population has the higher mean.

H_{0B} is used to test the null hypothesis when there is information that the mean of population 1 is less than or equal to the mean of population 2. H_{0C} is used to test the null hypothesis when there is information that the mean of population 1 is greater than or equal to the mean of population 2.

Even though information is available only from a sample, the null hypothesis is written in terms of the population parameters. This is because you are interested in the population of responses that might ever be studied. The sample statistics are used to make inferences about the population parameters. The logic and theory of hypothesis testing requires that the null hypothesis is considered true until evidence in the form of sample data indicates that it is false. If the null hypothesis is considered false, something else must be true.

Whenever a null hypothesis is specified, an **alternative hypothesis** or one that must be true if the null hypothesis is found to be false must also be specified. The alternative hypothesis (H_1) is the opposite of the null hypothesis (H_0). For the difference between the mean of the two groups, this is stated as either:

$$H_{1A}: \mu_1 \neq \mu_2 \text{ or } \mu_1 - \mu_2 \neq 0$$
$$H_{1B}: \mu_1 > \mu_2 \text{ or } \mu_1 - \mu_2 > 0$$
$$H_{1C}: \mu_1 < \mu_2 \text{ or } \mu_1 - \mu_2 < 0$$

H_{1A} is used to state the alternative hypothesis that there is a statistically significant difference between two population means when there is no information about which population has the higher mean. H_{1B} is used to state the alternative hypothesis that the mean of population 1 is statistically significantly greater than the mean of population 2. H_{1C} is used to state the alternative hypothesis that the mean of population 1 is statistically significantly less than the mean of population 2.

The alternative hypothesis represents the conclusion reached by rejecting the null hypothesis if there were sufficient evidence from sample information to decide that the null hypothesis is unlikely to be true. In the example concerning the difference between the mean waiting times in two banks, if the difference between the means is sufficiently large, you reject the null hypothesis in favor of the alternative hypothesis that the two mean waiting times are different.

Hypothesis testing procedures or statistical tests of significance are designed so that rejection of the null hypothesis is based on evidence from the sample that the alternative hypothesis is far more likely to be true. However, *failure to reject the null hypothesis is not proof that the null hypothesis is true.* If you fail to reject the null hypothesis, you can only conclude that there is insufficient evidence to warrant its rejection.

A summary of the null and alternative hypotheses is presented in Exhibit 7.1.

EXHIBIT 7.1   THE NULL AND ALTERNATIVE HYPOTHESES

The following key points summarize the null and alternative hypotheses:

1. The null hypothesis (H_0) represents the status quo or current belief in a situation; that is, that the CTP or X has no influence on the CTQ.
2. The alternative hypothesis (H_1) is the opposite of the null hypothesis and represents a research claim or specific inference you would like to study; that is, that the CTP or X has a statistically significant influence on the CTQ.
3. If you reject the null hypothesis, you have statistical proof that the alternative hypothesis is true.
4. If you do not reject the null hypothesis, you have failed to prove the alternative hypothesis. The failure to prove the alternative hypothesis does not mean that you have proven the null hypothesis.
5. The null hypothesis (H_0) always refers to a specified value of the *population parameter* (such as μ), not a *sample statistic* (such as $\bar{X}$).
6. The statement of the null hypothesis *always* contains an equal sign regarding the specified value of the parameter (for example, $H_0: \mu_1 = \mu_2$).
7. The statement of the alternative hypothesis *never* contains an equal sign regarding the specified value of the parameter (for example, $H_1: \mu_1 \neq \mu_2$).

The Critical Value of the Test Statistic

The logic behind hypothesis-testing methods is based on using sample information to determine the plausibility of the null hypothesis. The null hypothesis for the bank waiting times problem is that the mean waiting time for bank 1 is equal to the mean waiting time for bank 2: $H_0: \mu_1 = \mu_2$. You collect sample data and compute the sample mean waiting time for each of the two banks. The sample statistics computed are estimates of population parameters and will likely differ from the population parameters because of chance or sampling error. If there is no difference between the two banks, you expect the sample means to be very close to each other. When this occurs, there is insufficient evidence to reject the null hypothesis.

If there is a large difference between the sample statistics for the two groups, you conclude that the null hypothesis is unlikely to be true. Here, you reject the null hypothesis. In either case, you reach the decision because of the belief that randomly selected samples reflect the underlying populations from which they are selected.

Unfortunately, the decision-making process is not always so clear-cut and cannot be left to your subjective judgment as to the meaning of "very close" or "very different." Determining what is very close and what is very different is arbitrary without using operational definitions. Hypothesis testing procedures provide operational definitions for evaluating such differences and enable you to quantify the decision-making process by computing the probability of a given sample result if the null hypothesis were true. You calculate this probability by determining the sampling distribution for the sample statistic of interest, and then computing the particular **test statistic** based on the given sample result. The sampling distribution for the test statistic often follows a well-known statistical distribution, such as the normal distribution or the *t*-distribution. In such circumstances, you will be able to determine the likelihood of a null hypothesis being true.

Regions of Rejection and Nonrejection

The sampling distribution of the test statistic is divided into two regions: a **region of rejection** (sometimes called the **critical region**) and a **region of nonrejection** (see Figure 7.1). If the test statistic falls into the region of nonrejection, you do not reject the null hypothesis. In the test of waiting times of the two banks, you would conclude that the mean waiting time is the same for the two banks. If the test statistic falls into the rejection region, you reject the null hypothesis. In this case, you would conclude that the mean waiting time is different between the two banks.

FIGURE 7.1
Regions of Rejection and Nonrejection in Hypothesis Testing

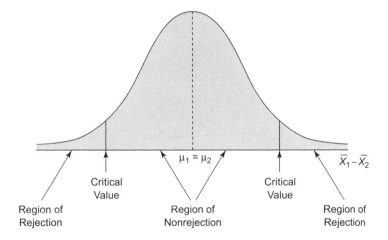

The region of rejection consists of the values of the test statistic that are unlikely to occur if the null hypothesis is true. These values are more likely to occur if the null hypothesis is false. Therefore, if a value of the test statistic falls into the *rejection region,* you reject the null hypothesis because that value is unlikely if the null hypothesis is true.

To make a decision concerning the null hypothesis, you first determine the **critical value** of the test statistic. The critical value divides the nonrejection region from the rejection region. However, the determination of the critical value is directly related to the risks involved in using only sample evidence to make decisions about a population parameter.

Risks in Decision Making Using Hypothesis-Testing Methodology

There are risks that you will reach an incorrect conclusion when using a sample statistic to make decisions about a population parameter. In fact, you can make two different types of errors when applying hypothesis-testing methodology: Type I and Type II.

> A **Type I error** occurs if you reject the null hypothesis H_0 when it is true and should not be rejected. The probability of a Type I error occurring is α. A good way to remember the definition of the Type I error is ART, <u>A</u>lpha-<u>R</u>eject H_0-<u>T</u>rue.
>
> A **Type II error** occurs if you do not reject the null hypothesis H_0 when it is false and should be rejected. The probability of a Type II error occurring is β. A good way to remember the definition of the Type II error is BAF, <u>B</u>eta-<u>A</u>ccept H_0-<u>F</u>alse.

In the bank waiting time example, the Type I error occurs if you conclude (based on sample information) that the mean waiting time is different between the two banks when there is no difference. On the other hand, the Type II error occurs if you conclude (based on sample information) that the mean waiting time is not different between the two banks when there is a difference.

Level of Significance

The probability of committing a Type I error, denoted by α, is called the **level of significance** of the statistical test. Traditionally, you control the Type I error by deciding the risk level of α you are willing to tolerate in rejecting the null hypothesis when it is true. Because you specify the level of significance before the hypothesis test is performed, you directly control the risk of committing a Type I error, α. Traditionally, you select an α level of 0.05 or 0.01. The choice of a particular risk level for making a Type I error depends on the cost of making a Type I error. After you specify the value for α, you know the size of the rejection region, because α is the probability of rejection under the null hypothesis. From this fact, you can determine the critical value or values that divide the rejection and nonrejection regions.

The Confidence Coefficient

The complement $(1 - \alpha)$ of the probability of a Type I error is called the **confidence coefficient**. When multiplied by 100%, the confidence coefficient yields the confidence level studied in Sections 6.2–6.5.

> The **confidence coefficient**, $1 - \alpha$, is the probability that you will not reject the null hypothesis H_0 when it is true and should not be rejected.

In hypothesis-testing methodology, this coefficient represents the probability of concluding that the value of the parameter as specified in the null hypothesis is plausible when it is true. In the bank waiting times example, the confidence coefficient measures the probability of concluding that there is no statistically significant difference between the two banks when there is actually no difference.

The β Risk

The probability of committing a Type II error, called β, is often referred to as the *consumer's risk* level. Unlike the Type I error, which you control by the selection of α, the probability of making a Type II error depends on the difference between the hypothesized and actual value of the population parameter. Because large differences are easier to find, if the difference between the hypothesized value and the corresponding population parameter is large, β, the probability of committing a Type II error, will likely be small. If the difference between the hypothesized value and the corresponding parameter value is small, the probability of committing a Type II error β is large.

The Power of a Test

The complement $(1 - β)$ of the probability of a Type II error is called the power of a statistical test.

> The **power of a statistical test**, $1 - β$, is the probability of rejecting the null hypothesis when it is false and should be rejected.

In the bank waiting times example, the power of the test is the probability of concluding that there is a statistically significant difference in the means of the two banks when there actually is a difference. Table 7.1 illustrates the results of the two possible decisions (do not reject H_0 or reject H_0) that can occur in any hypothesis test. Depending on the specific decision, one of two types of errors may occur or one of two types of correct conclusions will be reached.

TABLE 7.1   Hypothesis Testing and Decision Making

	Actual Situation	
Statistical Decision	**H_0 True**	**H_0 False**
Do not reject H_0	Correct decision confidence = $1 - α$	Type II error P (Type II error) = $β$
Reject H_0	Type I error P (Type I error) = $α$	Correct decision power = $1 - β$

One way you can control the probability of making a Type II error in a study is to increase the size of the sample. Large sample sizes generally permit you to detect even very small differences between the hypothesized values and the population parameters. For a given level of α, increasing the sample size will decrease β, and therefore increase the power of the test to detect that the null hypothesis H_0 is false. Of course, there is always a limit to resources. Thus, for a given sample size, you must consider the trade-off between the two possible types of errors. Because you can directly control the risk of the Type I error, you can reduce your risk by selecting a lower level for α. For example, if the negative consequences associated with making a Type I error are substantial, you can select α to be 0.01 instead of 0.05. However, when you decrease α, you increase β, so reducing the risk of a Type I error will result in an increased risk of Type II error. If you wish to reduce β, the risk of Type II error, you could select a larger value for α. Therefore, if it is important to try to avoid a Type II error, you can select α to be 0.05 instead of 0.01.

Now that the level of significance has been defined, you need to make a distinction between a statistically significant difference and a practically significant difference. Given a large enough sample size, it is always possible that you will detect a statistically significant difference. This is because no two things in nature are exactly equal. So with a large enough sample size, you can always detect the natural difference between two populations. Thus, you need to be aware of the real-world practical implications of the statistical significance.

The steps of hypothesis testing are summarized in Exhibit 7.2.

EXHIBIT 7.2   SEVEN-STEP METHOD OF HYPOTHESIS TESTING

1. State the null hypothesis, H_0, and the alternative hypothesis H_1. The null hypothesis must be stated in statistical terms, using population parameters. In testing whether there is a difference in the means of the two populations, the null hypothesis states that $\mu_1 = \mu_2$ and the alternative hypothesis states that $\mu_1 \neq \mu_2$.

2. Choose the level of significance, α. The level of significance is specified according to the relative importance of the risks of committing Type I and Type II errors in the problem. In other words, the Type I error is set by the decision maker as the probability she or he is willing to accept in rejecting the null hypothesis when it is true. The smaller the value of α, the less risk there is in making a Type I error.

3. Choose the sample size, n. The sample size is determined after taking into account the specified risks of committing Type I and Type II errors (i.e., selected levels of α and β) and considering budget constraints in carrying out the study.

4. Determine the appropriate test statistic.

5. Determine the critical values that divide the rejection and nonrejection regions.

6. Collect the data and compute the value of the test statistic.

7. Make the statistical decision. Compare the computed value of the test statistic with the critical values for the appropriate sampling distribution to determine whether the test statistic falls into the rejection or nonrejection region. If the test statistic falls into the nonrejection region, you do not reject the null hypothesis H_0. If the test statistic falls into the rejection region, you reject the null hypothesis in favor of the alternative hypothesis. Express the statistical decision in terms of the problem.

The *p*-Value Approach to Hypothesis Testing

Modern statistical software, including Minitab and JMP, computes a probability value known as the *p*-value. This approach to hypothesis testing has increasingly gained acceptance and is commonly substituted for the critical value approach.

The **p-value** is the probability that the test statistic will be equal to or more extreme than the sample result, given that the null hypothesis H_0 is true.

The *p*-value, often referred to as the *observed level of significance*, is the smallest level at which H_0 can be rejected for a given set of data. The decision rule in the *p*-value approach for rejecting H_0 is:

- If the *p*-value is greater than or equal to α, do not reject the null hypothesis.
- If the *p*-value is less than α, reject the null hypothesis.

Many people confuse this rule, mistakenly believing that a high *p*-value is grounds for rejection. You can avoid this confusion by informally remembering the following mantra:

"If the *p*-value is *low*, then H_0 must go."

Exhibit 7.3 displays a summary of the *p*-value approach for hypothesis testing.

EXHIBIT 7.3   SIX STEPS OF HYPOTHESIS TESTING USING THE *p*-VALUE APPROACH

1. State the null hypothesis, H_0, and the alternative hypothesis, H_1.
2. Choose the level of significance (α) and the sample size, n.
3. Determine the appropriate test statistic and sampling distribution.
4. Collect the data and compute the sample value of the appropriate test statistic.
5. Calculate the *p*-value based on the test statistic and compare the *p*-value to α.
6. Make the statistical decision. If the *p*-value is greater than or equal to α, you do not reject the null hypothesis. If the *p*-value is less than α, you reject the null hypothesis. Express the statistical decision in the context of the problem.

7.2   TESTING FOR THE DIFFERENCE BETWEEN TWO PROPORTIONS

Often, you want to analyze differences between two populations in the number of nonconforming or defective occurrences. The sample statistics needed to analyze these differences are the proportion of occurrences in population 1 and the proportion of occurrences in population 2. With a sufficient sample size in each group, the sampling distribution of the difference between the two proportions approximately follows a normal distribution.

Table 7.2 summarizes some findings from a study that was conducted at a resort hotel. Management of the hotel had a business objective of increasing the return rate of guests at the hotel. Management decided to focus on the critical first impressions of the service that the hotel provides. To accomplish this objective, such questions were asked: "Is the assigned hotel room ready when a guest checks in? Are all expected amenities, such as extra towels and a complementary guest basket, in the room when the guest first walks in? Are the video-entertainment center and high-speed Internet access working properly?" Because the hotel contained two wings, each of which had its own housekeeping and maintenance teams, on a certain day, a sample of 200 rooms were selected in each wing. There were 8 rooms in Wing A and 14 rooms in Wing B that had some nonconformance that would make the room not ready for arrival of the guest.

TABLE 7.2   Cross-Classification of Room Readiness and Hotel Wing

	Wing		
Room Is Ready	*A*	*B*	**Total**
No	8	14	22
Yes	192	186	378
Total	200	200	400

The objective of the hypothesis test is to determine whether the proportion of rooms not ready is the same for Wing A and Wing B, using a level of significance of $\alpha = 0.05$. For these data, the proportion of rooms not ready for Wing A is $8/200 = 0.04$, and the proportion of rooms not ready for Wing B is $14/200 = 0.07$.

Because the number of "successes" (rooms not ready) in the groups (8 and 14) is sufficiently large, as is the number of "failures" (rooms ready) in the groups (192 and 186), the sampling distribution for the difference between the two proportions is approximately normally distributed. The null and alternative hypotheses are:

$H_0: \pi_1 = \pi_2$ or $\pi_1 - \pi_2 = 0$ (No difference between the two proportions.)
$H_1: \pi_1 \neq \pi_2$ or $\pi_1 - \pi_2 \neq 0$ (There is a difference between the two proportions.)

Figure 7.2 illustrates Minitab output for the study of rooms not ready.

FIGURE 7.2
Minitab Output for the Difference Between Two Proportions for the Rooms Not Ready Study

```
Test and CI for Two Proportions

Sample   X    N   Sample p
1        8   200  0.040000
2       14   200  0.070000


Difference = p (1) - p (2)
Estimate for difference:  -0.03
95% CI for difference:  (-0.0745865, 0.0145865)
Test for difference = 0 (vs not = 0):  Z = -1.32  P-Value = 0.188
```

As stated earlier, there are two approaches to making a decision using a hypothesis test: the critical value approach and the p-value approach. In this first example, both approaches will be illustrated. For other tests of hypothesis discussed in this book, because Minitab and JMP software will be used, the p-value approach will be emphasized.

Using the critical value approach, you first need to define regions of rejection and nonrejection. As stated previously, the sampling distribution of the difference between two proportions approximately follows the normal distribution. Selecting a level of significance of 0.05 provides a lower tail area of 0.025 and an upper tail area of 0.025. Using the cumulative normal distribution table (Table C.1 in Appendix C, "Statistical Tables"), the lower tail area of 0.025 corresponds to a lower critical value of $Z = -1.96$, and the upper tail area of 0.025 (cumulative area of 0.975) corresponds to an upper critical value of $Z = +1.96$ (see Figure 7.3). The decision rule is as follows:

Reject H_0 if $Z < -1.96$ or if $Z > +1.96$; otherwise, do not reject H_0.

FIGURE 7.3
Testing a Hypothesis for the Difference Between Two Proportions at the 0.05 Level of Significance

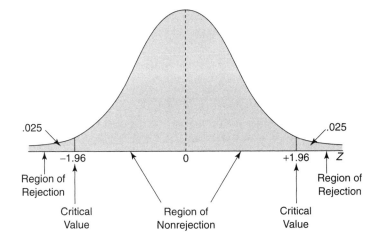

From Figure 7.2, the test statistic $Z = -1.32$. Because $Z = -1.32$ is greater than the lower critical value of -1.96 and less than the upper critical value of +1.96 ($-1.96 < Z = -1.32 < +1.96$), you do not reject the null hypothesis. Alternatively, using the p-value approach, the p-value $= 0.188$. Because the p-value $= 0.188$ is *greater than* the level of significance $\alpha = 0.05$, you do not reject the null hypothesis. This means that the chance that the Z value is less than -1.32 or greater than +1.32 is 0.188. You conclude that there is insufficient evidence of a difference in the proportion of rooms not ready between Wing A and Wing B of the hotel.

The steps of the critical value approach for this example are summarized as follows:

Step 1:
$H_0: \pi_1 = \pi_2$ (no difference between the two proportions)
$H_1: \pi_1 \neq \pi_2$ (statistically significant difference between the two proportions)

Step 2:
$\alpha = 0.05$

Step 3:
Samples of 200 rooms in Wing A and 200 rooms in Wing B are selected.

Step 4:
The test for the difference between two proportions approximately follows a normal distribution.

Step 5:
The decision rule is reject H_0 if $Z < -1.96$ or if $Z > +1.96$; otherwise, do not reject H_0.

Step 6:
$Z = -1.32$; $-1.96 < Z = -1.32 < +1.96$.

Step 7:
Do not reject the null hypothesis. You conclude that there is insufficient evidence of a difference in the proportion of rooms not ready between Wing A and Wing B of the hotel.

The steps of the p-value approach for this example are summarized as follows:

Steps 1–3:
Same as steps 1–4 of the critical value approach.

Step 4:
$Z = -1.32$

Step 5:

The p-value (computed by Minitab) is 0.188, which is greater than $\alpha = 0.05$.

Step 6:

Do not reject the null hypothesis. You conclude that there is insufficient evidence of a difference in the proportion of rooms not ready between Wing A and Wing B of the hotel.

You can use these steps for hypothesis testing for all hypothesis tests subsequently discussed in this book.

EQUATION FOR THE Z TEST FOR THE DIFFERENCE BETWEEN TWO PROPORTIONS {OPTIONAL}

$$Z = \frac{(p_1 - p_2) - (\pi_1 - \pi_2)}{\sqrt{\bar{p}(1-\bar{p})\left(\frac{1}{n_1} + \frac{1}{n_2}\right)}} \qquad (7.1)$$

with

$$\bar{p} = \frac{X_1 + X_2}{n_1 + n_2} \quad p_1 = \frac{X_1}{n_1} \quad p_2 = \frac{X_2}{n_2}$$

where

$p_1 =$ proportion of successes in sample 1

$X_1 =$ number of successes in sample 1

$n_1 =$ sample size from population 1

$\pi_1 =$ proportion of successes in population 1

$p_2 =$ proportion of successes in sample 2

$X_2 =$ number of successes in sample 2

$n_2 =$ sample size from population 2

$\pi_2 =$ proportion of successes in population 2

For the example concerning the rooms not ready in the hotel, using Equation (7.1), where:

$$p_1 = \frac{X_1}{n_1} = \frac{8}{200} = 0.04 \quad p_2 = \frac{X_2}{n_2} = \frac{14}{200} = 0.07$$

and

$$\bar{p} = \frac{X_1 + X_2}{n_1 + n_2} = \frac{8 + 14}{200 + 200} = \frac{22}{400} = 0.055$$

Continues

so that

$$Z = \frac{(0.04 - 0.07) - (0)}{\sqrt{0.055(1 - 0.055)\left(\dfrac{1}{200} + \dfrac{1}{200}\right)}}$$

$$= \frac{-0.03}{\sqrt{(0.051975)(0.01)}}$$

$$= \frac{-0.03}{\sqrt{0.0005197}}$$

$$= \frac{-0.03}{0.0228} = -1.32$$

7.3   TESTING FOR THE DIFFERENCE BETWEEN THE MEANS OF TWO INDEPENDENT GROUPS

Many studies are designed to compare two independent populations where the response of interest is a measurement on a continuous variable. Two different tests of hypotheses for the difference between the means are usually used: a pooled-variance t test in which the variances in the two populations are assumed to be equal and a separate-variance t test in which the variances in the two populations are not assumed to be equal.

Pooled-Variance t Test for the Difference in Two Means

The pooled-variance t test requires that the two sample variances be combined, or pooled, into one estimate of the variance common in the two groups, assuming that the population variances in the two populations are equal. The test statistic is based on the difference in the sample means of the two groups. The sampling distribution for the difference in the two sample means approximately follows the t distribution (see the assumptions on page 128).

The null hypothesis of no difference in the means of two independent populations is:

$H_0: \mu_1 = \mu_2$ (The two population means are equal.)

and the alternative hypothesis is:

$H_1: \mu_1 \neq \mu_2$ (The two population means are not equal.)

To illustrate this hypothesis test for the difference between two means, recall from Section 7.2 that hotel management was concerned with increasing the return rate for hotel guests. One aspect of first impressions by guests relates to the time it takes to deliver the guest's luggage to the room after check-in to the hotel. A random sample of 20 deliveries on a particular day were selected in Wing *A* of the hotel and a random sample of 20 deliveries were selected in Wing *B*. Management wanted to determine whether there was a difference in the mean delivery time in the two wings of the hotel. A level of significance of $\alpha = 0.05$ has been selected for making the decision. The results are displayed in Table 7.3.

TABLE 7.3   Luggage Delivery Time for 20 Deliveries to Wing *A* and 20 Deliveries to Wing *B* of the Hotel

Wing *A*	Wing *B*
10.70	7.20
9.89	6.68
11.83	9.29
9.04	8.95
9.37	6.61
11.68	8.53
8.36	8.92
9.76	7.95
13.67	7.57
8.96	6.38
9.51	8.89
10.85	10.03
10.57	9.30
11.06	5.28
8.91	9.23
11.79	9.25
10.59	8.44
9.13	6.57
12.37	10.61
9.91	6.77

LUGGAGE

Figure 7.4 illustrates Minitab output for the difference in the mean luggage delivery time between Wing *A* and Wing *B* of the hotel. Figure 7.5 illustrates JMP output.

FIGURE 7.4
Minitab Pooled-
Variance *t* Test Output
for the Difference in
the Mean Luggage
Delivery Time
Between Wing *A* and
Wing *B* of the Hotel

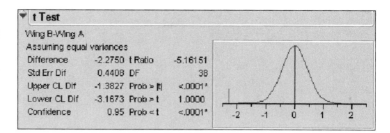

```
Two-sample T for Wing A vs Wing B

           N    Mean   StDev   SE Mean
Wing A    20   10.40    1.37     0.31
Wing B    20    8.12    1.42     0.32

Difference = mu (Wing A) - mu (Wing B)
Estimate for difference:  2.27500
95% CI for difference:  (1.38272, 3.16728)
T-Test of difference = 0 (vs not =): T-Value = 5.16  P-Value = 0.000  DF = 38
Both use Pooled StDev = 1.3938
```

FIGURE 7.5   JMP
Pooled-Variance *t* Test
Output for the Differ-
ence in the Mean Lug-
gage Delivery Time
Between Wing *A* and
Wing *B* of the Hotel

▼ **t Test**

Wing B-Wing A
Assuming equal variances

Difference	-2.2750	t Ratio	-5.16151
Std Err Dif	0.4408	DF	38
Upper CL Dif	-1.3827	Prob > |t|	<.0001*
Lower CL Dif	-3.1673	Prob > t	1.0000
Confidence	0.95	Prob < t	<.0001*

From Figure 7.4, the *t* statistic is +5.16 (Figure 7.5 shows a *t* statistic of -5.16 because it is computing the difference between Wing *B* and Wing *A*), and the *p*-value is 0.000. Because the *p*-value is 0.000, which is less than $\alpha = 0.05$, you reject the null hypothesis. This means that the chance of a *t* value greater than +5.16 or less than −5.16 is 0.000. You can conclude that the mean delivery time is higher for Wing *A* (sample mean of 10.40 minutes) than for Wing *B* (sample mean of 8.12 minutes). Management needs to study the reasons for the difference in order to reduce the luggage delivery time in Wing *A*.

CAUTION: CHECKING THE ASSUMPTIONS OF THE POOLED-VARIANCE *t* TEST

In testing for the difference between the means, you assume that the populations are normally distributed with equal variances. For situations in which the two populations have equal variances, the pooled-variance *t* test is robust (not sensitive) to moderate departures from the assumption of normality, provided that the sample sizes are large. In these situations, you can use the pooled-variance *t* test without serious effect on its power.

However, if you cannot assume that the data in each group are from normally distributed populations, you have two choices. You can use a *nonparametric* procedure, such as the *Wilcoxon rank sum test* (see Section 7.6 and Reference 1), that does not depend on the assumption of normality for the two populations. Alternatively, you can use a transformation [see References 2 and 4] on each of the values and then use the pooled-variance *t* test.

To check the assumption of normality in each of the two groups, Figure 7.6 displays a Minitab box-and-whisker plot and Figure 7.7 illustrates a JMP box-and-whisker plot.

From Figure 7.6 or 7.7, you can see that there is only moderate departure from normality, so the assumption of normality needed for the *t* test does not appear to be seriously violated.

FIGURE 7.6
Minitab Box-and-Whisker Plot of Luggage Delivery Times for Wing *A* and Wing *B*

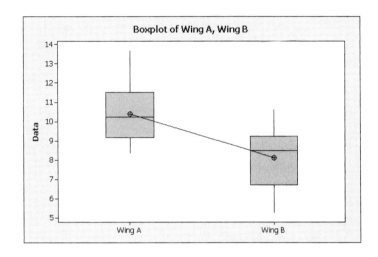

FIGURE 7.7 JMP Box-and-Whisker Plot of Luggage Delivery Times for Wing *A* and Wing *B*

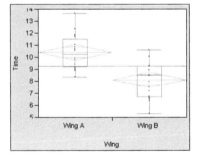

EQUATION FOR THE POOLED-VARIANCE *t* TEST FOR THE DIFFERENCE BETWEEN TWO MEANS {OPTIONAL}

$$t = \frac{(\bar{X}_1 - \bar{X}_2) - (\mu_1 - \mu_2)}{\sqrt{S_p^2 \left(\dfrac{1}{n_1} + \dfrac{1}{n_2} \right)}} \qquad (7.2)$$

Continues

where

$$S_p^2 = \frac{(n_1 - 1)S_1^2 + (n_2 - 1)S_2^2}{(n_1 - 1) + (n_2 - 1)}$$

and

S_p^2 = pooled variance

$\bar{X}_1$ = mean of the sample taken from population 1

S_1^2 = variance of the sample taken from population 1

n_1 = size of the sample taken from population 1

$\bar{X}_2$ = mean of the sample taken from population 2

S_2^2 = variance of the sample taken from population 2

n_2 = size of the sample taken from population 2

The test statistic t follows a t distribution with $n_1 + n_2 - 2$ degrees of freedom [see Reference 1]. There are $n_1 + n_2 - 2$ degrees of freedom because there are $n_1 - 1$ degrees of freedom in group 1 (the sample size minus 1) and $n_2 - 1$ degrees of freedom in group 2 (the sample size minus 1), for a total of $n_1 + n_2 - 2$ degrees of freedom.

For the example concerning the delivery time of luggage, using Equation (7.2):

$$t = \frac{(\bar{X}_1 - \bar{X}_2) - (\mu_1 - \mu_2)}{\sqrt{S_p^2 \left(\frac{1}{n_1} + \frac{1}{n_2} \right)}}$$

where

$$S_p^2 = \frac{(n_1 - 1)S_1^2 + (n_2 - 1)S_2^2}{(n_1 - 1) + (n_2 - 1)}$$

$$= \frac{19(1.37)^2 + 19(1.42)^2}{19 + 19} = 1.94665$$

Therefore:

$$t = \frac{10.398 - 8.123}{\sqrt{1.94665 \left(\frac{1}{20} + \frac{1}{20} \right)}} = \frac{2.275}{\sqrt{0.194665}} = +5.16$$

Using the $\alpha = 0.05$ level of significance, with $20 + 20 - 2 = 38$ degrees of freedom, the critical value of t (see Table C.2) is 2.0244 (0.025 in the upper tail of the t distribution). Because $t = +5.16 > 2.0244$, you reject H_0.

Separate-Variance *t* Test for Differences in Two Means

In the pooled-variance test for the difference between the means of two independent populations, the sample variances were pooled together into a common estimate because you assumed that the population variances were equal. However, if you cannot make this assumption, the pooled-variance *t* test is inappropriate. As a result, you can use the separate-variance *t* test [see References 1, 2, and 4]. Although the computations for the separate-variance *t* test are complicated, you can use Minitab or JMP to perform them. Figure 7.8 presents Minitab output of this separate-variance *t* test for the luggage delivery times. Figure 7.9 illustrates JMP output.

FIGURE 7.8
Minitab Output of the Separate-Variance *t* Test for the Luggage Delivery Data

```
Two-sample T for Wing A vs Wing B

          N   Mean  StDev  SE Mean
Wing A   20  10.40   1.37     0.31
Wing B   20   8.12   1.42     0.32


Difference = mu (Wing A) - mu (Wing B)
Estimate for difference:  2.27500
95% CI for difference:  (1.38193, 3.16807)
T-Test of difference = 0 (vs not =): T-Value = 5.16  P-Value = 0.000  DF = 37
```

FIGURE 7.9
JMP Output of the Separate-Variance *t* Test for the Luggage Delivery Data

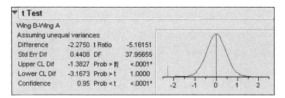

From Figure 7.8 or 7.9, the test statistic for $t = +5.16$ (there are 37 degrees of freedom), and the *p*-value is $0.000 < 0.05$. For these data, the results from the two different *t* tests led to the same decision and conclusions. The assumption of equality of population variances had no real effect on the results. Sometimes, however, the results from the pooled-variance and separate-variance *t* tests conflict because the assumption of equal variances is violated. This is why it is so important to evaluate the assumptions and use those results as a guide in the appropriate selection of a test procedure.

In the next section, the *F* test and the Levene test are used to determine whether there is evidence of a difference in the two population variances. The results of these tests can help you determine which of the *t* tests (pooled-variance or separate-variance) is more appropriate.

7.4   TESTING FOR THE DIFFERENCE BETWEEN TWO VARIANCES

Often, you need to test whether two independent populations have the same variance. One important reason to test for the difference in the variances of two populations is because you need to determine whether the pooled-variance *t* test is appropriate.

The *F* Test for the Ratio of Two Variances

The test statistic for the difference between the variances of two independent populations is based on the ratio of the two sample variances. The sampling distribution follows the *F* distribution (see the assumptions below).

The null hypothesis of equality of variances:

$$H_0: \quad \sigma_1^2 = \sigma_2^2$$

is tested against the alternative hypothesis that the two population variances are not equal:

$$H_1: \quad \sigma_1^2 \neq \sigma_2^2$$

To illustrate this test for the difference between two variances, return to the example previously discussed concerning luggage delivery times for the two wings of the hotel. The objective of the test of hypothesis is to determine whether the variance in luggage delivery time is the same for Wing A and Wing B of the hotel at the $\alpha = 0.05$ level of significance.

Figure 7.10 illustrates Minitab output for the difference in the variance of luggage delivery time between Wing A and Wing B of the hotel. Figure 7.11 illustrates JMP output.

In Figure 7.10, Minitab tests the variance in Wing A divided by the variance in Wing B, producing an F statistic of 0.93 and a p-value of 0.884. In Figure 7.11, JMP tests the larger variance (Wing B) divided by the smaller variance (Wing A), producing an F statistic of 1.07 and a p-value of 0.8842. Because the p-value is 0.884, which is greater than $\alpha = 0.05$, you do not reject the null hypothesis. You can conclude that there is insufficient evidence of a difference in the variance of the luggage delivery time between Wing A and Wing B of the hotel.

CAUTION: CHECKING THE ASSUMPTIONS OF THE F TEST FOR THE DIFFERENCES BETWEEN TWO VARIANCES

In testing for a difference in two variances using the *F* test, you assume that each of the two populations is normally distributed. This test is *very* sensitive to the normality assumption. If box-and-whisker plots or normal probability plots suggest even a mild departure from normality for either of the two populations, you should not use the *F* test. In such a case, you should use the Levene test.

FIGURE 7.10
Minitab Output of
Tests for Variances of
the Difference in Lug-
gage Delivery Time
Between Wing *A* and
Wing *B* of the Hotel

F-Test	
Test Statistic	0.93
P-Value	0.884
Levene's Test	
Test Statistic	0.06
P-Value	0.802

FIGURE 7.11
JMP Output of Tests
for Variances of the
Difference in Luggage
Delivery Time
Between Wing *A* and
Wing *B* of the Hotel

Level	Count	Std Dev	MeanAbsDif to Mean	MeanAbsDif to Median
Wing A	20	1.370032	1.113500	1.113500
Wing B	20	1.417195	1.209250	1.177500

Test	F Ratio	DFNum	DFDen	Prob > F
O'Brien[.5]	0.0291	1	38	0.8653
Brown-Forsythe	0.0637	1	38	0.8020
Levene	0.1761	1	38	0.6771
Bartlett	0.0212	1	.	0.8842
F Test 2-sided	1.0700	19	19	0.8842

EQUATION FOR THE *F* TEST FOR THE DIFFERENCE BETWEEN TWO VARIANCES {OPTIONAL}

$$F = \frac{S_1^2}{S_2^2} \quad (7.3)$$

where

n_1 = size of sample taken from population 1
n_2 = size of sample taken from population 2
n_1-1 = degrees of freedom from sample 1 (i.e., the numerator degrees of freedom)
n_2-1 = degrees of freedom from sample 2 (i.e., the denominator degrees of freedom)
S_1^2 = variance of sample 1
S_2^2 = variance of sample 2

The test statistic *F* follows an *F* distribution with $n_1 - 1$ and $n_2 - 1$ degrees of freedom. For the example concerning the luggage delivery times, using Equation (7.3):

$$F = \frac{S_1^2}{S_2^2}$$

$$= \frac{(1.37)^2}{(1.42)^2} = 0.93$$

The Levene Test for the Difference Between Variances

Although the *F* test for the ratio of two variances is a simple test, it is very sensitive to the assumption that each of the two populations follows the normal distribution. The Levene test for differences between variances is robust (not very sensitive) to lack of normality. The Levene test is based on the idea that if the variation in the two groups does not differ, a *t* test of the absolute differences from each group median can be used to test the null hypothesis of equal variances. Thus, the absolute value of the difference between each value and the median of the group is computed, and a one-way analysis of variance (see Section 7.5) is carried out on these *absolute differences*. Figure 7.10 provides Minitab output of the test statistic for the Levene test. The test statistic is 0.06, and the *p*-value is 0.802. Figure 7.11 provides JMP output of several tests of variances. The test labeled Levene by JMP is actually a test of the absolute differences between each value and the mean. The test labeled as Brown-Forsythe by JMP is the same as the test labeled Levene by Minitab. Because the *p*-value is 0.802, which is greater than $\alpha = 0.05$, you do not reject the null hypothesis. You can conclude that there is insufficient evidence of a difference in the variance of the luggage delivery time between the Wing *A* and Wing *B* of the hotel. For these data, the results of the *F* test for differences between variances and the Levene test are similar. However, remember that if there is any departure from normality in the data, the *F* test is inappropriate, and you should use the more robust Levene test.

7.5   ONE-WAY ANOVA: TESTING FOR DIFFERENCES AMONG THE MEANS OF THREE OR MORE GROUPS

Sometimes, a hypothesis test involves testing for differences in the mean level of a CTQ or *Y* for a CTP *(X)* with three or more levels. A factor *(X)*, such as baking temperature, may have several *numerical levels* (e.g., 300 degrees, 350 degrees, 400 degrees, 450 degrees) or a factor such as preferred level may have several *categorical levels* (low, medium, high). This type of hypothesis test is called a **completely randomized design**.

F Test for Differences in Three or More Means

When the numerical measurements (values of the CTQ) across the groups (levels of the CTP [*X*]) are continuous and certain assumptions are met (see pages 140-141), you use the **analysis of variance (ANOVA)** to compare the population means of the CTQ for each level of *X*. The ANOVA procedure used for completely randomized designs is referred to as a **one-way ANOVA** and is an extension of the *t* test for the difference between the means discussed in Section 7.3. Although ANOVA is an acronym for **an**alysis **of va**riance, the term is misleading because the objective is to analyze differences among the population means, not the variances. However, unlike the *t* test, which compares differences in two means, the one-way ANOVA simultaneously compares the differences among three or more population means. This is accomplished through an analysis of the variation among the populations and also within the populations. In ANOVA, the total variation of the measurements in all the populations is subdivided into variation that is due to differences *among* the populations and variation that is due to variation *within* the populations (see Figure 7.12). **Within-group variation** is considered random or experimental error. **Among-group variation** is attributable to **treatment effects**, which represent the effect of the CTP (levels of *X*), called a *factor*, used in the experiment on the CTQ or *Y*.

FIGURE 7.12

Partitioning the Total Variation in a One-Way ANOVA

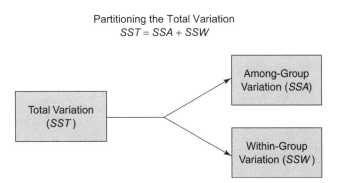

Partitioning the Total Variation
$SST = SSA + SSW$

The total variation of all the measurements is also called the **sum of squares total (SST)** because it represents the sum of the squared differences between each individual value and the **overall or grand mean**. The among-group variation, also called the **sum of squares among groups (SSA)**, represents the sum of the squared differences between the sample mean of each group and the overall or grand mean, weighted by the sample size in each group. The within-group variation, called the **sum of squares within groups (SSW)**, measures the difference between each value and the mean of its own group and cumulates the squares of these differences over all groups.

The ANOVA procedure derives its name from the fact that you compare the means of the groups by analyzing variances. In Section 4.2 on page 47, you computed the variance by dividing the sum of squared differences around the mean by the sample size minus 1. The sample size minus 1 represents the actual number of values that are free to vary once the mean is known and is called **degrees of freedom**. In the Analysis of Variance, there are three different variances: the variance among groups, the variance within groups, and the total variance. These variances are referred to in the ANOVA terminology as **mean squares**. The mean square among groups (*MSA*) is equal to the *SSA* divided by the number of groups minus 1. The mean square within groups (*MSW*) is equal to the *SSW* divided by the sample size minus the number of groups. The mean square total (*MST*) is equal to the *SST* divided by the sample size minus one.

To test the null hypothesis:

H_0: All the population means are equal; for example, H_0: $\mu_1 = \mu_2 = \mu_3$

against the alternative

H_1: Not all the population means are equal; for example, either H_1: $\mu_1 \neq \mu_2$ or $\mu_1 \neq \mu_3$ or $\mu_2 \neq \mu_3$ or $\mu_1 \neq \mu_2 \neq \mu_3$

the test statistic F is computed as the ratio of two of the variances, MSA to MSW.

The results of an analysis of variance are usually displayed in an ANOVA summary table, which is presented in Table 7.4. The entries in this table include the sources of variation (i.e., among-group, within-group, and total), the degrees of freedom, the sums of squares, the mean squares (i.e., the variances), and the calculated F statistic. In addition, Minitab and JMP include the p-value.

TABLE 7.4 Analysis of Variance Summary Table

Source	Degrees of Freedom	Sum of Squares	Mean Square (Variance)	F
Among groups	$c - 1$	SSA	$MSA = \dfrac{SSA}{c-1}$	$F = \dfrac{MSA}{MSW}$
Within groups	$\underline{n - c}$	$\underline{SSW}$	$MSW = \dfrac{SSW}{n-c}$	
Total	$n - 1$	SST		

where
  c = number of groups
  n = sample size

To illustrate the one-way ANOVA F test, consider a study undertaken by a hospital of the waiting time in its emergency room. The hospital has a main campus along with three satellite locations. Management had a business objective of reducing waiting time for emergency room cases that did not require immediate attention. To study this, a random sample of 15 emergency room cases at each location were selected on a particular day and the waiting time (measured from check-in to when the patient was called into the clinic area) was measured. The results are presented in Table 7.5.

TABLE 7.5 Emergency Room Waiting Time for Four Locations

Main	Satellite 1	Satellite 2	Satellite 3
120.08	30.75	75.86	54.05
81.90	61.83	37.88	38.82
78.79	26.40	68.73	36.85
63.83	53.84	51.08	32.83
79.77	72.30	50.21	52.94
47.94	53.09	58.47	34.13
79.88	27.67	86.29	69.37
48.63	52.46	62.90	78.52
55.43	10.64	44.84	55.95
64.06	53.50	64.17	49.61
64.99	37.28	50.68	66.40
53.82	34.31	47.97	76.06
62.43	66.00	60.57	11.37
65.07	8.99	58.37	83.51
81.02	29.75	30.40	39.17

ERWAITING

Figure 7.13 displays the Minitab ANOVA results for the four locations. Figure 7.14 illustrates JMP output.

FIGURE 7.13
Minitab ANOVA Results for the Four Locations

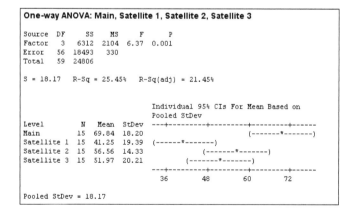
```
One-way ANOVA: Main, Satellite 1, Satellite 2, Satellite 3

Source  DF    SS    MS    F     P
Factor   3   6312  2104  6.37  0.001
Error   56  18493   330
Total   59  24806

S = 18.17   R-Sq = 25.45%   R-Sq(adj) = 21.45%


                                Individual 95% CIs For Mean Based on
                                Pooled StDev
Level         N   Mean  StDev  ---+---------+---------+---------+------
Main         15  69.84  18.20                       (-------*-------)
Satellite 1  15  41.25  19.39  (------*-------)
Satellite 2  15  56.56  14.33            (-------*-------)
Satellite 3  15  51.97  20.21         (-------*-------)
                                ---+---------+---------+---------+------
                                  36        48        60        72

Pooled StDev = 18.17
```

FIGURE 7.14   JMP ANOVA Results for the Four Locations

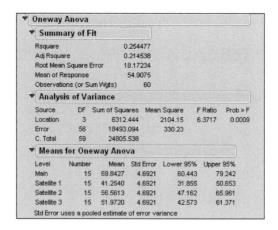

From Figure 7.13 or 7.14, the F statistic is 6.37, and the p-value is 0.001. Because the p-value is 0.001, which is less than $\alpha = 0.05$, you reject the null hypothesis. You can conclude that the mean waiting time in the emergency room is not the same for all the locations. From Figure 7.13 or 7.14, you see that the mean is 69.84 minutes for the main location; 41.25 minutes for satellite location 1; 56.56 minutes for satellite location 2; and 51.97 minutes for satellite location 3.

After performing the one-way ANOVA and finding a significant difference between the means of the locations, what you do not know is which means differ from each other. All that you know is that there is sufficient evidence that the population means are not all the same. In other words, at least one or some combination of means is statistically significantly different from some other means. To determine exactly which locations differ, all possible pairwise comparisons between the locations can be made using a procedure developed by John Tukey [see References 1–4].

Multiple Comparisons: The Tukey Procedure

In the hospital emergency room waiting time example, you used the one-way ANOVA F test to determine whether there was a difference between the locations. Once you find differences in the means of the groups, you should determine which group means are different.

Although many procedures are available [see References 2–4], the **Tukey multiple comparison procedure** is a simple procedure to determine which of the means are statistically different. This method is an example of a **post-hoc** comparison procedure, because the hypotheses of interest are formulated *after* the data have been inspected. The Tukey procedure enables you to simultaneously examine comparisons between all pairs of groups. Figure 7.15 represents Minitab output of the waiting time for all pairs of locations. Figure 7.16 presents JMP output.

USING THE CRITICAL VALUE APPROACH FOR ANOVA (OPTIONAL)

To use the critical value approach in ANOVA, you refer to the table of the F statistic (Table C.3 in Appendix C). Two sets of degrees of freedom are required to find the critical value of the F statistic: the numerator degrees of freedom, which are equal to the number of groups minus 1; and the denominator degrees of freedom, which are equal to the sample size minus the number of groups. For the emergency room waiting time example, because there are four groups of 15 patients and a total sample size of $(15)(4) = 60$ patients, the numerator degrees of freedom are equal to $4 - 1 = 3$, and the denominator degrees of freedom are equal to $60 - 4 = 56$. Selecting the $\alpha = 0.05$ level of significance, you see that in Table C.3, there is no entry for exactly 56 degrees of freedom, so you scan down to the intersection of the column with 3 degrees of freedom and the row with 60 degrees of freedom (the closest value to 56), and you find a critical value of F of 2.76.

Because the decision rule is to reject H_0 if $F >$ critical value of F, and $F = 6.37 > 2.76$, you reject H_0.

In Figure 7.15, the main location mean is compared with all satellite location means, then satellite 1 is compared with the remaining location means (satellites 2 and 3), and then the satellite 2 mean is compared with the remaining location mean (satellite 3). For each pairwise comparison, Minitab shows the lower and upper limits of the interval, the pairwise difference, and a plot of the interval. Any intervals that do *not* include zero are considered significant. The 95% simultaneous confidence tells you that there is 95% confidence that the *entire set of intervals* is correctly estimating the pairwise differences in the population means. Because the difference between the satellite 1 and main location has an interval of -46.14 to -11.04 minutes, and the difference between the satellite 3 and main location has an interval of -35.42 and -0.32 minutes, the mean waiting time at the main location is different from satellite 1 and satellite 3. These are the only locations that differ in mean waiting time. In Figure 7.16, you can observe that only the comparisons of the main location with satellite 1 and satellite 3 do *not* include 0 in their interval estimate of the mean waiting time.

FIGURE 7.15
Minitab Output of
Tukey Multiple Comparisons of the Emergency Room Waiting
Times for the Four
Locations

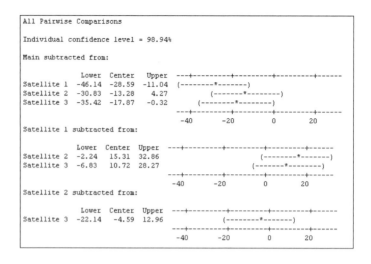

FIGURE 7.16
JMP Output of Tukey
Multiple Comparisons
of the Emergency
Room Waiting Times
for the Four Locations

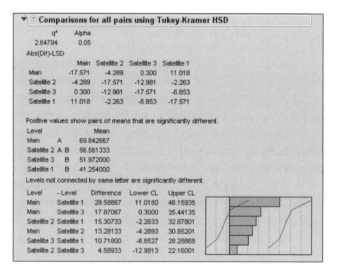

ANOVA Assumptions

To use the one-way ANOVA F test, you must make three assumptions about the underlying populations:

1. Randomness and independence.
2. Normality.
3. All populations have the same variance.

The first assumption, **randomness and independence**, always must be met because the validity of any experiment depends on random sampling and/or the randomization process. To avoid biases in the outcomes, you need to either select random samples from the populations or randomly assign the items or individuals to the levels of the factor of interest (i.e., the *CTP* categories, called *treatment groups or levels of X*). Departures from this assumption can seriously affect inferences from the ANOVA. These problems are discussed more thoroughly in Reference 5.

The second assumption, **normality**, states that the values in each group are from normally distributed populations. Just as in the case of the *t* test, the one-way ANOVA *F* test is fairly robust against departures from the normal distribution. As long as the distributions are not extremely different from a normal distribution, the level of significance of the ANOVA *F* test is usually not greatly affected by lack of normality, particularly for large samples. When only the normality assumption is seriously violated, *nonparametric* alternatives to the one-way ANOVA *F* test are available (see Section 7.7 and References 1−4).

The third assumption, **equal variance**, states that the variance within each population should be equal for all populations. This assumption is needed to combine or pool the variances within the groups into a single within-group source of variation *SSW*. If there are equal sample sizes in each group, inferences based on the *F* distribution may not be seriously affected by unequal variances. However, if there are unequal sample sizes in different groups, the unequal variances from group to group can have serious effects on any inferences developed from the ANOVA procedures. Thus, when possible, you should have equal sample sizes in all groups.

One way to evaluate the assumptions is to plot a side-by-side box-and-whisker plot of the groups to study their central tendency, variation, and shape. Figure 7.17 presents the Minitab box-and-whisker plot of the waiting time for the four locations. Figure 7.18 shows JMP output.

From Figures 7.17 or 7.18, there appears to be very little difference in the variation and very little skewness in the waiting time for the four locations.

FIGURE 7.17

Minitab Box-and-Whisker Plot of the Emergency Room Waiting Times for the Four Locations

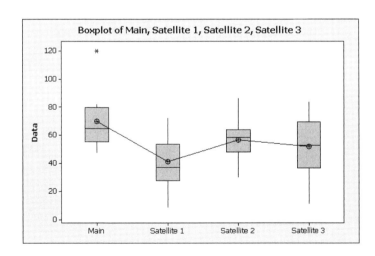

FIGURE 7.18
JMP Box-and-Whisker
Plot of the Emergency
Room Waiting Times
for the Four Locations

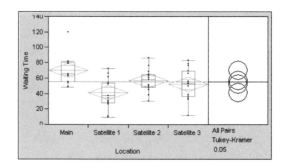

Levene's Test for Homogeneity of Variance

Although the one-way ANOVA F test is relatively robust with respect to the assumption of equal group variances, large departures from this assumption may seriously affect the level of significance and the power of the test. Therefore, various statistical procedures have been developed to test the assumption of homogeneity of variance. Perhaps the most powerful is the modified Levene test [see References 1—4]. You test for the equality of the population variances:

H_0: All the population variances are equal; for example, H_0: $\sigma_1 = \sigma_2 = \sigma_3$

against the alternative.

H_1: Not all the population variances are equal; for example,
$\sigma_1 \neq \sigma_2$ or $\sigma_1 \neq \sigma_3$ or $\sigma_2 \neq \sigma_3$ or $\sigma_1 \neq \sigma_2 \neq \sigma_3$

The Levene test is based on the idea that if the variation within the groups does not differ, you can use an ANOVA of the absolute differences from each group median to test the null hypothesis of equal variances. Thus, you compute the absolute value of the difference between each value and the median of the group, and carry out a one-way ANOVA on these *absolute differences.* Figure 7.19 presents Minitab output of the modified Levene test for the waiting time for the four locations. Figure 7.20 shows JMP output.

In Figure 7.19, the value of the F test statistic for the Levene test is 0.82, and the p-value is 0.488. In Figure 7.20, the test labeled Levene by JMP is actually a test of the absolute differences between each value and the mean. The test labeled as Brown-Forsythe by JMP is the same as the test labeled Levene by Minitab except for a correction that JMP makes when there are an odd number of values [see Reference 2]. Because the p-value of 0.488 shown in Minitab (or 0.4556 shown in JMP) is greater than $\alpha = 0.05$, you do not reject the null hypothesis. Thus, there is insufficient evidence to conclude that any of the variances in waiting time are different.

FIGURE 7.19
Minitab Output of the
Levene Test for the
Emergency Room
Waiting Time of the
Four Locations

Bartlett's Test	
Test Statistic	1.77
P-Value	0.622
Levene's Test	
Test Statistic	0.82
P-Value	0.488

FIGURE 7.20
JMP Output of the
Levene Test for the
Emergency Room
Waiting Time of the
Four Locations

Level	Count	Std Dev	MeanAbsDif to Mean	MeanAbsDif to Median
Main	15	18.20219	13.65120	12.69667
Satellite 1	15	19.39010	16.56560	16.49867
Satellite 2	15	14.33015	11.04924	10.93533
Satellite 3	15	20.20609	16.13653	16.14600

Test	F Ratio	DFNum	DFDen	Prob > F
O'Brien[.5]	0.4803	3	56	0.6973
Brown-Forsythe	0.8830	3	56	0.4556
Levene	0.9335	3	56	0.4307
Bartlett	0.5887	3	.	0.6224

7.6 WILCOXON RANK SUM TEST FOR THE DIFFERENCE BETWEEN TWO MEDIANS

In Section 7.3, you used the t test for the difference between the means of samples taken from two independent populations. If sample sizes are small and you cannot or do not want to assume that the data in each group are selected from normally distributed populations, you can use a nonparametric test (a test with relatively mild assumptions) called the **Wilcoxon rank sum test** for finding the difference between two medians. The Wilcoxon rank sum test is almost as powerful as the pooled-variance and separate-variance t tests under conditions appropriate to these tests and is likely to be more powerful when the assumptions of those t tests are not met. In addition, you can use the Wilcoxon rank sum test when you have only ordinal (ranked) data.

To perform the Wilcoxon rank sum test, you replace the values in the two samples with their combined ranks (unless the data contained the ranks initially). You assign the ranks so that rank 1 is given to the smallest of the values from the two groups, rank 2 is given to the second-smallest, and so on, until rank n is given to the largest. If several values are tied, you assign each the average of the ranks that would otherwise have been assigned had there been no ties.

The Wilcoxon rank sum test can be either a two-tail test or a one-tail test, depending on whether you are testing whether the two population medians are *different* or whether one median is *greater than* the other median.

Two-Tail Test	**One-Tail Test**	**One-Tail Test**
$H_0: M_1 = M_2$	$H_0: M_1 \geq M_2$	$H_0: M_1 \leq M_2$
$H_1: M_1 \neq M_2$	$H_1: M_1 < M_2$	$H_1: M_1 > M_2$

where

M_1 = median of population 1
M_2 = median of population 2

To illustrate the Wilcoxon rank sum test, recall that in Section 7.3, you used the t test to determine whether the mean luggage delivery time was different in Wing A and Wing B of the hotel. Now, you can determine whether the median luggage delivery time was different in Wing A and Wing B of the hotel.

Table 7.6 summarizes the delivery times and the combined ranks for the two wings of the hotel.

TABLE 7.6 Waiting Times and Ranks for Wings A and B

	Wing A		Wing B	
	Time	Rank	Time	Rank
	10.70	33	7.20	7
	9.89	27	6.68	5
	11.83	38	9.29	22
	9.04	18	8.95	16
	9.37	24	6.61	4
	11.68	36	8.53	12
	8.36	10	8.92	15
	9.76	26	7.95	9
	13.67	40	7.57	8
	8.96	17	6.38	2
	9.51	25	8.89	13
	10.85	34	10.03	29
	10.57	30	9.30	23
	11.06	35	5.28	1
	8.91	14	9.23	20
	11.79	37	9.25	21
	10.59	31	8.44	11
	9.13	19	6.57	3
	12.37	39	10.61	32
	9.91	28	6.77	6
Sum of Ranks		561		259

Figure 7.21 provides Minitab output. Figure 7.22 illustrates JMP output.

FIGURE 7.21
Minitab Wilcoxon
Rank Sum Test Output
for the Difference in
the Median Luggage
Delivery Time
Between Wing *A* and
Wing *B* of the Hotel

```
Mann-Whitney Test and CI: Wing A, Wing B

           N   Median
Wing A    20   10.240
Wing B    20    8.485


Point estimate for ETA1-ETA2 is 2.265
95.0 Percent CI for ETA1-ETA2 is (1.290,3.120)
W = 561.0
Test of ETA1 = ETA2 vs ETA1 not = ETA2 is significant at 0.0000
```

FIGURE 7.22   JMP
Wilcoxon Rank Sum
Test Output for the
Difference in the
Median Luggage
Delivery Time
Between Wing *A* and
Wing *B* of the Hotel

Wilcoxon / Kruskal-Wallis Tests (Rank Sums)				
Level	Count	Score Sum	Score Mean	(Mean-Mean0)/Std0
Wing A	20	561	28.0500	4.071
Wing B	20	259	12.9500	-4.071

2-Sample Test, Normal Approximation		
S	Z	Prob>|Z|
259	-4.07104	<.0001

In Figure 7.21, Minitab provides output for the *Mann-Whitney test*, which is numerically equivalent to the Wilcoxon rank sum test [see Reference 4]. From Figure 7.21, ETA1 and ETA2 refer to the hypothesized population medians M_1 and M_2. Also, the test statistic $W = 561$ is the sum of the ranks for Wing *A*. The *p*-value for this two-tail hypothesis test is 0.0000. Because the *p*-value = 0.0000 is less than $\alpha = 0.05$, you reject H_o and conclude that there is evidence of a significant difference in the median delivery time between Wing *A* and Wing *B*.

In Figure 7.22, JMP provides the sum of the ranks for each group and the normal approximation to the Wilcoxon rank sum statistic. Because the *p*-value (less than 0.0001) is less than $\alpha = 0.05$ (or $Z = -4.071 < -1.96$), you reject H_o and conclude that there is evidence of a significant difference in the median delivery time between Wing *A* and Wing *B*.

7.7   KRUSKAL-WALLIS RANK TEST: NONPARAMETRIC ANALYSIS FOR THE ONE-WAY ANOVA

If the assumptions of the one-way ANOVA *F* test are not met, you can use a nonparametric test called the Kruskal-Wallis rank test. The **Kruskal-Wallis rank test** for differences in medians is an extension of the Wilcoxon rank sum test for two independent samples, which is discussed in Section 7.6. The Kruskal-Wallis rank test has the same power relative to the one-way ANOVA *F* test that the Wilcoxon rank sum test has relative to the pooled-variance *t* test for two independent samples.

You use the Kruskal-Wallis rank test to test whether independent sample groups have equal medians. To use the Kruskal-Wallis rank test, you need to assume only that the measurements are ranks over all sample groups and the populations from which the samples are selected have the same variability and shape.

To use the Kruskal-Wallis rank test, you first replace the values in the samples with their combined ranks (if necessary). Rank 1 is given to the smallest of the combined values and rank n to the largest of the combined values. If any values are tied, you assign them the mean of the ranks they would have otherwise been assigned if ties had not been present in the data.

To illustrate the Kruskal-Wallis rank test, recall that in Section 7.5, you used the one-way ANOVA to determine whether the mean emergency room waiting time was different in four locations. Now you can determine whether the median emergency room waiting time was different in four locations. Table 7.7 summarizes the waiting times and the combined ranks for the four locations.

TABLE 7.7   Waiting Times and Ranks for Four Locations

	Main	Rank	Satellite 1	Rank	Satellite 2	Rank	Satellite 3	Rank
	120.08	60	30.75	8	75.86	50	54.05	31
	81.90	57	61.83	37	37.88	14	38.82	15
	78.79	53	26.40	4	68.73	47	36.85	12
	63.83	40	53.84	30	51.08	24	32.83	9
	79.77	54	72.30	49	50.21	22	52.94	26
	47.94	18	53.09	27	58.47	35	34.13	10
	79.88	55	27.67	5	86.29	59	69.37	48
	48.63	20	52.46	25	62.90	39	78.52	52
	55.43	32	10.64	2	44.84	17	55.95	33
	64.06	41	53.50	28	64.17	42	49.61	21
	64.99	43	37.28	13	50.68	23	66.40	46
	53.82	29	34.31	11	47.97	19	76.06	51
	62.43	38	66.00	45	60.57	36	11.37	3
	65.07	44	8.99	1	58.37	34	83.51	58
	81.02	56	29.75	6	30.40	7	39.17	16
Sum of Ranks		640		291		468		431

Locations

Figure 7.23 provides Minitab output. Figure 7.24 illustrates JMP output.

FIGURE 7.23
Minitab Kruskal-Wallis
Rank Test Output for
the Difference in the
Median Waiting Time
for Four Locations

```
Kruskal-Wallis Test: Waiting Time versus Location

Kruskal-Wallis Test on Waiting Time

Location    N   Median   Ave Rank      Z
1          15    64.99      42.7    3.12
2          15    37.28      19.4   -2.84
3          15    58.37      31.2    0.18
4          15    52.94      28.7   -0.45
Overall    60               30.5

H = 13.52   DF = 3   P = 0.004
```

FIGURE 7.24
JMP Kruskal-Wallis
Rank Test Output for
the Difference in the
Median Waiting Time
for Four Locations

```
▼ Wilcoxon / Kruskal-Wallis Tests (Rank Sums)
Level        Count   Score Sum   Score Mean   (Mean-Mean0)/Std0
Main           15        640      42.6667        3.107
Satellite 1    15        291      19.4000       -2.834
Satellite 2    15        468      31.2000        0.171
Satellite 3    15        431      28.7333       -0.444
▼ 1-way Test, ChiSquare Approximation
ChiSquare      DF   Prob>ChiSq
13.5172         3     0.0036
```

In Figure 7.23, Minitab provides the median waiting time at each location, the H test statistic ($H = 13.52$), and the p-value (= 0.004). In Figure 7.24, JMP provides the mean rank for each location, the test statistic (labeled as ChiSquare = 13.5172), and the p-value (= 0.0036). From Figure 7.23 or 7.24, you see that the p-value is approximately 0.004. Because the p-value is less than $\alpha = 0.05$, you reject H_o and conclude that there is evidence of a significant difference in the median emergency room waiting time between the four locations.

SUMMARY

This chapter introduced the fundamental concepts of hypothesis testing. You learned how to test for the difference in the proportions, means, and variances of two groups. In addition, the ANOVA testing method was developed to determine whether differences exist in the means of more than two groups. This ANOVA method will be extended in Chapter 8, "Design of Experiments," to the more general situation in which several factors are being studied. In addition, you studied two nonparametric tests that you can use when the assumptions of the tests for the difference between the means of two independent populations and the one-way ANOVA have been violated.

The roadmap in Figure 7.25 illustrates the steps needed to determine which test of hypothesis to use when dealing with two or more groups:

1. If you have two groups, what type of data do you have? If you have categorical variables, use the Z test for the difference between two proportions.

2. If you are analyzing a numerical variable for two groups, and if you are analyzing central tendency, determine whether you can assume that the two groups are normally distributed. If you cannot assume the groups are normally distributed, use the Wilcoxon rank sum test.

3. If you can assume that the two groups are normally distributed, can you assume that the variances in the two groups are equal? If you can assume that the variances in the two groups are equal, use the pooled-variance t test. If you cannot assume that the variances in the two groups are equal, use the separate-variance t test.

4. If you are analyzing a numerical variable for two groups, and if you are analyzing variation, use the F test only if you can assume the groups are normally distributed. Otherwise, use the Levene test.

5. If you have more than two groups and you are analyzing a numerical variable, use the analysis of variance (ANOVA), along with multiple comparisons and the Levene test. If you cannot assume that the groups are normally distributed, use the Kruskal-Wallis rank test.

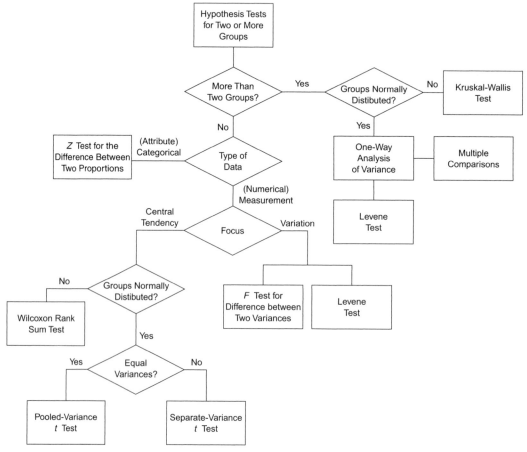

FIGURE 7.25   Roadmap for Hypothesis Testing

REFERENCES

1. Berenson, M. L., D. M. Levine, and T. C. Krehbiel. *Basic Business Statistics: Concepts and Applications*, 10th Ed. (Upper Saddle River, NJ: Prentice Hall, 2006).

2. *JMP Version 6* (Cary, NC: SAS Institute, 2005).

3. Kutner, M. H., C. Nachtsheim, J. Neter, and W. Li. *Applied Linear Statistical Models*, 5th Ed. (New York: McGraw-Hill-Irwin, 2005).

4. *Minitab for Windows Version 14* (State College, PA: Minitab, 2004).

5. Montgomery, D. C. *Design and Analysis of Experiments*, 6th Ed. (New York: John Wiley, 2005).

Appendix 7.1
Using Minitab for Hypothesis Testing

Testing for the Difference Between Two Proportions

To test the hypothesis for the difference in the proportion of rooms not ready between Wing *A* and Wing *B* illustrated in Figure 7.2 on page 123, select **Stat → Basic Statistics → 2 Proportions**.

1. In the 2 Proportions (Test and Confidence Interval) dialog box (see Figure A7.1), select the **Summarized data** option button. In the First: row, enter **200** in the Trials: edit box and **8** in the Events: edit box. In the Second: row, enter **200** in the Trials: edit box and **14** in the Events: edit box.

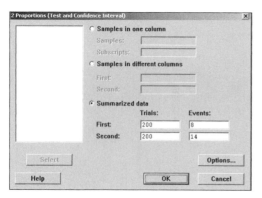

FIGURE A7.1
Minitab 2 Proportions (Test and Confidence Interval) Dialog Box

2. Click the **Options** button. In the 2 Proportions—Options dialog box (see Figure A7.2), enter **95** in the Confidence level: edit box. Enter **0.0** in the Test difference: edit box. Select **not equal** in the Alternative: drop-down list box. Select the **Use pooled estimate of p** for test check box (uncheck this if this selection is not desired). Click the **OK** button to return to the 2 Proportions (Test and Confidence Interval) dialog box. Click the **OK** button.

FIGURE A7.2
2 Minitab Proportions—Options Dialog Box

Testing for the Difference Between the Means of Two Independent Samples

To test for the difference in the mean delivery time between Wing *A* and Wing *B* illustrated in Figure 7.4 on page 128, open the

LUGGAGE.MTW worksheet. Select **Stat → Basic Statistics → 2-Sample t**.

1. In the 2-Sample t (Test and Confidence Interval) dialog box (see Figure A7.3), select the **Samples in different columns** option button. (If the samples are in one column, select the **Samples in one column** option button and enter the column number for the samples and the groups.) In the First: edit box, enter **C1** or **'Wing A'**. In the Second: edit box, enter **C2** or **'Wing B'**. (If you have summarized data instead of the actual data, select the **Summarized data** option button and enter values for the sample size, mean, and standard deviation.) For the pooled-variance *t* test, select the **Assume equal variances** check box. For the separate variance *t* test, leave this box unchecked.

2. Click the **Graphs** button. In the 2-Sample t–Graphs dialog box (see Figure A7.4), select the **Boxplots of data** check box. Click the **OK** button to return to the 2-Sample t (Test and Confidence Interval) dialog box.

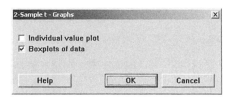

FIGURE A7.4   Minitab 2-Sample t— Graphs Dialog Box

3. Click the **Options** button. In the 2-Sample t–Options dialog box (see Figure A7.5), enter **95** in the Confidence level: edit box. Enter **0.0** in the Test difference: edit box. Select **not equal** in the Alternative: drop-down list box. Click the **OK** button to return to the 2-Sample t (Test and Confidence Interval) dialog box. Click the **OK** button.

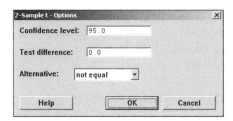

FIGURE A7.5   Minitab 2-Sample t— Options Dialog Box

FIGURE A7.3
Minitab 2-Sample t (Test and Confidence Interval) Dialog Box

Testing for the Difference Between Two Variances

To test for the difference in the variances of the waiting times in Wing *A* and Wing *B* illustrated in Figure 7.10 on page 133, open the **LUGGAGE.MTW** worksheet. Select **Stat → Basic Statistics → 2 Variances**.

1. In the 2 Variances dialog box (see Figure A7.6), select the **Samples in different columns** option button. (If the samples are in one column, select the **Samples in one column** option button and enter the column number for the samples and the groups.) In the First: edit box, enter **C1** or **'Wing A'**. In the Second: edit box, enter **C2** or **'Wing B'**. (If you have summarized data instead of the actual data, select the Summarized data option button and enter values for the sample size and variance.)
2. Click the **OK** button.

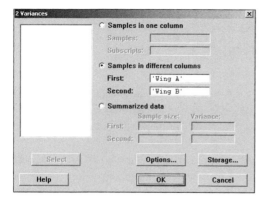

FIGURE A7.6
Minitab 2 Variances Dialog Box

Generating a One-Way ANOVA with Multiple Comparisons

To generate the one-way ANOVA for the waiting times for four locations illustrated in Figures 7.13, 7.15, and 7.17 on pages 137, 140, and 141, open the **ERWAITING.MTW** worksheet. The data in this worksheet have been stored in an unstacked format with each location in a separate column. Select **Stat → ANOVA → One-Way (Unstacked)**.

1. In the One-Way Analysis of Variance dialog box (see Figure A7.7), enter **C1** or **'Main'**, **C2** or **'Satellite 1'**, **C3** or **'Satellite 2'**, and **C4** or **'Satellite 3'** in the Responses (in separate columns): edit box. Enter **95** in the Confidence level: edit box.
2. Click the **Comparisons** button. In the One-Way Multiple Comparisons dialog box (see Figure A7.8), select the **Tukey's, family error rate:** check box. Enter **5** in the edit box for 95% simultaneous confidence intervals. Click the **OK** button to return to the One-Way Analysis of Variance dialog box.

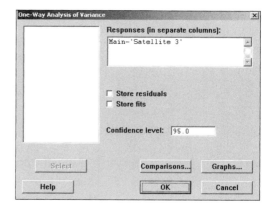

FIGURE A7.7
Minitab One-Way Analysis of Variance Dialog Box

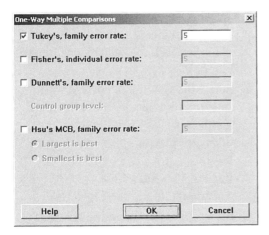

FIGURE A7.8
Minitab One-Way Multiple Comparisons Dialog Box

3. Click the **Graphs** button. In the One-Way Analysis of Variance—Graphs dialog box (see Figure A7.9), select the **Boxplots of data** check box. Click the **OK** button to return to the One-Way Analysis of Variance dialog box.

4. Click the **OK** button.

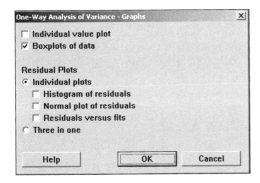

FIGURE A7.9
Minitab One-Way Analysis of Variance—Graphs Dialog Box

Testing for Equal Variances in the Analysis of Variance

To generate the Levene test for the difference in the variance of the waiting times of the locations illustrated in Figure 7.19 on page 143, open the **ERWAITING.MTW** worksheet. To perform the Levene test in the ANOVA, you need to stack the data. Select **Data → Stack → Columns**. Then, in the Stack Columns dialog box:

1. Enter **C1** or **'Main'**, **C2** or **'Satellite 1'**, **C3** or **'Satellite 2'**, and **C4** or **'Satellite 3'** in the Stack the following columns: edit box.

2. Select the **Column of current worksheet:** option button. Enter **C5** in the edit box. Enter **C6** in the Store the Subscript in: edit box. Click the **OK** button.

3. Label C5 **Waiting Time** and C6 **Location**.

4. Select **Stat → ANOVA → Test for Equal Variances**. In the Test for Equal Variances dialog box (see Figure A7.10), enter **C5** or **'Waiting Time'** in the Response: edit box and **C6** or **Location** in the Factors: edit box. Enter **95.0** in the Confidence level: edit box. Click the **OK** button.

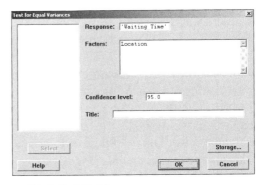

FIGURE A7.10
Minitab Test for Equal Variances Dialog Box

The Wilcoxon Rank Sum Test

To illustrate the use of Minitab for the Wilcoxon rank sum test, open the **LUGGAGE.MTW** worksheet. Select **Stat → Nonparametrics → Mann-Whitney**.

1. In the Mann-Whitney dialog box (see Figure A7.11) in the First Sample: edit box, enter **C1** or **'Wing A'**. In the Second Sample: edit box, enter C2 or **'Wing B'**. Click the **OK** button.

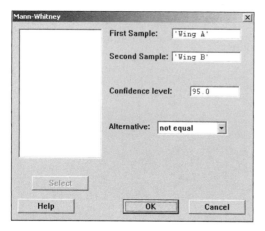

FIGURE A7.11
Minitab Mann-Whitney Dialog Box

The Kruskal-Wallis Rank Test

To illustrate the use of Minitab for the Kruskal-Wallis rank test, open the **ERWAITING.MTW** worksheet. The data have been stored in an unstacked format with each level in a separate column. To perform the Kruskal-Wallis rank test, you need to stack the data. To perform the Levene test in the ANOVA, you need to stack the data. Select **Data → Stack → Columns**. Then, in the Stack Columns dialog box:

1. Enter **C1** or **'Main'**, **C2** or **'Satellite 1'**, **C3** or **'Satellite 2'**, and **C4** or **'Satellite 3'** in the Stack the following columns: edit box.

2. Select the **Column of current worksheet:** option button. Enter **C5** in the edit box. Enter **C6** in the Store the Subscript in: edit box. Click the **OK** button.

3. Label C5 **Waiting Time** and C6 **Location**.

4. Select **Stat → Nonparametrics → Kruskal-Wallis**. In the Kruskal-Wallis dialog box (see Figure A7.12), enter **C5** or **'Waiting Time'** in the Response: edit box and **C6** or **Location** in the Factor: edit box. Click the **OK** button.

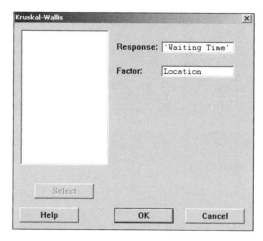

FIGURE A7.12
Minitab Kruskal-Wallis Dialog Box

Appendix 7.2
Using JMP for Hypothesis Testing

Stacking Data

In order to use JMP for hypothesis testing, you first need to make sure that the data are organized with the numerical variable of interest in one column and the categorical variable that defines the groups in a different column. If the data are organized with each group in a different column, you need to reorganize the data in a stacked format with the numerical variable of interest in one column and the categorical variable that defines the groups in a different column.

To illustrate how to stack data, open the **LUGGAGE.JMP** file. Select **Tables → Stack**. Then, in the Stack dialog box (see Figure A7.13):

1. Select **Wing A** and **Wing B** in the Select Columns edit box. Click the **Stack Columns** button to list Wing A and Wing B in the Stack Columns edit box.

2. Deselect all check boxes.
3. Enter **Time** as the label in the Stacked Data Column edit box. Enter **Wing** as the label in the Source Label Column.
4. Click the **OK** button. Save the stacked data set with the name **LUGGAGE2.JMP**.

Tests for the Difference Between Two Means, Tests for the Difference Between Two Variances, and the Wilcoxon Rank Sum Test

Open the **LUGGAGE2.JMP** data table. Select **Analyze → Fit Y by X**. Then, in the Report: Fit Y by X—Contextual dialog box (see Figure A7.14):

1. Enter **Time** in the Y, Response edit box and **Wing** in the X, Factor edit box. Click the **OK** button.

FIGURE A7.13
Stack Dialog Box

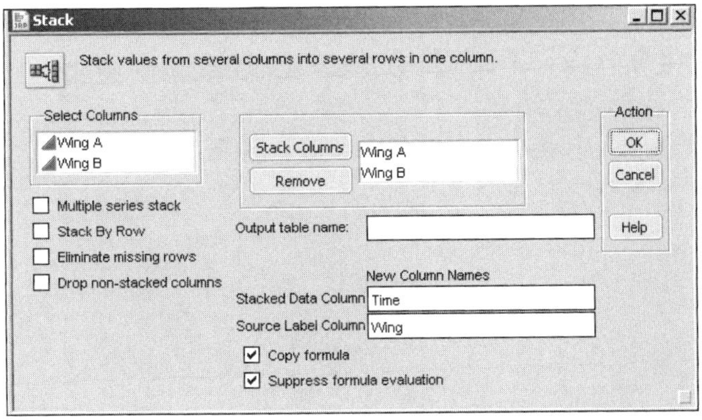

2. To generate a *t* test for the difference between the means assuming equal variances, click the red triangle next to Oneway Analysis of Time by Wing and select **Means / Anova / Pooled t**.

3. To generate a *t* test for the difference between the means assuming unequal variances, click the red triangle next to Oneway Analysis of Time by Wing and select **t Test**.

4. To produce a box-and-whisker plot, click the red triangle next to Oneway Analysis of Time by Wing and select **Quantiles**.

5. To generate tests for the difference between the variances, click the red triangle next to Oneway Analysis of Time by Wing and select **UnEqual** Variances.

6. To generate a Wilcoxon rank sum test, click the red triangle next to Oneway Analysis of Time by Wing and select **Nonparametric → Wilcoxon Test**.

The One-Way ANOVA, Tukey Multiple Comparisons, Tests for Variances, and the Kruskal-Wallis Rank Test

In order to perform the One-Way ANOVA using JMP, the data must be stacked with the numerical variable of interest in one column and the categorical grouping variable in another column. Open the **ERWAITING2.JMP** data table in which the data are already stacked. Select **Analyze → Fit Y by X**. Then in the Fit Y by X dialog box:

1. Enter **Waiting Time** in the Y, Response edit box and **Location** in the X, Factor edit box. Click the **OK** button.

2. To generate a One-Way ANOVA, click the red triangle next to Oneway Analysis of Waiting Time by Location and select **Means / Anova**.

3. To produce a box-and-whisker plot, click the red triangle next to Oneway Analysis of Waiting Time by Location and select **Quantiles**.

4. To generate tests for the difference between the variances, click the red triangle next to Oneway Analysis of Waiting Time by Location and select **UnEqual** Variances.

5. To generate Tukey multiple comparisons, click the red triangle next to Oneway Analysis of Waiting Time by Location and select **Compare Means → All Pairs, Tukey HSD**.

6. To generate a Kruskal-Wallis rank test, click the red triangle next to Oneway Analysis of Waiting Time by Location and select **Nonparametric → Wilcoxon Test**.

FIGURE A7.14

Report: Fit Y by X—Contextual Dialog Box

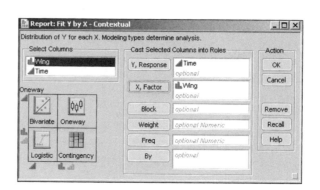

CHAPTER 8

Design of Experiments

INTRODUCTION

8.1 DESIGN OF EXPERIMENTS: BACKGROUND AND RATIONALE

8.2 TWO-FACTOR FACTORIAL DESIGNS

8.3 2^k FACTORIAL DESIGNS

8.4 FRACTIONAL FACTORIAL DESIGNS

SUMMARY

REFERENCES

APPENDIX 8.1 USING MINITAB FOR THE DESIGN OF EXPERIMENTS

APPENDIX 8.2 USING JMP FOR THE DESIGN OF EXPERIMENTS

LEARNING OBJECTIVES

After reading this chapter, you will be able to

- Understand the basic concepts of experimental design.
- Conduct 2^k factorial designs and interpret the effect of interactions.
- Conduct fractional factorial designs and interpret the effect of interactions.

INTRODUCTION

Design of Experiments (DoE) is a collection of statistical methods for studying the relationships between **independent variables**, the Xs or CTPs, and their interactions (also called *factors*, *input variables*, or *process variables*) on a **dependent variable**, the Y (or CTQ). Additionally, you can use design of experiments to minimize the effects of background variables on understanding the relationships between the CTPs or X(s) and CTQ or Y. A **background variable** (also called **noise variable** or **lurking variable**) is a variable that can potentially affect the dependent variable (Y or CTQ) in an experiment, but is not of interest as an independent variable (CTP or X).

The concepts of experimental design discussed in this chapter represent an *active* intervention into a process by Six Sigma team members. Process changes are planned and tested by team members, and the data that is collected from those changes is studied to determine the effect of the process change. This type of experiment does more than passively collect data from a functioning process. It actively intervenes in the function of the process to conduct experiments concerning the effects of the Xs and their interactions on a Y.

8.1   DESIGN OF EXPERIMENTS: BACKGROUND AND RATIONALE

The ideas involved in the design of experiments are not new. They were originally developed by R. A. Fisher in England early in the twentieth century [see References 1 and 4]. His original work focused on improving agricultural experimentation. Fisher's contributions to experimental design were based on several fundamental principles. First, Fisher developed an experimental strategy that purposely designed experiments to simultaneously study several factors (Xs) of interest on a CTQ (Y). This approach was considered novel, because it contrasted with the scientific method as practiced in the nineteenth century of varying only one factor at a time. Second, he developed the concept of randomization that allows for the control and measurement of variation resulting from factors (Xs) not considered in the experiment. Fisher realized that, in conducting an agricultural experiment in the field, not all factors could be foreseen (background variables). Thus, he determined the particular treatment levels received by each plot of land (the individual observations) by a method of random assignment. Any differences between different plots that received the same treatment could be considered to be due to random variation or experimental error.

The methods of experimental design have been used not only in agricultural experimentation, but also in industrial applications [see Reference 1]. They form a critical component of the statistical methods used in Six Sigma management, particularly in the Analyze and Improve Phases of the DMAIC model.

8.2   TWO-FACTOR FACTORIAL DESIGNS

This section begins the study of experimental designs in which more than one factor (X) is examined simultaneously. These experimental designs are called **factorial designs** because they simultaneously evaluate the effects of two or more factors (Xs). This section discusses the simplest factorial design: the two-factor design. In addition, although you can include any number of levels of a factor in a design, for pedagogical simplicity, only the special circumstance in which there are two levels (or treatments) for each factor of interest (CTP or X) will be considered in this book. Designs that contain more than two levels of a factor are logical extensions of the two-level case. In addition, this text only considers situations in which there are equal numbers of **replicates** (that is, the sample size) for each combination of the levels of the factors (Xs).

Owing to the complexity of the calculations involved, particularly as the number of levels of each factor increases and the number of *replications* in each cell increases, statistical software, such as Minitab and JMP, is used both to design experiments and to analyze data collected from them.

In the one-way completely randomized design model (see Section 7.5), the sum of squares total (SST) is subdivided into sum of squares among groups (SSA) and sum of squares within groups (SSW). For the two-factor factorial design model with equal replication in each cell, the **sum of squares total** (SST) is subdivided into **sum of squares due to factor A or X_A (SSA)**, **sum of squares due to factor B or X_B (SSB)**, **sum of squares due to the interacting effect of A and B ($SSAB$)**, and **sum of squares due to random error** (SSE). This partitioning of the SST is displayed in Figure 8.1.

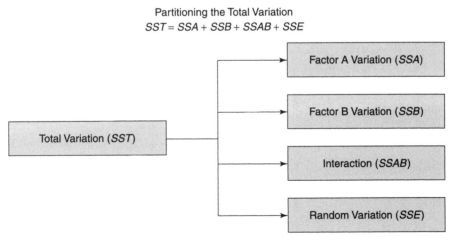

Partitioning the Total Variation
$SST = SSA + SSB + SSAB + SSE$

Total Variation (SST)

Factor A Variation (SSA)

Factor B Variation (SSB)

Interaction ($SSAB$)

Random Variation (SSE)

FIGURE 8.1   Partitioning the Total Variation in a Two-Factor Factorial Design Model

The *SST* represents the total variation among all the values around the grand mean of the CTQ. The *SSA* represents the differences among the various mean levels of factor *A* and the grand mean of the CTQ. The *SSB* represents the differences among the various mean levels of factor *B* and the grand mean of the CTQ. The *SSAB* represents the effect of the combinations of factor *A* and factor *B* on the CTQ. The *SSE* represents the differences among the individual values of the CTQ within each cell (combinations of one level of X_A and one level of X_B) and the corresponding cell mean. If each sum of squares is divided by its associated degrees of freedom, you have the four variances or mean square terms (*MSA*, *MSB*, *MSAB*, and *MSE*) needed for analysis of variance (ANOVA).

If the levels of factor *A* and factor *B* have been *specifically selected* for analysis (rather than being *randomly selected* from a population of possible levels[1]), there are three tests of hypotheses in the two-way ANOVA:

1. Test of no difference due to factor *A* (mean level of the CTQ is not affected by factor *A*):

H_0: All levels of factor *A* have the same mean value of the CTQ against the alternative.

H_1: Not all levels of factor *A* have the same mean value of the CTQ.

This test of hypothesis consists of an *F* test of *MSA* divided by *MSE*.

2. Test of no difference due to factor *B* (mean level of the CTQ is not affected by factor *B*):

H_0: All levels of factor *B* have the same mean value of the CTQ against the alternative.

H_1: Not all levels of factor *B* have the same mean value of the CTQ.

This test of hypothesis consists of an *F* test of *MSB* divided by *MSE*.

3. Test of no interaction of factors *A* and *B*:

H_0: The interaction between factors *A* and *B* on the CTQ does not affect the mean level of the CTQ against the alternative.

H_1: There is an interacting effect between factors *A* and *B* on the CTQ.

This test of hypothesis consists of an *F* test of *MSAB* divided by *MSE*.

The entire set of steps is summarized in the ANOVA table of Table 8.1.

---

[1] A discussion of random effects models is beyond the scope of this text [see References 7, 9, 12].

TABLE 8.1   ANOVA Table for the Two-Factor Model with Replication

Source	Degrees of Freedom	Sum of Squares	Mean Square (Variance)	F
A	$r-1$	SSA	$MSA = \dfrac{SSA}{r-1}$	$F = \dfrac{MSA}{MSE}$
B	$c-1$	SSB	$MSB = \dfrac{SSB}{c-1}$	$F = \dfrac{MSB}{MSE}$
AB	$(r-1)(c-1)$	SSAB	$MSAB = \dfrac{SSAB}{(r-1)(c-1)}$	$F = \dfrac{MSAB}{MSE}$
Error	$rc(n'-1)$	SSE	$MSE = \dfrac{SSE}{rc(n'-1)}$	
Total	$n-1$	SST		

where
r = number of levels of factor A
c = number of levels of factor B
n' = number of values (replications) for each cell, assuming that each cell has an equal number of replications
n = total number of observations in the experiment

To illustrate the two-way Analysis of Variance, a hotel wanted to develop a new system for delivering room service breakfasts. In the current system, an order form is left on the bed in each room. If the customer wishes to receive a room service breakfast, he or she places the order form on the doorknob before 11 P.M. The current system includes a delivery time that provides a 15-minute interval for desired delivery time (6:30–6:45 A.M., 6:45–7:00 A.M., and so on). The new system is designed to allow the customer to request a specific delivery time. The hotel wants to measure the difference between the actual delivery time and the requested delivery time of room service orders for breakfast. (A negative time means that the order was delivered before the requested time. A positive time means that the order was delivered after the requested time.) The factors included were the menu choice (X_1) [American or Continental] and the desired time period in which the order was to be delivered (X_2) [early time period (6:30–8:00 A.M.) or late time period (8:00–9:30 A.M.)]. Ten orders for each combination of menu choice and desired time period were studied on a particular day. Table 8.2 displays the results.

TABLE 8.2   Difference Between the Actual Delivery Time and the Requested Delivery Time of Room Service Orders (in Minutes) for Breakfast Based on Menu Choice and Desired Time Period

	Desired Time	
Delivery Time Difference (Minutes)	$X_2 =$ **Early Time Period**	$X_2 =$ **Late Time Period**
$X_1 =$ Continental	1.2	-2.5
	2.1	3.0
	3.3	-0.2
	4.4	1.2
	3.4	1.2
	5.3	0.7
	2.2	-1.3
	1.0	0.2
	5.4	-0.5
	1.4	3.8
$X_1 =$ American	4.4	6.0
	1.1	2.3
	4.8	4.2
	7.1	3.8
	6.7	5.5
	5.6	1.8
	9.5	5.1
	4.1	4.2
	7.9	4.9
	9.4	4.0

BREAKFAST

The design used in this example is called a 2×2 design with ten replications. The first number refers to the number of levels for the first factor, and the second number refers to the number of levels for the second factor. This design is also referred to as a 2^2 design, where the exponent indicates that there are two factors each with two treatment levels. Figure 8.2 represents Minitab output for these data. Figure 8.3 illustrates JMP output.

FIGURE 8.2
Minitab Output for
the Breakfast Delivery
Data

```
Source          DF      SS       MS       F      P
Menu Choice      1  112.560  112.560  30.44  0.000
Desired Time     1   46.010   46.010  12.44  0.001
Interaction      1    0.702    0.702   0.19  0.666
Error           36  133.105    3.697
Total           39  292.378

S = 1.923   R-Sq = 54.47%   R-Sq(adj) = 50.68%


                             Individual 95% CIs For Mean Based on
                             Pooled StDev
Menu Choice   Mean    ----+---------+---------+---------+-----
American      5.120                             (-----*-----)
Continental   1.765    (-----*-----)
                       ----+---------+---------+---------+-----
                        1.5       3.0       4.5       6.0


                             Individual 95% CIs For Mean Based on
Desired                      Pooled StDev
Time          Mean    -----+---------+---------+---------+----
Early         4.515                            (--------*--------)
Late          2.370    (--------*-------)
```

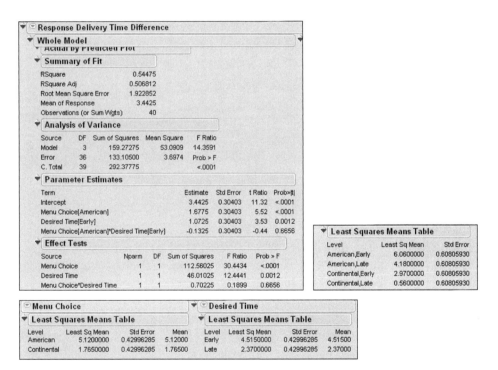

FIGURE 8.3   JMP Output for the Breakfast Delivery Data

From Figure 8.2 or 8.3, the tests of hypotheses are as follows (at the $\alpha = 0.05$ level of significance):

1. **Test for interaction:** Because the F statistic for the interaction effect = 0.19 and the p-value is $0.666 > 0.05$, you do not reject the null hypothesis. There is insufficient evidence of any interaction between menu choice and desired time period.

2. **Test for menu choice:** Because the F statistic for the menu choice = 30.44 and the p-value is $0.000 < 0.05$, you reject the null hypothesis. There is evidence of an effect of menu choice on the difference between actual delivery time and requested delivery time. The difference between actual delivery time and requested delivery time is higher for an American breakfast than for a Continental breakfast.

3. **Test for desired delivery time:** Because the F statistic for the desired delivery time = 12.44 and the p-value is $0.001 < 0.05$, you reject the null hypothesis. There is evidence of an effect of desired delivery time on the difference between actual delivery time and requested delivery time. The difference between actual delivery time and requested delivery time is higher for breakfast delivered earlier in the morning than later in the morning.

Table 8.3 summarizes the means for each combination of menu choice and desired delivery time.

TABLE 8.3   Mean Difference of Actual Delivery Time and the Requested Delivery Time (in Minutes) of Room Service Orders for Breakfast Based on Menu Choice and Desired Time Period

	Desired Time		
Delivery Time Difference	**Early**	**Late**	**Row Mean**
Continental	2.970	0.56	1.7650
American	6.060	4.18	5.1200
Column Mean	4.515	2.37	3.4425

From Table 8.3, you can reach several conclusions. In terms of the individual factors (called the main effects, Xs or CTPs), there is a difference in the mean delivery time difference (CTQ) between the Continental and American menu choices, or X_1 (1.765 vs. 5.12 minutes). The size of the effect for menu choice is $5.12 - 1.765 = 3.355$ minutes. There is also a difference in the mean delivery time difference (CTQ) between the early and late levels of desired delivery times, or X_2. The early level of desired delivery time has a mean delivery time difference of 4.515 minutes, and the late level of desired delivery time has a mean delivery time difference of 2.37 minutes. Thus, the effect due to desired delivery time is $4.515 - 2.37 = 2.145$ minutes. Figure 8.4 provides plots for these two main effects using Minitab. Figure 8.5 provides JMP output.

FIGURE 8.4
Minitab Main Effects
Plots of Menu Choice
and Desired Delivery
Time

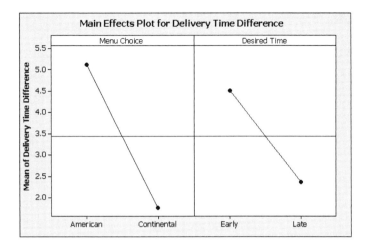

FIGURE 8.5
JMP Main Effects
Plots of Menu
Choice and Desired
Delivery Time

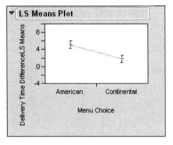 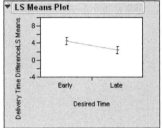

Now that the main effects of menu choice and desired delivery time have been studied, the question remains as to what is meant by interaction between factors? To understand the meaning of **interaction**, first consider what is meant by the absence of interaction:

If there is no interaction between two factors (A and B), then any difference in the dependent or response variable (CTQ) between the two levels of factor A (X_A) would be the same at each level of factor B (X_B).

In terms of the factors in this example, if there was no interaction between menu choice and desired delivery time, any difference in the delivery time difference between Continental and American breakfast would be the same for early delivery times as for late delivery times. From Table 8.3, you see that for a Continental breakfast, the difference in delivery time difference between early and late delivery times is 2.41 minutes, and for an American breakfast, the difference in delivery time difference between early and late delivery times is 1.88 minutes.

You can present the interaction between two factors in an interaction plot. If there is no interaction between the factors, the lines for the two levels will be approximately parallel. Figure 8.6 is a Minitab interaction plot for these data. Figure 8.7 is a JMP interaction plot.

FIGURE 8.6
Minitab Interaction
Plots for the Breakfast
Delivery Example

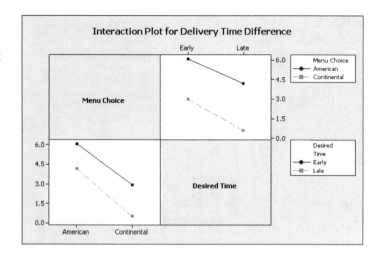

FIGURE 8.7
JMP Interaction Plots
for the Breakfast
Delivery Example

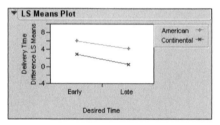

In the Minitab interaction plot displayed in Figure 8.6, you can use either the bottom-left or the top-right panels of this plot, depending on whether you want to focus on menu choice or desired delivery time. Referring to the upper-right panel, the levels on the horizontal axis represent the desired delivery time levels for each menu choice. Referring to the lower-left panel, the levels on the horizontal axis represent the menu choices for each desired delivery time. An examination of either panel shows that the lines are roughly parallel, indicating very little interaction between the menu choice and desired delivery time factors.

To study an example that has an interaction, suppose the results for the breakfast study of Table 8.2 were as in Table 8.4.

TABLE 8.4   Difference Between the Actual Delivery Time and the Requested Delivery Time of Room Service Orders (in Minutes) for Breakfast Based on Menu Choice and Desired Time Period

Delivery Time Difference (Minutes)	Desired Time	
	X_2 = Early	X_2 = Late
X_1 = Continental	1.2	-0.5
	2.1	5.0
	3.3	1.8
	4.4	3.2
	3.4	3.2
	5.3	2.7
	2.2	0.7
	1.0	2.2
	5.4	1.5
	1.4	5.8
X_1 = American	4.4	6.0
	1.1	2.3
	4.8	4.2
	7.1	3.8
	6.7	5.5
	5.6	1.8
	9.5	5.1
	4.1	4.2
	7.9	4.9
	9.4	4.0

🌐 **BREAKFAST2**

Figures 8.8 and 8.9 present the Minitab and JMP interaction plots for these data. Table 8.5 summarizes the means for each combination of menu choice and desired delivery time.

FIGURE 8.8
Minitab Interaction
Plots for the Revised
Breakfast Delivery
Example

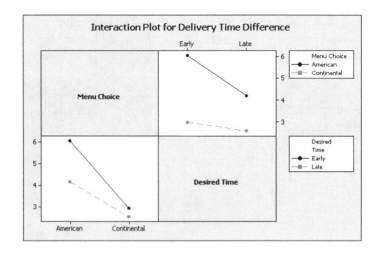

FIGURE 8.9
JMP Interaction Plot
for the Revised Break-
fast Delivery Example

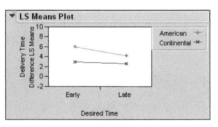

TABLE 8.5   Mean Difference of Actual Delivery Time and the Requested
Delivery Time of Room Service Orders (in Minutes) for Breakfast Based on Menu
Choice and Desired Time Period

	Desired Time		
Delivery Time Difference	**Early**	**Late**	**Row Mean**
Continental	2.970	2.56	2.7650
American	6.060	4.18	5.1200
Column Mean	4.515	3.37	3.9425

From Table 8.5 and Figures 8.8 and 8.9, observe that the difference in the actual and
desired delivery time for an American breakfast is much greater at the earlier time
than the later time. The difference in the actual and desired delivery time for a Continental breakfast is slightly higher for the early time than for the late time. The possible existence of an interaction effect complicates the interpretation of the main
effects. You may not be able to conclude that there is a difference in the actual and

desired delivery time between the two types of breakfast because the difference may not be the same for the two desired delivery time periods. Likewise, you may not be able to conclude that there is a difference between the time periods because the difference is not the same for the two types of breakfasts. In sum, the interaction effect takes precedence over any interpretation of main effects.

Notation for Interaction Effects. Determining the magnitude of the effect of each factor and interaction becomes complex when many factors are involved. The treatment combinations (the simultaneous combinations of the different levels of each of the Xs or factors) are represented using a special notation. The steps involved in this notation are as follows:

1. A shorthand notation is used to define the factors by assigning a letter, such as A, B, or C, to each factor.

2. One level of each factor is designated as the low level, and the other level is designated as the high level. The high and low levels are defined by the nature of the factor (e.g., high speed versus low speed). In cases where levels are not defined by the factor being studied, it is common practice to set the current operating level as the low level.

3. A table is developed in which the columns represent the factors and their interactions, and the rows represent the different combinations, called **treatment combinations**, created by setting the factors at their different levels. Treatment combinations are defined only by the high levels of the factors. For example, in a two-factor design, if only the high level of factor A is present, the treatment combination is specified as a. If only the high level of factor B is present, the treatment combination is specified as b. If the high levels of factors A and B are present, the treatment combination is specified as ab. The treatment combination that contains the low level of all the factors is specified as (1).

4. Each factor is listed in a column. For each factor, a minus (−) sign is included in the row if the low level is present and a plus (+) sign is included if the high level of the factor is present. The sign for an interaction effect is the product of the signs that define the interaction. Thus, the sign for the AB interaction is the product of the signs in the particular row for factors A and B (for example, if the row has a plus sign for A and a plus sign for B or a minus sign for A and a minus sign for B, the interaction AB sign is a plus. If the row has a plus sign for A and a minus sign for B or a minus sign for A and a plus sign for B, the interaction AB sign is a minus).

The treatment combinations for the data in Table 8.3 on page 164, using the special notation, are displayed in Table 8.6.

TABLE 8.6   Computing the Mean Effects for Factors A, B, and AB in the 2^2 Design for the Breakfast Delivery Data

Treatment Combination	Notation	Mean Response	Breakfast Type A	Time Period B	AB
Continental, early	(1)	2.97	−	−	+
American, early	a	6.06	+	−	−
Continental, late	b	0.56	−	+	−
American, late	ab	4.18	+	+	+

COMPUTING THE ESTIMATED EFFECTS {OPTIONAL}

You compute the mean effect for each factor or interaction by multiplying the mean response for the row by the sign in the column and summing these products over all the rows. You divide this sum by the number of plus signs used in computing the effect.

For a two-factor design, the mean effects for factor A, factor B, and the interaction of A and B are as follows:

$$A = \frac{1}{2}\left(a + ab - b - (1)\right) \qquad (8.1a)$$

$$B = \frac{1}{2}\left(b + ab - a - (1)\right) \qquad (8.1b)$$

$$AB = \frac{1}{2}\left(ab - a - b + (1)\right) \qquad (8.1c)$$

From Equations (8.1a–8.1c) and Table 8.6:

$$A = \frac{1}{2}\left(6.06 + 4.18 - 0.56 - 2.97\right)$$

$$= \frac{6.71}{2}$$

$$= 3.355$$

Thus, the mean difference in the actual and desired delivery time for an American breakfast is 3.355 minutes greater than the mean for a Continental breakfast, a conclusion previously stated on page 164.

$$B = \frac{1}{2}\left(0.56 + 4.18 - 6.06 - 2.97\right)$$

$$= -\frac{4.29}{2}$$

$$= -2.145$$

Thus, the difference in the actual and desired delivery time is 2.145 minutes less for late times than for early times.

$$AB = \frac{1}{2}\left(4.18 - 6.06 - 0.56 + 2.97\right)$$

$$= \frac{0.53}{2}$$

$$= 0.265$$

The interaction means that the mean effect of combining the high level of breakfast type and desired time is 0.265 minutes greater than the mean difference between desired times for the breakfast types. This occurs because the mean difference in the actual and desired delivery time is 3.62 minutes greater for an American breakfast at a late time than for a Continental breakfast at a late time (4.18 as compared to 0.56), while the mean difference in the actual and desired delivery time for an American breakfast as compared to a Continental breakfast is 5.12 − 1.765 = 3.355 minutes. The difference between 3.62 minutes and 3.355 minutes is the interaction effect of 0.265 minutes.

8.3   2^k FACTORIAL DESIGNS

The two-factor factorial design is the most elementary of all factorial designs. In this section, the concepts developed for the two-factor 2^2 design in Section 8.2 are extended to the more general factorial design that has three or more factors. With this design, there are 2^k treatment combinations, where k = the number of factors (CTPs or Xs); for example, 2^3 = 2 × 2 × 2 = 8 treatment combinations. Table 8.7 extends the format of Table 8.6 to the 2^3 design in standard order. **Standard order** is an arrangement for listing trials in which the first factor alternates between − and +, the second factor alternates between −,− and +,+, the third factor alternates between −,−,−,− and +,+,+,+, and so on.

To illustrate the 2^3 design, suppose that the hotel also wanted to study the process of delivering room service meals at dinner time. Three factors were to be considered in studying the delivery time. They were as follows:

1. Complexity of the meal: low versus high.
2. Elevator used for delivering the meal: service versus main.
3. Order volume in the kitchen at the time of the order: low versus high.

TABLE 8.7   Computing Effects for Factors A, B, C, and Interactions AB, AC, BC, and ABC in the 2^3 Design in Standard Order

Notation	A	B	C	AB	AC	BC	ABC
				Effect			
(1)	–	–	–	+	+	+	–
a	+	–	–	–	–	+	+
b	–	+	–	–	+	–	+
ab	+	+	–	+	–	–	–
c	–	–	+	+	–	–	+
ac	+	–	+	–	+	–	–
bc	–	+	+	–	–	+	–
abc	+	+	+	+	+	+	+

Each treatment combination consists of five replications. The results from this experiment are presented in Table 8.8.

TABLE 8.8   Results for a 2^3 Design Involving the Delivery Time (CTQ) Based on Complexity of the Meal (X_A), Elevator Used (X_B), and Order Volume in the Kitchen (X_C) Treatment Combinations

Complexity	Elevator	Order Volume	Notation	Delivery Time
Low	Service	Low	1	31.4, 31.6, 28.6, 36.3, 30.6
High	Service	Low	a	42.7, 30.6, 38.5, 28.2, 41.4
Low	Main	Low	b	41.5, 33.5, 39.0, 31.1, 39.1
High	Main	Low	ab	35.1, 32.0, 36.9, 39.9, 36.0
Low	Service	High	c	44.1, 35.5, 40.5, 34.8, 42.4
High	Service	High	ac	50.4, 49.3, 45.1, 44.0, 51.3
Low	Main	High	bc	43.4, 45.0, 28.1, 33.4, 45.0
High	Main	High	abc	45.2, 52.1, 49.5, 47.3, 47.3

DINNER

Figure 8.10 presents the eight treatment combinations (and their average responses) in the form of a cube.

FIGURE 8.10

Geometric Represen-
tation of the 2³ Design
(Source: Table 8.8)

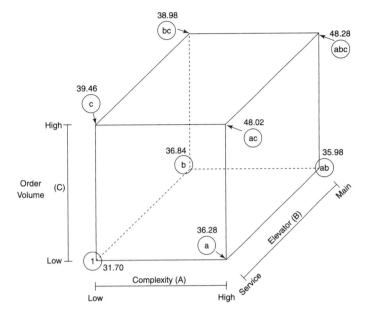

Figure 8.11 represents Minitab ANOVA output of the estimated effects of meal complexity, elevator, and order volume on the delivery time of room service dinners. Figure 8.12 is JMP output. The coefficients shown in the JMP output are half the value of the effects.

FIGURE 8.11

Minitab ANOVA
Output of Meal Com-
plexity, Elevator, and
Order Volume on the
Delivery Time of
Room Service Dinners

```
Estimated Effects and Coefficients for Delivery Time (coded units)

Term                              Effect     Coef  SE Coef       T      P
Constant                                  39.4425   0.7346   53.69  0.000
Complexity                        5.3950   2.6975   0.7346    3.67  0.001
Elevator                          1.1550   0.5775   0.7346    0.79  0.438
Order Volume                      8.4850   4.2425   0.7346    5.77  0.000
Complexity*Elevator              -1.1750  -0.5875   0.7346   -0.80  0.430
Complexity*Order Volume           3.5350   1.7675   0.7346    2.41  0.022
Elevator*Order Volume            -1.2650  -0.6325   0.7346   -0.86  0.396
Complexity*Elevator*Order Volume  1.5450   0.7725   0.7346    1.05  0.301


S = 4.64632   R-Sq = 63.52%   R-Sq(adj) = 55.54%


Analysis of Variance for Delivery Time (coded units)

Source              DF   Seq SS   Adj SS   Adj MS      F      P
Main Effects         3  1024.35  1024.35   341.45  15.82  0.000
2-Way Interactions   3   154.77   154.77    51.59   2.39  0.087
3-Way Interactions   1    23.87    23.87    23.87   1.11  0.301
Residual Error      32   690.82   690.82    21.59
  Pure Error        32   690.82   690.82    21.59
Total               39  1893.82
```

FIGURE 8.12
JMP ANOVA Output of Meal Complexity, Elevator, and Order Volume on the Delivery Time of Room Service Dinners

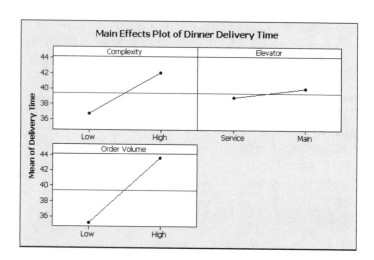

Figures 8.13 and 8.14 display the main effects plot for these data, and Figures 8.15 and 8.16 present the interaction plots.

FIGURE 8.13
Minitab Main Effects Plots for the Delivery Time of Room Service Dinners in the 2^3 Experiment

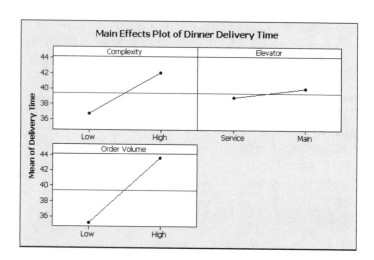

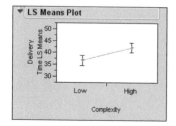
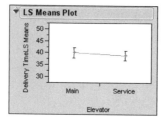
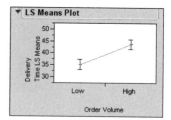

FIGURE 8.14   JMP Main Effects Plots for the Delivery Time of Room Service Dinners in the 2^3 Experiment

FIGURE 8.15

Minitab Interaction
Plots for the Delivery
Time of Room Service
Dinners in the 2^3
Experiment

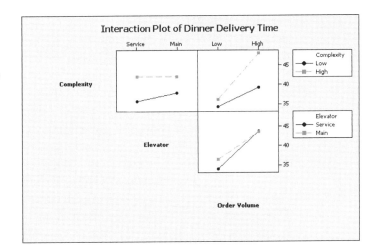

FIGURE 8.16   JMP Interaction Plots for the Delivery Time of Room Service
Dinners in the 2^3 Experiment

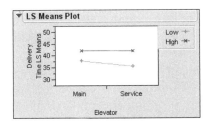
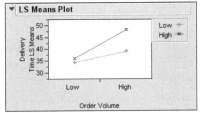
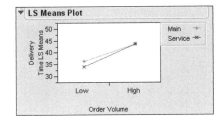

From the ANOVA results of Figures 8.11 and 8.12, the main effects plot illustrated
in Figures 8.13 and 8.14, and the interaction plots in Figures 8.15 and 8.16, you can
conclude that:

1. The mean delivery time is significantly higher (p-value = 0.001) for meals
   that are highly complex to prepare than for meals that have a low complexity
   in their preparation. The highly complex meals have a mean delivery time of
   5.395 minutes higher than low complex meals.

2. There is insufficient evidence of a statistically significant difference in the
   mean delivery time based on the elevator used to deliver the meals.

The mean delivery time for meals delivered using the main elevator is 1.155 minutes higher than for meals delivered using the service elevator.

3. The mean delivery time is significantly higher (p-value = 0.000) when the order volume in the kitchen is high than when the order volume in the kitchen is low. The mean delivery time is 8.485 minutes more when the order volume in the kitchen is high than when the order volume in the kitchen is low.

4. Only the interaction between meal complexity and order volume is statistically significant (p-value = 0.022). The effects of A (Meal Complexity) and C (Order Volume) are interacting due to the large effect caused by the presence of the high level of meal complexity and the high level of order volume. The interpretation of this interacting effect is that the mean difference in the delivery time for highly complex meals as compared with meals of low complexity is 3.535 minutes more when there is high order volume than for the mean of low and high order volume.

In many instances, you may not be able to or it may be prohibitively expensive to take more than one replication for each treatment combination. When this is the case, you are unable to compute a separate measure of the error variance and, therefore, not able to conduct an ANOVA of the effects and interactions. However, you can carry out a preliminary screening step using a **half-normal plot** [see Reference 5] to screen out interactions that do not appear to have any effect and combine them into an error variance. This half-normal plot is a type of normal probability plot in which the absolute value of the estimated effects is plotted on normal probability paper in rank order. Figures 8.17 and 8.18 show the estimated effects and their associated cumulative probabilities for the dinner delivery time example in the normal and half-normal probability plot.

FIGURE 8.17
Minitab Normal Probability Plot for the 2^3 Design for the Dinner Delivery Time Example

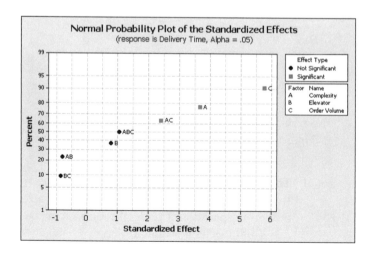

FIGURE 8.18

JMP Half-Normal Probability Plot for the 2^3 Design for the Dinner Delivery Time Example

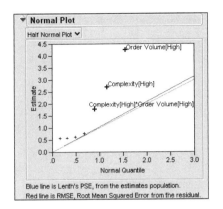

When there is only one replication per treatment combination, you use the normal probability plot [see Reference 10] to determine which factors and interaction effects are not important (and thus, not different from zero). In the normal probability plot, any factors or interactions whose observed effects are due to chance are expected to be randomly distributed around zero, with some being slightly below zero and others being slightly above zero. (In the half-normal plot, negative values are converted to positive values.) These effects will tend to fall along a straight line. The effects that may be important have mean values different from zero and are located a substantial distance away from the hypothetical vertical line that represents no effect.

From Figure 8.17 and 8.18, observe that the most important effects are A, C, and AC. These results are consistent with those seen in the ANOVA, main effects plot, and the interaction plot of Figures 8.11–8.16.

Table 8.9 reorganizes the results of Table 8.8 to focus on factors A and C.

TABLE 8.9   Mean Delivery Time (in Minutes) by Complexity of Meal and Order Volume

Meal Complexity	Order Volume	
	Low	High
Low	34.27	39.22
High	36.13	48.15

From Table 8.9, the mean delivery time for high meal complexity is 1.86 minutes higher than for low meal complexity when there is low order volume, but is 8.93 minutes higher for high meal complexity than for low meal complexity when there is high order volume. The difference of 8.93 – 1.86 = 7.07, divided by 2 (to account for the two levels of factor C), represents the interaction effect of 3.535 for factors A (meal complexity) and C (order volume).

COMPUTING THE ESTIMATED EFFECTS AND INTERACTION EFFECTS {OPTIONAL}

For each of the main effects, the estimated effect consists of the mean at the high level of the factor minus the mean at the low level of the factor. Thus, for factors A, B, and C:

$$A = \frac{1}{4}\left[a + ab + ac + abc - (1) - b - c - bc\right] \qquad (8.2a)$$

$$B = \frac{1}{4}\left[b + ab + bc + abc - (1) - a - c - ac\right] \qquad (8.2b)$$

$$C = \frac{1}{4}\left[c + ac + bc + abc - (1) - a - b - ab\right] \qquad (8.2c)$$

The two-way interactions are measured as one-half the difference in the average of one effect at the two levels of the other effect. Thus, for the interactions AB, AC, and BC:

$$AB = \frac{1}{4}\left[abc - bc + ab - b - ac + c - a + (1)\right] \qquad (8.3a)$$

$$AC = \frac{1}{4}\left[(1) - a + b - ab - c + ac - bc + abc\right] \qquad (8.3b)$$

$$BC = \frac{1}{4}\left[(1) + a - b - ab - c - ac + bc + abc\right] \qquad (8.3c)$$

The ABC interaction is defined as the average difference in the AB interaction for the two levels of factor C. Thus:

$$ABC = \frac{1}{4}\left[abc - bc - ac + c - ab + b + a - (1)\right] \qquad (8.4)$$

Table 8.10 represents the format needed to compute the effects for the delivery time example.

TABLE 8.10   Computing Effects for Factors A, B, and C and Interactions AB, AC, BC, and ABC in the 2^3 Design

		Effect						
Notation Delivery Time	Mean	A	B	C	AB	AC	BC	ABC
(1)	31.70	–	–	–	+	+	+	–
a	36.28	+	–	–	–	–	+	+
b	36.84	–	+	–	–	+	–	+
ab	35.98	+	+	–	+	–	–	–

Effect Notation Delivery Time	Mean	A	B	C	AB	AC	BC	ABC
c	39.46	–	–	+	+	–	–	+
ac	48.02	+	–	+	–	+	–	–
bc	38.98	–	+	+	–	–	+	–
abc	48.28	+	+	+	+	+	+	+

From Table 8.10 and Equations (8.2), (8.3), and (8.4):

$$A = \frac{-31.70 + 36.28 - 36.84 + 35.98 - 39.46 + 48.02 - 38.98 + 48.28}{4}$$

$$= \frac{21.58}{4}$$

$$= 5.395$$

$$B = \frac{-31.70 - 36.28 + 36.84 + 35.98 - 39.46 - 48.02 + 38.98 + 48.28}{4}$$

$$= \frac{4.62}{4}$$

$$= 1.155$$

$$C = \frac{-31.70 - 36.28 - 36.84 - 35.98 + 39.46 + 48.02 + 38.98 + 48.28}{4}$$

$$= \frac{33.94}{4}$$

$$= 8.485$$

$$AB = \frac{+31.70 - 36.28 - 36.84 + 35.98 + 39.46 - 48.02 - 38.98 + 48.28}{4}$$

$$= \frac{-4.7}{4}$$

$$= -1.175$$

$$AC = \frac{+31.70 - 36.28 + 36.84 - 35.98 - 39.46 + 48.02 - 38.98 + 48.28}{4}$$

$$= \frac{14.14}{4}$$

$$= 3.535$$

$$BC = \frac{+31.70 + 36.28 - 36.84 - 35.98 - 39.46 - 48.02 + 38.98 + 48.28}{4}$$

$$= \frac{-5.06}{4}$$

$$= -1.265$$

Continues

$$ABC = \frac{-31.70+36.28+36.84-35.98+39.46-48.02-38.98+48.28}{4}$$

$$= \frac{6.18}{4}$$

$$= 1.545$$

To study a factorial design that has more than three factors (Xs), consider an experiment involving a cake mix. Each year, millions of cake mixes are sold by food processing companies. A cake mix consists of a packet containing flour, shortening, and egg powder that will (it is hoped) provide a good-tasting cake. One difficulty in determining the amount of these ingredients to include in the packet to maximize the tastiness of the cake relates to the fact that consumers might not precisely follow the recommended oven temperature and baking time. An experiment is conducted in which each factor is tested at a higher level than called for in the instructions and at a lower level than called for in the instructions. The goal of the experiment is to determine which factors have an effect on the taste rating of the cake and the levels of the factors that will provide the cake with the highest taste rating. Five factors were to be considered: flour, shortening, egg powder, oven temperature, and baking time. Only one observation for each of the $2^5 = 32$ treatment combinations was collected. Table 8.11 presents the taste rating for each treatment combination obtained from a taste testing expert.

TABLE 8.11   Taste Rating for Cake Mix Combinations

Treatment Combinations	Flour (A)	Shortening (B)	Egg Powder (C)	Oven Temp (D)	Bake Time (E)	Rating Score (Y)
(1)	–	–	–	–	–	1.1
a	+	–	–	–	–	3.8
b	–	+	–	–	–	3.7
ab	+	+	–	–	–	4.5
c	–	–	+	–	–	4.2
ac	+	–	+	–	–	5.2
bc	–	+	+	–	–	3.1
abc	+	+	+	–	–	3.9

Treatment Combinations	Flour (A)	Shortening (B)	Egg Powder (C)	Oven Temp (D)	Bake Time (E)	Rating Score (Y)
d	−	−	−	+	−	5.7
ad	+	−	−	+	−	4.9
bd	−	+	−	+	−	5.1
abd	+	+	−	+	−	6.4
cd	−	−	+	+	−	6.8
acd	+	−	+	+	−	6.0
bcd	−	+	+	+	−	6.3
abcd	+	+	+	+	−	5.5
e	−	−	−	−	+	6.4
ae	+	−	−	−	+	4.3
be	−	+	−	−	+	6.7
abe	+	+	−	−	+	5.8
ce	−	−	+	−	+	6.5
ace	+	−	+	−	+	5.9
bce	−	+	+	−	+	6.4
abce	+	+	+	−	+	5.0
de	−	−	−	+	+	1.3
ade	+	−	−	+	+	2.1
bde	−	+	−	+	+	2.9
abde	+	+	−	+	+	5.2
cde	−	−	+	+	+	3.5
acde	+	−	+	+	+	5.7
bcde	−	+	+	+	+	3.0
abcde	+	+	+	+	+	5.4

 CAKE

Figure 8.19 presents the Minitab output of the estimated effects for the cake mix design. Figure 8.20 illustrates JMP output of the coefficients, which are half the value of the effects.

FIGURE 8.19
Minitab Estimated
Effects for the Cake
Mix Example

```
Estimated Effects and Coefficients for Rating (coded units)

Term                                    Effect     Coef
Constant                                           4.759
Flour                                    0.431     0.216
Shortening                               0.344     0.172
Egg Powder                               0.781     0.391
ovenTemp                                -0.044    -0.022
BakeTime                                -0.006    -0.003
Flour*Shortening                         0.131     0.066
Flour*Egg Powder                        -0.081    -0.041
Flour*ovenTemp                           0.394     0.197
Flour*BakeTime                          -0.094    -0.047
Shortening*Egg Powder                   -0.994    -0.497
Shortening*ovenTemp                      0.131     0.066
Shortening*BakeTime                      0.244     0.122
Egg Powder*ovenTemp                      0.294     0.147
Egg Powder*BakeTime                      0.056     0.028
ovenTemp*BakeTime                       -2.194    -1.097
Flour*Shortening*Egg Powder             -0.231    -0.116
Flour*Shortening*ovenTemp                0.344     0.172
Flour*Egg Powder*ovenTemp                0.006     0.003
Flour*Shortening*BakeTime                0.131     0.066
Flour*Egg Powder*BakeTime                0.394     0.197
Flour*ovenTemp*BakeTime                  1.194     0.597
Shortening*Egg Powder*ovenTemp           0.069     0.034
Shortening*Egg Powder*BakeTime          -0.044    -0.022
Shortening*ovenTemp*BakeTime             0.256     0.128
Egg Powder*ovenTemp*BakeTime             0.394     0.197
Flour*Shortening*Egg Powder*ovenTemp    -0.194    -0.097
Flour*Shortening*Egg Powder*BakeTime    -0.181    -0.091
Flour*Shortening*ovenTemp*BakeTime      -0.181    -0.091
Flour*Egg Powder*ovenTemp*BakeTime       0.056     0.028
Shortening*Egg Powder*ovenTemp*         -0.406    -0.203
  BakeTime
Flour*Shortening*Egg Powder*             0.281     0.141
  ovenTemp*BakeTime
```

FIGURE 8.20
JMP Estimated
Coefficients for the
Cake Mix Example

Response Rating				
Parameter Estimates				
Term	Estimate	Std Error	t Ratio	Prob>|t|
Intercept	4.759375			
Flour[low]	-0.215625			
Shortening[low]	-0.171875			
Flour[low]*Shortening[low]	0.065625			
Egg Powder[low]	-0.390625			
Flour[low]*Egg Powder[low]	-0.040625			
Shortening[low]*Egg Powder[low]	-0.496875			
Flour[low]*Shortening[low]*Egg Powder[low]	0.115625			
ovenTemp[low]	0.021875			
Flour[low]*ovenTemp[low]	0.196875			
Shortening[low]*ovenTemp[low]	0.065625			
Flour[low]*Shortening[low]*ovenTemp[low]	-0.171875			
Egg Powder[low]*ovenTemp[low]	0.146875			
Flour[low]*Egg Powder[low]*ovenTemp[low]	-0.003125			
Shortening[low]*Egg Powder[low]*ovenTemp[low]	-0.034375			
Flour[low]*Shortening[low]*Egg Powder[low]*ovenTemp[low]	-0.096875			
BakeTime[low]	0.003125			
Flour[low]*BakeTime[low]	-0.046875			
Shortening[low]*BakeTime[low]	0.121875			
Flour[low]*Shortening[low]*BakeTime[low]	-0.065625			
Egg Powder[low]*BakeTime[low]	0.028125			
Flour[low]*Egg Powder[low]*BakeTime[low]	-0.196875			
Shortening[low]*Egg Powder[low]*BakeTime[low]	0.021875			
Flour[low]*Shortening[low]*Egg Powder[low]*BakeTime[low]	-0.090625			
ovenTemp[low]*BakeTime[low]	-1.096875			
Flour[low]*ovenTemp[low]*BakeTime[low]	-0.596875			
Shortening[low]*ovenTemp[low]*BakeTime[low]	-0.128125			
Flour[low]*Shortening[low]*ovenTemp[low]*BakeTime[low]	-0.090625			
Egg Powder[low]*ovenTemp[low]*BakeTime[low]	-0.196875			
Flour[low]*Egg Powder[low]*ovenTemp[low]*BakeTime[low]	0.028125			
Shortening[low]*Egg Powder[low]*ovenTemp[low]*BakeTime[low]	-0.203125			
Flour[low]*Shortening[low]*Egg Powder[low]*ovenTemp[low]*BakeTime[low]	-0.140625			

Figures 8.21 and 8.22 are a Minitab normal probability plot and a JMP half-normal plot of the estimated effects for the cake mix design.

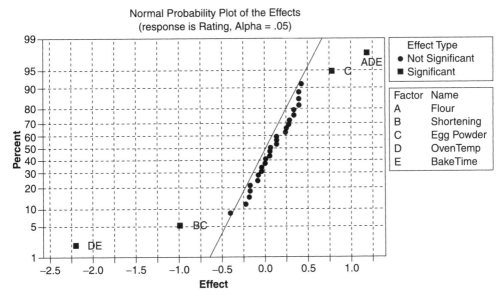

FIGURE 8.21
Minitab Normal Probability Plot of the Estimated Effects for the Cake Mix Design

FIGURE 8.22
JMP Half-Normal
Probability Plot of the
Estimated Effects for
the Cake Mix Design

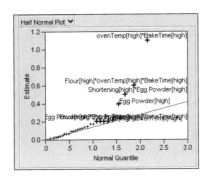

From Figure 8.21 or 8.22, you see that only effects C, BC, DE, and ADE plot far away from a straight line that is approximately zero on the X axis. Minitab indicates that these terms are statistically significant, according to criteria developed by Lenth [see Reference 10]. From Figure 8.21 or 8.22, factor C (Egg Powder), the BC (Shortening–Egg Powder) interaction, the DE (Oven Temperature–Bake Time) interaction, and the ADE (Flour–Oven Temperature–Bake Time) interaction are far from a hypothetical vertical line at zero. Thus, you can consider all third-order interactions (except ADE), all fourth-order interactions, and the single fifth-order interaction ($ABCDE$) as consisting only of random error. You can eliminate these effects from the ANOVA model and combine them into an estimate of the error variance. The ANOVA model computed by Minitab with these effects combined into an error variance is displayed in Figure 8.23. The model computed by JMP is displayed in Figure 8.24.

FIGURE 8.23
Minitab ANOVA
Model for the Cake
Mix Example

Term	Effect	Coef	SE Coef	T	P
Constant		4.759	0.1240	38.40	0.000
Flour	0.431	0.216	0.1240	1.74	0.102
Shortening	0.344	0.172	0.1240	1.39	0.186
Egg Powder	0.781	0.391	0.1240	3.15	0.007
ovenTemp	-0.044	-0.022	0.1240	-0.18	0.862
BakeTime	-0.006	-0.003	0.1240	-0.03	0.980
Flour*Shortening	0.131	0.066	0.1240	0.53	0.604
Flour*Egg Powder	-0.081	-0.041	0.1240	-0.33	0.748
Flour*ovenTemp	0.394	0.197	0.1240	1.59	0.133
Flour*BakeTime	-0.094	-0.047	0.1240	-0.38	0.711
Shortening*Egg Powder	-0.994	-0.497	0.1240	-4.01	0.001
Shortening*ovenTemp	0.131	0.066	0.1240	0.53	0.604
Shortening*BakeTime	0.244	0.122	0.1240	0.98	0.341
Egg Powder*ovenTemp	0.294	0.147	0.1240	1.18	0.254
Egg Powder*BakeTime	0.056	0.028	0.1240	0.23	0.824
ovenTemp*BakeTime	-2.194	-1.097	0.1240	-8.85	0.000
Flour*ovenTemp*BakeTime	1.194	0.597	0.1240	4.82	0.000

Analysis of Variance for Rating (coded units)

Source	DF	Seq SS	Adj SS	Adj MS	F	P
Main Effects	5	7.332	7.332	1.4663	2.98	0.046
2-Way Interactions	10	49.231	49.231	4.9231	10.01	0.000
3-Way Interactions	1	11.400	11.400	11.4003	23.19	0.000
Residual Error	15	7.375	7.375	0.4916		

FIGURE 8.24
JMP ANOVA Model
for the Cake Mix
Example

▼ Response Rating

▶ Actual by Predicted Plot

▶ Summary of Fit

▼ Analysis of Variance

Source	DF	Sum of Squares	Mean Square	F Ratio
Model	16	67.962500	4.24766	8.6397
Error	15	7.374688	0.49165	Prob > F
C. Total	31	75.337188		<.0001*

▼ Parameter Estimates

Term	Estimate	Std Error	t Ratio	Prob>|t|
Intercept	4.759375	0.123951	38.40	<.0001*
Flour[low]	-0.215625	0.123951	-1.74	0.1024
Shortening[low]	-0.171875	0.123951	-1.39	0.1858
Egg Powder[low]	-0.390625	0.123951	-3.15	0.0066*
ovenTemp[low]	0.021875	0.123951	0.18	0.8623
BakeTime[low]	0.003125	0.123951	0.03	0.9802
Flour[low]*Shortening[low]	0.065625	0.123951	0.53	0.6042
Flour[low]*Egg Powder[low]	-0.040625	0.123951	-0.33	0.7476
Flour[low]*ovenTemp[low]	0.196875	0.123951	1.59	0.1331
Flour[low]*BakeTime[low]	-0.046875	0.123951	-0.38	0.7106
Shortening[low]*Egg Powder[low]	-0.496875	0.123951	-4.01	0.0011*
Shortening[low]*ovenTemp[low]	0.065625	0.123951	0.53	0.6042
Shortening[low]*BakeTime[low]	0.121875	0.123951	0.98	0.3411
Egg Powder[low]*ovenTemp[low]	0.146875	0.123951	1.18	0.2545
Egg Powder[low]*BakeTime[low]	0.028125	0.123951	0.23	0.8236
ovenTemp[low]*BakeTime[low]	-1.096875	0.123951	-8.85	<.0001*
Flour[low]*ovenTemp[low]*BakeTime[low]	-0.596875	0.123951	-4.82	0.0002*

From Figure 8.23 or 8.24, using the 0.05 level of significance, you see that factor C (Egg Powder) with a p-value of 0.007, the BC (Shortening–Egg Powder) interaction (p-value = 0.001), the DE (Oven Temperature–Bake Time) interaction (p-value = 0.000), and the ADE (Flour–Oven Temperature–Bake Time) interaction (p-value = 0.000) are all highly significant. The significance of these interactions complicates any interpretation of the main effects. Although egg powder significantly affects taste rating (with high amount providing a better rating than low amount), the significance of the shortening–egg powder interaction means that the difference in egg powder is not the same for the two levels of shortening. Because neither effect D

nor E was significant, the significance of the DE (Oven Temperature–Bake Time) interaction indicates a crossing effect (see Figures 8.27 and 8.28). This occurs because the rating is high for low oven temperature and high baking time and for high oven temperature and low baking time. The significance of the ADE (Flour–Oven Temperature–Bake Time) interaction means that the interaction of oven temperature and baking time is not the same for low and high amounts of flour.

Figure 8.25 and 8.26 present main effects plots, and Figures 8.27 and 8.28 are interaction plots for the cake mix design.

FIGURE 8.25

Minitab Main Effects Plots for the Cake Mix Design

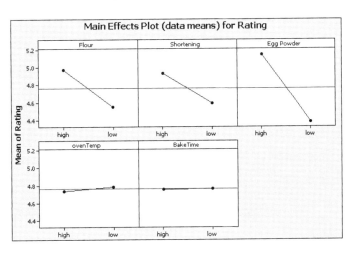

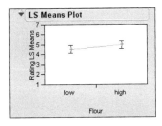 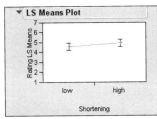 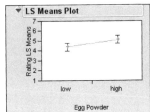

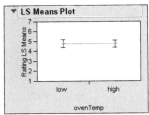 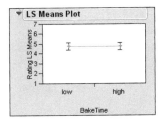

FIGURE 8.26   JMP Main Effects Plots for the Cake Mix Design

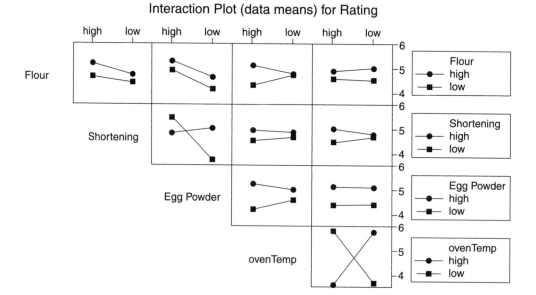

FIGURE 8.27   Minitab Interaction Plots for the Cake Mix Design

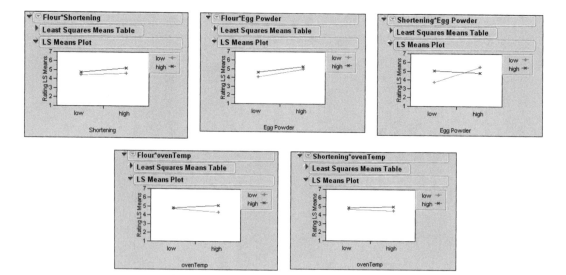

FIGURE 8.28   JMP Interaction Plots for the Cake Mix Design (Continues)

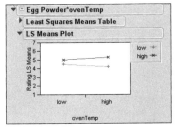
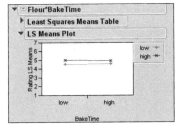
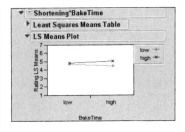

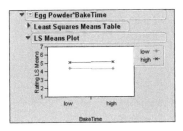
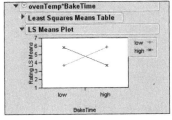

FIGURE 8.28   JMP Interaction Plots for the Cake Mix Design (Continued)

To further your understanding of these results, you can examine the interaction plots in Figures 8.27 and 8.28 along with Tables 8.12–8.15, which provide the mean values for combinations of shortening and egg powder, oven temperature and baking temperature, and oven temperature and baking time for each level of flour.

TABLE 8.12   Mean Rating for Each Level of Shortening and Egg Powder

	Egg Powder	
Shortening	**Low**	**High**
Low	3.7000	5.475
High	5.0375	4.825

TABLE 8.13   Mean Rating for Each Level of Oven Temperature and Baking Time

	Baking Time	
Oven Temperature	**Low**	**High**
Low	3.6875	5.8750
High	5.8375	3.6375

TABLE 8.14   Mean Rating for Each Level of Oven Temperature and Baking Time for the Low Level of Flour

Oven Temperature	Baking Time	
	Low	**High**
Low	3.025	6.500
High	5.975	2.675

TABLE 8.15   Mean Rating for Each Level of Oven Temperature and Baking Time for the High Level of Flour

Oven Temperature	Baking Time	
	Low	**High**
Low	4.35	5.25
High	5.70	4.60

From Figures 8.27 and 8.28 and Table 8.12, you see that for low levels of shortening, the mean rating is much better for the high level of egg powder (5.475) than for the low level of egg powder (3.70). For a high level of shortening, the results are quite different. The rating is slightly better for low egg powder (5.0375) than for high egg powder (4.825).

Turning to the interaction of oven temperature and baking time, from Figures 8.27 and 8.28 and Table 8.13, you see that the mean rating is best for low oven temperature and high baking time (5.875) or high oven temperature and low baking time (5.8375). The rating is worse when there is both low oven temperature and low baking time (3.6875) or high oven temperature and high baking time (3.6375). However, the interaction of oven temperature and baking time is different for each of the two levels of flour. From Tables 8.14 and 8.15, the interaction seen in Table 8.13 is much more pronounced for the low level of flour than for the high level of flour.

Thus, how can you choose the level of flour, shortening, and egg powder that will result in the highest rating? Based on these results, you probably should choose high flour, low shortening, and high egg powder. The rationale for this is as follows:

1. Based on Tables 8.14 and 8.15, using a high level of flour will improve the rating and reduce the effect of oven temperature and baking time.
2. Based on Table 8.12, using a low level of shortening and a high level of egg powder provides the best rating.
3. In addition, the consumer should be warned not to use oven temperature and baking time that are both too low or both too high.

8.4 FRACTIONAL FACTORIAL DESIGNS

When you are considering four or more factors (Xs), simultaneously running all possible treatment combinations often becomes costly or impossible. For example, 4 factors each with 2 levels involve 16 treatment combinations; 5 factors each with 2 levels involve 32 treatment combinations; and 7 factors each with 2 levels involve 128 treatment combinations. Thus, as the number of factors in an experiment increases, Six Sigma team members need to have a rational way of choosing a subset of the treatment combinations so that they can conduct a cost-effective experiment with meaningful results. One way to do this is through the use of a fractional factorial design.

In a **fractional factorial design**, you use only a subset of all possible treatment combinations. However, as a consequence of reducing experimental size, you will not be able to independently estimate all the effects. In other words, there is a loss of information. If you design the experiment appropriately, higher order interactions often can be confounded with lower order terms. You assume that the higher order interaction effects are negligible, so what remains are relatively good estimates of the lower order interactions. If you reduce the experimental size too much, lower order interactions, such as two-factor interactions, may become confounded with main effects or other two-factor interactions. It is advantageous to use fractional designs that allow good estimates of main effects and two-factor interactions. One approach is to choose the treatment combinations so that each main effect can be independently estimated without being confused or confounded with any estimate of the two-factor interactions. When a main effect or an interaction is **confounded**, its effect cannot be isolated from the main effect of some other factor or interaction.

Designs in which main effects are confounded with two-way interactions (such as A being confounded with BC) are called **Resolution III designs**. In other words, confounding main effects (one factor) with two-way interactions (two factors) yields Resolution III designs (one factor + two-way interaction = Resolution III design).

In **Resolution IV designs**, a two-way interaction, such as AB, is confounded with another two-way interaction, such as CD (two-way interaction + two-way interaction = Resolution IV design), or a main effect such as A is confounded with a three-way interaction, such as BCD (one factor + three-way interaction = Resolution IV design).

In **Resolution V designs**, main effects and two-way interactions are confounded with three-way or higher order interactions (such as ABC or $ABCD$). In other words, confounding main effects (one factor) with four-way interactions (four factors) yields Resolution V designs (one factor + four-way interaction = Resolution V design). Also, confounding two-way interactions (two factors) with three-way interactions (three factors) yields Resolution V designs (two-way interaction + three-way interaction = Resolution V design).

Choosing the Treatment Combinations

To choose a subset of the treatment combinations, you can begin with the 2^4 design. Table 8.16 presents the 16 possible treatment combinations for this full factorial design, along with the pattern of pluses and minuses for the main effects (the columns headed by $A, B, C,$ and D) and the $ABCD$ interaction.

TABLE 8.16   Treatment Combinations for the 2^4 Design in Standard Order

Notation	A	B	C	D	ABCD
(1)	–	–	–	–	+
a	+	–	–	–	–
b	–	+	–	–	–
ab	+	+	–	–	+
c	–	–	+	–	–
ac	+	–	+	–	+
bc	–	+	+	–	+
abc	+	+	+	–	–
d	–	–	–	+	–
ad	+	–	–	+	+
bd	–	+	–	+	+
abd	+	+	–	+	–
cd	–	–	+	+	+
acd	+	–	+	+	–
bcd	–	+	+	+	–
abcd	+	+	+	+	+

In a fractional factorial design with four factors in which half the treatment combinations are chosen, only eight treatment combinations are available from the possible 16 combinations. With only eight treatment combinations, you cannot estimate as many effects as compared with the full factorial 2^4 design, in which there are 16 combinations. If you are willing to assume that the four-way interaction, $ABCD$, is not significant, the fraction or subset of eight treatment combinations (called a *half-replicate*) out of the possible 16 could be selected, so that either:

1. The eight treatment combinations all have a plus sign in the column headed by $ABCD$.

2. The eight treatment combinations all have a minus sign in the column headed by $ABCD$.

If you use such a design, the $ABCD$ interaction is the **defining contrast**, from which the factors and interactions that are confounded with each other can be determined. With $ABCD$ as the defining contrast, factor A is confounded with interaction BCD because A and $ABCD$ differ only by BCD. BCD is also called an **alias** of A, because the effects of BCD and A cannot be separated in this fractional factorial design. Thus, the A main effect is equivalent to the BCD interaction. If you are willing to assume that the BCD interaction is negligible, when you evaluate the mean main effect of A, you state that this is the effect of factor A (even though it could have been the effect of the BCD interaction). If the half-replicate chosen has a plus sign in column $ABCD$, then A is confounded with BCD. If the half-replicate chosen has a minus sign in column $ABCD$, then A is confounded with $-BCD$. In a similar manner, B is confounded with ACD, C is confounded with ABD, D is confounded with ABC, AB is confounded with CD, AC is confounded with BD, and AD is confounded with BC. Thus, this design is a Resolution IV design.

From this pattern of confounded effects, observe that in this design (which is called a 2^{4-1} fractional factorial design), the two-factor interaction terms are confounded with each other. Thus, you cannot separate AB and CD, AC and BD, and AD and BC. If any of these interaction terms are found to be important, you will not be able to know whether the effect is due to one term or the other.

As a first example of a fractional factorial design, a 2^{4-1} design in which eight treatments have been chosen from the total of 16 possible combinations and the defining contrast is $ABCD$ is considered. In addition to the experimental design used in Section 8.3 on page 171, the hotel decided to conduct an experiment in its restaurant kitchen to measure the preparation time for various meals. The four factors studied were whether there was a dessert (no or yes), the number of side dishes (less than two or two or more), whether the side dishes included a potato (no or yes), and the type of entrée (fish or meat). The restaurant was only able to conduct this experiment with eight meals at a particular time. A half-replicate of a full factorial design was used. Table 8.17 shows the full factorial design.

The half-replicate (using only the plus signs from the $ABCD$ column) from the defining contrast ($ABCD$) is shown in Table 8.18.

TABLE 8.17   Sixteen Treatment Combinations in a 2^4 Experiment in Standard Order

Notation	Mean Preparation Time (Y)	A	B	C	D	Defining Contrast ABCD
(1)		−	−	−	−	+
a		+	−	−	−	−
b		−	+	−	−	−
ab		+	+	−	−	+
c		−	−	+	−	−
ac		+	−	+	−	+
bc		−	+	+	−	+
abc		+	+	+	−	−
d		−	−	−	+	−
ad		+	−	−	+	+
bd		−	+	−	+	+
abd		+	+	−	+	−
cd		−	−	+	+	+
acd		+	−	+	+	−
bcd		−	+	+	+	−
abcd		+	+	+	+	+

TABLE 8.18   Preparation Time for Eight Treatment Combinations in the 2^{4-1} Experiment in Standard Order

Notation	Preparation Time	A	B	C	D	AB+ CD	AC+ BD	AD+ BC
(1)	17.7	−	−	−	−	+	+	+
ab	24.0	+	+	−	−	+	−	−
ac	21.7	+	−	+	−	−	+	−
bc	22.8	−	+	+	−	−	−	+
ad	27.2	+	−	−	+	−	−	+
bd	28.3	−	+	−	+	−	+	−
cd	30.4	−	−	+	+	+	−	−
abcd	36.5	+	+	+	+	+	+	+

In this design, the two-way interactions are confounded with each other; specifically, AB with CD, AC with BD, and AD with BC. This is a Resolution IV design.

Using the results presented in Table 8.18, for this 2^{4-1} design, you can evaluate $2^{4-1} - 1 = 7$ effects (A, B, C, D, AB, AC, and AD), as long as you realize that A is confounded with BCD, B is confounded with ACD, C is confounded with ABD, D is confounded with ABC, AB is confounded with CD, AC is confounded with BD, and AD is confounded with BC. Figure 8.29 provides the mean effects for these factors computed by Minitab. Figure 8.30 includes the coefficients (half the effects) computed by JMP.

FIGURE 8.29
Minitab Estimated Effects for the Meal Preparation Fractional Factorial Design

```
Estimated Effects and Coefficients for Preparation Time (coded units)

Term                    Effect      Coef
Constant                          26.0750
Dessert                 2.5500    1.2750
Side Dishes             3.6500    1.8250
Potato                  3.5500    1.7750
Entree                  9.0500    4.5250
Dessert*Side Dishes     2.1500    1.0750
Dessert*Potato         -0.0500   -0.0250
Dessert*Entree         -0.0500   -0.0250
```

FIGURE 8.30
JMP Estimated Coefficients for the Meal Preparation Fractional Factorial Design

Response Preparation Time				
▶ **Summary of Fit**				
▶ **Analysis of Variance**				
▼ **Parameter Estimates**				
Term	Estimate	Std Error	t Ratio	Prob>|t|
Intercept	26.075	.	.	.
Dessert[No]	-1.275	.	.	.
Side Dishes[Less than two]	-1.825	.	.	.
Potato[No]	-1.775	.	.	.
Entree[Fish]	-4.525	.	.	.
Dessert[No]*Side Dishes[Less than two]	1.075	.	.	.
Dessert[No]*Potato[No]	-0.025	.	.	.
Dessert[No]*Entree[Fish]	-0.025	.	.	.

These mean effects are depicted in Figures 8.31 and 8.32 in a normal probability plot and a half-normal probability plot.

FIGURE 8.31
Minitab Normal Probability Plot for the 2^{4-1} Design for the Meal Preparation Experiment

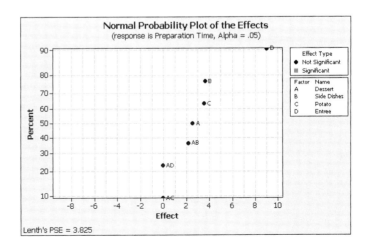

FIGURE 8.32
JMP Half-Normal
Probability Plot for
the 2^{4-1} Design for the
Meal Preparation
Experiment

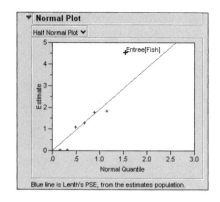

Figures 8.33 and 8.34 are main effects plots, and Figures 8.35 and 8.36 are interaction plots.

FIGURE 8.33
Minitab Main Effects
Plots for the 2^{4-1}
Design for the
Meal Preparation
Experiment

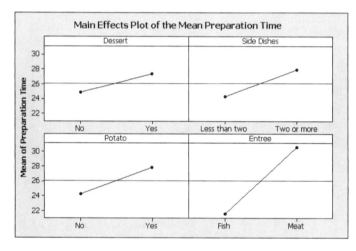

FIGURE 8.34
JMP Main Effects
Plots for the 2^{4-1}
Design for the
Meal Preparation
Experiment

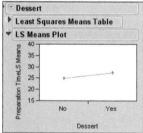
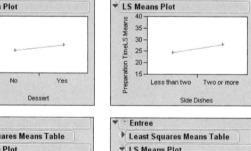
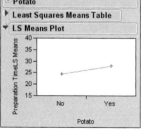
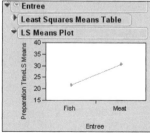

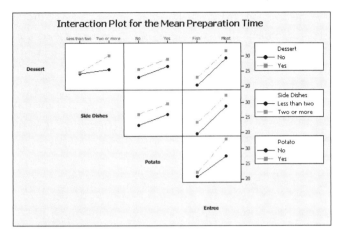

FIGURE 8.35   Minitab Interaction Plots for the 2^{4-1} Design for the Meal Preparation Experiment

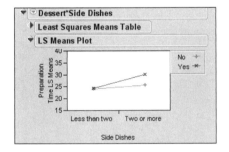

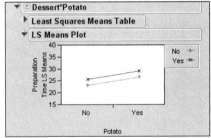

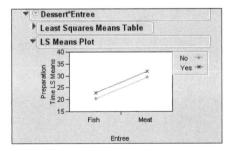

FIGURE 8.36   JMP Interaction Plots for the 2^{4-1} Design for the Meal Preparation Experiment

From Figure 8.31 or 8.32, you see that factor D appears to plot away from a straight line that is approximately zero on the X axis. From Figure 8.33 or 8.34, you can see that that the mean preparation time is higher for meat than for fish entrées. From Figure 8.35 or 8.36, only the interaction of dessert and number of side dishes might be important.

After considering the results of this experiment, management of the hotel decided to conduct another experiment to study the preparation time of meals that involved five factors (Xs). These factors were (A), the type of entrée (fish or meat); (B), the type of beverage (cold versus warm); (C), the order volume in the kitchen at the time of the order (low versus high); (D), whether there was a dessert (no or yes); and (E), the complexity of the meal (low versus high). Because the restaurant was only able to study 16 different treatment combinations, a 2^{5-1} design, a half-replicate of a 2^5 design, was used. The standard order matrix for a full factorial 2^5 design is shown in Table 8.19.

TABLE 8.19   Standard Order Design Matrix for a Full Factorial 2^5 Experiment

Notation	Response Variable (Y)	A	B	C	D	E	ABCDE
(1)		−	−	−	−	−	−
a		+	−	−	−	−	+
b		−	+	−	−	−	+
ab		+	+	−	−	−	−
c		−	−	+	−	−	+
ac		+	−	+	−	−	−
bc		−	+	+	−	−	−
abc		+	+	+	−	−	+
d		−	−	−	+	−	+
ad		+	−	−	+	−	−
bd		−	+	−	+	−	−
abd		+	+	−	+	−	+
cd		−	−	+	+	−	−
acd		+	−	+	+	−	+
bcd		−	+	+	+	−	+
abcd		+	+	+	+	−	−
e		−	−	−	−	+	+
ae		+	−	−	−	+	−
be		−	+	−	−	+	−
abe		+	+	−	−	+	+
ce		−	−	+	−	+	−
ace		+	−	+	−	+	+
bce		−	+	+	−	+	+
abce		+	+	+	−	+	−

Notation	Response Variable (Y)	A	B	C	D	E	ABCDE
de		−	−	−	+	+	−
ade		+	−	−	+	+	+
bde		−	+	−	+	+	+
abde		+	+	−	+	+	−
cde		−	−	+	+	+	+
acde		+	−	+	+	+	−
bcde		−	+	+	+	+	−
abcde		+	+	+	+	+	+

Table 8.20 presents the results of the half-replicate experiment (using the minus signs in the $ABCDE$ column).

TABLE 8.20   Data for the Meal Preparation Study Involving Five Factors

Treatment Combination	Preparation Time	Treatment Combination	Preparation Time
(1)	10.3	ae	27.9
ab	26.4	be	18.5
ac	32.8	ce	30.9
bc	26.8	abce	43.1
ad	24.6	de	20.9
bd	16.8	abde	29.7
cd	27.6	acde	44.6
abcd	33.8	bcde	38.0

PREPARATION2

The subset or fraction of 16 treatment combinations used in Table 8.20 is based on the five-factor interaction $ABCDE$ as the defining contrast. This produces a Resolution V design in which you can estimate all main effects and two-factor interactions independently of each other. Each main effect is confounded with a four-factor interaction, and each two-factor interaction is confounded with a three-factor interaction. For this design, Table 8.21 summarizes the set of confounded effects.

TABLE 8.21   Confounded Effects for the 2^{5-1} Design with *ABCDE* as the Defining Contrast

Effect	Confounded With	Effect	Confounded With
A	*BCDE*	*AE*	*BCD*
B	*ACDE*	*BC*	*ADE*
C	*ABDE*	*BD*	*ACE*
D	*ABCE*	*BE*	*ACD*
E	*ABCD*	*CD*	*ABE*
AB	*CDE*	*CE*	*ABD*
AC	*BDE*	*DE*	*ABC*
AD	*BCE*		

Figure 8.37 provides the mean effects for these factors computed by Minitab. Figure 8.38 includes the coefficients (half the effects) computed by JMP.

FIGURE 8.37
Estimated Effects from Minitab for the Five-Factor Meal Preparation Fractional Factorial Design

```
Estimated Effects and Coefficients for Preparation Time (coded units)

Term                       Effect      Coef
Constant                              28.2938
Entree                     9.1375     4.5688
Beverage                   1.6875     0.8438
Order Volume              12.8125     6.4063
Dessert                    2.4125     1.2063
Complexity                 6.8125     3.4063
Entree*Beverage           -0.9125    -0.4563
Entree*Order Volume       -1.3875    -0.6937
Entree*Dessert            -1.7875    -0.8938
Entree*Complexity          0.1125     0.0563
Beverage*Order Volume     -0.2375    -0.1187
Beverage*Dessert          -1.5375    -0.7688
Beverage*Complexity       -0.4375    -0.2187
Order Volume*Dessert       0.1875     0.0938
Order Volume*Complexity    2.0875     1.0437
Dessert*Complexity         0.7875     0.3938
```

FIGURE 8.38
Estimated Coefficients from JMP for the Five-Factor Meal Preparation Fractional Factorial Design

```
▼ ▽ Response Preparation Time
  ▶ Summary of Fit
  ▼ Parameter Estimates
    Term                                   Estimate   Std Error  t Ratio  Prob>|t|
    Intercept                              28.29375       .         .        .
    Entree[Fish]                           -4.56875       .         .        .
    Beverage[Cold]                         -0.84375       .         .        .
    Order Volume[Low]                      -6.40625       .         .        .
    Dessert[No]                            -1.20625       .         .        .
    Complexity[Low]                        -3.40625       .         .        .
    Entree[Fish]*Beverage[Cold]            -0.45625       .         .        .
    Entree[Fish]*Order Volume[Low]         -0.69375       .         .        .
    Entree[Fish]*Dessert[No]               -0.89375       .         .        .
    Entree[Fish]*Complexity[Low]            0.05625       .         .        .
    Beverage[Cold]*Order Volume[Low]       -0.11875       .         .        .
    Beverage[Cold]*Dessert[No]             -0.76875       .         .        .
    Beverage[Cold]*Complexity[Low]         -0.21875       .         .        .
    Order Volume[Low]*Dessert[No]           0.09375       .         .        .
    Order Volume[Low]*Complexity[Low]       1.04375       .         .        .
    Dessert[No]*Complexity[Low]             0.39375       .         .        .
```

Figure 8.39 and 8.40 are a Minitab normal probability plot and a JMP half-normal plot for the meal preparation experiment.

FIGURE 8.39
Minitab Normal Probability Plot for the Meal Preparation Experiment

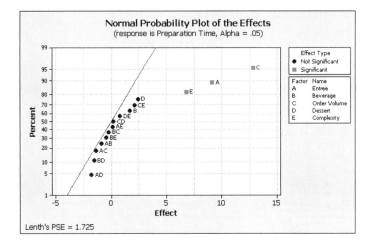

FIGURE 8.40
JMP Half-Normal Probability Plot for the Meal Preparation Experiment

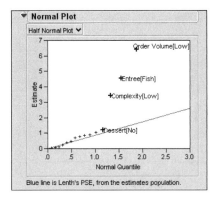

From Figures 8.39 or 8.40, you see that factors A, C, and E plot far away from the straight line that is approximately zero on the X axis. Minitab indicates that these terms are statistically significant according to criteria developed by Lenth [see Reference 10]. Thus, you can consider all interactions as consisting only of random error. You can eliminate these interaction effects from the ANOVA model and combine them to estimate an error variance. Figures 8.41 and 8.42 represent The ANOVA model with these interaction effects combined into an error variance.

FIGURE 8.41
ANOVA Model from
Minitab for the Meal
Preparation
Experiment

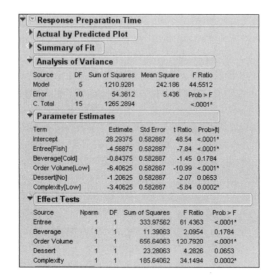

```
Estimated Effects and Coefficients for Preparation Time (coded units)

Term            Effect     Coef   SE Coef      T      P
Constant                28.2938    0.5829   48.54  0.000
Entree          9.1375   4.5688    0.5829    7.84  0.000
Beverage        1.6875   0.8438    0.5829    1.45  0.178
Order Volume   12.8125   6.4063    0.5829   10.99  0.000
Dessert         2.4125   1.2062    0.5829    2.07  0.065
Complexity      6.8125   3.4063    0.5829    5.84  0.000


S = 2.33155   R-Sq = 95.70%   R-Sq(adj) = 93.56%


Analysis of Variance for Preparation Time (coded units)

Source          DF   Seq SS   Adj SS   Adj MS      F      P
Main Effects     5  1210.93  1210.93  242.186  44.55  0.000
Residual Error  10    54.36    54.36    5.436
Total           15  1265.29
```

FIGURE 8.42
ANOVA Model from
JMP for the Meal
Preparation
Experiment

▼ ⊟ **Response Preparation Time**
▶ **Actual by Predicted Plot**
▶ **Summary of Fit**
▼ **Analysis of Variance**

Source	DF	Sum of Squares	Mean Square	F Ratio
Model	5	1210.9281	242.186	44.5512
Error	10	54.3612	5.436	Prob > F
C. Total	15	1265.2894		<.0001*

▼ **Parameter Estimates**

Term	Estimate	Std Error	t Ratio	Prob>|t|
Intercept	28.29375	0.582887	48.54	<.0001*
Entree[Fish]	-4.56875	0.582887	-7.84	<.0001*
Beverage[Cold]	-0.84375	0.582887	-1.45	0.1784
Order Volume[Low]	-6.40625	0.582887	-10.99	<.0001*
Dessert[No]	-1.20625	0.582887	-2.07	0.0653
Complexity[Low]	-3.40625	0.582887	-5.84	0.0002*

▼ **Effect Tests**

Source	Nparm	DF	Sum of Squares	F Ratio	Prob > F
Entree	1	1	333.97562	61.4363	<.0001*
Beverage	1	1	11.39063	2.0954	0.1784
Order Volume	1	1	656.64063	120.7920	<.0001*
Dessert	1	1	23.28063	4.2826	0.0653
Complexity	1	1	185.64062	34.1494	0.0002*

From Figures 8.41 or 8.42, you see that the main effects of entrée, order volume, and complexity of the meal are highly significantly with p-values of 0.000.

Figures 8.43 and 8.44 are main effects plots, and Figures 8.45 and 8.46 are interaction plots.

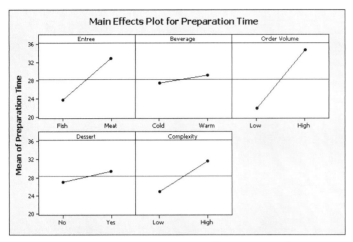

FIGURE 8.43   Minitab Main Effects Plots for the Meal Preparation Experiment

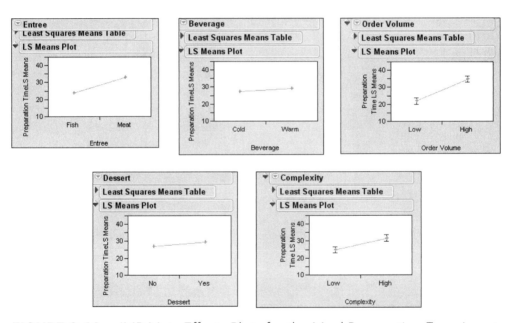

FIGURE 8.44   JMP Main Effects Plots for the Meal Preparation Experiment

FIGURE 8.45
Minitab Interaction
Plots for the Meal
Preparation
Experiment

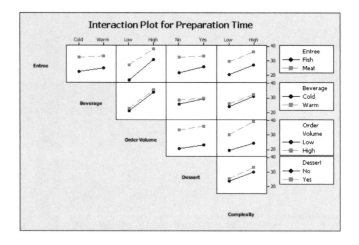

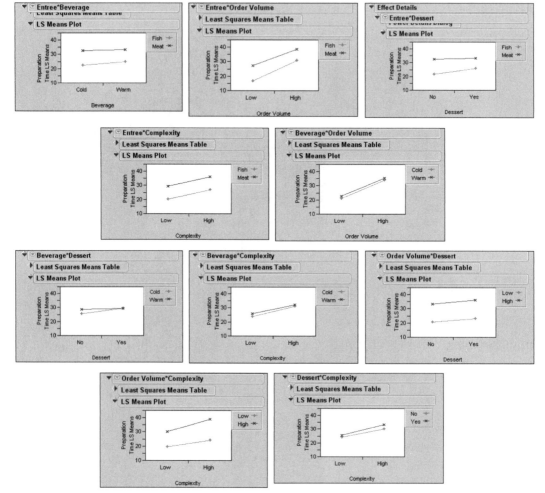

FIGURE 8.46   JMP Interaction Plots for the Meal Preparation Experiment

From Figures 8.41 and 8.42, you see that the mean preparation time is higher by 9.1375 minutes for meat entrées as compared to fish entrées, is higher by 1.6875 minutes for warm beverages than for cold beverages, is higher by 12.8125 minutes when there is high order volume, is higher by 2.4125 minutes when there is a dessert ordered, and is higher by 6.8125 minutes when the meal is highly complex. Consistent with the results of Figure 8.39 or 8.40 on page 199, none of the interactions appear to be important.

In this section, two fractional factorial designs that you can use when it is not feasible to evaluate all possible treatment combinations have been discussed. These two designs are only a small subset of the many fractional factorial designs that you can use. The 2^{4-1} and 2^{5-1} designs are examples of designs that involve the selection of a half-replicate (8 out of 16 or 16 out of 32 treatment combinations) of a full factorial design. Other designs you can consider involve a quarter-replicate (such as 2^{5-2} and 2^{6-2} designs) or even smaller replicates in which only main effects can be estimated (for instance, a 2^{15-11} design). For further information, see References 7, 9, and 12.

S U M M A R Y

In this chapter, the basic aspects of Design of Experiments were developed. You have seen how the factorial design, by allowing for the measurement of the size of interaction effects, offers a substantial benefit as compared with the one-factor design. Although several designs were discussed, be aware that the topics covered in this book have barely "scratched the surface" of the subject of the Design of Experiments. For further information, see References 7, 9, and 12.

R E F E R E N C E S

1. Bisgaard, S. "Industrial Use of Statistically Designed Experiments: Case Study References and Some Historical Anecdotes." *Quality Engineering*, 4, 1992, 547–562.

2. Box, G.E.P. "Do Interactions Matter?" *Quality Engineering*, 2, 1990, 365–369.

3. Box, G.E.P. "What Can You Find Out from Eight Experimental Runs." *Quality Engineering*, 4, 1992, 619–627.

4. Box, J. F. "R. A. Fisher and the Design of Experiments." *American Statistician*, 34, 1980. 1–10.

5. Daniel, C. "Use of Half-Normal Plots in Interpreting Factorial Two-Level Experiments." *Technometrics*, 1, 1959, 311–341.

6. Gitlow, H.S. and D. M. Levine. *Six Sigma for Green Belts and Champions* (Upper Saddle River, NJ: Financial Times Prentice Hall, 2005).

7. Hicks, C. R. and K. V. Turner. *Fundamental Concepts in the Design of Experiments*, 5th Ed. (New York: Oxford University Press, 1999).

8. *JMP Version 6* (Cary, NC: SAS Institute, 2005).

9. Kutner, M. H., C. Nachtsheim, J. Neter, and W. Li. *Applied Linear Statistical Models*, 5th Ed. (New York: McGraw-Hill-Irwin, 2005).

10. Lenth, R. V. "Quick and Easy Analysis of Unreplicated Factorials." *Technometrics*, 31, 1989, 469–473.

11. *Minitab for Windows Version 14* (State College, PA: Minitab, 2004).

12. Montgomery, D. C. *Design and Analysis of Experiments*, 6th Ed. (New York: John Wiley, 2005).

Appendix 8.1
Using Minitab for the Design of Experiments

Two-Way ANOVA

To generate a two-way ANOVA, open the **BREAKFAST.MTW** worksheet. Select **Stat → ANOVA → Two-Way**, then do the following:

1. In the Two-Way Analysis of Variance dialog box (see Figure A8.1), enter **C1** or **'Delivery Time Difference'** in the Response: edit box.

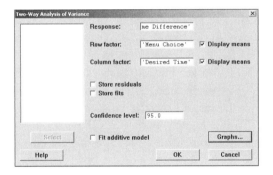

FIGURE A8.1
Minitab Two-Way Analysis of Variance Dialog Box

2. In the Row Factor: edit box, enter **C2** or **'Menu Choice'**. Select the **Display means** check box.
3. In the Column Factor: edit box, enter **C3** or **'Desired Time'**. Select the **Display means** check box.
4. Click the **OK** button.

Main Effects Plot

To generate a main effects plot using Minitab, open the **BREAKFAST.MTW** worksheet. Select **Stat → ANOVA → Main Effects Plot**, then do the following:

1. In the Main Effects Plot dialog box (see Figure A8.2), enter **C1** or **'Delivery Time Difference'** in the Responses: edit box.

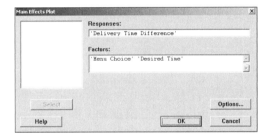

FIGURE A8.2
Minitab Main Effects Plot Dialog Box

2. In the Factors: edit box, enter **C2** or **'Menu Choice'** and **C3** or **'Desired Time'**.
3. Click the **OK** button.

Interaction Plot

To generate an interaction plot using Minitab, open the **BREAKFAST.MTW** worksheet. Select **Stat → ANOVA → Interactions Plot**, then do the following:

1. In the Interactions Plot dialog box (see Figure A8.3), enter **C1** or **'Delivery Time Difference'** in the Responses: edit box.

FIGURE A8.3
Minitab Interactions Plot Dialog Box

2. In the Factors: edit box, enter **C2** or **'Menu Choice'** and **C3** or **'Desired Time'**.
3. Click the **OK** button.

Factorial Design

To compute the estimated effects and ANOVA in a factorial design along with a normal probability plot of the effects, open the **CAKE.MTW** worksheet. Select **Stat → DOE → Factorial → Analyze Factorial Design**, then do the following:

1. Click **Yes** in the Minitab dialog box (see Figure A8.4) that appears because Minitab has not yet created a design.
2. In the Define Custom Factorial Design dialog box (see Figure A8.5), enter **C1** or **Flour**, **C2** or **Shortening**, **C3** or **Egg Powder**, **C4** or **ovenTemp**, and **C5** or **BakeTime** in the Factors: edit box. Select the **2-level factorial** option button. Click the **Low/High** button.

FIGURE A8.4
Minitab Dialog Box to Create a Design

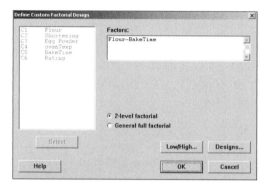

FIGURE A8.5
Minitab Define Custom Factorial Design Dialog Box

3. Enter the low and high values for each factor in the Design Custom Factorial Design—Low/High dialog box (see Figure A8.6). Click the **OK** button to return to the Design Custom Factorial Design dialog box. Click the **OK** button.
4. In the Analyze Factorial Design dialog box (see Figure A8.7), enter **C6** or **Rating** in the Responses: edit box.

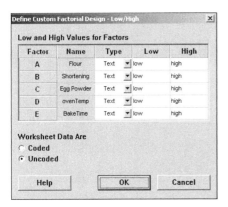

FIGURE A8.6
Minitab Define Custom Factorial
Design—Low/High Dialog Box

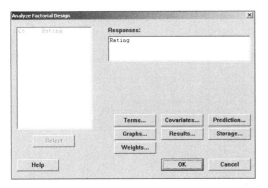

FIGURE A8.7
Minitab Analyze Factorial Design
Dialog Box

5. Click the **Terms** button. In the Analyze Factorial Design—Terms dialog box (see Figure A8.8), because this is a full factorial design, enter **5** in the Include terms in the model up through order: drop-down list box. (Use arrow keys to add terms and delete terms if desired.) Click the **OK** button.

FIGURE A8.8
Minitab Analyze Factorial Design—
Terms Dialog Box

6. In the Analyze Factorial Design dialog box (see Figure A8.7), click the **Graphs** button. In the Analyze Factorial Design—Graphs dialog box (see Figure A8.9), under Effects Plots, select the **Normal** check box to generate a normal probability plot for the effects. (Select Pareto to generate a Pareto diagram of the effects.) Click the **OK** button.

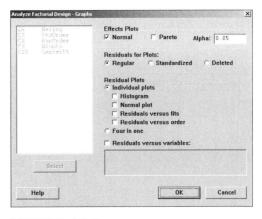

FIGURE A8.9
Minitab Analyze Factorial Design—
Graphs Dialog Box

7. In the Analyze Factorial Design dialog box (see Figure A8.7), click the **OK** button.

8. To label all the effects on the normal probability plot, right-click on the normal probability plot and select **Graph Options**. Select the **Label all effects** option button.

Fractional Factorial Design

Follow the steps shown for the factorial design, except for step 5. In the Analyze Factorial Design—Terms dialog box, enter the value in the edit box that indicates the highest interactions included in the model. For example, in the 2^{4-1} fractional factorial design used for the meal preparation example, open the **PREPARATION.MTW** worksheet. In the Analyze Factorial Design—Terms dialog box (see Figure A8.10), enter **2** in the Include terms in the model up through order: edit box because only the AB, AC, AD, BC, BD, and CD interactions are to be included.

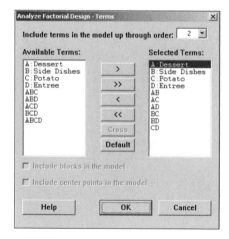

FIGURE A8.10
Minitab Analyze Factorial Design—Terms Dialog Box

Appendix 8.2
Using JMP for the Design of Experiments

You use the **Analyze → Fit Model** selection on the menu bar to generate a two-way ANOVA, a factorial design, or a fractional factorial design.

Two-Way ANOVA

To generate a two-way ANOVA, open the **BREAKFAST.JMP** data table. Select **Analyze → Fit Model**. Then, do the following:

1. In the Model Specification dialog box (see Figure A8.11), select **Delivery Time Difference** and click the **Y** button.

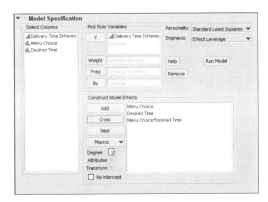

FIGURE A8.11
JMP Fit Model Dialog Box for the Two-Way ANOVA

2. Select **Menu Choice** and click the **Add** button. Select **Desired Time** and click the **Add** button.

3. Select **Menu Choice** and **Desired Time** and click the **Cross** button.

   (Note: Instead of steps 2 and 3, you could select **Menu Choice** and **Desired Time** and select **Full Factorial** in the Macros pop-up menu.)

4. In the Personality drop-down list box, select **Standard Least Squares**.

5. Click the **Run Model** button.

6. To generate a Main Effects Plot, click on the red triangle next to the main effect of interest and select **LSMeans Plot**. For example, to generate a Main Effects Plot for Menu Choice, click the red triangle next to **Menu Choice** and select **LSMeans Plot** (see Figure A8.12).

7. To generate an interaction plot, click the red triangle next to **Menu Choice*Desired Time** and select **LSMeans Plot** (see Figure A8.12).

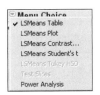

FIGURE A8.12
Generating a JMP Main Effects or Interaction Plot

Factorial Design

To generate a factorial design, open the **DINNER.JMP** data table. Select **Analyze → Fit Model**. Then, do the following:

1. In the Model Specifications dialog box (see Figure A8.11), select **Delivery Time** and click the **Y** button.
2. Select **Complexity**, **Elevator**, and **Order Volume**. In the Macros pop-up menu, select **Full Factorial**.
3. In the Personality drop-down list box, select **Standard Least Squares**.
4. Click the **Run Model** button.
5. To generate a Main Effects Plot, click the red triangle next to the main effect of interest and select **LSMeans Plot**. For example, to generate a Main Effects Plot for Complexity, click the red triangle next to **Complexity** and select **LSMeans Plot**. To generate an interaction plot, click the red triangle next to **Complexity *Order Volume** and select **LSMeans Plot**.
6. To generate a normal probability plot, click the arrow next to the response variable of interest and select **Effect Screening → Normal Plot** (see Figure A8.13). To change the normal probability plot into a half-normal plot in which all the estimates are positive, click the arrow next to **Normal Plot** just above the normal probability plot, and select **Half Normal Plot**.

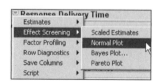

FIGURE A8.13
Generating a JMP Normal Probability Plot

Fractional Factorial Design

Follow all steps shown for the factorial design except for step 2. Open the **PREPARATION.JMP** data table. Select **Analyze → Fit Model**. Then, do the following:

1. In the Fit Model dialog box (see Figure A8.11), select **Preparation Time** and click the **Y** button.
2. Select **Dessert**, **Side Dishes**, **Potato**, and **Entree**. In the Macros pop-up menu, select **Factorial to degree**. Enter **2** in the Degree edit box. Because this is a fractional factorial design with confounded two-factor interactions, select **Side Dishes*Potato**, **Side Dishes * Entree**, and **Potato *Entrée** and click the **Remove** button.
3. In the Personality drop-down list box, select **Standard Least Squares**.
4. Click the **Run Model** button.
5. To generate a Main Effects Plot, click Effect Details, then click the red triangle next to the main effect of interest and select **LSMeans Plot**. For example, to generate a Main Effects Plot for Dessert, click the arrow next to **Dessert** and select **LSMeans Plot**. To generate an interaction plot, click the arrow next to **Dessert * Side Dishes** and select **LSMeans Plot**.
6. To generate a normal probability plot, click the red triangle next to the response variable of interest and select **Effect Screening → Normal Plot** (see Figure A8.13). To change the normal probability plot into a half-normal plot in which the estimates are positive, select **Normal Plot** right above the normal probability plot, and select **Half-Normal**.

CHAPTER 9

Simple Linear Regression

INTRODUCTION

9.1 TYPES OF REGRESSION MODELS

9.2 DETERMINING THE SIMPLE LINEAR REGRESSION EQUATION

9.3 MEASURES OF VARIATION

9.4 ASSUMPTIONS

9.5 RESIDUAL ANALYSIS

9.6 INFERENCES ABOUT THE SLOPE

9.7 ESTIMATION OF PREDICTED VALUES

9.8 PITFALLS IN REGRESSION ANALYSIS

SUMMARY

REFERENCES

APPENDIX 9.1 USING MINITAB FOR SIMPLE LINEAR REGRESSION

APPENDIX 9.2 USING JMP FOR SIMPLE LINEAR REGRESSION

LEARNING OBJECTIVES

After reading this chapter, you will be able to

- Understand how to use regression analysis to predict the value of a dependent variable (CTQ) based on an independent variable (CTP or X).

- Interpret the meaning of the regression coefficients b_0 (Y intercept) and b_1 (slope).

- Evaluate the assumptions of regression analysis and know what to do if the assumptions are violated.

- Make inferences about the slope (b_1).

- Estimate mean values and predict individual values.

INTRODUCTION

In this and the following chapter, you will learn how **regression analysis** allows you to develop a model to predict the values of a numerical variable (CTQ or Y) based on the values of one or more other variables (CTPs or Xs). In regression analysis, the variable you wish to predict is called the **dependent variable** or CTQ. The variables used to make the prediction are called **independent variables** (CTPs or Xs). In addition to predicting values of the dependent variable, regression analysis also allows you to identify the type of mathematical relationship that exists between a dependent and independent variable, to quantify the effect that changes in the independent variable have on the dependent variable, and to identify unusual observations. This chapter discusses **simple linear regression** in which a *single* numerical independent variable X is used to predict the numerical dependent variable Y. Chapter 10, "Multiple Regression," discusses *multiple regression models* that use several independent variables to predict a dependent variable Y.

9.1   TYPES OF REGRESSION MODELS

In Section 3.2, you used the run chart to plot a numerical variable over time. In regression analysis, you use the **scatter plot** to plot the relationship between an X variable on the horizontal axis and a Y variable on the vertical axis. The nature of the relationship between two variables can take many forms, ranging from simple to extremely complicated mathematical functions; for example, from a simple linear relationship to a complex curvilinear or exponential relationship. Figure 9.1 shows the different types of patterns that you could discover when plotting the values of the X and Y variables.

The patterns shown in Figure 9.1 can be described as follows:

- Panel A, positive straight line or linear relationship.
- Panel B, negative straight line or linear relationship.
- Panel C, a positive curvilinear relationship between X and Y. The values of Y are increasing as X increases, but this increase tapers off beyond certain values of X.
- Panel D, a U-shaped relationship between X and Y. As X increases, at first Y decreases. However, as X continues to increase, Y not only stops decreasing but actually increases above its minimum value.
- Panel E, an exponential relationship between X and Y. In this case, Y decreases very rapidly as X first increases, but then decreases much less rapidly as X increases further.
- Panel F, where there is very little or no relationship between X and Y. High and low values of Y appear at each value of X.

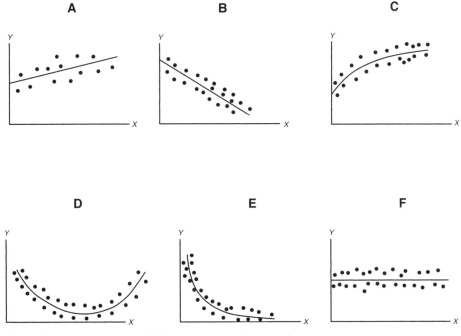

FIGURE 9.1 Types of Patterns in Relationships

Scatter plots only informally help you identify the relationship between the dependent Y and the independent X variables in a simple regression. To specify the numeric relationship between the variables, you need to develop an equation that best represents the relationship.

9.2 DETERMINING THE SIMPLE LINEAR REGRESSION EQUATION

The Y Intercept and the Slope

Once you determine that a straight-line relationship exists between a dependent variable Y and the independent variable X, you need to find the straight line that is the best fit to the data. Two values define any straight line: the Y intercept and the slope.

The **Y intercept** is the value of Y when $X = 0$, represented by the symbol b_0. The **slope** is the change in Y per unit change in X represented by the symbol b_1. A positive slope means Y increases as X increases. A negative slope means Y decreases as X increases. Figure 9.2 illustrates the Y intercept and the slope.

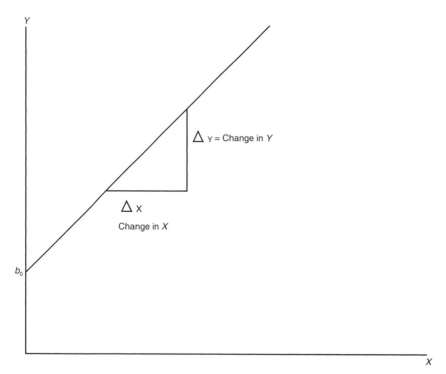

FIGURE 9.2   A Straight Line

You use the Y intercept and the slope to develop the prediction for the dependent variable Y.

$$\text{Predicted } Y = Y \text{ intercept} + (\text{slope} \times X \text{ value})\qquad(9.1a)$$

or

$$\text{Predicted } Y = b_0 + b_1 X\qquad(9.1b)$$

The Y intercept (b_0) and the slope (b_1) are known as the **regression coefficients**. Multiplying a specific X value by the slope and then adding the Y intercept generates the predicted Y value. The equation Predicted $Y = b_0 + b_1 X$ is used to express this relationship for the regression line from the smallest to the largest values of the independent variable (X). It is dangerous to extend the regression line beyond the range of the independent variable because the nature of the relationship between X and Y may change; for example, from linear to curvilinear.

Least-Squares Method

The most common method for finding the Y intercept and the slope is the **least-squares method**. This method minimizes the sum of the squared differences between the actual values of the dependent variable (Y) and the predicted values of the dependent variable.

For plotted sets of X and Y values, there are many possible straight lines, each with their own values of b_0 and b_1, that might seem to fit the data. The least-squares method finds the values for the Y intercept and the slope that makes the sum of the squared differences between the actual values of the dependent variable Y and the predicted values of Y as small as possible.

Calculating the Y intercept and the slope using the least-squares method is tedious and can be subject to rounding errors if you use a simple four-function calculator. You will get more accurate results much faster if you use regression software available in Minitab or JMP to perform the calculations.

You can use simple linear regression analysis to assist a moving company owner to develop a more accurate method of predicting the labor hours needed for a moving job by using the volume of goods (in cubic feet) that are being moved. The manager has collected the following data (shown in Table 9.1) for a random sample of 36 moves for 2005 and has eliminated the travel time portion of the time needed for the move.

TABLE 9.1 Hours and Cubic Feet Moved for a Sample of 36 Moves

Hours	Cubic Feet Moved	Hours	Cubic Feet Moved
24.00	545	25.00	557
13.50	400	45.00	1,028
26.25	562	29.00	793
25.00	540	21.00	523
9.00	220	22.00	564
20.00	344	16.50	312
22.00	569	37.00	757
11.25	340	32.00	600
50.00	900	34.00	796
12.00	285	25.00	577
38.75	865	31.00	500
40.00	831	24.00	695
19.50	344	40.00	1,054
18.00	360	27.00	486
28.00	750	18.00	442
27.00	650	62.50	1,249
21.00	415	53.75	995
15.00	275	79.50	1,397

MOVING

Figure 9.3 is a Minitab scatter plot of the relationship between cubic feet moved and hours. Figure 9.4 is a JMP scatter plot.

FIGURE 9.3
Minitab Scatter
Plot for the Moving
Company Data

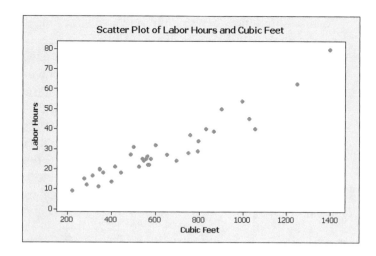

FIGURE 9.4
JMP Scatter Plot for
the Moving Company
Data

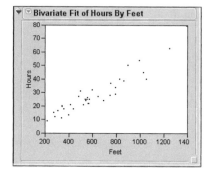

The scatter plot indicates an increasing relationship between cubic feet moved (X) and labor hours (Y). As the cubic footage moved increases, labor hours increase approximately as a straight line.

Figures 9.5 and 9.6 provide Minitab and JMP regression results for the moving company data. Figure 9.7 is a Minitab scatter plot that includes the regression line.

The results show that the slope $b_1 = 0.05008$ and the Y intercept (called constant by Minitab) $b_0 = -2.37$. Thus, the equation for the best straight line for these data is as follows:

Predicted value of labor hours = -2.37 + (0.05 × cubic feet moved)

The slope b_1 was computed as +0.05. This means that for each increase of 1 unit in X, the mean value of Y is estimated to increase by 0.05 units. In other words, for each increase of 1 cubic foot in the amount to be moved, the fitted model predicts that the expected labor hours are estimated to increase by 0.05 hours. The Y intercept b_0 was computed to be -2.37. The Y intercept represents the mean value of Y when X

equals 0. Because the cubic feet moved cannot be below 0, the Y intercept has no practical interpretation. The sample linear regression line for these data, along with the actual observations, is shown in the Figure 9.7.

FIGURE 9.5
Minitab Regression
Results for the Moving
Company Data

```
The regression equation is
Labor Hours = - 2.37 + 0.0501 Cubic Feet

Predictor        Coef    SE Coef      T      P
Constant       -2.370      2.073  -1.14  0.261
Cubic Feet   0.050080   0.003031  16.52  0.000

S = 5.03143    R-Sq = 88.9%   R-Sq(adj) = 88.6%

Analysis of Variance

Source        DF       SS       MS       F      P
Regression     1   6910.7   6910.7  272.99  0.000
Residual Error 34    860.7     25.3
Total         35   7771.4

Predicted Values for New Observations

New
Obs     Fit  SE Fit       95% CI              95% PI
  1  22.670   0.921  (20.799, 24.542)  (12.276, 33.065)
Values of Predictors for New Observations
New   Cubic
Obs    Feet
  1     500
```

FIGURE 9.6
JMP Regression
Results for the Moving
Company Data

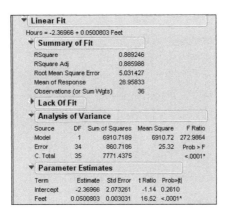

FIGURE 9.7
Minitab Scatter Plot
with Regression Line
for the Moving Com-
pany Data

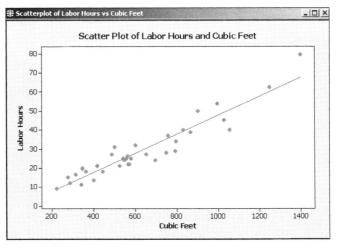

Regression Model Prediction

To reiterate an important point, you can use a regression model for predicting values of a dependent variable (Y) from an independent variable (X) only within the **relevant range** of the independent variable. Again, this range is all values from the smallest to the largest X used to develop the regression model. You should not extrapolate beyond the range of X values. For example, when you use the model developed for the moving company data, predictions of labor hours should be made *only* for moves of 220 through 1,397 cubic feet.

Using the regression model already developed, to predict the mean labor hours for a moving job that consists of 500 cubic feet, you do the following.

$$\text{Prediction line for } Y = Y \text{ intercept} + (\text{slope} \times X \text{ value})$$
$$= \text{-}2.37 + (0.05008 \times 500) = 22.67$$

You predict that the mean labor hours for a move with 500 cubic feet are 22.67 hours.

COMPUTING THE Y INTERCEPT b_0, AND THE SLOPE, b_1 {OPTIONAL}

You use symbols for the Y intercept, b_0, the slope, b_1, the sample size, n, and the following:

- The subscripted YHat, $\hat{Y}_i$, for predicted Y values.
- The subscripted italic capital X for the independent X values.
- The subscripted italic capital Y for the dependent Y values.
- $\bar{X}$ for the arithmetic mean of the X values.
- $\bar{Y}$ for the arithmetic mean of the Y values.

to write the equation for a simple linear regression model:

$$\hat{Y}_i = b_0 + b_1 X_i$$

You use this equation and these summations:

- $\sum_{i=1}^{n} X_i$, the sum of the X values.

- $\sum_{i=1}^{n} Y_i$, the sum of the Y values.

- $\sum_{i=1}^{n} X_i^2$, the sum of the squared X values.

- $\sum_{i=1}^{n} X_i Y_i$, the sum of the product of X and Y.

to define the equation of the slope, b_1, as:

$$b_1 = \frac{SSXY}{SSX} \qquad (9.2)$$

in which

$$SSXY = \sum_{i=1}^{n}(X_i - \bar{X})(Y_i - \bar{Y}) = \sum_{i=1}^{n} X_i Y_i - \frac{\left(\sum_{i=1}^{n} X_i\right)\left(\sum_{i=1}^{n} Y_i\right)}{n}$$

and

$$SSX = \sum_{i=1}^{n}(X_i - \bar{X})^2 = \sum_{i=1}^{n} X_i^2 - \frac{\left(\sum_{i=1}^{n} X_i\right)^2}{n}$$

These equations allow you to define the Y intercept as:

$$b_0 = \bar{Y} - b_1\bar{X} \qquad (9.3)$$

For the moving company problem, these sums and the sum of the squared Y values ($\sum_{i=1}^{n} Y_i^2$) used for calculating the sum of squares total (SST) on page 223 are shown in Table 9.2.

TABLE 9.2 Computations for the Moving Company Example

Move	Hours(Y)	Cubic Feet Moved(X)	X^2	Y^2	XY
1	24.00	545	297,025	576.0000	13,080.00
2	13.50	400	160,000	182.2500	5400.00
3	26.25	562	315,844	689.0625	14,752.50
4	25.00	540	291,600	625.0000	13,500.00
5	9.00	220	48,400	81.0000	1,980.00
6	20.00	344	118,336	400.0000	6,880.00
7	22.00	569	323,761	484.0000	12,518.00
8	11.25	340	115,600	126.5625	3,825.00
9	50.00	900	810,000	2,500.0000	45,000.00
10	12.00	285	81,225	144.0000	3,420.00
11	38.75	865	748,225	1,501.5625	33,518.75

Continues

TABLE 9.2   Computations for the Moving Company Example (Continued)

Move	Hours(Y)	Cubic Feet Moved(X)	X^2	Y^2	XY
12	40.00	831	690,561	1,600.0000	33,240.00
13	19.50	344	118,336	380.2500	6,708.00
14	18.00	360	129,600	324.0000	6,480.00
15	28.00	750	562,500	784.0000	21,000.00
16	27.00	650	422,500	729.0000	17,550.00
17	21.00	415	172,225	441.0000	8,715.00
18	15.00	275	75,625	225.0000	4,125.00
19	25.00	557	310,249	625.0000	13,925.00
20	45.00	1,028	1,056,784	2,025.0000	46,260.00
21	29.00	793	628,849	841.0000	22,997.00
22	21.00	523	273,529	441.0000	10,983.00
23	22.00	564	318,096	484.0000	12,408.00
24	16.50	312	97,344	272.2500	5,148.00
25	37.00	757	573,049	1,369.0000	28,009.00
26	32.00	600	360,000	1,024.0000	19,200.00
27	34.00	796	633,616	1,156.0000	27,064.00
28	25.00	577	332,929	625.0000	14,425.00
29	31.00	500	250,000	961.0000	15,500.00
30	24.00	695	483,025	576.0000	16,680.00
31	40.00	1,054	1,110,916	1,600.0000	42,160.00
32	27.00	486	236,196	729.0000	13,122.00
33	18.00	442	195,364	324.0000	7,956.00
34	62.50	1,249	1,560,001	3,906.2500	78,062.50
35	53.75	995	990,025	2,889.0625	53,481.25
36	79.50	1,397	1,951,609	6,320.2500	111061.50
Sums:	1,042.50	22,520	16,842,944	37,960.5000	790,134.50

Using these sums, you can compute the values of the slope b_1:

$$SSXY = \sum_{i=1}^{n}(X_i - \bar{X})(Y_i - \bar{Y}) = \sum_{i=1}^{n} X_i Y_i - \frac{\left(\sum_{i=1}^{n} X_i\right)\left(\sum_{i=1}^{n} Y_i\right)}{n}$$

$$SSXY = 790,134.5 - \frac{(22,520)(1,042.5)}{36}$$

$$= 790,134.5 - 652,141.66$$
$$= 137,992.84$$

$$SSX = \sum_{i=1}^{n}(X_i - \bar{X})^2 = \sum_{i=1}^{n}X_i^2 - \frac{\left(\sum_{i=1}^{n}X_i\right)^2}{n}$$

$$= 16,842,944 - \frac{(22,520)^2}{36}$$
$$= 16,842,944 - 14,087,511.11$$
$$= 2,755,432.889$$

because

$$b_1 = \frac{SSXY}{SSX}$$

$$b_1 = \frac{137,992.84}{2,755,432.889}$$

$$= 0.05008$$

With the value for the slope b_1, you can calculate the Y intercept as follows:

1. First, calculate the mean Y ($\bar{Y}$) and the mean X ($\bar{X}$) values:

$$\bar{Y} = \frac{\sum_{i=1}^{n}Y_i}{n} = \frac{1,042.5}{36} = 28.9583$$

$$\bar{X} = \frac{\sum_{i=1}^{n}X_i}{n} = \frac{22,520}{36} = 625.5555$$

2. Then use these results in the equation:

$$b_0 = \bar{Y} - b_1\bar{X}$$
$$b_0 = 28.9583 - (0.05008)(625.5555)$$
$$= -2.3695$$

9.3   MEASURES OF VARIATION

Once a regression model has been fit to a set of data, three measures of variation determine how much of the variation in the dependent variable Y can be explained by variation in the independent variable X. The first measure, the **total sum of squares (SST)**, is a measure of variation of the Y values around their mean, $\bar{Y}$. In a regression analysis, the **total variation** or total sum of squares is subdivided into **explained variation or regression sum of squares (SSR)**, that which is due to the relationship between X and Y, and **unexplained variation or error sum of squares (SSE)**, that which is due to factors other than the relationship between X and Y.

$$\text{Total sum of squares} = \text{regression sum of squares} + \text{error sum of squares} \qquad (9.4)$$

The total sum of squares (SST) is the measure of variation of the Y_i values around their mean. The total sum of squares (SST) is equal to the sum of the squared differences between each observed Y value and the mean value of Y,

$$SST = \text{sum (observed } Y \text{ value} - \text{mean } Y \text{ value)}^2 \qquad (9.5)$$

The total sum of squares is also equal to the sum of the regression sum of squares and the error sum of squares.

The regression sum of squares (SSR) is the variation that is due to the relationship between X and Y. The regression sum of squares (SSR) is equal to the sum of the squared differences between the Y that is predicted from the regression equation and the mean value of Y:

$$SSR = \text{sum (predicted } Y \text{ value} - \text{mean } Y \text{ value)}^2 \qquad (9.6)$$

The error sum of squares (SSE) is the variation that is due to factors other than the relationship between X and Y. The error sum of squares (SSE) is equal to the sum of the squared differences between each observed Y value and the predicted value of Y:

$$SSE = \text{sum (observed } Y \text{ value} - \text{predicted } Y \text{ value)}^2 \qquad (9.7)$$

For the moving company data, from Figure 9.5 or 9.6 on page 217, SSR (called Regression by Minitab and Model by JMP) = 6,910.7189, SSE (called residual error by Minitab and error by JMP) = 860.7186, and SST = 7,771.4375. (Note that 7,771.4375 is the sum of 6,910.7189 and 860.7186.)

COMPUTING THE MEASURES OF VARIATION {OPTIONAL}

The equation for total sum of squares SST is expressed as follows:

$$SST = \sum_{i=1}^{n}(Y_i - \bar{Y})^2 \text{ which is equivalent to} \sum_{i=1}^{n}Y_i^2 - \frac{\left(\sum_{i=1}^{n}Y_i\right)^2}{n} \qquad (9.8)$$

or as

$$SST = SSR + SSE \qquad (9.8b)$$

The equation for the regression sum of squares (SSR) is:

$$SSR = \text{explained variation or regression sum of squares}$$

$$= \sum_{i=1}^{n}(\hat{Y}_i - \bar{Y})^2 \qquad (9.9)$$

which is equivalent to

$$= b_0 \sum_{i=1}^{n} Y_i + b_1 \sum_{i=1}^{n} X_i Y_i - \frac{\left(\sum\limits_{i=1}^{n} Y_i\right)^2}{n}$$

The equation for the error sum of squares (SSE) is:

$$SSE = \text{unexplained variation or error sum of squares}$$

$$= \sum_{i=1}^{n}(Y_i - \hat{Y}_i)^2 \text{ which is equivalent to} \qquad (9.10)$$

$$= \sum_{i=1}^{n} Y_i^2 - b_0 \sum_{i=1}^{n} Y_i - b_1 \sum_{i=1}^{n} X_i Y_i$$

For the moving company problem on page 219:

$$SST = \text{total sum of squares} = \sum_{i=1}^{n}(Y_i - \bar{Y})^2 = \sum_{i=1}^{n} Y_i^2 - \frac{\left(\sum\limits_{i=1}^{n} Y_i\right)^2}{n}$$

$$= 37,960.5 - \frac{(1,042.5)^2}{36}$$

$$= 37,960.5 - 30,189.0625$$

$$= 7,771.4375$$

$$SSR = \text{regression sum of squares}$$

$$= \sum_{i=1}^{n}(\hat{Y}_i - \bar{Y})^2$$

$$= b_0 \sum_{i=1}^{n} Y_i + b_1 \sum_{i=1}^{n} X_i Y_i - \frac{\left(\sum\limits_{i=1}^{n} Y_i\right)^2}{n}$$

$$= (-2.3695)(1,042.5) + (0.05008)(790,134.5) - \frac{(1,042.5)^2}{36}$$

$$= 6,910.671$$

SSE = error sum of squares

$$= \sum_{i=1}^{n}(Y_i - \hat{Y}_i)^2$$

$$= \sum_{i=1}^{n}Y_i^2 - b_0\sum_{i=1}^{n}Y_i - b_1\sum_{i=1}^{n}X_iY_i$$

$$= 37,960.5 - (-2.3695)(1,042.5) - (0.05008)(790,134.5)$$

$$= 860.768$$

The Coefficient of Determination

By themselves, SSR, SSE, and SST provide little that can be directly interpreted. The **coefficient of determination** (r^2) is the ratio of the regression sum of squares (SSR) to the total sum of squares (SST). It measures the proportion of variation in Y that is explained by the independent variable (X) in the regression model. The ratio is expressed as:

$$r^2 = \frac{\text{regression sum of squares}}{\text{total sum of squares}} = \frac{SSR}{SST} \qquad (9.11)$$

For the moving company data, $SSR = 6,910.7189$ and $SST = 7,771.4375$ (see Figures 9.5 and 9.6 on page 217). Therefore:

$$r^2 = \frac{6,010.7189}{7,771.4375} = 0.8892$$

This value means that 89% of the variation in labor hours can be explained by the variability in the cubic footage moved. This shows a strong positive linear relationship between two variables because the use of a regression model has reduced the variability in predicting labor hours by 89%. Only 11% of the sample variability in labor hours can be explained by factors other than what is accounted for by the linear regression model that uses only cubic footage.

The Coefficient of Correlation

The **coefficient of correlation** is the measure of the strength of the linear relationship between two variables, represented by the symbol r. The values of this coefficient vary from -1, which indicates perfect negative correlation, to +1, which indicates perfect positive correlation. In simple linear regression, the sign of the correlation coefficient r is the same as the sign of the slope. If the slope is positive, r is positive. If the slope is negative, r is negative. In simple linear regression, the coefficient of correlation (r) is the square root of the coefficient of determination r^2.

For the moving company data, the coefficient of correlation, r, is $+0.943$ (because the slope is positive), the square root of 0.8892 (r^2). Because the coefficient is very close to $+1.0$, you can say that the relationship between cubic footage moved and labor hours is very strong. You can plausibly conclude that the increased volume moved is associated with increased labor hours.

In general, you must remember that just because two variables are strongly correlated, you cannot conclude that there is a cause-and-effect relationship between the variables. You can say that causation implies correlation, but correlation alone does not imply causation.

Standard Error of the Estimate

The **standard error of the estimate** is the standard deviation around the fitted line of regression that measures the variability of the actual Y values from the predicted Y, represented by the symbol S_{YX}. Although the least-squares method results in the line that fits the data with the minimum amount of variation, unless the coefficient of determination $r^2 = 1.0$, the regression equation is not a perfect predictor.

The variability around the line of regression was illustrated in Figure 9.7 on page 217, which showed the scatter plot and the line of regression for the moving company data. You can see from Figure 9.7 that there are values above the line of regression, as well as values below the line of regression. For the moving company problem, the standard error of the estimate is equal to 5.03 hours (see Figure 9.5 or 9.6 on page 217).

Just as the standard deviation measures variability around the mean, the standard error of the estimate measures variability around the fitted line of regression. As you will see in Section 9.6, you can use the standard error of the estimate to determine whether a statistically significant relationship exists between the two variables.

COMPUTING THE STANDARD ERROR OF THE ESTIMATE {OPTIONAL}

$$S_{YX} = \sqrt{\frac{SSE}{n-2}} = \sqrt{\frac{\sum_{i=1}^{n}(Y_i - \hat{Y}_i)^2}{n-2}} \qquad (9.12)$$

For the moving company problem, with $SSE = 860.7186$,

$$S_{YX} = \sqrt{\frac{860.7186}{36-2}}$$

$$S_{YX} = 5.0314$$

9.4   ASSUMPTIONS

The discussion of hypothesis testing and the analysis of variance in Chapter 7, "Hypothesis Testing," emphasized the importance of the assumptions to the validity of any conclusions reached. The assumptions necessary for regression are similar to those of the analysis of variance because both topics fall under the general heading of *linear models* [see Reference 4].

The four **assumptions of regression** (known by the acronym LINE) are as follows:

- Linearity between Y and X
- Independence of errors between the actual and predicted values of Y
- Normality of the distribution of error terms (differences between the actual and predicted values of Y)
- Equal variance (also called *homoscedasticity*) for the distribution of Y for each level of the independent variable (X)

The first assumption, **linearity**, states that the relationship between Y and X is linear. The second assumption, **independence of errors**, requires that the errors around the regression line (to be evaluated in Section 9.5) are independent from one another. This assumption is particularly important when data are collected over a period of time. In such situations, the errors for a specific time period are often correlated with those of the previous time period [see References 2 and 4]. The third assumption, **normality**, requires that the errors are normally distributed at each value of X. Like the t test and the ANOVA F test, regression analysis is fairly robust against departures from the normality assumption. As long as the distribution of the errors at each level of X is not extremely different from a normal distribution, inferences about the Y intercept and the slope are not seriously affected. The fourth assumption, **equal variance** or **homoscedasticity**, requires that the variance of the errors are constant for all values of X. In other words, the variability of Y values will be the same when X is a low value as when X is a high value. The equal variance assumption is important for using the least-squares method of determining the regression coefficients. If there are serious departures from this assumption, you can use either data transformations or weighted least-squares methods [see Reference 4].

9.5   RESIDUAL ANALYSIS

The graphical method **residual analysis** allows you to evaluate whether the regression model that has been fitted to the data is an appropriate model *and* determine whether there are violations of the assumptions of the regression model.

The **residual** is the difference between the observed and predicted values of the dependent variable for a given value of X.

$$\text{Residual} = (\text{Observed value of } Y) - (\text{Predicted value of } Y) \qquad (9.13)$$

Evaluating the Assumptions

Recall from Section 9.4 that the four **assumptions of regression** (known by the acronym LINE) are linearity, independence, normality, and equal variance.

Linearity. To evaluate linearity, you plot the residuals on the vertical axis against the corresponding X values of the independent variable on the horizontal axis. If the fitted model is appropriate for the data, there will be no apparent pattern in this plot; that is, there will only be random variation of the residuals around the mean value of Y over all values of X. However, if the fitted model is not appropriate, there will be a clear relationship between the X values and the residuals.

Figures 9.8 and 9.9 are Minitab and JMP residual plots for the moving company data with cubic feet plotted on the horizontal X axis and the residuals plotted on the vertical Y axis.

FIGURE 9.8
Minitab Residual
Plot for the Moving
Company Data

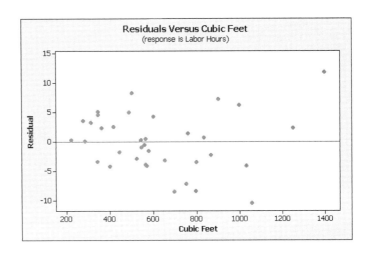

FIGURE 9.9
JMP Residual Plot for
the Moving Company
Data

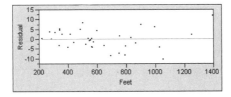

You see that although there is widespread scatter in the residual plot, there is no apparent pattern or relationship between the residuals and X. The residuals appear to be evenly spread above and below 0 for the differing values of X. This result enables you to conclude that the fitted straight-line model is appropriate for the moving company data.

Independence. You can evaluate the assumption of independence of the errors by plotting the residuals in the order or sequence in which the observed data were collected. Data collected over periods of time sometimes exhibit an *autocorrelation* effect among successive residuals. If this relationship exists (which violates the assumption of independence), it will be apparent in the plot of the residuals versus the time in which the data were collected. You can also test for autocorrelation using the Durbin-Watson statistic [see References 2 and 4]. Since the moving company data considered in this chapter were collected during the same time period, you do not need to evaluate the independence assumption for these data.

Normality. To evaluate the assumption of normality of the variation around the line of regression, you plot the residuals in a histogram (see Section 3.2), box-and-whisker plot (see Section 4.3), or a normal probability plot (see Section 5.7). From the histogram shown in Figure 9.10 for the moving company data, you can see that the data appear to be approximately normally distributed, with most of the residuals concentrated in the center of the distribution.

FIGURE 9.10
Minitab Moving Company Histogram of Residuals

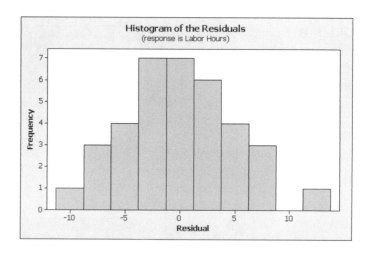

Equal variance. To evaluate the equal variance assumption, you examine the same plot that you used to evaluate the aptness of the fitted model. For the residual plots shown in Figures 9.8 and 9.9, there do not appear to be major differences in the variability of the residuals for different X values. You can conclude that for this fitted model, there is no apparent violation in the assumption of equal variation at each level of X.

9.6   INFERENCES ABOUT THE SLOPE

After using residual analysis to show that the assumptions of a least-squares regression model have not been seriously violated and that the straight-line model is appropriate, you can make inferences about the linear relationship between the dependent and independent variables in a population based on your sample results.

t Test for the Slope

You can determine the existence of a significant relationship between the X and Y variables by testing whether β_1 (the population slope) is equal to 0. If you reject this hypothesis, you conclude that there is evidence of a linear relationship between Y and X. The null and alternative hypotheses are as follows:

H_0: $\beta_1 = 0$ (There is no linear relationship.)
H_1: $\beta_1 \neq 0$ (There is a linear relationship.)

The test statistic follows the t distribution with the degrees of freedom equal to the sample size minus 2. The test statistic is equal to the sample slope divided by the standard error of the slope.

$$t = \frac{\text{sample slope}}{\text{standard error of the slope}}$$

For the moving company data, the critical value of t for level of significance $\alpha = 0.05$ is 2.0322, the value of t is 16.52, and the p-value is 0.000 (see Figure 9.5 or 9.6 on page 217). Using the p-value approach, you reject H_0 because the p-value of 0.000 is less than $\alpha = 0.05$. Using the critical value approach, you reject H_0 because $t = 16.52 > 2.0322$. You can conclude that there is a significant linear relationship between labor hours and the cubic footage moved.

TESTING A HYPOTHESIS FOR A POPULATION SLOPE (β_1) USING THE t TEST {OPTIONAL}

$$S_{b_1} = \frac{S_{YX}}{\sqrt{SSX}}$$

You use the standard error of the slope, S_{b_1} to define t:

$$t = \frac{b_1 - \beta_1}{S_{b_1}} \qquad (9.14)$$

Continues

The test statistic t follows a t distribution with $n - 2$ degrees of freedom.
For the moving company data, to test whether there is a significant relationship
between the cubic footage and the labor hours at the level of significance $\alpha = 0.05$,
refer to the calculation of SSX on page 219 and the standard error of the estimate on
page 225.

$$S_{b_1} = \frac{S_{YX}}{\sqrt{SSX}}$$

$$= \frac{5.0314}{\sqrt{2,755,432.889}}$$

$$= 0.00303$$

Therefore, to test the existence of a linear relationship at the 0.05 level of significance,
with:

$$b_1 = +0.05008 \quad n = 36 \quad S_{b_1} = 0.00303$$

$$t = \frac{b_1 - \beta_1}{S_{b_1}}$$

$$= \frac{0.05008 - 0}{0.00303} = 16.52$$

F Test for the Slope

You can also use an F test to determine whether the slope in simple linear regression is statistically significant. Recall from Section 7.5 and Chapter 8 that you used the F distribution for the Analysis of Variance. In testing for the significance of the slope, the F test is the ratio of the variance that is due to the regression (MSR) divided by the error variance (MSE). Table 9.3 is the Analysis of Variance summary table.

For the moving company data, since $n = 36$ and $k = 1$ independent variable, the critical value of F for level of significance $\alpha = 0.05$ with one degree of freedom in the numerator and $36 - 1 - 1 = 34$ degrees of freedom in the denominator is approximately 4.13. From Figure 9.5 or 9.6 on page 217, the value of F is 272.986, and the p-value is 0.000. Using the p-value approach, you reject H_0 because the p-value of 0.000 is less than $\alpha = 0.05$. Using the critical value approach, you reject H_0 because $F = 272.986 > 4.13$. You can conclude that there is a significant linear relationship between labor hours and the cubic footage moved.

TABLE 9.3   ANOVA Table for Testing the Significance of a Regression Coefficient

Source	df	Sum of Squares	Mean Square (Variance)	F
Regression	k	SSR	$MSR = \dfrac{SSR}{k}$	$F = \dfrac{MSR}{MSE}$
Error	$n - k - 1$	$\underline{SSE}$	$MSE = \dfrac{SSE}{n - k - 1}$	
Total	$n - 1$	SST		

where

n = sample size

k = number of independent variables

Confidence Interval Estimate of the Slope (β_1)

You can also test the existence of a linear relationship between the variables by calculating a confidence interval estimate of β_1 and determining whether the hypothesized value ($\beta_1 = 0$) is included in the interval.

You calculate the confidence interval estimate of β_1 by multiplying the t statistic by the standard error of the slope, and then adding and subtracting this product to the sample slope:

$$\text{Sample slope} \pm t \text{ statistic (standard error of the slope)} \qquad (9.15)$$

For the moving company data, using the Minitab and JMP regression results in Figures 9.5 and 9.6 on page 217, you calculate the lower and upper limits of the confidence interval estimate for the slope of cubic footage and labor hours as follows:

$$\text{Sample slope} \pm t \text{ statistic (standard error of the slope)}$$

Thus:

$$+0.05008 \pm (2.0322)(0.00303)$$
$$+0.05008 \pm 0.00616$$

With 95% confidence, the lower limit is 0.0439 and the upper limit is 0.0562.

Because this interval does not contain 0, you conclude that there is a significant linear relationship between labor hours and cubic footage moved. Had the interval included 0, you would have concluded that no relationship exists between the variables. The confidence interval indicates that for each increase of 1 cubic foot moved, mean labor hours are estimated to increase by at least 0.0439 hour but less than 0.0562 hour.

9.7   ESTIMATION OF PREDICTED VALUES

In Section 9.2, you made predictions of Y for a given X. You predicted that for a move with 500 cubic feet, the mean labor hours is 22.67 hours. This estimate, however, is a *point estimate* of the population mean. In Section 6.3, you studied the concept of the confidence interval as an estimate of the population mean. In regression, you can form a confidence interval estimate for the mean response of Y for a given X. Figure 9.5 on page 217 provides a confidence interval estimate for the mean response of Y for a given X. For the moving company example, you have 95% confidence that the mean moving time for 500 cubic feet is between 20.799 and 24.5419 hours.

The width of the confidence interval depends on several factors. For a given level of confidence, increased variation around the prediction line (as measured by the standard error of the estimate) results in a wider interval. However, as you would expect, increased sample size reduces the width of the interval. In addition, the width of the interval also varies at different values of X. When you predict Y for values of X close to the mean, the interval is narrower than for predictions for X values more distant from the mean.

The Prediction Interval

In addition to the confidence interval estimate for the mean value, you often want to predict the response for an *individual* value. Although the form of the **prediction interval** is similar to the confidence interval estimate, the prediction interval is predicting an individual value, not estimating the mean value. Figure 9.5 provides this prediction interval estimate. For the moving company example, you have 95% confidence that the estimated labor hours for an individual move that consists of 500 cubic feet is between 12.276 and 33.065 hours. If you compare the results of the confidence interval estimate and the prediction interval, you see that the width of the prediction interval for an individual move is much wider than the confidence interval estimate for the mean labor hours. Remember that there is much more variation in predicting an individual value than in estimating a mean value.

9.8   PITFALLS IN REGRESSION ANALYSIS

Some of the pitfalls people encounter when using regression analysis are the following:

- Lacking an awareness of the assumptions of least-squares regression.
- Knowing how to evaluate the assumptions of least-squares regression.
- Knowing what are the alternatives to least-squares regression if a particular assumption is violated.

- Using a regression model without knowledge of the subject matter.
- Predicting Y outside the relevant range of X.

When you use regression analysis, you need to be aware of these pitfalls since most regression software does not automatically check for them. You must evaluate the assumptions of regression and whether they have been seriously violated, rather than just compute basic statistics such as the Y intercept, slope, coefficient of determination, and test of significance of the slope.

The data in Table 9.4 illustrates the need to go beyond these basics of regression.

TABLE 9.4 Four Sets of Artificial Data

Data Set A		Data Set B		Data Set C		Data Set D	
X_i	Y_i	X_i	Y_i	X_i	Y_i	X_i	Y_i
10	8.04	10	9.14	10	7.46	8	6.58
14	9.96	14	8.10	14	8.84	8	5.76
5	5.68	5	4.74	5	5.73	8	7.71
8	6.95	8	8.14	8	6.77	8	8.84
9	8.81	9	8.77	9	7.11	8	8.47
12	10.84	12	9.13	12	8.15	8	7.04
4	4.26	4	3.10	4	5.39	8	5.25
7	4.82	7	7.26	7	6.42	19	12.50
11	8.33	11	9.26	11	7.81	8	5.56
13	7.58	13	8.74	13	12.74	8	7.91
6	7.24	6	6.13	6	6.08	8	6.89

Source: F. J. Anscombe, "Graphs in Statistical Analysis," *American Statistician*, Vol. 27 (1973), pp. 17–21. Reprinted with permission from *The American Statistician*. Copyright 1973 by the American Statistical Association. All rights reserved.

ANSCOMBE

Anscombe [see Reference 1] showed that for the four data sets, the regression results are identical:

$$\text{predicted value of } Y = 3.0 + 0.5X_i$$

$$\text{standard error of the estimate} = 1.237$$
$$r^2 = 0.667$$
$$SSR = \text{regression sum of squares} = 27.51$$
$$SSE = \text{error sum of squares} = 13.76$$
$$SST = \text{total sum of squares} = 41.27$$

The scatter diagrams of Figure 9.11 and the residual plots of Figure 9.12 reveal that the four data sets are actually quite different.

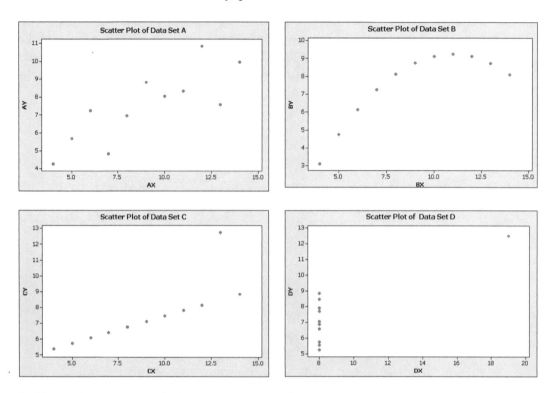

FIGURE 9.11   Minitab Scatter Diagrams for Four Data Sets

From the scatter diagrams and the residual plots, you see the difference in the data sets. The only data set that seems to follow an approximate straight line is data set A. The residual plot for data set A does not show any obvious patterns or outlying residuals. This is certainly not the case for data sets B, C, and D. The scatter plot for data set B shows that you should fit a curvilinear regression model. This conclusion is reinforced by the residual plot for B which shows a clear curvilinear pattern. The scatter diagram and the residual plot for data set C clearly show what is an extreme value in the upper part of the plot. The scatter diagram for data set D represents the unusual situation in which the fitted model is heavily dependent on the outcome of a single observation ($X = 19$ and $Y = 12.50$). Any regression model fit for these data should be evaluated cautiously since its regression coefficients are heavily dependent on a single observation.

To avoid the common pitfalls of regression analysis, you can use the following strategy:

• Always start with a scatter plot to observe the possible relationship between X and Y. Look at your data.

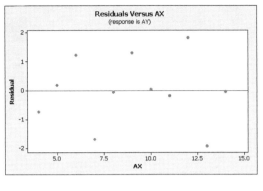

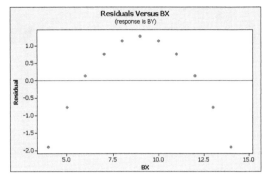

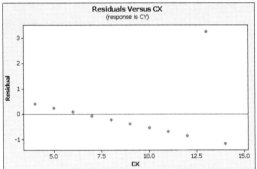

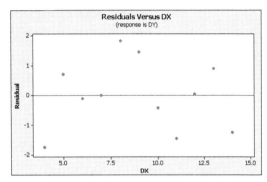

FIGURE 9.12   Minitab Residual Plots for Four Data Sets

- Check the assumptions of regression after the regression model has been fit, before using the results of the model.
- Plot the residuals versus the independent variable. This will enable you to determine whether the model fit to the data is an appropriate one and will allow you to check visually for violations of the equal variation assumption.
- Use a histogram, box-and-whisker plot, or normal probability plot of the residuals to graphically evaluate whether the normality assumption has been seriously violated.
- If the evaluation of the residuals indicates violations in the assumptions, use alternative methods to least-squares regression or alternative least-squares models [see Reference 4], depending on what the evaluation has indicated.
- If the evaluation of the residuals does not indicate violations in the assumptions, then you can undertake the inferential aspects of the regression analysis. Tests for the significance of the slope, confidence interval estimates of the slope, confidence intervals for the mean response, and prediction intervals for an individual response can be carried out. Avoid making predictions outside the relevant range of the independent variable.

SUMMARY

This chapter develops the simple linear regression model and discusses the assumptions and how to evaluate them. Once you are assured that the model is appropriate, you can predict values using the prediction line and test for the significance of the slope using the t or F test. In Chapter 10, the discussion of regression analysis is extended to situations where more than one independent variable is used to predict the value of a dependent variable.

REFERENCES

1. Anscombe, F. J. "Graphs in Statistical Analysis." *The American Statistician,* 27 (1973): 17–21.

2. Berenson, M. L., D. M. Levine, and T. C. Krehbiel. *Basic Business Statistics: Concepts and Applications,* 10th Ed. (Upper Saddle River, NJ: Prentice Hall, 2006).

3. *JMP Version 6* (Cary, NC: SAS Institute, 2005).

4. Kutner, M. H., C. Nachtsheim, J. Neter, and W. Li. *Applied Linear Statistical Models,* 5th Ed. (New York: McGraw-Hill-Irwin, 2005).

5. Minitab for Windows Version 14 (State College, PA: Minitab Inc., 2004).

Appendix 9.1
Using Minitab for Simple Linear Regression

Scatter Plot

To produce the scatter plot of cubic feet and labor hours, open the **MOVING.MTW** worksheet. Select **Graph → Scatterplot**.

1. In the Scatterplots dialog box (see Figure A9.1), select **Simple**. (To generate a scatter plot with a line of regression, select **With Regression**.) Click the **OK** button.

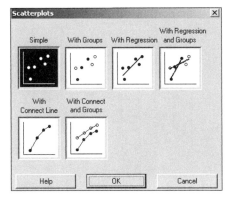

FIGURE A9.1
Minitab Scatterplots Dialog Box

2. In the Scatterplot—Simple dialog box (see Figure A9.2), enter **'Labor Hours'** or **C1** in the Y variables: edit box in row 1. Enter **'Cubic Feet'** or **C3** in the X variables: edit box in row 1. Click the **OK** button.

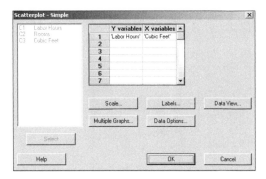

FIGURE A9.2
Minitab Scatterplot—Simple Dialog Box

Simple Linear Regression

To illustrate the use of Minitab for simple linear regression with the moving company example of this chapter, open the **MOVING.MTW** worksheet and select **Stat → Regression → Regression**.

1. In the Regression dialog box (see Figure A9.3), enter **'Labor Hours'** or **C1** in the Response: edit box and **'Cubic Feet'** or **C3** in the Predictors: edit box. Click the **Graphs** button.

2. In the Regression—Graphs dialog box (see Figure A9.4), select the **Regular** option button under Residuals for Plots. Under Residual Plots, select the **Histogram of residuals**, **Normal plot of residuals**, **Residuals versus fits**, and

Residuals versus order check boxes. In the Residuals versus the variables: edit box, enter **'Cubic Feet'** or **C3**. Click the **OK** button to return to the Regression dialog box.

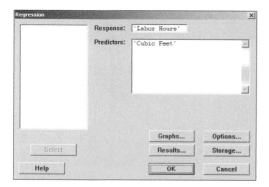

FIGURE A9.3
Minitab Regression Dialog Box

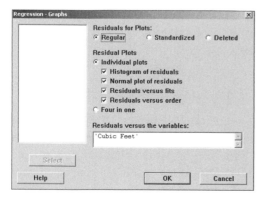

FIGURE A9.4
Minitab Regression—Graphs Dialog Box

3. Click the **Results** option button. In the Regression—Results dialog box (see Figure A9.5), select the **Regression equation, table of coefficients, s, R-squared, and basic analysis of variance** option button. Click the **OK** button to return to the Regression dialog box.

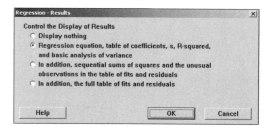

FIGURE A9.5
Minitab Regression—Results Dialog Box

4. Click the **Options** button. In the Regression—Options dialog box (see Figure A9.6), in the Prediction intervals for new observations: edit box, enter **500**. In the Confidence level: edit box, enter **95**. Click the **OK** button to return to the Regression dialog box. Click the **OK** button.

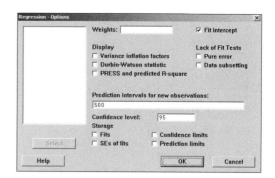

FIGURE A9.6
Minitab Regression—Options Dialog Box

Appendix 9.2
Using JMP for Simple Linear Regression

To produce the scatter plot of cubic feet and labor hours and the simple linear regression analysis to predict labor hours based on cubic feet, open the **MOVING.JMP** data table. Select **Analyze → Fit Y by X.** Then, do the following:

1. In the Report: Fit Y by X—Contextual dialog box (see Figure A9.7), enter **Hours** in the Y, Response edit box and **Feet** in the X, Factor edit box. Click the **OK** button.

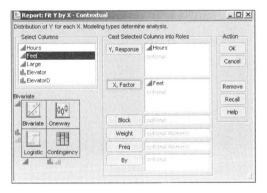

FIGURE A9.7
JMP Report: Fit Y by X—Contextual Dialog Box

2. To generate a scatter plot with a linear regression line and the regression statistics, click the red triangle to the left of Bivariate Fit. On the pop-up menu that appears, select **Fit Line**.

3. To generate a residual plot, click the red triangle next to Linear Fit below the scatter plot with the regression line. In the pop-up menu that appears, select **Plot Residuals**.

4. To save residuals so you can generate a histogram or normal probability plot of the residuals, click the red triangle next to Linear Fit below the scatter plot with the regression line. In the pop-up menu that appears, select **Save Residuals**.

CHAPTER 10

Multiple Regression

INTRODUCTION

10.1 DEVELOPING THE MULTIPLE REGRESSION MODEL

10.2 COEFFICIENT OF MULTIPLE DETERMINATION AND THE OVERALL *F* TEST

10.3 RESIDUAL ANALYSIS FOR THE MULTIPLE REGRESSION MODEL

10.4 INFERENCES CONCERNING THE POPULATION REGRESSION COEFFICIENTS

10.5 USING DUMMY VARIABLES AND INTERACTION TERMS IN REGRESSION MODELS

10.6 COLLINEARITY

10.7 MODEL BUILDING

10.8 LOGISTIC REGRESSION

SUMMARY

REFERENCES

APPENDIX 10.1 USING MINITAB FOR MULTIPLE REGRESSION

APPENDIX 10.2 USING JMP FOR MULTIPLE REGRESSION

LEARNING OBJECTIVES

After reading this chapter, you will be able to

- Develop a multiple regression model.
- Interpret the regression coefficients in a multiple regression model.
- Determine which independent variables to include in the regression model.
- Use categorical independent variables in a regression model.
- Build a multiple regression model.
- Predict a categorical dependent variable using logistic regression.

INTRODUCTION

Chapter 9, "Simple Linear Regression," focused on the simple linear regression model that uses one numerical independent variable X (CTP) to predict the value of a numerical dependent variable Y (CTQ). Often, you can make better predictions if you use more than one independent variable. This chapter introduces you to **multiple regression models** that use two or more independent variables (Xs) to predict the value of a dependent variable (Y).

10.1 DEVELOPING THE MULTIPLE REGRESSION MODEL

In Chapter 9, when analyzing the moving company data, you used the cubic footage to be moved to predict the labor hours (CTQ). In addition to cubic footage (X_1), now you are also going to consider the number of pieces of large furniture (such as beds, couches, china closets, and dressers) that need to be moved (X_2 = LARGE = number of pieces of large furniture to be moved). Table 10.1 presents the results.

TABLE 10.1   Labor Hours, Cubic Feet, and Number of Pieces of Large Furniture

Hours	Feet	Large	Hours	Feet	Large
24.00	545	3	25.00	557	2
13.50	400	2	45.00	1,028	5
26.25	562	2	29.00	793	4
25.00	540	2	21.00	523	3
9.00	220	1	22.00	564	3
20.00	344	3	16.50	312	2
22.00	569	2	37.00	757	3
11.25	340	1	32.00	600	3
50.00	900	6	34.00	796	3
12.00	285	1	25.00	577	3
38.75	865	4	31.00	500	4
40.00	831	4	24.00	695	3
19.50	344	3	40.00	1,054	4
18.00	360	2	27.00	486	3
28.00	750	3	18.00	442	2
27.00	650	2	62.50	1,249	5
21.00	415	2	53.75	995	6
15.00	275	2	79.50	1,397	7

MOVING

With two independent variables and a dependent variable, the data are in three dimensions. Figure 10.1 illustrates a three-dimensional graph constructed by Minitab.

FIGURE 10.1
Minitab 3D Graph of Labor Hours, Cubic Feet, and Number of Pieces of Large Furniture

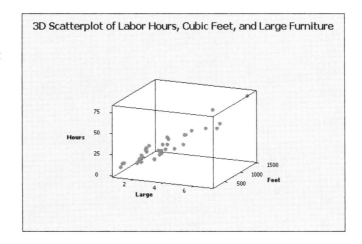

Interpreting the Regression Coefficients

When there are several independent variables, you can extend the simple linear regression model of Equation (9.1) on page 214 by assuming a straight-line or linear relationship between each independent variable and the dependent variable. For example, with two independent variables, the multiple regression model is:

Predicted $Y = Y$ intercept + (slope with $X_1 \times X_1$ value) + (slope with $X_2 \times X_2$ value)

$$(10.1a)$$

or

$$\text{Predicted } Y = b_0 + b_1 X_1 + b_2 X_2 \qquad (10.1b)$$

In the simple regression model, the slope represents the change in the mean of Y per unit change in X and does not take into account any other variables besides the single independent variable included in the model. In the multiple regression model with two independent variables, the slope of Y with X_1 represents the change in the mean of Y per unit change in X_1, taking into account the effect of X_2. This slope is called a **net regression coefficient**. (Some statisticians refer to net regression coefficients as *partial regression coefficients*.)

As in simple linear regression, you use the least-squares method and software such as Minitab or JMP to compute the regression coefficients. Figure 10.2 presents Minitab output for the moving company data and Figure 10.3 illustrates JMP output.

FIGURE 10.2

Partial Minitab Output for the Moving Company Data

```
The regression equation is
Hours = - 3.92 + 0.0319 Feet + 4.22 Large

Predictor      Coef    SE Coef      T      P
Constant     -3.915      1.674  -2.34  0.026
Feet       0.031924   0.004604   6.93  0.000
Large        4.2228     0.9142   4.62  0.000

S = 3.98000   R-Sq = 93.3%   R-Sq(adj) = 92.9%

Analysis of Variance
Source           DF      SS      MS       F      P
Regression        2  7248.7  3624.4  228.80  0.000
Residual Error   33   522.7    15.8
Total            35  7771.4

Predicted Values for New Observations
New
Obs      Fit  SE Fit         95% CI            95% PI
  1   24.715   0.852  (22.981, 26.450)  (16.434, 32.996)

Values of Predictors for New Observations
New
Obs  Feet  Large
  1   500   3.00
```

FIGURE 10.3

Partial JMP Output for the Moving Company Data

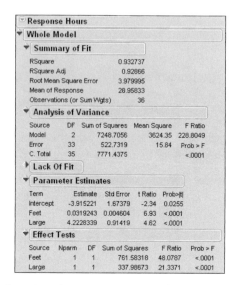

The results show that the slope of Y with X_1 (b_1 = 0.0319), the slope of Y with X_2 (b_2 = 4.2228), and the Y intercept b_0 = -3.915. Thus, the multiple regression equation is as follows:

$$\text{Predicted value of labor hours} = -3.915 + (0.0319 \times \text{cubic feet moved})$$
$$+ (4.2228 \times \text{large furniture})$$

The slope b_1 was computed as +0.0319. This means that for each increase of 1 unit in X_1, the mean value of Y is estimated to increase by 0.0319 units, holding constant the effect of X_2. In other words, holding constant the number of pieces of large furniture, for each increase of 1 cubic foot in the amount to be moved, the fitted model predicts that the expected labor hours are estimated to increase by 0.0319 hours. The slope b_2 was computed as +4.2228. This means that for each increase of

1 unit in X_2, the mean value of Y is estimated to increase by 4.2228 units, holding constant the effect of X_1. In other words, holding constant the amount to be moved, for each additional piece of large furniture, the fitted model predicts that the expected labor hours are estimated to increase by 4.2228 hours. The Y intercept b_0 was computed to be -3.915. The Y intercept represents the mean value of Y when X equals 0. Because the cubic feet moved cannot be less than 0, the Y intercept has no practical interpretation. Recall, that a regression model is only valid within the ranges of the independent variables.

Regression coefficients in multiple regression are called net regression coefficients and measure the mean change in Y per unit change in a particular X, *holding constant the effect of the other X variables*. For example, in the moving company study, for a move with a given number of pieces of large furniture, the mean labor hours are estimated to increase by 0.0319 hours for each 1 cubic foot increase in the amount to be moved. Another way to interpret this "net effect" is to think of two moves with an equal number of pieces of large furniture. If the first move consists of 1 cubic foot more than the other move, the "net effect" of this difference is that the first move is predicted to take 0.0319 more labor hours than the other move. To interpret the net effect of the number of pieces of large furniture, you can consider two moves that have the same cubic footage. If the first move has one additional piece of large furniture, the net effect of this difference is that the first move is predicted to take 4.2228 more labor hours than the other move.

Predicting the Dependent Variable Y

As in simple linear regression, you can use the multiple regression equation to predict values of the dependent variable. For example, the predicted labor hours for a move with 500 cubic feet with three large pieces of furniture to be moved is as follows:

$$
\begin{aligned}
\text{Predicted } Y &= Y \text{ intercept} + (\text{slope with } X_1 \times X_1 \text{ value}) + (\text{slope with } X_2 \times X_2 \text{ value}) \\
&= -3.915 + (0.0319 \times 500) + (4.2228 \times 3) = 24.715
\end{aligned}
$$

You predict that the mean labor hours for a move with 500 cubic feet and three large pieces of furniture to be moved are 24.715 hours.

As was the case in simple linear regression, after you have predicted Y and done a residual analysis (see Section 10.3), you can construct a confidence interval estimate of the mean response and a prediction interval for an individual response. Figure 10.2 on page 244 presents confidence and prediction intervals computed using Minitab for predicting the labor hours. The 95% confidence interval estimate of the mean labor hours with 500 cubic feet and three large pieces of furniture to be moved is between 22.981 and 26.45 hours. The prediction interval for an individual move is between 16.434 and 32.996 hours.

10.2 COEFFICIENT OF MULTIPLE DETERMINATION AND THE OVERALL *F* TEST

Coefficients of Multiple Determination

In Section 9.3, you computed the coefficient of determination (r^2) that measures the variation in Y that is explained by the independent variable X in the simple linear regression model. In multiple regression, the **coefficient of multiple determination** represents the proportion of the variation in Y that is explained by the set of independent variables selected. In the moving company example, from Figures 10.2 or 10.3 on page 244, $SSR = 7{,}248.7$, $SST = 7{,}771.4$. Thus:

$$r^2 = \frac{\text{regression sum of squares}}{\text{total sum of squares}} = \frac{SSR}{SST}$$
$$= \frac{7{,}248.7}{7{,}771.4}$$
$$= 0.933$$

The coefficient of multiple determination, $(r^2 = 0.933)$, indicates that 93.3% of the variation in labor hours is explained by the variation in the cubic footage and the variation in the number of pieces of large furniture to be moved.

Test for the Significance of the Overall Multiple Regression Model

The **overall *F* test** is used to test for the significance of the overall multiple regression model. You use this test to determine whether there is a significant relationship between the dependent variable and the entire set of independent variables. Because there is more than one independent variable, you have the following null and alternative hypotheses:

H_0: No linear relationship between the dependent variable and the independent variables ($\beta_1 = \beta_2 = \beta_3 = \cdots = \beta_k = 0$, where k = the number of independent variables).

H_1: Linear relationship between the dependent variable and at least one of the independent variables ($\beta_i \neq \beta_j$, for at least one i and j).

Table 10.2 presents the ANOVA summary table.

From Figures 10.2 or 10.3 on page 244, the F statistic given in the ANOVA summary table is 228.80 and the p-value = 0.000. Because the p-value = $0.000 < 0.05$, you reject H_0 and conclude that at least one of the independent variables (cubic footage and/or the number of pieces of large furniture moved) is related to labor hours.

TABLE 10.2   ANOVA Summary Table for the Overall F Test

Source	Degrees of Freedom	Sum of Squares	Mean Square (Variance)	F
Regression	k	SSR	$MSR = \dfrac{SSR}{k}$	$F = \dfrac{MSR}{MSE}$
Error	$n-k-1$	$\underline{SSE}$	$MSE = \dfrac{SSE}{n-k-1}$	
Total	$n-1$	SST		

where

n = sample size

k = number of independent variables

10.3 RESIDUAL ANALYSIS FOR THE MULTIPLE REGRESSION MODEL

In Section 9.5, you used residual analysis to evaluate the appropriateness of using the simple linear regression model for a set of data. For the multiple regression model with two independent variables, you need to construct and analyze the following residual plots:

1. Residuals versus the predicted value of Y
2. Residuals versus the first independent variable X_1
3. Residuals versus the second independent variable X_2
4. Residuals versus time (if the data has been collected in time order)

The first residual plot examines the pattern of residuals versus the predicted values of Y. If the residuals show a pattern for different predicted values of Y, there is evidence of a possible curvilinear effect in at least one independent variable, a possible violation to the assumption of equal variance, and/or the need to transform the Y variable. The second and third residual plots involve the independent variables. Patterns in the plot of the residuals versus an independent variable may indicate the existence of a curvilinear effect and, therefore, indicate the need to add a curvilinear independent variable to the multiple regression model [see References 1 and 4]. The fourth type of plot is used to investigate patterns in the residuals to validate the independence assumption when the data are collected in time order.

Figures 10.4 and 10.5 on page 248 are the Minitab and JMP residual plots for the moving company example. In Figures 10.4 or 10.5, there is very little or no pattern in the relationship between the residuals and the cubic feet moved (X_1), the number of pieces of large furniture moved (X_2), or the predicted value of Y. Thus, you can conclude that the multiple regression model is appropriate for predicting labor hours.

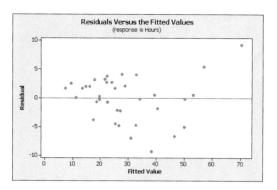
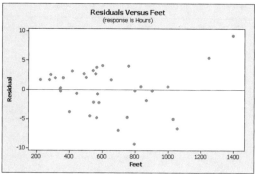

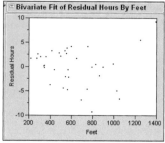

FIGURE 10.4 Minitab Residual Plots for the Moving Company Model: Residuals Versus Predicted Y, Residuals Versus Cubic Feet Moved, Residuals Versus the Number of Pieces of Large Furniture Moved

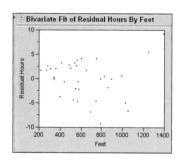
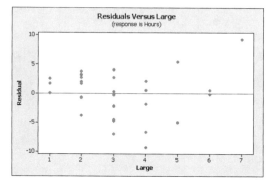
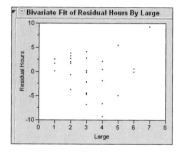

FIGURE 10.5 JMP Residual Plots for the Moving Company Model: Residuals Versus Predicted Y, Residuals Versus Cubic Feet Moved, Residuals Versus the Number of Pieces of Large Furniture Moved

10.4 INFERENCES CONCERNING THE POPULATION REGRESSION COEFFICIENTS

In Section 9.6, you tested the existence of the slope in a simple linear regression model to determine the significance of the relationship between X and Y. In addition, you constructed a confidence interval of the population slope. In this section, these procedures are extended to the multiple regression model.

Tests of Hypothesis

In a simple linear regression model, to test a hypothesis concerning the population slope, you used the t test:

$$t = \frac{\text{sample slope}}{\text{standard error of the slope}} = \frac{b_1 - 0}{S_{b_1}}$$

To test the significance of the cubic feet moved (X_1) or the number of pieces of large furniture moved (X_2), refer to Figures 10.2 or 10.3 on page 244. The null hypothesis for each independent variable is that there is no linear relationship between labor hours and the independent variable holding constant the effect of the other independent variables. The alternative hypothesis is that there is a linear relationship between labor hours and the independent variable holding constant the effect of the other independent variables.

For the cubic feet moved, the t statistic is 6.93 and the p-value is 0.000. Because the p-value is $0.000 < 0.05$, you reject the null hypothesis and conclude that there is a linear relationship between labor hours and the cubic feet moved (X_1). For the number of pieces of large furniture moved, the t statistic is 4.62 and the p-value is 0.000. Because the p-value is $0.000 < 0.05$, you reject the null hypothesis and conclude that there is a linear relationship between labor hours and the number of pieces of large furniture moved (X_2).

The t test of significance for a particular regression coefficient is actually a test for the significance of adding a particular variable into a regression model given that the other variable is included. Because each of the two independent variables is significant, both should be included in the regression model. Therefore, the t test for the regression coefficient is equivalent to testing for the contribution of each independent variable.

Confidence Interval Estimation

As you did in simple linear regression (see Section 9.6), you can construct confidence interval estimates of the slope. You calculate the confidence interval estimate of the population slope by multiplying the t statistic by the standard error of the slope and then adding and subtracting this product to the sample slope.

$$\text{Confidence interval of slope} = \text{sample slope} \pm t \text{ statistic}$$
$$\times (\text{standard error of the slope})$$

For the moving company data, using the Minitab and JMP regression results in Figures 10.2 and 10.3 on page 244, you calculate the lower and upper limits of the 95% confidence interval estimate for the slope of cubic footage and labor hours as follows:

There are $36 - 2 - 1 = 33$ degrees of freedom; hence, the t statistic is 2.0345. Thus:

$$\text{Confidence interval of slope} = \text{Sample slope} \pm t \text{ statistic}$$
$$(\text{standard error of the slope})$$
$$= 0.0319 \pm (2.0345)(0.0046)$$
$$= 0.0319 \pm 0.0094$$

With 95% confidence, the lower limit is 0.0225 hours and the upper limit is 0.0413 hours. The confidence interval indicates that for each increase of 1 cubic foot moved, mean labor hours are estimated to increase by at least 0.0225 hours but less than 0.0413 hours, holding constant the number of pieces of large furniture moved.

To calculate the confidence interval estimate of the slope of the number of pieces of large furniture moved and labor hours, you have the following:

$$\text{Sample slope} \pm t \text{ statistic (standard error of the slope)}$$
$$4.2228 \pm (2.0345)(0.9142)$$
$$4.2228 \pm 1.8599$$

With 95% confidence, the lower limit is 2.3629 hours and the upper limit is 6.0827 hours. The confidence interval indicates that for each increase of one piece of large furniture moved, mean labor hours are estimated to increase by at least 2.3629 hours but less than 6.0827 hours holding constant the cubic footage moved.

10.5   USING DUMMY VARIABLES AND INTERACTION TERMS IN REGRESSION MODELS

The multiple regression models discussed in Sections 10.1–10.4 assumed that each independent variable is numerical. However, in some situations, you might want to include categorical variables as independent variables in the regression model. The use of **dummy variables** allows you to include categorical independent variables as part of the regression model. If a given categorical independent variable has two categories, then you need only one dummy variable to represent the two categories. A particular dummy variable, say X_3, is defined as:

$X_3 = 0$ if the observation is in category 1
$X_3 = 1$ if the observation is in category 2

To illustrate the application of dummy variables in regression, consider the moving company example in which you are predicting labor hours based on the cubic feet moved and whether the apartment building had an elevator. To include the categorical variable concerning the presence of an elevator, you define the dummy variable as:

$X_3 = 0$ if the apartment building does not have an elevator
$X_3 = 1$ if the apartment building has an elevator

Table 10.3 lists the labor hours, cubic feet to be moved, and presence of an elevator in the apartment building. In the last column of Table 10.3, you can see how the categorical data are converted to numerical values.

TABLE 10.3   Labor Hours, Cubic Feet to Be Moved, and Presence of an Elevator

Hours (Y)	Feet (X_1)	Elevator (X_2)	Elevator (Coded) (X_3)
24.00	545	Yes	1
13.50	400	Yes	1
26.25	562	No	0
25.00	540	No	0
9.00	220	Yes	1
20.00	344	Yes	1
22.00	569	Yes	1
11.25	340	Yes	1
50.00	900	Yes	1
12.00	285	Yes	1
38.75	865	Yes	1
40.00	831	Yes	1
19.50	344	Yes	1
18.00	360	Yes	1
28.00	750	Yes	1
27.00	650	Yes	1
21.00	415	No	0
15.00	275	Yes	1
25.00	557	Yes	1
45.00	1,028	Yes	1
29.00	793	Yes	1
21.00	523	Yes	1

Continues

TABLE 10.3   Labor Hours, Cubic Feet to Be Moved, and Presence of an Elevator (Continued)

Hours (Y)	Feet (X_1)	Elevator (X_2)	Elevator (Coded) (X_3)
22.00	564	Yes	1
16.50	312	Yes	1
37.00	757	No	0
32.00	600	No	0
34.00	796	Yes	1
25.00	577	Yes	1
31.00	500	Yes	1
24.00	695	Yes	1
40.00	1,054	Yes	1
27.00	486	Yes	1
18.00	442	Yes	1
62.50	1,249	No	0
53.75	995	Yes	1
79.50	1,397	No	0

MOVING

Assuming that the slope of labor hours with the cubic feet moved is the same for apartments that have and do not have an elevator, the multiple regression model is:

Predicted labor hours = Y intercept + slope with cubic feet × cubic feet value
+ slope with presence of elevator × coded elevator value

Figures 10.6 and 10.7 provide Minitab and JMP output for this model.

FIGURE 10.6
Minitab Output for the Moving Company Dummy Variable Model

```
The regression equation is
Hours = 2.45 + 0.0482 Feet - 4.53 ElevatorD


Predictor      Coef    SE Coef      T       P
Constant      2.451     2.984    0.82   0.417
Feet       0.048205  0.003010   16.01   0.000
ElevatorD    -4.528     2.104   -2.15   0.039


S = 4.78249   R-Sq = 90.3%   R-Sq(adj) = 89.7%


Analysis of Variance

Source          DF      SS      MS       F       P
Regression       2  7016.7  3508.3  153.39   0.000
Residual Error  33   754.8    22.9
Total           35  7771.4
```

FIGURE 10.7

JMP Output for the
Moving Company
Dummy Variable
Model

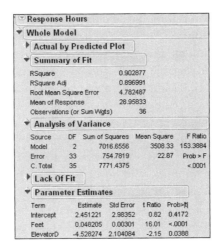

From Figure 10.6 or 10.7, the regression equation is:

$$\text{Predicted labor hours} = 2.451 + (0.0482 \times \text{cubic feet value})$$
$$- (4.528 \times \text{coded elevator value})$$

For moves in buildings without an elevator, you substitute 0 as the coded elevator value into the regression equation:

$$\text{Predicted labor hours} = 2.451 + (0.0482 \times \text{cubic feet value}) - [4.528 \times (0)]$$
$$\text{Predicted labor hours} = 2.451 + (0.0482 \times \text{cubic feet value})$$

For moves in buildings with an elevator, you substitute 1 as the coded elevator value into the regression equation:

$$\text{Predicted labor hours} = 2.451 + (0.0482 \times \text{cubic feet value}) - [4.528 \times (1)]$$
$$\text{Predicted labor hours} = 2.451 + (0.0482 \times \text{cubic feet value}) - 4.528$$
$$\text{Predicted labor hours} = -2.077 + (0.0482 \times \text{cubic feet value})$$

In this model, you interpret the regression coefficients as follows:

1. Holding constant whether or not the move occurs in an apartment building with an elevator, for each increase of 1.0 cubic feet in the amount moved, the mean labor hours are estimated to increase by 0.0482 hours.

2. Holding constant the number of cubic feet moved, the presence of an elevator in the apartment building where the move takes place decreases the mean estimated labor hours by 4.528 hours.

In Figures 10.6 or 10.7, the t statistic for the slope of cubic feet with labor hours is 16.01 and the p-value is approximately 0.000. The t statistic for presence of an elevator is -2.15 and the p-value is 0.039. Thus, each of the two variables makes a significant contribution to the model at a level of significance of 0.05. In addition, the coefficient of multiple determination indicates that 90.3% of the variation in labor hours is explained by variation in the cubic feet and whether or not the apartment building has an elevator.

In all the regression models discussed so far, the *effect* an independent variable has on the dependent variable was assumed to be statistically independent of the other independent variables in the model. An **interaction** occurs if the *effect* of an independent variable on the dependent variable is related to the *value* of a second independent variable.

To model an interaction effect in a regression model, you use an **interaction term** (sometimes referred to as a **cross-product term**). To illustrate the concept of interaction and use of an interaction term, return to the moving company example. In the regression model of Figures 10.6 and 10.7, you assumed that the effect that cubic feet has on the labor hours is independent of whether or not the apartment building has an elevator. In other words, you assumed that the slope of labor hours with cubic feet is the same for moves from apartment buildings with an elevator as it is for apartment buildings without an elevator. If these two slopes are different, an interaction between cubic feet and elevator exists.

To evaluate a hypothesis of equal slopes of a dependent Y variable with the independent variable X, you first define an **interaction term** that consists of the product of the independent variable X_1 and the dummy variable X_2. You then test whether this interaction variable makes a significant contribution to a regression model that contains the other X variables. If the interaction is significant, you cannot use the original model for prediction. For the data of Table 10.3 on page 251, you define the new variable as the product of cubic feet and the elevator dummy variable.

Figure 10.8 illustrates Minitab output for this regression model, which includes the cubic feet X_1, the presence of an elevator X_2, and the interaction of cubic feet X_1 and the presence of an elevator X_2 (which is defined as X_3). Figure 10.9 displays JMP output.

FIGURE 10.8

Minitab Output for a Regression Model That Includes Cubic Feet, Presence of an Elevator, and Interaction of Cubic Feet and an Elevator

```
The regression equation is
Hours = - 4.73 + 0.0573 Feet + 5.46 ElevatorD - 0.0139 Feet*ElevatorD

Predictor          Coef    SE Coef      T      P
Constant         -4.726      4.153  -1.14  0.264
Feet           0.057306   0.004808  11.92  0.000
ElevatorD         5.461      4.705   1.16  0.254
Feet*ElevatorD -0.013899   0.005941  -2.34  0.026

S = 4.48799    R-Sq = 91.7%    R-Sq(adj) = 90.9%

Analysis of Variance

Source          DF      SS      MS       F      P
Regression       3  7126.9  2375.6  117.94  0.000
Residual Error  32   644.5    20.1
Total           35  7771.4
```

FIGURE 10.9

JMP Output for a Regression Model That Includes Cubic Feet, Presence of an Elevator, and Interaction of Cubic Feet and an Elevator

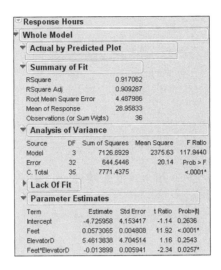

To test for the existence of an interaction, you use the null hypothesis that there is no interaction between cubic feet and an elevator versus the alternative hypothesis that there is an interaction between cubic feet and an elevator. In Figure 10.8 or 10.9, the t statistic for the interaction of cubic feet and an elevator is -2.34. Because the p-value = 0.026 < 0.05, you reject the null hypothesis. Therefore, the interaction term make a significant contribution to the model given that cubic feet and presence of an elevator are already included. Therefore, you need to use a regression model that includes cubic feet, presence of an elevator, and the interaction of cubic feet and presence of an elevator.

From Figure 10.8, this regression model is:

$$\text{Predicted labor hours} = -4.726 + (0.0573 \times \text{cubic feet value})$$
$$+ (5.461 \times \text{coded elevator value})$$
$$- (0.0139 \times \text{cubic feet value} \times \text{coded elevator value})$$

10.6 COLLINEARITY

One important problem in the application of multiple regression analysis involves the possible **collinearity** of the independent variables. This condition refers to situations in which one or more of the independent variables are highly correlated with each other. In such situations, the different variables do not provide new information, and it is difficult to separate the effect of such variables on the dependent variable. When collinearity exists, the values of the regression coefficients for the correlated variables may fluctuate drastically, depending on which independent variables are included in the model.

One method of measuring collinearity is the **variance inflationary factor (*VIF*)** for each independent variable. The *VIF* is directly related to the coefficient of determination between a particular independent variable and all the other independent variables. When a particular independent variable has a small coefficient of determination with the other independent variables, its *VIF* will be small (below 5). When a particular independent variable has a large coefficient of determination with the other independent variables, its *VIF* will be large (above 5). You compute *VIF* as follows:

$$VIF = \frac{1}{1 - R^2} \qquad (10.2)$$

where R^2 is the coefficient of multiple determination of an independent variable with all other independent variables.

If there are only two independent variables, R_1^2 is the coefficient of determination between X_1 and X_2. It is identical to R_2^2 which is the coefficient of determination between X_2 and X_1. If, for example, there are three independent variables, then R_1^2 is the coefficient of multiple determination of X_1 with X_2 and X_3; R_2^2 is the coefficient of multiple determination of X_2 with X_1 and X_3; and R_3^2 is the coefficient of multiple determination of X_3 with X_1 and X_2.

If a set of independent variables is uncorrelated, each *VIF* is equal to 1. If the set is highly intercorrelated, then a *VIF* might even exceed 10. Many statisticians [see Reference 7] have suggested that you use alternatives to least-squares regression if the maximum *VIF* is greater than 5.

You need to proceed with extreme caution when using a multiple regression model that has one or more large *VIF* values. You can use the model to predict values of the dependent variable *only* in the case where the values of the independent variables used in the prediction are consistent with the values observed in the data set. However, you cannot extrapolate to values of the independent variables not observed in the sample data, and because the independent variables contain overlapping information, you should always avoid interpreting the coefficient estimates (i.e., there is no way to accurately estimate the individual effects of the independent variables). One solution to the problem is to delete the variable with the largest *VIF* value. The reduced model (i.e., the model with the independent variable with the largest *VIF* value deleted) is often free of collinearity problems. If you determine that all the independent variables are needed in the model, you can use methods discussed in References 4, 5, and 7.

In the moving company data of Section 10.1, the correlation between the two independent variables, cubic feet, and number of pieces of large furniture is 0.854. Therefore, because there are only two independent variables in the model, using Equation (10.2):

$$VIF_1 = VIF_2 = \frac{1}{1 - (0.854)^2}$$

$$= 3.69$$

Thus, you can conclude that there is some collinearity for the moving company data. However, because the *VIF* is below 5, you can include both independent variables in the regression model.

10.7 MODEL BUILDING

This chapter and Chapter 9 introduced you to many different topics in regression analysis. In this section, you learn a structured approach to building the most appropriate regression model.

To begin, the director of operations for a television station needs to look for ways to reduce labor expenses. Currently, the unionized graphic artists at the station receive hourly pay for a significant number of hours in which they are idle. These hours are called *standby hours*. You have collected data concerning standby hours and four factors that you suspect are related to the excessive number of standby hours the station is currently experiencing: the total number of staff present, remote hours, Dubner hours, and total labor hours. You plan to build a multiple regression model to help determine which factors most heavily affect standby hours. You believe that an appropriate model will help you to predict the number of future standby hours, identify the root causes for excessive amounts of standby hours, and allow you to reduce the total number of future standby hours. How do you build the model with the most appropriate mix of independent variables? Table 10.4 presents the data.

TABLE 10.4   Predicting Standby Hours Based on Total Staff Present, Remote Hours, Dubner Hours, and Total Labor Hours

Week	Standby Hours	Total Staff Present	Remote Hours	Dubner Hours	Total Labor Hours
1	245	338	414	323	2,001
2	177	333	598	340	2,030
3	271	358	656	340	2,226
4	211	372	631	352	2,154
5	196	339	528	380	2,078
6	135	289	409	339	2,080
7	195	334	382	331	2,073
8	118	293	399	311	1,758
9	116	325	343	328	1,624
10	147	311	338	353	1,889
11	154	304	353	518	1,988

Continues

TABLE 10.4   Predicting Standby Hours Based on Total Staff Present, Remote Hours, Dubner Hours, and Total Labor Hours (Continued)

Week	Standby Hours	Total Staff Present	Remote Hours	Dubner Hours	Total Labor Hours
12	146	312	289	440	2,049
13	115	283	388	276	1,796
14	161	307	402	207	1,720
15	274	322	151	287	2,056
16	245	335	228	290	1,890
17	201	350	271	355	2,187
18	183	339	440	300	2,032
19	237	327	475	284	1,856
20	175	328	347	337	2,068
21	152	319	449	279	1,813
22	188	325	336	244	1,808
23	188	322	267	253	1,834
24	197	317	235	272	1,973
25	261	315	164	223	1,839
26	232	331	270	272	1,935

🌐 **STANDBY**

Before you develop a model to predict standby hours, you need to consider the principle of parsimony. **Parsimony** means that you want to develop a regression model that includes the fewest number of independent variables that permit an adequate interpretation of the dependent variable. Regression models with fewer independent variables are easier to interpret, particularly because they are less likely affected by collinearity problems (described in Section 10.6).

The selection of an appropriate model when many independent variables are under consideration involves complexities that are not present with a model with only two independent variables. The evaluation of all possible regression models is more computationally complex, and although you can quantitatively evaluate competing models, there may not be a *uniquely best* model but rather several *equally appropriate* models.

To begin analyzing the standby hours data, the *VIF* [see Equation (10.2) on page 256] is computed to measure the amount of collinearity among the independent variables. Figure 10.10 shows Minitab output of the *VIF* values along with the regression equation. Observe that all the *VIF* values are relatively small, ranging from a high of 2.0 for the total labor hours to a low of 1.2 for remote hours. Thus, on the basis of the criteria developed by Snee that all *VIF* values should be less than 5.0 [see Reference 7], there is little evidence of collinearity among the set of independent variables.

FIGURE 10.10

Minitab Regression Model to Predict Standby Hours Based on Four Independent Variables

```
The regression equation is
Standby = - 331 + 1.25 Staff - 0.118 Remote - 0.297 Dubner + 0.131 Labor


Predictor      Coef   SE Coef      T      P    VIF
Constant     -330.8     110.9  -2.98  0.007
Staff        1.2456    0.4121   3.02  0.006   1.7
Remote     -0.11842   0.05432  -2.18  0.041   1.2
Dubner      -0.2971    0.1179  -2.52  0.020   1.5
Labor       0.13053   0.05932   2.20  0.039   2.0


S = 31.8350   R-Sq = 62.3%   R-Sq(adj) = 55.1%


Analysis of Variance

Source           DF     SS    MS     F      P
Regression        4  35182  8795  8.68  0.000
Residual Error   21  21283  1013
Total            25  56465
```

The Stepwise Regression Approach to Model Building

You continue your analysis of the standby hours data by attempting to determine the subset of all independent variables that yield an adequate and appropriate model. The first approach described here is stepwise regression, which attempts to find the "best" regression model without examining all possible models.

In Section 9.6, you used the t test or F test to determine whether a particular slope made a significant contribution to a multiple regression model. Stepwise regression extends these tests to a model with any number of independent variables. An important feature of this stepwise approach is that an independent variable that has entered into the model at an early stage may subsequently be removed after other independent variables are considered. Thus, in stepwise regression, variables are either added to or deleted from the regression model at each step of the model-building process. The stepwise procedure terminates with the selection of a best-fitting model when no additional variables can be added to or deleted from the last model evaluated.

Figure 10.11 represents Minitab stepwise regression output for the standby hours data, while Figure 10.12 illustrates JMP output. For this example, a significance level of 0.05 is used to enter a variable into the model or to delete a variable from the model. The first variable entered into the model is total staff, the variable that correlates most highly with the dependent variable standby hours. Because the p-value of 0.001 is less than 0.05, total staff is included in the regression model.

FIGURE 10.11
Minitab Stepwise
Regression Output for
the Standby Hours
Data

```
Alpha-to-Enter: 0.05   Alpha-to-Remove: 0.05

Response is Standby on 4 predictors, with N = 26

Step                 1       2
Constant         -272.4  -330.7

Staff              1.42    1.76
T-Value            3.72    4.66
P-Value           0.001   0.000

Remote                    -0.139
T-Value                    -2.36
P-Value                    0.027

S                  38.6    35.4
R-Sq              36.60   48.99
R-Sq(adj)         33.96   44.56
Mallows C-p        13.3     8.4
```

FIGURE 10.12
JMP Stepwise Regres-
sion Output for the
Standby Hours Data

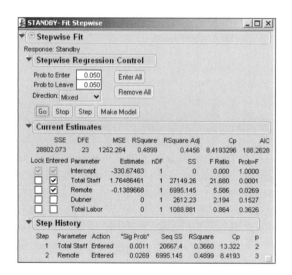

The next step involves selecting a second variable for the model. The second variable chosen is one that makes the largest contribution to the model, given that the first independent variable has been selected. For this model, the second variable is remote hours. Because the p-value of 0.027 for remote hours is less than 0.05, remote hours is included in the regression model.

After remote hours is entered into the model, the stepwise procedure determines whether total staff is still an important contributing variable or whether it can be eliminated from the model. Because the p-value of 0.0001 for total staff is less than 0.05, total staff remains in the regression model.

The next step involves selecting a third independent variable for the model. Because none of the other variables meets the 0.05 criterion for entry into the model, the stepwise procedure terminates with a model that includes total staff present and the number of remote hours.

This stepwise regression approach to model building was originally developed more than four decades ago, in an era in which regression analysis on mainframe computers involved the costly use of large amounts of processing time. Under such conditions, stepwise regression became widely used, although it provides a limited evaluation of alternative models. With today's extremely fast personal computers, the evaluation of many different regression models is completed quickly at a very small cost. Thus, a more general way of evaluating alternative regression models, in this era of fast computers, is the best subsets approach discussed next. Stepwise regression is not obsolete, however. Today, many businesses use stepwise regression as part of a new research technique called **data mining**, where huge data sets are explored to discover significant statistical relationships among a large number of variables. These data sets are so large that the best-subsets approach is impractical.

The Best-Subsets Approach to Model Building

The **best-subsets approach** evaluates either all possible regression models for a given set of independent variables or the best subsets of models for a given number of independent variables. Figure 10.13 presents Minitab output of all possible regression models for the standby hours data, while Figure 10.14 illustrates JMP output.

FIGURE 10.13
Minitab Best-Subsets Regression Output for the Standby Hours Data

```
Response is Standby

                                                R D
                                              S e u L
                                              t m b a
                                              a o n b
                                    Mallows    f t e o
Vars  R-Sq  R-Sq(adj)      C-p        S     f e r r
  1   36.6      34.0     13.3   38.621   X
  1   17.1      13.7     24.2   44.162           X
  1    6.0       2.1     30.4   47.035       X
  2   49.0      44.6      8.4   35.387   X X
  2   45.0      40.2     10.6   36.749   X   X
  2   42.9      37.9     11.8   37.447       X X
  3   53.8      47.5      7.8   34.443   X   X X
  3   53.6      47.3      7.8   34.503   X X X
  3   50.9      44.2      9.3   35.492   X X   X
  4   62.3      55.1      5.0   31.835   X X X X
```

FIGURE 10.14
JMP All Possible Regression Models Output for the Standby Hours Data

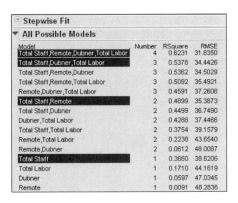

Model	Number	RSquare	RMSE
Total Staff,Remote,Dubner,Total Labor	4	0.6231	31.8350
Total Staff,Dubner,Total Labor	3	0.5378	34.4426
Total Staff,Remote,Dubner	3	0.5362	34.5029
Total Staff,Remote,Total Labor	3	0.5092	35.4921
Remote,Dubner,Total Labor	3	0.4591	37.2608
Total Staff,Remote	2	0.4899	35.3873
Total Staff,Dubner	2	0.4499	36.7490
Dubner,Total Labor	2	0.4288	37.4466
Total Staff,Total Labor	2	0.3754	39.1579
Remote,Total Labor	2	0.2238	43.6540
Remote,Dubner	2	0.0612	48.0087
Total Staff	1	0.3660	38.6206
Total Labor	1	0.1710	44.1619
Dubner	1	0.0597	47.0345
Remote	1	0.0091	48.2636

A criterion often used in model building is the adjusted r^2, which adjusts the r^2 of each model to account for the number of variables in the model as well as for the sample size. Because model building requires you to compare models with different numbers of independent variables, the adjusted r^2 is more appropriate than r^2.

Referring to Figure 10.13, you see that the adjusted r^2 reaches a maximum value of 0.551 when all four independent variables plus the intercept term (for a total of five estimated regression coefficients) are included in the model. Observe that Figure 10.14 provides only the r^2 value for each model, but highlights the model with the highest r^2 for a given number of independent variables. You can then use the stepwise features of JMP to compute the adjusted r^2 for any model along with the C_p statistic, which will be discussed next.

A second criterion often used in the evaluation of competing models is the C_p statistic developed by Mallows [see Reference 4]. The C_p statistic[1] measures the differences between a fitted regression model and a *true* model, along with random error.

When a regression model with k independent variables contains only random differences from a *true* model, the mean value of C_p is the number of regression coefficients including the Y intercept in the model. Thus, in evaluating many alternative regression models, the goal is to find models whose C_p is close to or less than the number of regression coefficients including the Y intercept in the model.

In Figure 10.13, you see that only the model with all four independent variables considered contains a C_p value close to or below the number of regression coefficients including the Y intercept in the model. Therefore, you should choose this model. Although it was not the case here, the C_p statistic often provides several alternative models for you to evaluate in greater depth using other criteria such as parsimony, interpretability, and departure from model assumptions (as evaluated by residual analysis). The model selected using stepwise regression has a C_p value of 8.4, which is substantially above the suggested criterion of the number of regression coefficients including the Y intercept in the model (equals 3 for that model).

When you finish selecting the independent variables to include in the model, perform a residual analysis to evaluate the aptness of the selected model. Figure 10.15 presents Minitab residual analysis output.

You see that the plots of the residuals versus the total staff, the remote hours, the Dubner hours, and the total labor hours all reveal no apparent pattern. In addition, a histogram of the residuals (not shown here) indicates only moderate departure from normality.

---

[1] The C_p presented in this section is entirely different from the C_p statistic that measures the capability of a process.

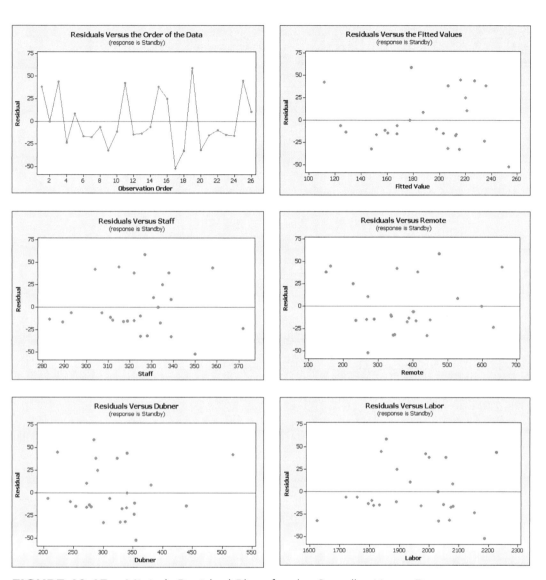

FIGURE 10.15 Minitab Residual Plots for the Standby Hours Data

Thus, from Figure 10.10 on page 259, the regression equation is:

Predicted standby hours = -330.83 + 1.2456 × total staff hours – 0.1184
× total remote hours – 0.2971 × Dubner hours + 0.1305 × total labor hours

THE C_p STATISTIC {OPTIONAL}

$$C_p = \frac{(1-R_k^2)(n-T)}{1-R_T^2} - \left[n-2(k+1)\right] \qquad (10.3)$$

where

k = number of independent variables included in a regression model

T = total number of regression coefficients (including the intercept) to be estimated in the full regression model

R_k^2 = coefficient of multiple determination for a regression model that has k independent variables

R_T^2 = coefficient of multiple determination for a full regression model that contains all T estimated regression coefficients

Using Equation (10.3) to compute C_p for the model containing total staff present and remote hours,

$$n = 26 \quad k = 2 \quad T = 4+1 = 5 \quad R_k^2 = 0.490 \quad R_T^2 = 0.623$$

so that

$$C_p = \frac{(1-0.49)(26-5)}{1-0.623} - [26-2(2+1)]$$
$$= 8.42$$

To summarize, follow these steps when building a regression model:

1. Compile a list of all potential independent variables.
2. Fit a regression model that includes all the independent variables under consideration and determine the *VIF* for each independent variable. Three possible results can occur:
   a. None of the independent variables have a *VIF* > 5; proceed to step 3.
   b. One of the independent variables has a *VIF* > 5; eliminate that independent variable and proceed to step 3.
   c. More than one of the independent variables has a *VIF* > 5; eliminate the independent variable that has the highest *VIF*, and repeat step 2.
3. Perform a best-subsets or all-subsets regression with the remaining independent variables and determine the C_p statistic and/or the adjusted r^2 for each model.

4. List all models that have C_p close to or less than $(k + 1)$ and/or a high adjusted r^2.

5. From those models listed in step 4, choose a best model.

6. Perform a complete analysis of the model chosen, including a residual analysis.

7. Depending on the results of the residual analysis, add curvilinear terms, transform variables, possibly delete individual observations if necessary [see References 1 and 4 for further discussion], and reanalyze the data.

8. Use the selected model for prediction and inference.

Figure 10.16 represents a road map for these steps in model building.

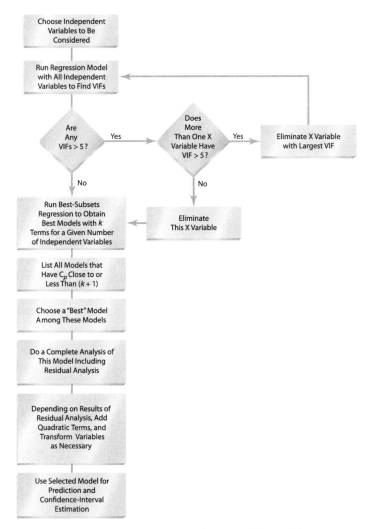

FIGURE 10.16 Road Map for Model Building

Model Validation

The final step in the model-building process is to validate the regression model. This step involves checking the model against data that was not part of the analyzed sample. Several ways of validating a regression model are as follows:

1. Collect new data and compare the results.
2. Compare the results of the regression model to theoretical expectations or previous results.
3. If the data set is large, split the data into two parts: the main sample and a hold-out sample. You use the main sample to develop your regression model and the hold-out sample to validate the regression model. The hold-out sample provides an opportunity to test the validity of the regression model on a data set other than the data set (the main sample) used to develop the regression model. Perhaps the best way of validating a regression model is by collecting new data. If the results with new data are consistent to the fitted regression model, you have strong reason to believe that the fitted regression model is applicable in a wide set of circumstances. If it is not possible to collect new data, you can compare your regression coefficients and predictions to theoretical expectations or other empirical results.

10.8 LOGISTIC REGRESSION

The discussion of the simple linear regression model in Chapter 9 and the multiple regression models in Sections 10.1–10.7 only considered numerical dependent variables. However, sometimes, the dependent variable is a categorical variable that takes on one of only two possible values. For example, a customer is satisfied or a customer is not satisfied. The use of simple or multiple least-squares regression for a two category response variable (CTQ or Y) often violates the normality assumption and can lead to impossible values of the CTQ (Y).

An alternative approach, **logistic regression**, originally applied in the health sciences [see Reference 2] enables you to use regression models to predict the probability of a particular categorical binary response for a given set of independent variables (CTPs or Xs). This logistic regression model is based on the **odds ratio**, which represents the probability of a success compared with the probability of failure.

$$\text{Odds ratio} = \frac{\text{probability of success}}{1 - \text{probability of success}} \qquad (10.4)$$

Using Equation (10.4), if the probability of success for an event is 0.50, the odds ratio is:

$$\text{Odds ratio} = \frac{0.50}{1 - 0.50} = 1.0, \text{ or } 1 \text{ to } 1$$

If the probability of success for an event is 0.75, the odds ratio is:

$$\text{Odds ratio} = \frac{0.75}{1 - 0.75} = 3.0, \text{ or } 3 \text{ to } 1$$

The logistic regression model is based on the natural logarithm (LN) of this odds ratio. (For more information on logarithms, see below.) The logistic regression model for two independent variables is:

$$\text{LN(estimated odds ratio)} = Y \text{ intercept} \qquad (10.5a)$$
$$+ \text{ (slope with } X_1 \times X_1 \text{ value)} + \text{ (slope with } X_2 \times X_2 \text{ value)}$$

or

$$\text{LN(estimated odds ratio)} = b_0 + b_1 X_1 + b_2 X \qquad (10.5b)$$

A mathematical method called *maximum likelihood estimation* is usually used to develop a regression equation to predict the natural logarithm of this odds ratio. Once you determine the logistic regression equation, you compute the estimated odds ratio:

$$\text{Estimated odds ratio} = e^{\text{LN(estimated odds ratio)}} \qquad (10.6)$$

where e is the mathematical constant 2.718282.

Once you have computed the estimated odds ratio, you find the estimated probability of success:

$$\text{Estimated probability of success} = \frac{\text{estimated odds ratio}}{1 + \text{estimated odds ratio}} \qquad (10.7)$$

LOGARITHMS {OPTIONAL}

The logarithm of a number is the power that the base number needs to be raised to in order to equal the number of interest. For example:

$$10 \times 10 = 10^2 = 100$$

The number 10 raised to the second power (squared) equals 100. Base 10 logarithms are called common logarithms (and use the symbol LOG). Because 100 is equal to 10 raised to the second power, the logarithm of 100 is 2.

Continues

Using another example, the logarithm of 80 is approximately 1.903. (You can use a scientific calculator to compute this.) This means that 10 raised to the 1.903 power equals 80.

Natural logarithms (which use the symbol LN) have a base that is the mathematical constant e, approximately equal to 2.718282. The natural logarithm of 100 is approximately equal to 4.6052. This means that e ($e = 2.718282$) raised to the 4.6052 power equals 100.

To illustrate the logistic regression model, recall from Chapter 8, "Design of Experiments," that a hotel that served many business customers had instituted a new process of delivering breakfast via room service. When customers finished breakfast, they were asked to indicate whether they were satisfied with the delivery process. Table 10.5 summarizes the results from a random sample of 30 customers, along with the delivery time difference and whether the customer had previously stayed at the hotel.

TABLE 10.5   Customer Satisfaction, Delivery Time Difference, and Previous Stay at Hotel

Satisfaction	Delivery Time Difference	Previous
No	6.1	No
Yes	4.5	Yes
Yes	0.8	No
Yes	1.3	Yes
Yes	3.6	Yes
Yes	2.7	Yes
No	5.9	No
Yes	4.5	Yes
No	4.8	Yes
Yes	2.1	No
Yes	4.1	Yes
No	5.6	Yes
Yes	3.8	Yes
Yes	2.3	No
No	3.2	No
Yes	3.6	Yes
No	6.0	No
Yes	4.4	Yes

Satisfaction	Delivery Time Difference	Previous
Yes	0.9	No
Yes	1.2	Yes
No	3.8	No
Yes	3.5	Yes
No	4.0	Yes
Yes	4.3	Yes
No	4.9	Yes
Yes	2.3	No
Yes	3.8	Yes
No	5.9	Yes
Yes	3.7	Yes
Yes	2.5	No

SATISFACTION

Figures 10.17 and 10.18 represent Minitab and JMP output for the logistic regression model. There are two independent variables: X_1 (delivery time difference) and X_2 (previous stay at hotel).

FIGURE 10.17
Minitab Logistic Regression Output for the Hotel Satisfaction Data

```
Logistic Regression Table
                                                              95%
                                                              CI
Predictor                    Coef  SE Coef     Z     P  Odds Ratio Lower
Constant                  14.7567  6.56055   2.25 0.024
Delivery Time Difference  -5.05457 2.27853  -2.22 0.027       0.01  0.00
Previous
  1                        8.43943 4.29026   1.97 0.049    4625.91  1.03

Predictor                     Upper
Constant
Delivery Time Difference       0.56
Previous
  1                     20755983.77


Log-Likelihood = -5.629
Test that all slopes are zero: G = 26.933, DF = 2, P-Value = 0.000


Goodness-of-Fit Tests

Method          Chi-Square  DF     P
Pearson           22.7232   23  0.477
Deviance          11.2581   23  0.980
Hosmer-Lemeshow    8.9074    8  0.350
```

FIGURE 10.18

JMP Logistic Regression Output for the Hotel Satisfaction Data

Nominal Logistic Fit for Satisfaction

▶ Iteration History

▼ **Whole Model Test**

Model	-LogLikelihood	DF	ChiSquare	Prob>ChiSq
Difference	13.466395	2	26.93279	<.0001*
Full	5.629030			
Reduced	19.095425			

RSquare (U)	0.7052
Observations (or Sum Wgts)	30

Converged by Gradient

▼ **Lack Of Fit**

Source	DF	-LogLikelihood	ChiSquare
Lack Of Fit	23	5.6290301	11.25806
Saturated	25	0.0000000	Prob>ChiSq
Fitted	2	5.6290301	0.9804

▼ **Parameter Estimates**

Term	Estimate	Std Error	ChiSquare	Prob>ChiSq
Intercept	-14.756524	6.5604911	5.06	0.0245*
Delivery Time Difference	5.05451072	2.2785101	4.92	0.0265*
Previous	-8.439329	4.2902227	3.87	0.0492*

For log odds of 0/1

▼ **Effect Likelihood Ratio Tests**

Source	Nparm	DF	L-R ChiSquare	Prob>ChiSq
Delivery Time Difference	1	1	25.8008399	<.0001*
Previous	1	1	10.159666	0.0014*

(Because the first value for satisfaction is not satisfied (0), JMP is predicting the probability of not being satisfied while Minitab is predicting the probability of being satisfied. Thus, the signs of the regression coefficients are the opposite of those shown by Minitab.)

From Figure 10.17, the regression model is stated as:

$$\text{LN(estimated odds ratio)} = 14.7567 - 5.05457X_1 + 8.43943X_2$$

The regression coefficients are interpreted as follows:

1. The regression constant is 14.7567. Thus, for a customer who did not have any delivery time difference and who did not stay at the hotel previously, the estimated natural logarithm of the odds ratio of being satisfied with the delivery service is 14.7567.

2. The regression coefficient for delivery time difference is -5.05457. Therefore, holding constant the effect of whether the customer had previously stayed at the hotel, for each increase of one minute in the delivery time difference, the estimated natural logarithm of the odds ratio of being satisfied with the delivery service decreases by 5.05457. Therefore, the longer the delivery time difference, the less likely the customer is to be satisfied with the delivery service.

3. The regression coefficient for previous stay at the hotel is 8.43943. Holding constant the delivery time difference, the estimated natural logarithm of the odds ratio of being satisfied with the delivery service increases by 8.43943 for customers who have previously stayed at the hotel compared with customers

who have not previously stayed at the hotel. Therefore, customers who have previously stayed at the hotel are more likely to be satisfied with the delivery service.

As was the case with least-squares regression models, a main purpose of performing logistic regression analysis is to provide predictions of a dependent variable. For example, consider a customer who had a delivery time difference of four minutes and previously stayed at the hotel. What is the probability this customer will be satisfied with the delivery service? Using delivery time difference = 4 minutes and previous stay = Yes ($X_2 = 1$) from Figure 10.17, you have the following:

$$\text{LN(estimated odds ratio)} = 14.7567 - (5.05457 \times 4) + (8.43943 \times 1) = 2.97785$$

Using Equation (10.6) on page 267, estimated odds ratio = $e^{2.97785}$ = 19.6455

Therefore, the odds are 19.6455 to 1 that a customer who had a delivery time difference of 4 minutes and previously stayed at the hotel will be satisfied with the delivery service. Using Equation (10.7) on page 267, this odds ratio can be converted to a probability:

$$\text{estimated probability of being satisfied with the delivery service} = \frac{19.6455}{1 + 19.6455}$$
$$= 0.9516$$

Thus, the estimated probability is 0.9516 that a customer who had a delivery time difference of 4 minutes and previously stayed at the hotel will be satisfied with the delivery service. In other words, 95.16% of such individuals are expected to be satisfied with the delivery service.

Now that you have used the logistic regression model for prediction, you can consider whether the model is a good-fitting model and whether each of the independent variables included in the model makes a significant contribution to the model. The **deviance statistic** is frequently used to determine whether or not the current model provides a good fit to the data. This statistic measures the fit of the current model compared with a model that has as many parameters as there are data points (what is called a *saturated* model). The null and alternative hypotheses are as follows:

H_0: The model is a good-fitting model.
H_1: The model is not a good-fitting model.

When using the deviance (or lack of fit) statistic for logistic regression, the null hypothesis represents a good-fitting model, which is the opposite of the null hypothesis when using the F test for the multiple regression model (see Section 10.2). From Figure 10.17 on page 269, the deviance (or lack of fit) = 11.2581 and the p-value = 0.980 > 0.05. Thus, you do not reject H_0, and you conclude that the model is a good-fitting one.

Now that you have concluded that the model is a good-fitting one, you need to evaluate whether each of the independent variables makes a significant contribution to the model in the presence of the others. As was the case with linear regression in Section 10.6, the test statistic is based on the ratio of the regression coefficient to the standard error of the regression coefficient. In logistic regression, this ratio is defined by the **Wald statistic**, which approximately follows the normal distribution. From Figure 10.17, the Wald statistic $Z = -2.22$ for delivery time difference and 1.97 for previous stay at the hotel. In Figure 11.18, the square of the Wald statistic, labeled as Chisquare, is provided (for these data, $(-2.22)^2 = 4.92$ and $(1.97)^2 = 3.87$). Because $-2.22 < 1.96$ and $1.97 > 1.96$ and the p-values are 0.027 and 0.049, you can conclude that each of the two explanatory variables makes a contribution to the model in the presence of the other. Therefore, you should include both these independent variables in the model.

SUMMARY

In this chapter, you learned how to use several independent variables to predict a dependent variable (CTQ). You used independent and dependent variables that were either numerical or categorical and also applied both stepwise and all possible regression approaches.

REFERENCES

1. Berenson, M. L., D. M. Levine, and T. C. Krehbiel. *Basic Business Statistics: Concepts and Applications*, 10th Ed. (Upper Saddle River, NJ: Prentice Hall, 2006).

2. Hosmer, D. W. and S. Lemeshow. *Applied Logistic Regression*, 2nd Ed. (New York: Wiley, 2001).

3. *JMP Version 6* (Cary, NC: SAS Institute, 2005).

4. Kutner, M. H., C. Nachtsheim, J. Neter, and W. Li. *Applied Linear Statistical Models*, 5th Ed. (New York: McGraw-Hill-Irwin, 2005).

5. Marquardt, D. W. "You should standardize the predictor variables in your regression models," discussion of "A critique of some ridge regression methods," by G. Smith and F. Campbell. *Journal of the American Statistical Association*, 75 (1980): 87–91.

6. *Minitab for Windows Version 14* (State College, PA: Minitab Inc., 2004).

7. Snee, R. D. "Some aspects of nonorthogonal data analysis, part I. Developing prediction equations." *Journal of Quality Technology*, 5 (1973): 67–79.

Appendix 10.1
Using Minitab for Multiple Regression

Generating a Multiple Regression Equation

In Appendix 9.1, you used Minitab for generating a simple linear regression model. The same set of instructions is valid in using Minitab for multiple regression. To carry out a multiple regression analysis for the moving company data, open the **MOVING.MTW** worksheet and select **Stat → Regression → Regression**.

1. Enter **C1** or **Hours** in the Response: edit box and **C2** or **Feet** and **C3** or **Large** in the Predictors: edit box. Click the **Graphs** button.

2.. In the Regression-Graphs dialog box, in the Residuals for Plots: edit box, select the **Regular** option button. For Residual Plots, select the **Histogram of residuals** and the **Residuals versus fits** check boxes. In the Residuals versus the variables: edit box, select **C2** or **Feet** and **C3** or **Large**. Click the **OK** button to return to the Regression dialog box.

3. Click the **Results** option button. In the Regression Results dialog box, click the **In addition, the full table of fits and residuals** option button. Click the **OK** button to return to the Regression dialog box.

4. Click the **Options** button. Select the **Variance inflation factors** check box. In the Prediction interval for new observations: edit box, enter the desired values for Feet and Large. Enter **95** in the Confidence level: edit box. Click the **OK** button to return to the Regression dialog box. Click the **OK** button.

Using Minitab for a Three-Dimensional Plot

You can use Minitab to construct a three-dimensional plot when there are two independent variables in the regression model. To illustrate the three-dimensional plot with the moving company data, open the **MOVING.MTW** worksheet. Select **Graph → 3D Scatterplot**.

1. In the 3D Scatterplots dialog box, select the **Simple** button.

2. In the 3D Scatterplot—Simple dialog box (see Figure A10.1), enter **C1** or **Hours** in the Z variable edit box, **C2** or **Feet** in the *Y* variable edit box, and **C3** or **Large** in the X variable edit box. Click the **OK** button.

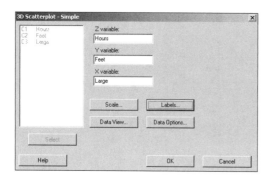

FIGURE A10.1
Minitab 3D Scatterplot—Simple
Dialog Box

Using Minitab for Dummy Variables and Interactions

In order to perform regression analysis with dummy variables, the categories of the dummy variable are coded as 0 and 1. If the dummy variable has not already been coded as a 0–1 variable, Minitab can recode the variable. To illustrate this with the moving company data, open the **MOVING. MTW** worksheet. In this worksheet, the elevator variable in column C4 has been entered as Yes and No. To recode this variable using Minitab, select **Calc → Make Indicator Variables**. In the Indicator variables for: edit box, enter **Elevator** or **C4**. In the Store results in: edit box, enter **C5 C6**, because you need to specify a column for each possible definition of the dummy variable, even though only one column (C6) will be used in the regression analysis. Click the **OK** button. Observe that No is coded as 1 in C5, and Yes is coded as 1 in C6. Label C6 as **ElevatorD**.

To define an interaction term that is the product of cubic feet and the dummy variable elevator, select **Calc → Calculator**. In the Store result in variable: edit box,

enter **C7**. In the Expression: edit box, enter **Feet * ElevatorD** or **C2 * C6**. Click the **OK** button. C7 now contains a new X variable that is the product of C2 and C6. Label C7 as **Feet * ElevatorD**.

Using Minitab for Stepwise Regression and Best-Subsets Regression

You can use Minitab for model building with either stepwise regression or best-subsets regression. To illustrate model building with the standby hours data, open the **STANDBY.MTW** worksheet. To perform stepwise regression, select **Stat → Regression → Stepwise**.

1. In the Stepwise Regression dialog box (see Figure A10.2), in the Response: edit box, enter **STANDBY** or **C1**.

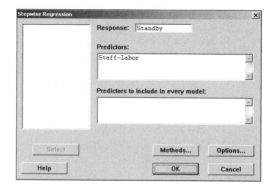

FIGURE A10.2
Minitab Stepwise Regression Dialog Box

2. In the Predictors: edit box, enter **Staff** or **C2**, **Remote** or **C3**, **Dubner** or **C4**, and **Labor** or **C5**. Click the **Methods** button.

3. In the Stepwise-Methods dialog box (see Figure A10.3), select the **Stepwise** option button. Enter **0.05** in the Alpha to enter: edit box and **0.05** in the Alpha to remove edit box. Enter **4** in the *F* to enter: edit box and **4** in the *F* to remove: edit box. Click the **OK** button to return to the Stepwise Regression dialog box. Click the **OK** button.

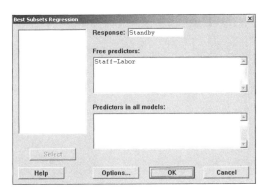

FIGURE A10.4
Minitab Best Subsets Regression Dialog Box

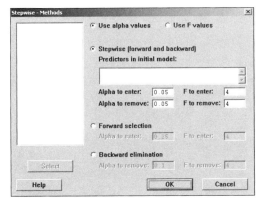

FIGURE A10.3
Minitab Stepwise-Methods Dialog Box

To perform a best-subsets regression, select **Stat → Regression → Best Subsets**.

1. In the Best Subsets Regression dialog box (see Figure A10.4), in the Response: edit box, enter **Standby** or **C1**.

2. In the Free Predictors: edit box, enter **Staff** or **C2**, **Remote** or **C3**, **Dubner** or **C4**, and **Labor** or **C5**. Click the **Options** button. Enter **3** in the Models of each size to print edit box. Click the **OK** button to return to the Best Subsets Regression dialog box. Click the **OK** button.

Using Minitab for Logistic Regression

To illustrate the use of Minitab for logistic regression with the room service delivery satisfaction example, open the **SATISFAC-TION.MTW** worksheet. To perform a logistic regression, select **Stat → Regression → Binary Logistic Regression**.

In the Binary Logistic Regression dialog box (see Figure A10.5), in the Response: edit box, enter **C1** or **Satisfaction**. In the Model: edit box, enter **C2** or **Delivery Time Difference** and **C3** or **Previous**. In the Factors: edit box, enter **C3** or **Previous** because it is a categorical variable. Click the **OK** button.

FIGURE A10.5
Minitab Binary
Regression Dialog
Box

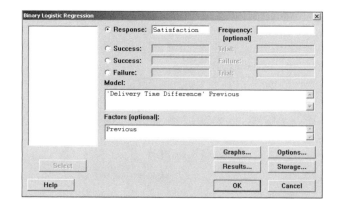

Appendix 10.2
Using JMP for Multiple Regression

Generating a Multiple Regression Equation

In Appendix 9.1, you used JMP for generating a simple linear regression model. To carry out a multiple regression analysis for the moving company data, open the **MOVING.JMP** data table and select **Analyze → Fit Model**.

1. Select **Hours** and click the **Y** button.
2. Select **Feet** and **Large** and click the **Add** button. Click the **Run Model** button.
3. To generate residual plots for each independent variable, click the red triangle to the left of Response Hours. Select **Save Columns → Residuals** (see Figure A10.6).

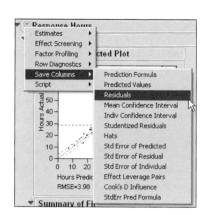

FIGURE A10.6
Using JMP to Save Residuals

4. Select **Analyze → Fit Y by X**. Enter **Residual Hours** in the **Y, Response** box. Enter **Feet** in the **X, Factor** edit box. Click the **OK** button.

5. Select **Analyze → Fit Y by X**. Enter **Residual Hours** in the **Y, Response** box. Enter **Large** in the **X, Factor** edit box. Click the **OK** button.

Using JMP for Dummy Variables

To create a dummy variable for presence of an elevator coded as a 0 – 1 variable for the moving company data, open the **MOVING.JMP** Data Table. Select **Cols → New Column**. Then select **Column Properties → Formula → Conditional → If** and do the following (see Figure A10.7):

1. If you do not code Elevator as a continuous variable, JMP uses a -1, 0, +1 coding scheme instead of a 0 and 1 coding scheme [see Reference 3]. With this coding scheme, the regression coefficients are interpreted as how much the response for each level differs from the average across all levels.

2. Enter **Elevator = =“Yes”** in the expression area.

3. Enter **1** as the clause in the then area.

4. Enter **0** as the clause in the else area.

5. Click the **OK** button.

6. Select **Continuous** in the Modeling Type option box. Provide a name for the variable in the Column Name edit box. Click the **OK** button.

7. Select **Analyze → Fit Model**.

8. Select **Hours** and click the **Y** button.

9. Select **Feet** and **ElevatorD** (or the name of the variable you just created) and click the **Add** button. Click the **Run Model** button.

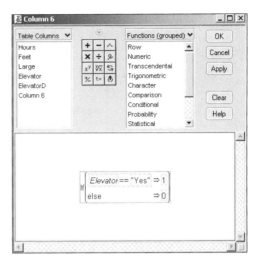

FIGURE A10.7
Using JMP to Create a Dummy Variable

To generate residual plots for each independent variable, click the red triangle to the left of Response Hours. Select **Save Columns → Residuals**.

1. Select **Analyze → Fit Y by X**. Enter **Residual Hours** in the **Y, Response** box. Enter **Feet** in the **X, Factor** edit box. Click the **OK** button.

2. Select **Analyze → Fit Y by X**. Enter **Residual Hours** in the **Y, Response** box. Enter **ElevatorD** in the **X, Factor** edit box. Click the **OK** button.

Using JMP for Interactions

To generate a regression model with an interaction term, open the **MOVING.JMP** Data Table. Select **Cols → New Column → Column Properties → Formula** and do the following:

1. Enter **Feet* ElevatorD** in the expression area. Click the **OK** button.
2. Enter **Feet* ElevatorD** in the Column Name edit box. Click the **OK** button.
3. Select **Analyze → Fit Model**.
4. Select **Hours** and click the **Y** button.
5. Select **Feet**, **ElevatorD**, and **Feet* ElevatorD** and click the **Add** button.
6. Click the **Run Model** button.

Using JMP for Stepwise Regression and All Possible Regressions

You can use JMP for model building with either stepwise regression or all possible regressions. To illustrate model building with the standby hours data, open the **STANDBY.JMP** worksheet. Select **Analyze → Fit Model**.

1. Select **Standby** and click the **Y** button.
2. Select **Total Staff**, **Remote**, **Dubner**, and **Labor Hours** and click the **Add** button.
3. In the Personality: edit box, select **Stepwise**. Select **Run Model**.
4. In the Stepwise Regression Control area (see Figure A10.8), enter **0.05** in the Prob to Enter: edit box. Enter **0.05** in the Prob to Leave: edit box. Select **Mixed** in the Direction drop-down list box. Click the **Go** button.
5. To generate all possible regression models, click the red triangle to the left of Stepwise Fit. Select **All Possible Models**. Click the **Go** button.

FIGURE A10.8
JMP Stepwise Fit Dialog Box

Using JMP for Logistic Regression

To illustrate the use of JMP for logistic regression with the room service delivery satisfaction example, open the **SATISFACTION.JMP** worksheet.

1. Highlight the **Satisfaction** column. Select **Cols → Col Info**. Select **Nominal** in the Modeling Type options box. Click the **OK** button. Do the same for the **Previous** column.
2. To perform a logistic regression, select **Analyze → Fit Model**.
3. Select **Satisfaction** and click the **Y** button.
4. Select **Delivery Time Difference** and **Previous** and click the **Add** button. Click the **Run Model** button.

The regression coefficients computed by JMP are not the same as those computed by Minitab. This occurs because JMP uses a -1, 0, +1 coding scheme instead of a 0 and 1 coding scheme [see Reference 3]. With this coding scheme, the regression coefficients are interpreted as how much the response for each level differs from the average across all levels.

CHAPTER 11

Control Charts for Six Sigma Management

11.1 BASIC CONCEPTS OF CONTROL CHARTS

11.2 CONTROL LIMITS AND PATTERNS

11.3 RULES FOR DETERMINING OUT-OF-CONTROL POINTS

11.4 THE p-CHART

11.5 THE c-CHART

11.6 THE u-CHART

11.7 CONTROL CHARTS FOR THE MEAN AND RANGE

11.8 CONTROL CHARTS FOR THE MEAN AND THE STANDARD DEVIATION

11.9 INDIVIDUAL VALUE AND MOVING RANGE CHARTS

SUMMARY

REFERENCES

APPENDIX 11.1 USING MINITAB FOR CONTROL CHARTS

APPENDIX 11.2 USING JMP FOR CONTROL CHARTS

LEARNING OBJECTIVES

After reading this chapter, you will be able to

- Understand the purpose of control charts.
- Know which control chart to use for a particular type of data.
- Construct and interpret various control charts.

11.1 BASIC CONCEPTS OF CONTROL CHARTS

The **control chart** is a tool for distinguishing between the common causes of variation (variation due to the system itself) and special causes of variation (variation due to factors external to the system) for a CTQ or a CTP (X). Control charts are used to assess and monitor the stability of a CTQ or an X (presence of only common causes of variation). The data for a control chart are collected from a subgroup or sample of items selected at each observation session.

Control charts can be divided into two categories that are determined by the type of data used to monitor a process. These two broad categories are called **attribute control charts** and **measurement (variable) control charts**.

In Chapter 2, "Introduction to Statistics," attribute data was defined as classification data (e.g., conforming or nonconforming) or count data (e.g., number of defects per area of opportunity). Attribute control charts are used to evaluate CTQs or Xs that are defined by attribute data. The attribute control charts covered in this chapter are as follows:

1. Proportion nonconforming charts (p-charts) for classification data:
   a. Proportion of nonconformities for constant subgroup size.
   b. Proportion of nonconformities for variable subgroup size.
2. Area of opportunity charts for count data:
   a. Number of defects charts (c-charts) for constant areas of opportunity.
   b. Number of defects per unit charts (u-charts) for variable areas of opportunity.

If the CTQ or X is measured on a continuous scale, such as height, weight, or cycle time, a variables control chart is used. Variables (measurement) control charts contain two sections. One section examines process variability, and the other section examines central tendency. The variables control charts covered in this chapter are the following:

1. Charts based on subgroups of $n \geq 2$:
   a. Mean and range charts ($\bar{X}$ and R-charts) for subgroups of $2 \leq n \leq 10$.
   b. Mean and standard deviation charts ($\bar{X}$ and S-charts) for subgroups of $n > 10$.
2. Charts based on individual measurements (X and moving range charts) for subgroups of $n = 1$.

Figure 11.17 on page 310 is a flow diagram that can help you to determine which type of chart is most appropriate for a given situation. Control charts are an important statistical tool in Six Sigma management. They are used at every stage of the DMAIC model (see Table 1.1 on page 5).

The distinction between the two causes of variation is crucial because special causes of variation are considered to be those that are not due to the process, whereas common causes of variation are due to the process. Only management can change the process.

> **Special or assignable causes of variation** create fluctuations or patterns in data that are not inherent to a process. Special causes of variation are the responsibility of workers and engineers. Workers and engineers identify and, if possible, resolve special causes of variation. If they cannot resolve a special cause of variation, they enlist the aid of management.
>
> **Chance or common causes of variation** create fluctuations or patterns in data that are due to the system itself; for example, the fluctuations caused by hiring, training, and supervisory policies and practices. Common causes of variation are the responsibility of management. Only management can change the policies and procedures that define the common causes of variation in a system.

One experiment that is useful to help you appreciate the distinction between common and special causes of variation was developed by Walter Shewhart more than 80 years ago. The experiment requires that you repeatedly write the letter "A" over and over again in a horizontal line across a piece of paper.

AAAAAAAAAAAAAAAAA

When you do this, you will immediately notice that the "A"s are all similar, but not exactly the same. Additionally, you may notice as much as a 10%, 20%, or even 30% difference in the size of the "A"s from letter to letter. This difference is due to common cause variation. Nothing special happened that caused the differences in the size of the "A"s. If you had gotten more sleep last night, or drank less coffee today, your hand might be steadier, and your "A"s might be more similar. You probably realize that it would be foolish to try to explain why the largest "A" was so big and the smallest "A" was so small.

There are two types of errors that control charts help prevent. The first type of error involves the belief that an observed value represents special cause variation when it is due to the common cause variation of the system. Treating common causes of variation as special cause variation can result in tampering with or overadjustment of a process with an accompanying increase in variation. The second type of error involves treating special cause variation as though it were common cause variation and not taking corrective action when it is necessary. Although these errors can still occur when a control chart is used, they are far less likely.

11.2 CONTROL LIMITS AND PATTERNS

The most typical form of a control chart sets control limits at plus or minus three standard deviations of the statistic of interest (the mean, the range, the proportion, etc.). In general, control limits are computed as follows:

COMPUTING CONTROL LIMITS

Process mean of the statistic $\pm$ 3 standard deviations of the statistic   (11.1)

so that

Upper control limit (UCL) = process mean of the statistic + 3 standard deviations of the statistic

Lower control limit (LCL) = process mean of the statistic – 3 standard deviations of the statistic

Once you compute these control limits from the data, you evaluate the control chart by determining whether any nonrandom pattern exists in the data. Figure 11.1 illustrates three different patterns.

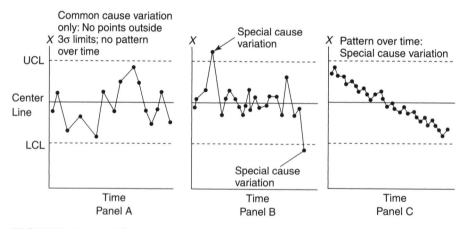

FIGURE 11.1   Three Control Chart Patterns

In panel A of Figure 11.1, there does not appear to be any pattern in the ordering of values over time, and there are no points that fall outside the three standard deviation control limits. The process appears to be stable; that is, it contains only common cause variation. Panel B, on the contrary, contains two points that fall outside the three standard deviation control limits. Each of these points should be investigated to determine if special causes led to their occurrence. Although panel C does not have any points outside the control limits, there are a series of consecutive points above the mean value (the center line), a series of consecutive points below the mean value, as well as a clearly visible long-term overall downward trend in the value of the variable.

Control limits are often called **Three-Sigma limits**. In practice, virtually all the output of a process will be located within a Three-Sigma interval of the process mean, provided that the process is stable; that is, it exhibits only common cause variation. Further, virtually all the sample means for a given subgroup size will be located within the Three-Sigma limits around the process mean, provided that the process is stable. This provides a basis for distinguishing between common and special variation for the process statistics.

11.3   RULES FOR DETERMINING OUT-OF-CONTROL POINTS

The simplest rule for detecting the presence of a special cause is one or more points falling beyond the Three-Sigma limits. The control chart can be made more sensitive and effective in detecting out-of-control points by considering other signals and patterns that are unlikely to occur by chance alone. For example, if only common causes are operating, you would expect the points plotted to approximately follow a bell-shaped normal distribution. Figure 11.2 presents a control chart in which the area between the *UCL* and *LCL* is subdivided into bands, each of which is 1 standard deviation wide. These additional limits, or **zone boundaries**, are useful in detecting other unlikely patterns of data points.

Exhibit 11.1 provides some rules for deciding when a process is out of control.

If only common causes are operating in a process, each of these events is statistically unlikely to occur. For example, the probability that you will observe eight consecutive points on a given side of the center line by chance alone is $(0.5)^8 = 0.0039$. (This is based on the binomial distribution [see Section 5.4].) Consequently, either a low-probability event occurred (eight points in a row on one side of the center line) or a special cause of variation is present in the process. Many statisticians agree that if the probability of an event is less than 1/100 (in this case, 0.0039), it is reasonable to assume the event is likely due to a special cause of variation, not due to the occurrence of a low-probability common cause of variation (event).

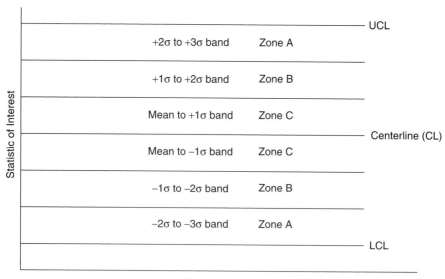

FIGURE 11.2   A Control Chart Showing Bands, Each of Which Is 1 Standard Deviation Wide

---

EXHIBIT 11.1   SOME RULES FOR DECIDING WHEN A PROCESS IS OUT OF CONTROL

You conclude that the process is out of control (not stable) if any of the following events occur:

1. A point falls above the *UCL* or below the *LCL*.

2. Two of three *consecutive points* fall above the mean + 2 standard deviation limits or two of three *consecutive points* fall below the mean – 2 standard deviation limits.

3. Four of five *consecutive points* fall above the mean + 1 standard deviation limit or four of five *consecutive points* fall below the mean – 1 standard deviation limit.

4. Eight or more *consecutive points* lie above the center line or eight or more *consecutive points* lie below the center line.

5. Eight or more *consecutive points* move upward in value or eight or more *consecutive points* move downward in value.

6. An unusually small number of consecutive points above and below the centerline are present (a sawtooth pattern).[1]

7. Thirteen consecutive points fall within the ± 1 standard deviation limits on either side of the centerline.

---

[1] Rules 6 and 7 are used to determine whether a process is unusually noisy (high variability) or unusually quiet (low variability).

The presence of one or more of these low-probability events indicates that one or more special causes *may* be operating, thereby resulting in a process that is out of a state of statistical control. Rules 2–7 should be used with statistical knowledge because, in some situations, they can increase the false alarm rate. Other rules for special causes have been developed and are incorporated within the control chart features of Minitab and JMP. Different rules may be considered appropriate for specific charts (see Appendixes 11.1 and 11.2).

11.4 THE *p*-CHART

The *p*-chart is used to study classification type attribute (nominal scaled) data; for example, the proportion of nonconforming items by month. Subgroup sizes in a *p*-chart may remain constant or may vary. The *p*-chart assumes that:

1. There are only two possible outcomes for an event. An item must be classified as either conforming or nonconforming.
2. The probability, *p*, of a nonconforming item is constant over time.
3. Successive items are independent over time.
4. Subgroups are of sufficient size to detect an out-of-control event. A general rule for subgroup size for a *p*-chart is that the subgroup size should be large enough to detect a special cause of variation if it exists. Frequently, subgroup sizes are between 50 and 500 per subgroup, depending on the variable being studied.
5. Subgroup frequency, how often you draw a subgroup from the process under study, should be often enough to detect changes in the process under study. This requires expertise in the process under study. If the process can change very quickly, more frequent sampling is needed to detect special causes of variation. If the process changes slowly, less frequent sampling is needed to detect a special cause of variation.

As an illustration of the *p*-chart, consider the resort hotel discussed in Section 7.2 on page 122. Management of the hotel had a business objective of increasing the return rate of guests at the hotel. Management decided to focus on the critical first impressions of the service that the hotel provides to accomplish this objective. Is the assigned hotel room ready when a guest checks in? Are all expected amenities, such as extra towels and a complimentary guest basket, in the room when the guest first walks in? Are the video-entertainment center and high-speed Internet access working properly? Data on the nonconformances were collected daily from a sample of 200 rooms. Table 11.1 lists the number and proportion of nonconforming rooms for each day in the four-week period.

TABLE 11.1   Nonconforming Hotel Rooms at Check-In Over a 20-Day Period

Day	Rooms Studied	Rooms Not Ready	Proportion	Day	Rooms Studied	Rooms Not Ready	Proportion
1	200	16	0.080	15	200	18	0.090
2	200	7	0.035	16	200	13	0.065
3	200	21	0.105	17	200	15	0.075
4	200	17	0.085	18	200	10	0.050
5	200	25	0.125	19	200	14	0.070
6	200	19	0.095	20	200	25	0.125
7	200	16	0.080	21	200	19	0.095
8	200	15	0.075	22	200	12	0.060
9	200	11	0.055	23	200	6	0.030
10	200	12	0.060	24	200	12	0.060
11	200	22	0.110	25	200	18	0.090
12	200	20	0.100	26	200	15	0.075
13	200	17	0.085	27	200	20	0.100
14	200	26	0.130	28	200	22	0.110

ROOMSREADY

These data are appropriate for a p-chart because each room is classified as ready or not ready. The probability of a room that is not ready is assumed to be constant from room to room, and each room is considered independent of the other rooms.

Figure 11.3 illustrates the Minitab p-chart for the hotel rooms data. Figure 11.4 shows JMP output.

FIGURE 11.3
Minitab p-Chart for the Hotel Rooms Data

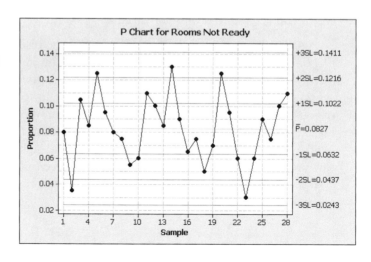

FIGURE 11.4
JMP p-Chart for the
Hotel Rooms Data

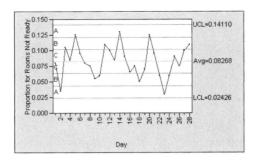

From Figures 11.3 and 11.4, you see that the process is in control. None of the points are outside the control limits, and none of the rules concerning consecutive points have been violated. Thus, any improvement in the proportion of rooms not ready must come from management changing the system.

COMPUTING THE CONTROL LIMITS FOR THE p-CHART {OPTIONAL}

$$UCL = \bar{p} + 3\sqrt{\frac{\bar{p}(1-\bar{p})}{\bar{n}}} \qquad (11.2a)$$

$$LCL = \bar{p} - 3\sqrt{\frac{\bar{p}(1-\bar{p})}{\bar{n}}} \qquad (11.2b)$$

where

X_i = number of nonconforming items in subgroup i

n_i = sample or subgroup size for subgroup i

$p_i = \dfrac{X_i}{n_i}$ = proportion of nonconforming items in subgroup i

k = number of subgroups taken

$\bar{n}$ = mean subgroup size

$\bar{p}$ = mean proportion of nonconforming items

$$\bar{n} = \frac{\sum_{i=1}^{k} n_i}{k} = \frac{\text{total sample size}}{\text{number of groups}}$$

$$\bar{p} = \frac{\sum_{i=1}^{k} X_i}{\sum_{i=1}^{k} n_i} = \frac{\text{total number of nonconformances}}{\text{total sample size}}$$

Continues

For the data of Table 11.1, the number of rooms not ready is 463, and the total sample size is 5,600. Thus:

$$\bar{p} = \frac{463}{5,600} = 0.0827 \text{ and } \bar{n} = 200$$

so that using Equation (11.2):

$$UCL = 0.0827 + 3\sqrt{\frac{(0.0827)(1-0.0827)}{200}}$$

$$= 0.0827 + 0.0584$$

$$= 0.1411$$

$$LCL = 0.0827 - 3\sqrt{\frac{(0.0827)(1-0.0827)}{200}}$$

$$= 0.0827 - 0.0584$$

$$= 0.0243$$

In many instances, unlike the example concerning the hotel rooms, the subgroup size will vary. Consider a hospital administrator who is concerned with the time to process patients' medical records after discharge. She determined that all records should be processed within five days of discharge. Thus, any record not processed within five days of a patient's discharge is nonconforming. Table 11.2 shows the number of patients discharged and the number of records not processed within the 5-day standard for a 30-day period.

TABLE 11.2   Number of Patients Discharged and the Number of Records Not Processed Within the 5-Day Standard

Day	Discharged Patients	Records Not Processed	Day	Discharged Patients	Records Not Processed
1	54	13	10	92	24
2	63	23	11	105	27
3	110	38	12	112	43
4	105	35	13	120	25
5	131	40	14	95	21
6	137	44	15	72	11
7	80	16	16	128	24
8	63	21	17	126	33
9	75	18	18	106	38

Day	Discharged Patients	Records Not Processed	Day	Discharged Patients	Records Not Processed
19	129	39	25	124	57
20	136	74	26	113	28
21	94	31	27	140	38
22	74	15	28	83	21
23	107	45	29	62	10
24	135	53	30	106	45

MEDREC

Figure 11.5 illustrates the Minitab *p*-chart. Figure 11.6 presents JMP output.

FIGURE 11.5
Minitab p-Chart for the Discharge Records

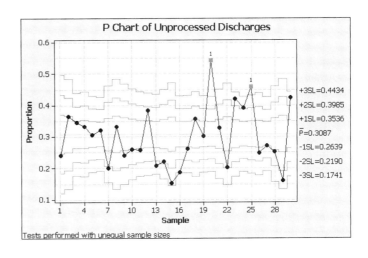

FIGURE 11.6
JMP *p*-Chart for the Discharge Records

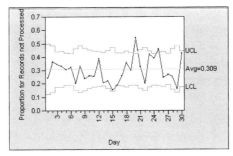

Due to the different subgroup sizes, the values for the *UCL*, *LCL*, and the zones are different for each subgroup. From Figure 11.5 or 11.6, observe that the process lacks control. On day 20, the proportion of discharges not processed within five days

(74/136 = 0.544) is above the upper control limit, and on day 25, the proportion of discharges not processed within five days (57/124 = 0.46) is above the upper control limit. None of the other rules presented in Exhibit 11.1 seems to be violated. There are no instances when two out of three consecutive points lie in zone A on one side of the centerline; there are no instances when four out of five consecutive points lie in zone B or beyond on one side of the centerline; there are no instances when eight consecutive points move upward or downward; nor are there eight consecutive points on one side of the centerline.

Nevertheless, the processing of patient medical records after discharge from the hospital needs further examination. The special causes of these erratic shifts in the proportion of records not processed within five days should be studied and eliminated so that the process can be stabilized. Only after this is done can improvements be made in the process.

11.5 THE c-CHART

A defective item is a nonconforming unit. It must be discarded, reworked, returned, sold, scrapped, or downgraded. It is unusable for its intended purpose in its present form. A defect, however, is an imperfection of some type that does not necessarily render the entire item defective or unusable, but is undesirable. One or more defects may not make an entire item defective. An assembled piece of machinery, such as a car, dishwasher, or air conditioner, may have one or more defects that may not render the entire item defective, but may cause it to be downgraded or may necessitate its being reworked.

When there are multiple opportunities for defects or imperfections in a given continuous unit (such as a large sheet of fabric or a week in a call center), each unit is called an **area of opportunity**. Each area of opportunity is a subgroup. The c-chart is used when the areas of opportunity are of constant size. The u-chart is used when the areas of opportunity differ in size.

Subgroups should be of sufficient size to detect an out-of-control event. A general rule for subgroup size for a c-chart is that the subgroup size should be large enough to detect a special cause of variation if it exists. This is operationally defined as the mean number of defects per area of opportunity being at least 2.0. Additionally, subgroup frequency should be often enough to detect changes in the process under study. This requires expertise in the process under study. If the process can change very quickly, more frequent sampling is needed to detect special causes of variation. If the process changes slowly, less frequent sampling is needed to detect a special cause of variation.

To illustrate the c-chart, consider the number of customer complaints received by a company per week. Each week is an area of opportunity. Results of the complaints per week produce the data in Table 11.3.

TABLE 11.3 Complaints Per Week for 25 Weeks

Week	Number of Complaints	Week	Number of Complaints
1	4	14	9
2	5	15	0
3	5	16	2
4	10	17	6
5	6	18	10
6	4	19	3
7	5	20	7
8	6	21	4
9	3	22	8
10	6	23	7
11	6	24	9
12	7	25	7
13	11		

COMPLAINTS

The assumptions necessary for using the *c*-chart are well met here because the weeks are long enough to be considered continuous areas of opportunity; complaints are discrete events and seem to be independent of one another, and they are relatively rare. Even if these conditions are not precisely met, the *c*-chart is fairly robust, or insensitive to small departures from the assumptions.

Figures 11.7 and 11.8 illustrate the *c*-chart generated by Minitab and JMP for the number of complaints per week.

FIGURE 11.7
Minitab *c*-Chart for the Number of Complaints Per Week

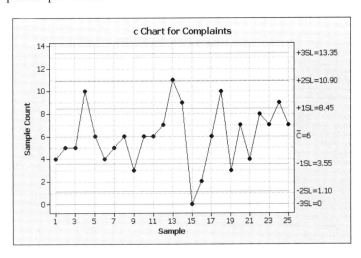

FIGURE 11.8
JMP c-Chart for the Number of Complaints Per Week

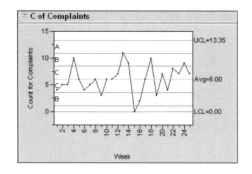

From Figures 11.7 or 11.8, the number of complaints appears to be stable around a center line or mean of 6.0. None of the weeks is outside the control limits, and none of the rules concerning zones have been violated.

COMPUTING CONTROL LIMITS FOR THE c-CHART {OPTIONAL}

$$UCL = \bar{c} + 3\sqrt{\bar{c}}$$
$$LCL = \bar{c} - 3\sqrt{\bar{c}} \qquad (11.3)$$

where

$$\bar{c} = \frac{\sum_{i=1}^{k} c_i}{k} = \frac{\text{total number of occurrences}}{\text{number of units}}$$

$\bar{c}$ = mean number of occurrences

k = number of units sampled

c_i = number of occurrences in unit i

For the data of Table 11.3, the total number of complaints is 150 for the 25 weeks. Thus:

$$\bar{c} = \frac{\text{total number of occurrences}}{\text{number of units}}$$

$$= \frac{150}{25} = 6.0$$

$$UCL = 6.0 + 3\sqrt{6.0}$$
$$= 6.0 + 7.35 = 13.35$$

$$LCL = 6.0 - 3\sqrt{6.0}$$
$$= 6.0 - 7.35 = -1.35 \text{ so } LCL = 0.0$$

11.6 THE *u*-CHART

In some applications, the areas of opportunity vary in size. Generally, the construction and interpretation of control charts are easier when the area of opportunity remains constant, but sometimes changes in the area may be unavoidable. For example, samples taken from a roll of paper may need to be manually torn from rolls, so that the areas of opportunity will vary; and the number of typing errors in a document will have areas of opportunity that will vary with the lengths of the documents. When the areas vary, the control chart you use is a *u*-chart.

The *u*-chart is similar to the *c*-chart because it is a control chart for the count of the number of events, such as the number of defects (nonconformities over a given area of opportunity). The fundamental difference lies in the fact that during construction of a *c*-chart, the area of opportunity remains constant from observation to observation, whereas this is not a requirement for the *u*-chart. Instead, the *u*-chart considers the number of events (such as complaints or other defects) as a fraction of the total size of the area of opportunity in which these events were possible, thus circumventing the problem of having different areas of opportunity for different observations. The characteristic used for the chart, *u,* is the ratio of the number of events to the area of opportunity in which the events occur.

As with the *c*-chart, subgroups should be of sufficient size to detect an out-of-control event. A general rule for subgroup size for a *u*-chart is that the subgroup size should be large enough to detect a special cause of variation if it exists. Additionally, subgroup frequency should be often enough to detect changes in the process under study. This requires expertise in the process under study. If the process can change very quickly, more frequent sampling is needed to detect special causes of variation. If the process changes slowly, less frequent sampling is needed to detect a special cause of variation.

To illustrate a *u*-chart, consider a software company that monitors the number of coding errors in programs under development. Because the number of lines of code written in a day varies, you should use the *u*-chart. Table 11.4 shows the number of lines written and the number of errors in the initial version of programs written for 40 consecutive days.

TABLE 11.4   Coding Errors in Computer Programs

Number of Lines	Number of Code Errors	Number of Lines	Number of Code Errors
367	33	254	23
264	25	429	28
235	15	541	28
243	18	995	84
289	18	400	27
270	25	369	35
962	33	548	33
365	29	615	21
343	23	427	36
917	41	428	14
251	22	636	15
224	19	287	11
486	21	334	13
398	17	881	31
977	33	277	14
203	15	966	75
314	15	512	26
761	20	214	12
728	22	217	24
252	17	521	21

ERRORCODE

Figure 11.9 illustrates the Minitab u-chart for the programming errors, while Figure 11.10 shows the JMP u-chart.

From Figures 11.9 or 11.10, you see that the process lacks control. On days 24, 26, and 39, the proportion of programming errors is above the UCL, while on days 18 and 31, the proportion of programming errors is below the LCL. None of the rules presented in Exhibit 11.1 on page 284 are violated. The programming system needs to be stabilized, and then improved, to reduce the number of programming errors. The erratic shifts in the number of errors per line of code should be studied to determine the reasons for the large number of errors and the small number of errors. Only then can improvements be made in the process.

FIGURE 11.9
Minitab *u*-Chart for
Programming Errors

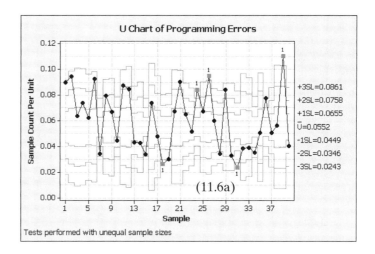

(11.6a)

FIGURE 11.10
JMP *u*-Chart for
Programming Errors

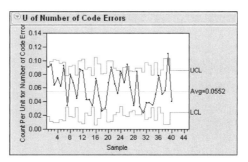

COMPUTING CONTROL LIMITS FOR THE *U*-CHART {OPTIONAL}

where

$$u_i = \frac{c_i}{a_i} \qquad (11.4)$$

c_i = number of events observed in inspection unit i

a_i = the size of the area of opportunity, inspection unit, or subgroup of items i

The mean number of events per area of opportunity equals:

$$\bar{u} = \frac{\sum\limits_{i=1}^{k} c_i}{\sum\limits_{i=1}^{k} a_i} \qquad (11.5)$$

Continues

where

c_i = number of events observed in inspection unit i

a_i = the size of the ith area of opportunity, inspection unit, or subgroup

k = number of areas of opportunity

$$UCL = \bar{u} + 3\sqrt{\frac{\bar{u}}{a_i}} \qquad (11.6a)$$

$$LCL = \bar{u} - 3\sqrt{\frac{\bar{u}}{a_i}} \qquad (11.6b)$$

For the data of Table 11.4:

Total number of events (programming errors) = 1,032, total area of opportunity (lines of code) = 18,700

$$\bar{u} = \frac{\sum_{i=1}^{k} c_i}{\sum_{i=1}^{k} a_i}$$

$$\bar{u} = \frac{1,032}{18,700}$$

$$= 0.0552$$

$$UCL = 0.0552 + 3\sqrt{\frac{0.0552}{a_i}}$$

$$LCL = 0.0552 - 3\sqrt{\frac{0.0552}{a_i}}$$

The control limits will vary according to the area of opportunity for each subgroup.

11.7 CONTROL CHARTS FOR THE MEAN AND RANGE

Variables control charts are used to study a process when a characteristic is a measurement; for example, cycle time, processing time, waiting time, height, area, temperature, cost, or revenue. Measurement data provides more information than attribute data. Therefore, variables charts are more sensitive in detecting special cause variation than are attribute charts. Variables charts are typically used in pairs. One chart studies the variation in a process, and the other studies the variation in the process mean. You *must* examine the chart that studies variability before the chart that studies the process mean. You do this because the chart that studies the process mean assumes that the process variability is stable over time. One of the most commonly employed pair of charts is the $\bar{X}$ chart and the R-chart. When these charts are used, the subgroup range, R, is plotted on the R-chart, which monitors process variability, and the subgroup mean, $\bar{X}$, is plotted on the $\bar{X}$ chart, which monitors the central tendency of the process.

Subgroups should be of sufficient size to detect an out-of-control event, as with attribute control charts. The common subgroup sizes for $\bar{X}$–R-charts are between 2 and 10 items. If a larger subgroup size is required, you can use $\bar{X}$–S-chart to detect special causes of variation in the process. Additionally, subgroup frequency should be often enough to detect changes in the process under study. This requires expertise in the process under study. If the process can change very quickly, more frequent sampling is needed to detect special causes of variation. If the process changes slowly, less frequent sampling is needed to detect a special cause of variation.

To illustrate the R- and $\bar{X}$ charts, consider a bank whose management has embarked on a program of statistical process control and has decided to use variables control charts to study the waiting time of customers during the peak noon to 1 p.m. lunch hour to detect special causes of variation. Four customers are selected during the one-hour period; the first customer to enter the bank every 15 minutes. Each set of four measurements makes up a subgroup. Table 11.5 lists the waiting time (operationally defined as the time from when the customer enters the line until he or she begins to be served by the teller) for 20 days.

TABLE 11.5 Waiting Time for Customers at a Bank

Day	Time in Minutes			
1	7.2	8.4	7.9	4.9
2	5.6	8.7	3.3	4.2
3	5.5	7.3	3.2	6.0
4	4.4	8.0	5.4	7.4
5	9.7	4.6	4.8	5.8
6	8.3	8.9	9.1	6.2
7	4.7	6.6	5.3	5.8
8	8.8	5.5	8.4	6.9
9	5.7	4.7	4.1	4.6
10	3.7	4.0	3.0	5.2
11	2.6	3.9	5.2	4.8
12	4.6	2.7	6.3	3.4
13	4.9	6.2	7.8	8.7
14	7.1	6.3	8.2	5.5

Continues

Day	Time in Minutes			
15	7.1	5.8	6.9	7.0
16	6.7	6.9	7.0	9.4
17	5.5	6.3	3.2	4.9
18	4.9	5.1	3.2	7.6
19	7.2	8.0	4.1	5.9
20	6.1	3.4	7.2	5.9

BANKTIME

Figures 11.11 and 11.12 illustrate the Minitab and JMP R- and $\bar{X}$ charts for the bank waiting time data.

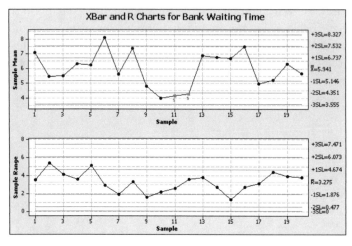

FIGURE 11.11   Minitab R- and $\bar{X}$ Charts for the Bank Waiting Time Data

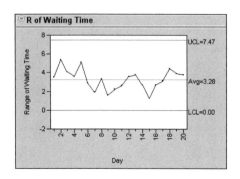
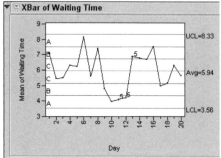

FIGURE 11.12   JMP R- and $\bar{X}$ Charts for the Bank Waiting Time Data

In Figure 11.11, the bottom portion is the R-chart, and the top portion is the $\bar{X}$ chart. In Figure 11.12, the first panel is the R-chart and the second panel is the $\bar{X}$ chart. First, you examine the R-chart for signs of special variation. None of the points on the R-chart is outside the control limits, and there are no other signals indicating a lack of control. Thus, there are no indications of special sources of variation on the R-chart.

Now you can examine the $\bar{X}$ chart. Notice that days 11 and 12 are below the mean $- 2$ standard deviations (2 out of 3 points 2 sigma or beyond rule). This indicates a lack of control. Further investigation is warranted to determine the source(s) of these special variations that may have caused a low waiting time on these days. Once the special sources of variation have been identified and incorporated into the system since they are beneficial, a revised process can be developed and put in place.

COMPUTING THE CONTROL LIMITS FOR THE RANGE {OPTIONAL}

$$UCL = \bar{R} + 3\bar{R}\frac{d_3}{d_2} \qquad (11.7a)$$

$$LCL = \bar{R} - 3\bar{R}\frac{d_3}{d_2} \qquad (11.7b)$$

where

$$\bar{R} = \frac{\sum_{i=1}^{k} R_i}{k} = \frac{\text{sum of the ranges}}{\text{number of subgroups}}$$

Referring to Equations (11.7a) and (11.7b), instead of using the d_2 and d_3 factors, the calculations can be simplified by utilizing the **D_3 factor**, equal to $1 - 3(d_3/d_2)$, and the **D_4 factor**, equal to $1 + 3(d_3/d_2)$, to compute the control limits, as shown in Equations (11.8a) and (11.8b). Values for these factors for different subgroup sizes are listed in Table C.4.

$$UCL = D_4\bar{R} \qquad (11.8a)$$

$$LCL = D_3\bar{R} \qquad (11.8b)$$

For the data of Table 11.5:

Sum of the ranges = 65.5 and the number of subgroups = 20.

Continues

Thus:

$$\bar{R} = \frac{\text{sum of the ranges}}{\text{number of subgroups}}$$

$$= \frac{65.5}{20} = 3.275$$

For a subgroup size $= 4$, $D_3 = 0$, and $D_4 = 2.282$:

$$UCL = (2.282)(3.275) = 7.47$$
$$LCL = (0)(3.275) = 0$$

COMPUTING CONTROL LIMITS FOR THE MEAN {OPTIONAL}

$$UCL = \bar{\bar{X}} + 3\frac{\bar{R}}{d_2\sqrt{n}} \qquad (11.9a)$$

$$LCL = \bar{\bar{X}} - 3\frac{\bar{R}}{d_2\sqrt{n}} \qquad (11.9b)$$

where

$$\bar{\bar{X}} = \frac{\sum_{i=1}^{k} \bar{X}_i}{k} = \frac{\text{sum of the sample means}}{\text{number of subgroups}}$$

$$\bar{R} = \frac{\sum_{i=1}^{k} R_i}{k} = \frac{\text{sum of the ranges}}{\text{number of subgroups}}$$

$\bar{X}_i =$ the sample mean of n observations at time i

$R_i =$ the range of n observations at time i

$k =$ number of subgroups

Referring to Equations (11.9a) and (11.9b), the calculations are simplified by utilizing the **A$_2$ factor**, equal to $3/(d_2\sqrt{n})$, to compute the control limits, as displayed in Equations (11.10a) and (11.10b). Values for these factors for different subgroup sizes are listed in Table C.4, in Appendix C.

$$UCL = \bar{\bar{X}} + A_2\bar{R} \qquad (11.10a)$$
$$LCL = \bar{\bar{X}} - A_2\bar{R} \qquad (11.10b)$$

For the data of Table 11.5:

Sum of the ranges = 65.5, the sum of the sample means = 118.825, and the number of subgroups = 20.

Thus:

$$\bar{R} = \frac{\text{sum of the ranges}}{\text{number of subgroups}}$$

$$= \frac{65.5}{20} = 3.275$$

$$\bar{\bar{X}} = \frac{\text{sum of the sample means}}{\text{number of subgroups}}$$

$$= \frac{118.825}{20} = 5.94125$$

For a subgroup size = 4, $A_2 = 0.729$:

$$UCL = 5.94125 + (0.729)(3.275) = 8.327$$
$$LCL = 5.94125 - (0.729)(3.275) = 3.555$$

11.8 CONTROL CHARTS FOR THE MEAN AND THE STANDARD DEVIATION

As the sample size n increases, the range becomes increasingly less efficient as a measure of variability. This is the case because the range ignores all information between the two most extreme values; as the sample size increases, the range will use a smaller proportion of the information available in a sample. In addition, the probability of observing an extreme value in a sample increases as n gets larger. A single extreme value will result in an unduly large value for the sample range and will inflate the estimate of process variability. Thus, as the subgroup size increases, the individual subgroup standard deviations provide a better estimate of the process standard deviation than does the range.

Subgroups should be of sufficient size to detect an out-of-control event, as with $\bar{X}$-R-charts. The common subgroup sizes for $\bar{X}$-S-charts are 11 or more items. Additionally, subgroup frequency should be often enough to detect changes in the process under study. This requires expertise in the process under study. If the process can change very quickly, more frequent sampling is needed to detect special causes of variation. If the process changes slowly, less frequent sampling is needed to detect a special cause of variation.

To illustrate the $\bar{X}$-S-charts, consider the cycle time for a banking operation. Cycle time data is collected for the first 10 transactions every half-hour for 20 time periods, as summarized in Table 11.6.

TABLE 11.6   Cycle Times for the First 10 Transactions for 20 Time Periods

8:30	9:00	9:30	10:00	10:30	11:00	11:30
2.08	2.14	2.30	2.01	2.06	2.14	2.07
2.26	2.02	2.10	2.10	2.12	2.22	2.05
2.13	2.14	2.20	2.15	1.98	2.18	1.97
1.94	1.94	2.25	1.97	2.12	2.27	2.05
2.30	2.30	2.05	2.25	2.20	2.17	2.16
2.15	2.08	1.95	2.12	2.02	2.26	2.02
2.07	1.94	2.10	2.10	2.19	2.15	2.02
2.02	2.12	2.16	1.90	2.03	2.07	2.14
2.22	2.15	2.37	2.04	2.02	2.02	2.07
2.18	2.36	1.98	2.08	2.09	2.36	2.00

12:00	12:30	13:00	13:30	14:00	14:30	15:00
2.08	2.13	2.13	2.24	2.25	2.03	2.08
2.31	1.90	2.16	2.34	1.91	2.10	1.92
2.12	2.12	2.12	2.40	1.96	2.24	2.14
2.18	2.04	2.22	2.26	2.04	2.20	2.20
2.15	2.40	2.12	2.13	1.93	2.25	2.02
2.17	2.12	2.07	2.15	2.08	2.03	2.04
1.98	2.15	2.04	2.08	2.29	2.06	1.94
2.05	2.01	2.28	2.02	2.42	2.19	2.05
2.00	2.30	2.12	2.05	2.10	2.13	2.12
2.26	2.14	2.10	2.18	2.00	2.20	2.06

15:30	16:00	16:30	17:00	17:30	18:00	
2.04	1.92	2.12	1.98	2.08	2.22	
2.14	2.10	2.30	2.30	2.12	2.05	
2.18	2.13	2.01	2.31	2.11	1.93	
2.12	2.02	2.20	2.12	2.22	2.08	
2.00	1.93	2.11	2.08	2.00	2.15	
2.02	2.17	1.93	2.10	1.95	2.27	
2.05	2.24	2.02	2.15	2.15	1.95	
2.34	1.98	2.25	2.35	2.14	2.11	
2.12	2.34	2.05	2.12	2.28	2.12	
2.05	2.12	2.10	2.26	2.31	2.10	

CYCLETIME2

Figures 11.13 and 11.14 illustrate the Minitab and JMP $\bar{X}$-S-charts for the cycle times data.

In Figure 11.13, the bottom portion is the S-chart, and the top portion is the $\bar{X}$ chart. In Figure 11.14, the first panel is the S-chart and the second panel is the $\bar{X}$ chart. First, the S-chart is examined for signs of special variation. None of the points on the S-chart is outside of the control limits, and there are no other signals indicating a lack of control. Thus, there are no indications of special sources of variation on the S-chart. Now the $\bar{X}$ chart can be examined. There are no indications of a lack of control, so the process can be considered to be stable and the output to be predictable with respect to time, as long as conditions remain the same.

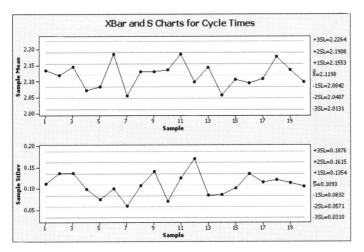

FIGURE 11.13   Minitab $\bar{X}$–S-Charts for the Cycle Times Data

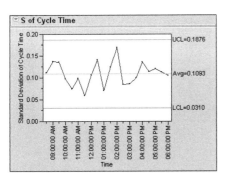
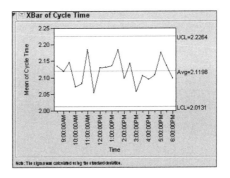

FIGURE 11.14   JMP $\bar{X}$–S-Charts for the Cycle Times Data

COMPUTING THE CONTROL LIMITS FOR THE STANDARD DEVIATION {OPTIONAL}

$$\bar{S} = \frac{\sum_{i=1}^{k} S_i}{k} = \frac{\text{sum of the sample standard deviations}}{\text{number of subgroups}}$$

where

S_i = the sample standard deviation for sample or subgroup i

k = the number of subgroups

$$UCL(S) = \bar{S} + 3\bar{S}\frac{\sqrt{1-c_4^2}}{c_4} \qquad (11.11a)$$

$$LCL(S) = \bar{S} - 3\bar{S}\frac{\sqrt{1-c_4^2}}{c_4} \qquad (11.11b)$$

where c_4 is a control chart factor (see Table C.4) that represents the relationship between the sample standard deviations and the process standard deviation for varying subgroup sizes.

Because c_4 is constant for a given sample size, the term $\left(1 + \frac{3\sqrt{1-c_4^2}}{c_4}\right)$ can be replaced by tabled values of control chart factor B_4, and the term $\left(1 - \frac{3\sqrt{1-c_4^2}}{c_4}\right)$ can be replaced by control chart factor B_3 (see Table C.4). The factors B_4, and B_3 can be used to simplify Equations (11.11a) and (11.11b), respectively.

$$UCL(S) = B_4\bar{S} \qquad (11.12a)$$

and

$$LCL(S) = B_3\bar{S} \qquad (11.12b)$$

For the data of Table 11.6, the sum of the sample standard deviations = 2.19 and the number of subgroups = 20.

$$\bar{S} = \frac{\text{sum of the sample standard deviations}}{\text{number of subgroups}}$$

$$= \frac{2.19}{20} = 0.11$$

With a subgroup size of 10, $B_4 = 1.716$ and $B_3 = 0.284$:

$UCL = (1.716)(0.11) = 0.188$

$LCL = (0.284)(0.11) = 0.031$

COMPUTING CONTROL LIMITS FOR THE MEAN {OPTIONAL}

$$UCL(\bar{X}) = \bar{\bar{X}} + 3\frac{\bar{S}}{c_4\sqrt{n}} \qquad \text{(11.13a)}$$

and

$$LCL(\bar{X}) = \bar{\bar{X}} - 3\frac{\bar{S}}{c_4\sqrt{n}} \qquad \text{(11.13b)}$$

where c_4 is a control chart factor that represents the relationship between subgroup standard deviations and the process standard deviation for varying subgroup sizes.

n = the subgroup size

Because $\dfrac{3}{c_4\sqrt{n}}$ is a constant term for a given subgroup size, the equations for the upper and lower control limits can be simplified by using tabled values (see Table C.4) of $\dfrac{3}{c_4\sqrt{n}}$ called A_3.

$$UCL(\bar{X}) = \bar{\bar{X}} + A_3\bar{S} \qquad \text{(11.14a)}$$
$$LCL(\bar{X}) = \bar{\bar{X}} - A_3\bar{S} \qquad \text{(11.14b)}$$

For the data of Table 11.6, the sum of the sample standard deviations = 2.19, the sum of the sample means = 42.43, and the number of subgroups = 20.

$$\bar{S} = \frac{\text{sum of the sample standard deviations}}{\text{number of subgroups}}$$

$$= \frac{2.19}{20} = 0.11$$

$$\bar{\bar{X}} = \frac{\text{sum of the sample means}}{\text{number of subgroups}}$$

$$= \frac{42.43}{20} = 2.12$$

With a subgroup size of 10, A_3 = 0.975:

UCL = 2.12 + (0.975)(0.11) = 2.226

LCL = 2.12 + (0.975)(0.11) = 2.013

11.9 INDIVIDUAL VALUE AND MOVING RANGE CHARTS

Often, you are only able to measure a single value per subgroup. Perhaps measurements must be taken at relatively long intervals, or the measurements are destructive and/or expensive; or perhaps they represent a single batch where only one measurement is appropriate, such as the total yield of a homogeneous chemical batch process; or the measurements may be monthly or quarterly revenue or cost data. Whatever the case, there are circumstances when data must be taken as individual units that cannot be conveniently divided into subgroups.

Individual value charts have two parts, one that charts the process variability and the other that charts the process average. The two parts are used in tandem, as with the $\bar{X}$ and R-charts. Stability must first be established in the portion charting the variability because the estimate of the process variability provides the basis for the control limits of the portion charting the process mean.

Single measurements of variables are considered a subgroup of size one. Hence, there is no variability within the subgroups themselves. An estimate of the process variability must be made in some other way. The estimate of variability used for individual value charts is based on the observaton-to-observaation variation in the sequence of single values, measured by the moving range (the absolute value of the difference between each data value and the one that immediately precedes it).

As before, subgroup frequency should be often enough to detect changes in the process under study. This requires expertise in the process under study. If the process can change very quickly, more frequent sampling is needed to detect special causes of variation. If the process changes slowly, less frequent sampling is needed to detect a special cause of variation.

To illustrate the individual value chart, consider the monthly revenues for a chemical company of a liquid chemical product. Shipments of the product to customers are made each month. Table 11.7 shows the monthly revenues for the product.

TABLE 11.7 Revenues in Millions for 30 Months for a Liquid Chemical Product

Month	Revenue (000, 000)	Month	Revenue (000, 000)
January 2003	1.242	April 2004	1.253
February 2003	1.289	May 2004	1.257
March 2003	1.186	June 2004	1.275
April 2003	1.197	July 2004	1.232
May 2003	1.252	August 2004	1.201
June 2003	1.221	September 2004	1.281
July 2003	1.299	October 2004	1.274
August 2003	1.323	November 2004	1.234
September 2003	1.323	December 2004	1.187

Month	Revenue (000, 000)	Month	Revenue (000, 000)
October 2003	1.314	January 2005	1.196
November 2003	1.299	February 2005	1.282
December 2003	1.225	March 2005	1.322
January 2004	1.185	April 2005	1.258
February 2004	1.194	May 2005	1.261
March 2004	1.235	June 2005	1.201

REVENUE

Figures 11.15 and 11.16 illustrate the Minitab and JMP moving range and individual value charts for the monthly revenue data.

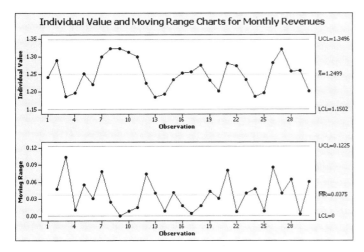

FIGURE 11.15   Minitab Moving Range and Individual Value Charts for Monthly Revenue

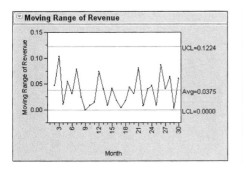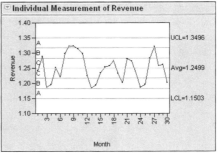

FIGURE 11.16   JMP Moving Range and Individual Value Charts for Monthly Revenue

In Figure 11.15, the bottom portion is the moving range chart, and the top portion is the individual value chart. In Figure 11.16, the first panel is the moving range chart and the second panel is the individual value chart. First, you examine the moving range chart for signs of special variation. None of the points on the moving range chart is outside of the control limits, and there are no other signals indicating a lack of control. Thus, there are no indications of special sources of variation on the moving range chart. Now you examine the individual value chart. There are no indications of a lack of control, so the process can be considered to be stable and the revenue to be predictable with respect to time, as long as conditions remain the same.

COMPUTING CONTROL LIMITS FOR THE MOVING RANGE {OPTIONAL}

$$MR_i = |X_{i+1} - X_i| \qquad (11.15)$$

where

   k = the number of samples or subgroups

   | | = the absolute value

   X_{i+1} is the value for observation $i + 1$

   X_i is the value for observation i

Because each value of MR_i requires two successive observations for its calculation, for any set of k observations, there will be only $k - 1$ values of the moving range. For example, the first moving range value $MR_1 = |X_2 - X_1|$, the second moving range value $MR_2 = |X_3 - X_2|$, and the last moving range value $MR_{k-1} = |X_k - X_{k-1}|$.

$$\overline{MR} = \frac{\sum_{i=1}^{k-1} MR_i}{k-1} = \frac{\text{sum of the moving ranges}}{\text{number of subgroups} - 1} \qquad (11.16)$$

$$UCL(MR) = D_4 \overline{MR} \qquad (11.17a)$$

$$LCL(MR) = D_3 \overline{MR} \qquad (11.17b)$$

where D_4 and D_3 are control chart factors from Table C.4.

Because each moving range value is based on two consecutive observations, the subgroup size for each moving range is 2. From Table C.4, with $n = 2$, D_4 is 3.267 and D_3 is 0.00. Therefore:

$$UCL(MR) = 3.267 \overline{MR} \qquad (11.18a)$$

$$LCL(MR) = 0.00 \overline{MR} \qquad (11.18b)$$

For the data of Table 11.7, the sum of the moving ranges = 1.087. Thus:

$$\overline{MR} = \frac{\text{sum of the moving ranges}}{\text{number of subgroups} - 1}$$

$$= \frac{1.087}{29} = 0.037$$

$$UCL = (3.267)(0.037) = 0.122$$

$$LCL = (0)(0.037) = 0$$

COMPUTING CONTROL LIMITS FOR THE INDIVIDUAL VALUE CHART {OPTIONAL}

$$UCL(X) = \bar{X} + 3\frac{\overline{MR}}{d_2} \qquad (11.19a)$$

$$LCL(X) = \bar{X} - 3\frac{\overline{MR}}{d_2} \qquad (11.19b)$$

Because $3/d_2$ is a constant for a given subgroup size, the control chart factor E_2 presented in Table C.4 can be used, so that:

$$UCL(X) = \bar{X} + E_2\overline{MR} \qquad (11.20a)$$

$$LCL(X) = \bar{X} - E_2\overline{MR} \qquad (11.20b)$$

Because each of the moving ranges used to compute $\overline{MR}$ is calculated from two consecutive observations, the subgroup size is equal to 2. Whenever $n = 2$, the value of $E_2 = 2.66$. Therefore:

$$UCL(X) = \bar{X} + 2.66\overline{MR} \qquad (11.21a)$$

$$LCL(X) = \bar{X} - 2.66\overline{MR} \qquad (11.21b)$$

For the data of Table 11.7, the sum of the revenues = 37.498 and the sum of the moving ranges = 1.087. Thus,

$$\overline{MR} = \frac{\text{sum of the moving ranges}}{\text{number of subgroups} - 1}$$

$$= \frac{1.087}{29} = 0.037$$

$$\bar{X} = \frac{37.498}{30}$$

$$= 1.25$$

$$UCL = 1.25 + 2.66(0.037) = 1.349$$

$$LCL = 1.25 - 2.66(0.037) = 1.15$$

SUMMARY

In this chapter, both attribute and variables control charts have been discussed. As a road map for this chapter, Figure 11.17 presents a flow diagram useful in selecting the control chart appropriate for monitoring your process.

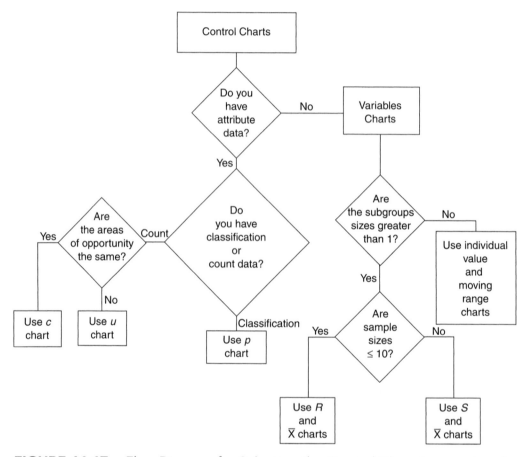

FIGURE 11.17   Flow Diagram for Selecting the Control Chart Appropriate for Monitoring a Process

REFERENCES

1. Deming, W. Edwards. *Out of the Crisis* (Cambridge, MA: Massachusetts Institute for Technology Center for Advanced Engineering Study, 1986).

2. Deming, W. Edwards. *The New Economics for Industry, Government, Education* (Cambridge, MA: Massachusetts Institute for Technology Center for Advanced Engineering Study, 1993).

3. Gitlow, H. G., A. Oppenheim, R. Oppenheim, and D. M. Levine. *Quality Management,* 3rd Ed. (New York: McGraw-Hill-Irwin, 2005).

4. *JMP Version 6* (Cary, NC: SAS Institute, 2005).

5. Levine, D. M., P. C. Ramsey, and R. K. Smidt. *Applied Statistics for Engineers and Scientists Using Microsoft Excel and Minitab* (Upper Saddle River, NJ: Prentice Hall, 2001).

6. *Minitab for Windows Version 14* (State College, PA: Minitab, 2004).

7. Montgomery, D. C. *Introduction to Statistical Quality Control,* 5th Ed. (New York: John Wiley, 2005).

8. Shewhart, W. A. *Economic Control of Quality of Manufactured Product* (New York: Van Nostrand-Reinhard, 1931, reprinted by the American Society for Quality Control, Milwaukee, 1980).

9. Shewhart, W. A. and W. E. Deming. *Statistical Methods from the Viewpoint of Quality Control* (Washington, D.C.: Graduate School, Department of Agriculture, 1939; Dover Press, 1986).

10. Western Electric. *Statistical Quality Control Handbook* (Indianapolis, IN: Western Electric Corporation, 1956).

Appendix 11.1
Using Minitab for Control Charts

Generating Zone Limits

To plot zone limits on any of the control charts discussed in this appendix, open to the initial dialog box for the control chart being developed and do the following:

1. Click the **Scale** button. Click the **Gridlines** tab. Select the **Y major ticks**, **Y minor ticks**, and **X major ticks** check boxes. Click the **OK** button to return to the previous dialog box.

2. Click the **Options** button for the chart (for example, P Chart Options for the *p*-chart). Select the **S limits** tab. In the Display control limits at: edit box, enter **1 2 3** in the edit box. Click the **OK** button to return to the initial dialog box.

The *p*-Chart

To illustrate how to produce a *p*-chart, refer to the data of Figure 11.3 on page 286 concerning the number of rooms not ready. Open the **ROOMSREADY.MTW** worksheet.

1. Select **Stat → Control Charts → Attribute Charts → P**. In the P Chart dialog box (see Figure A11.1), enter **C3** or **'Not Ready'** in the Variables: edit box. Because the subgroup sizes

are equal, enter **200** in the **Subgroup sizes:** edit box. Click the **P Chart Options** button.

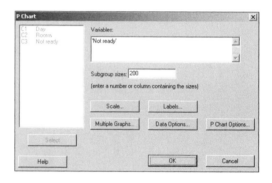

FIGURE A11.1
Minitab P Chart Dialog Box

2. In the P Chart—Options dialog box, click the **Tests** tab (see Figure A11.2). In the drop-down list box, select **Perform all tests for special causes**. Click the **OK** button to return to the P Chart dialog box. (These values will stay intact until Minitab is restarted.)

3. If there are points that should be omitted when estimating the center line and control limits, click the **Estimate** tab in the P Chart—Options dialog box (see Figure A11.3). Enter the points to be omitted in the edit box shown. Click the **OK** button to return to the P Chart dialog box. In the P Chart dialog box, click the **OK** button to generate the *p*-chart.

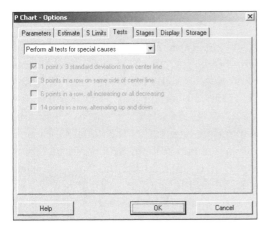

FIGURE A11.2
Minitab P Chart—Options Dialog Box, Tests Tab

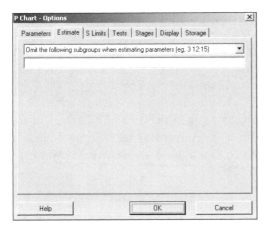

FIGURE A11.3
Minitab P Chart—Options Dialog Box, Estimate Tab

The c-Chart

To illustrate how to produce a c-chart, refer to the data of Figure 11.7 on page 291 concerning the number of customer complaints. Open the **COMPLAINTS.MTW** worksheet.

1. Select **Stat → Control Charts → Attribute Charts → C**. In the C Chart dialog box (see Figure A11.4), enter **C2** or **COMPLAINTS** in the Variables: edit box.

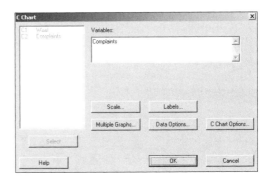

FIGURE A11.4
Minitab C Chart Dialog Box

2. Click the **C Chart Options** button. In the C Chart—Options dialog box, click the **Tests** tab. In the drop-down list box, select **Perform all tests for special causes**. Click the **OK** button to return to the C Chart dialog box. (These values will stay intact until Minitab is restarted.) Click the **OK** button to produce the c-chart.

3. If there are points that should be omitted when estimating the center line and control limits, click the **Estimate** tab in the C Chart—Options dialog box. Enter the points to be omitted in the edit box shown. Click the **OK** button to return to the C Chart dialog box.

The u-Chart

To illustrate how to generate a u-chart, refer to the data of Figure 11.9 on page 295 concerning the number of coding errors.

Open the **ERRORCODE.MTW** work-sheet.

1. Select **Stat → Control Charts → Attribute Charts → U**. In the U Chart dialog box (see Figure A11.5), enter **C2** or **Number of Code Errors** in the Variables: edit box. In the Subgroups sizes: edit box, enter **C1** or **'Number of Lines'**.

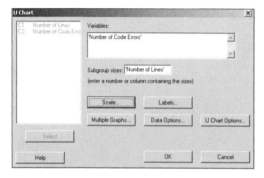

FIGURE A11.5
Minitab U Chart Dialog Box

2. In the U Chart—Options dialog box, click the **Tests** tab. In the drop-down list box, select **Perform all tests for special causes**. Click the **OK** button to return to the U Chart dialog box. (These values will stay intact until Minitab is restarted.) Click the **OK** button to generate the *u*-chart.

3. If there are points that should be omitted when estimating the center line and control limits, click the **Estimate** tab in the U Chart—Options dialog box. Enter the points to be omitted in the edit box shown. Click the **OK** button to return to the U Chart dialog box.

R and $\bar{X}$ Charts

You generate R and $\bar{X}$ charts from Minitab by selecting **Stat → Control Charts → Variable Charts for Subgroups → Xbar-R** from the menu bar. The format for entering the variable name is different, depending on whether the data are stacked down a single column or unstacked across a set of columns, with the data for each time period located in a single row. If the data for the variable of interest are stacked down a single column, choose **All observations for a chart are in one column** in the drop-down list box and enter the variable name in the edit box below. If the subgroups are unstacked with each row representing the data for a single time period, choose **Observations for a subgroup are in one row of columns** in the drop-down list box and enter the variable names for the data in the edit box below.

To illustrate how to generate R and $\bar{X}$ charts, refer to the data of Figure 11.11 on page 298 concerning the waiting time at a bank. Open the **BANKTIME.MTW** work-sheet.

1. Select **Stat → Control Charts → Variable Charts for Subgroups → Xbar-R**. Because the data are unstacked, select **Observations for a subgroup are in one row of columns** in the drop-down list box. In the Xbar-R Chart dialog box (see Figure A11.6), enter **C2** or **1**, **C3** or **2**, **C4** or **3**, and **C5** or **4**, in the edit box. Click the **Xbar-R Options** button.

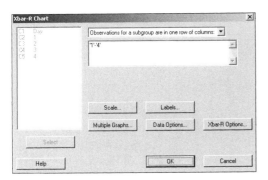

FIGURE A11.6
Minitab Xbar-R Chart Dialog Box

2. In the Xbar-R Chart—Options dialog box (see Figure A11.7), click the **Tests** tab. In the drop-down list box, select **Perform all tests for special causes**. Click the **OK** button to return to the Xbar-R Chart dialog box. (These values will stay intact until Minitab is restarted.)

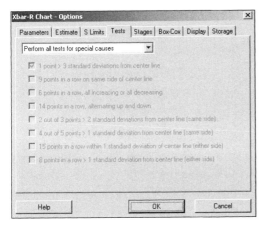

FIGURE A11.7
Minitab Xbar-R Chart—Options Dialog Box, Tests Tab

3. Click the **Estimate** tab in the Xbar-R Chart—Options dialog box (see Figure A11.8). Click the **Rbar** option button. If there are points that should

be omitted when estimating the center line and control limits, enter the points to be omitted in the edit box shown. Click the **OK** button to return to the Xbar-R Chart dialog box. (Note: When generating more than one set of R and $\bar{X}$ charts in the same session, be sure to reset the values of the points to be omitted before generating new charts.)

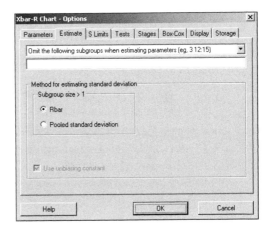

FIGURE A11.8
Minitab Xbar-R Chart—Options Dialog Box, Estimate Tab

4. In the Xbar-R Chart dialog box, click the **OK** button to produce the R and $\bar{X}$ charts.

S and $\bar{X}$ Charts

You can use Minitab to produce S and $\bar{X}$ charts by selecting **Stat → Control Charts → Variable Charts for Subgroups → Xbar-S** from the menu bar. The format for entering the variable name is different, depending on whether the data are stacked down a single column or unstacked across a set of columns with the data for each time period in a single row. If the data for the variable of interest are stacked down a single column, choose **All observations for a chart are in one column** in the drop-down list box and enter the variable name in the edit box below. If the subgroups are unstacked with each row representing the data for a single time period, choose **Observations for a subgroup are in one row of columns** in the drop-down list box and enter the variable names for the data in the edit box below.

To illustrate how to generate S and $\bar{X}$ charts, refer to the data of Figure 11.13 on page 303 concerning the cycle time of transactions. Open the **CYCLETIME2. MTW** worksheet.

1. Select **Stat → Control Charts → Variable Charts for Subgroups → Xbar-S**. Because the data are stacked, select **All observations for a chart are in one column** in the drop-down list box. In the Xbar-S Chart dialog box (see Figure A11.9), enter **C3** or **'Cycle Time'** in the edit box. In the Subgroup sizes, edit box, enter **10**. Click the **Xbar-S Options** button.

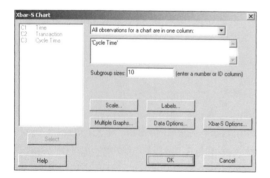

FIGURE A11.9
Minitab Xbar-S Chart Dialog Box

2. In the Xbar-S Chart—Options dialog box, click the **Tests** tab. In the drop-down list box, select **Perform all tests for special causes**. Click the **OK** button to return to the Xbar-S Chart dialog box. (These values will stay intact until Minitab is restarted.)

3. Click the **Estimate** tab in the Xbar-S Chart—Options dialog box. Click the **Sbar** option button. If there are points that should be omitted when estimating the center line and control limits, enter the points to be omitted in the edit box shown. Click the **OK** button to return to the Xbar-S Chart dialog box. (Note: When generating more than one set of S and $\bar{X}$ charts in the same session, be sure to reset the values of the points to be omitted before generating new charts.)

4. In the Xbar-S Chart dialog box, click the **OK** button to produce the S and $\bar{X}$ charts.

Individual Value and Moving Range Charts

You use Minitab to generate individual value and moving range charts by selecting **Stat → Control Charts → Variable Charts for Individuals → I-MR** from the menu bar. To illustrate how to generate individual value and moving range charts, refer to the data of Figure 11.15 on page 307 concerning monthly revenues. Open the **REVENUE.MTW** worksheet.

1. Select **Stat → Control Charts → Variable Charts for Individuals → I-MR**. In the Individuals-Moving Range Chart dialog box (see Figure A11.10),

enter **C2** or **REVENUE** in the Variable(s): edit box. Click the **I-MR Options** button.

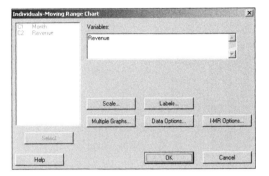

FIGURE A11.10
Minitab Individuals-Moving Range Chart Dialog Box

2. In the Individuals-Moving Range Chart — Options dialog box, click the **Tests** tab. Select the **Perform the following tests for special causes** in the drop-down list box. Select the **1 point > 3 standard deviations from center line** check box. Click the **OK** button to return to the I-MR Chart dialog box. (These values will stay intact until Minitab is restarted.)

3. Click the **Estimate** tab in the Individual-Moving Range Chart — Options dialog box. Click the **Average moving range** option button. If there are points that should be omitted when estimating the center line and control limits, enter the points to be omitted in the edit box shown. Click the **OK** button to return to the Individuals-Moving Range Chart dialog box. (Note: When generating more than one set of individual value and moving range

charts in the same session, be sure to reset the values of the points to be omitted before generating new charts.)

4. In the Individuals-Moving Range Chart dialog box, click the **OK** button to produce the individual value and moving range charts.

Appendix 11.2
Using JMP for Control Charts

The *p*-Chart

To illustrate how to produce a *p*-chart, refer to the data of Figure 11.4 on page 287 concerning the number of rooms not ready. Open the **ROOMSREADY.JMP** data table.

1. Select **Graph → Control Chart → P.** In the P Control Chart dialog box (see Figure A11.11), enter **Rooms Not Ready** in the Process edit box. Enter **Day** in the **Sample Label** edit box. Select the **KSigma** options button and enter **3** in the edit box. Because the sample size is constant, enter **200** in the Constant Size: edit box. (If the sample size varies, enter the variable for the sample size in the Sample Size edit box.) Click the **OK** button.

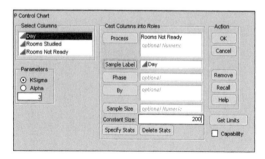

FIGURE A11.11
JMP Control Chart Dialog Box for a *p*-Chart

2. Click the red triangle to the left of P of Rooms Not Ready (see Figure A11.12). Select **Show Zones**.

FIGURE A11.12
Selecting Zones in a JMP Control Chart

3. Click the red triangle to the left of P of Rooms Not Ready. Select **Tests → All Tests**.

The *c*-Chart

To illustrate how to produce a *c*-chart, refer to the data of Figure 11.8 on page 292 concerning the number of complaints. Open the **COMPLAINTS.JMP** data table.

1. Select **Graph → Control Chart → C.** In the C Control Chart dialog box (see Figure A11.13), enter **Complaints** in the Process edit box. Enter **Week** in

the **Sample Label** edit box. Select the **KSigma** options button and enter **3** in the edit box. Click the **OK** button.

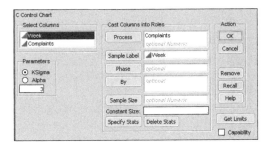

FIGURE A11.13
JMP Control Chart Dialog Box for a c-Chart

2. Click the red triangle to the left of C of Complaints. Select **Show Zones**.

3. Click the red triangle to the left of C of Complaints. Select **Tests → All Tests**

The *u*-Chart

To illustrate how to produce a *u*-chart, refer to the data of Figure 11.10 on page 295 concerning the number of programming errors. Open the **ERRRORCODE.JMP** data table.

1. Select **Graph → Control Chart → U.** In the U Control Chart dialog box (see Figure A11.14), enter **Day** in the Sample Label edit box. Enter **Number of Code Errors** in the Process edit box. Enter **Number of Lines** in the Unit Size edit box. Select the **KSigma** options button and enter **3** in the edit box. Click the **OK** button.

2. Click the red triangle to the left of U of Number of Code Errors. Select **Tests → All Tests**.

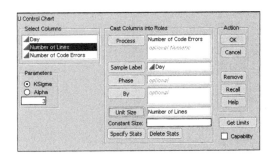

FIGURE A11.14
JMP Control Chart Dialog Box for a *u*-Chart

$\bar{X}$ and *R*-Charts

To illustrate how to produce $\bar{X}$ and *R*-charts, refer to the data of Figure 11.12 on page 298 concerning the waiting times at a bank. Open the **BANKTIME.JMP** data table.

1. Select **Graph → Control Chart → XBar.** In the XBar Control Chart dialog box (see Figure A11.15), select the **XBar** and **R** check boxes. Enter **Waiting Time** in the Process edit box. Enter **Day** in the Sample Label edit box. Select the **KSigma** options button and enter **3** in the edit box. Select the **Sample Size Constant** option button. Enter **4** in the edit box. Click the **OK** button.

2. Click the red triangle to the left of XBar of Waiting Time. Select **Show Zones**.

3. Click the red triangle to the left of XBar of Waiting Time. Select **Tests → All Tests**.

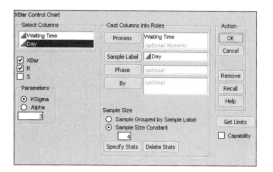

FIGURE A11.15
JMP Control Chart Dialog Box for $\bar{X}$ and R-Charts

$\bar{X}$ and S-Charts

To illustrate how to produce $\bar{X}$ and S-charts, refer to the data of Figure 11.14 on page 303 concerning cycle times. Open the **CYCLETIME2.JMP** data table.

1. Select **Graph → Control Chart → XBar.** In the XBar Control Chart dialog box (see Figure A11.16), select the **XBar** and **S** check boxes. Enter **Cycle Time** in the Process edit box. Enter **Time** in the Sample Label edit box. Select the **KSigma** options button and enter **3** in the edit box. Select the **Sample Size Constant** option button. Enter **10** in the edit box. Click the **OK** button.

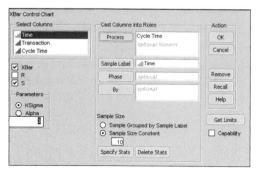

FIGURE A11.16
JMP Control Chart Dialog Box for $\bar{X}$ and S-Charts

2. Click the red triangle to the left of XBar of Cycle Time. Select **Show Zones**.

3. Click the red triangle to the left of XBar of Cycle Time. Select **Tests → All Tests**.

Individual Value and Moving Range Charts

To illustrate how to produce individual value and moving range charts, refer to the data of Figure 11.16 on page 307 concerning revenues. Open the **REVENUE.JMP** data table.

1. Select **Graph → Control Chart → IR.** In the IR Control Chart dialog box (see Figure A11.17), select the **Individual Measurement** and **Moving Range** check boxes. Enter **Revenue** in the Process edit box. Enter **Month** in the Sample Label edit box. Select the **KSigma** options button and enter **3** in the edit box. Enter **2** in the Range Span edit box. Click the **OK** button.

2. Click the red triangle to the left of Individual Measurement of Revenue. Select **Show Zones**.

3. Click the red triangle to the left of Individual Measurement of Revenue. Select **Tests → Test 1**.

FIGURE A11.17
JMP Control Chart Dialog Box for Individual Value Charts

APPENDIX A

Review of Arithmetic and Algebra

In writing this book, I realize that there are wide differences in the mathematical background of readers. Some readers may have taken courses in calculus and matrix algebra, whereas others may not have taken any mathematics courses in a long, long time. Because the emphasis in this book is on statistical concepts and the interpretation of Minitab and JMP output, no prerequisite beyond elementary algebra is needed. To assess your arithmetic and algebraic skills, I suggest that you answer the following questions, then read the review that follows.

PART 1   FILL IN THE CORRECT ANSWER

1. $\dfrac{\frac{1}{2}}{3} =$

2. $(0.4)^2 =$

3. $1 + \dfrac{2}{3} =$

4. $\left(\dfrac{1}{3}\right)^4 =$

5. $\dfrac{1}{5} =$ (in decimals)

6. $1 - (-0.3) =$

7. $4 \times 0.2 \times (-8) =$

8. $\left(\dfrac{1}{4} \times \dfrac{2}{3}\right) =$

9. $\left(\dfrac{1}{100}\right) + \left(\dfrac{1}{200}\right) =$

10. $\sqrt{16} =$

PART 2   SELECT THE CORRECT ANSWER

1. If $a = bc$, then $c =$
   a. ab
   b. b/a
   c. a/b
   d. None of the above

2. If $x + y = z$, then y
   a. z/x
   b. $z + x$
   c. $z - x$
   d. None of the above

3. $(x^3)(x^2) =$
   a. x^5
   b. x^6
   c. x^1
   d. None of the above

4. $x^0 =$
   a. x
   b. 1
   c. 0
   d. None of the above

5. $x(y - z) =$
   a. $xy - xz$
   b. $xy - z$
   c. $(y - z)/x$
   d. None of the above

6. $(x + y)/z =$
   a. $(x/z) + y$
   b. $(x/z) + (y/z)$
   c. $x + (y/z)$
   d. None of the above

7. $x/(y + z) =$
   a. $(x/y) + (1/z)$
   b. $(x/y) + (x/z)$
   c. $(y + z)/x$
   d. None of the above

8. If $x = 10$, $y = 5$, $z = 2$, and $w = 20$, then $(xy - z^2)/w =$
   a. 5
   b. 2.3
   c. 46
   d. None of the above

9. $(8x^4)/(4x^2) =$
   a. $2x^2$
   b. 2
   c. $2x$
   d. none of the above

10. $\sqrt{\dfrac{X}{Y}} =$
   a. $\sqrt{Y}/\sqrt{X}$
   b. $\sqrt{1}/\sqrt{XY}$
   c. $\sqrt{X}/\sqrt{Y}$
   d. none of the above

The answers to both parts of the quiz appear at the end of this appendix.

SYMBOLS

Each of the four basic arithmetic operations—addition, subtraction, multiplication, and division—is indicated by an appropriate symbol:

> [+] add
> [×] or [·] multiply
> [–] subtract
> [÷] or [/] divide

In addition to these operations, the following symbols are used to indicate equality or inequality:

> = equals
> ≠ not equal
> ≡ approximately equal to
> > greater than
> < less than
> ≥ greater than or equal to
> ≤ less than or equal to

Addition

Addition refers to the summation of a set of numbers. In adding numbers, there are two basic laws: the commutative law and the associative law.

The *commutative law* of addition states that the order in which numbers are added is irrelevant. This can be seen in the following two examples:

> $1 + 2 = 3$ $2 + 1 = 3$
> $x + y = z$ $y + x = z$

In each example, it does not matter which number is listed first and which number is listed second.

The *associative law* of addition states that in adding several numbers, any subgrouping of the numbers can be added first, last, or in the middle. This is seen in the following examples:

1. $2 + 3 + 6 + 7 + 4 + 1 = 23$
2. $(5) + (6 + 7) + 4 + 1 = 23$
3. $5 + 13 + 5 = 23$
4. $5 + 6 + 7 + 4 + 1 = 23$

In each example, the order in which the numbers have been added has no effect on the results.

Subtraction

The process of **subtraction** is the opposite, or inverse, of addition. The operation of subtracting 1 from 2 (i.e., $2 - 1$) means that one unit is to be taken away from two units, leaving a remainder of one unit. In contrast to addition, the commutative and associative laws do not hold for subtraction, as indicated in the following examples:

$8 - 4 = 4$	but	$4 - 8 = -4$
$3 - 6 = -3$	but	$6 - 3 = 3$
$8 - 3 - 2 = 3$	but	$3 - 2 - 8 = -7$
$9 - 4 - 2 = 3$	but	$2 - 4 - 9 = -11$

When subtracting negative numbers, remember that the same result occurs when subtracting a negative number as when adding a positive number. Thus:

$4 - (-3) = +7$	$4 + 3 = 7$
$8 - (-10) = +18$	$8 + 10 = 18$

Multiplication

The operation of **multiplication** is a shortcut method of addition when the same number is to be added several times. For example, if 7 is to be added three times ($7 + 7 + 7$), you could multiply 7 by 3 to obtain the product of 21.

In multiplication, as in addition, the commutative laws and associative laws are in operation, so that:

$$a \times b = b \times a$$
$$4 \times 5 = 5 \times 4 = 20$$
$$(2 \times 5) \times 6 = 10 \times 6 = 60$$

A third law of multiplication, the *distributive law*, applies to the multiplication of one number by the sum of several numbers:

$$a(b + c) = ab + ac$$
$$2(3 + 4) = 2(7) = 2(3) + 2(4) = 14$$

The resulting product is the same, regardless of whether b and c are summed and multiplied by a, or a is multiplied by b and by c, then the two products are added together. You also need to remember that when multiplying negative numbers, a negative number multiplied by a negative number equals a positive number. Thus,

$$(-a) \times (-b) = ab$$
$$(-5) \times (-4) = +20$$

Division

Just as subtraction is the opposite of addition, **division** is the opposite, or inverse, of multiplication. Division can be viewed as a shortcut to subtraction. When 20 is divided by 4, you are actually determining the number of times that 4 can be subtracted from 20. In general, however, the number of times one number can be divided by another may not be an exact integer value, because there could be a remainder. For example, if 21 is divided by 4, the answer is 5¼ or 5 with a remainder of 1. In division, the number on top is called the *numerator* and the number on the bottom is called the *denominator*.

As in the case of subtraction, neither the commutative nor the associative law of addition and multiplication holds for division:

$$a \div b \neq b \div a$$
$$9 \div 3 \neq 3 \div 9$$
$$6 \div (3 \div 2) = 4$$
$$(6 \div 3) \div 2 = 1$$

The distributive law will hold only when the numbers to be added are contained in the numerator, not the denominator. Thus:

$$\frac{a+b}{c} = \frac{a}{c} + \frac{b}{c} \quad \text{but} \quad \frac{a}{b+c} \neq \frac{a}{b} + \frac{a}{c}$$

For example:

$$\frac{6+9}{3} = \frac{6}{3} + \frac{9}{3} = 2 + 3 = 5$$

$$\frac{1}{2+3} = \frac{1}{5} \quad \text{but} \quad \frac{1}{2+3} \neq \frac{1}{2} + \frac{1}{3}$$

The last important property of division states that if the numerator and the denominator are both multiplied or divided by the same number, the resulting quotient will not be affected. Therefore:

$$\frac{80}{40} = 2$$

then

$$\frac{5(80)}{5(40)} = \frac{400}{200} = 2$$

and

$$\frac{80 \div 5}{40 \div 5} = \frac{16}{8} = 2$$

Fractions

A **fraction** is a number that consists of a combination of whole numbers and/or parts of whole numbers. For instance, the fraction 1/3 consists of only one portion of a number, whereas the fraction 7/6 consists of the whole number 1 plus the fraction 1/6. Each of the operations of addition, subtraction, multiplication, and division can be used with fractions. When adding and subtracting fractions, you must find the lowest common denominator for each fraction prior to adding or subtracting them. Thus, in adding,

$$\frac{1}{3} + \frac{1}{5}$$

the lowest common denominator is 15, so:

$$\frac{5}{15} + \frac{3}{15} = \frac{8}{15}$$

In subtracting,

$$\frac{1}{4} - \frac{1}{6}$$

the same principles apply, so that the lowest common denominator is 12, producing a result of:

$$\frac{3}{12} - \frac{2}{12} = \frac{1}{12}$$

Multiplying and dividing fractions do not have the lowest common denominator requirement associated with adding and subtracting fractions. Thus, if a/b is multiplied by c/d, the result is

$$\frac{ac}{bd}$$

The resulting numerator, ac, is the product of the numerators a and c, and the denominator, bd, is the product of the two denominators b and d. The resulting fraction can sometimes be reduced to a lower term by dividing the numerator and denominator by a common factor. For example, taking

$$\frac{2}{3} \times \frac{6}{7} = \frac{12}{21}$$

and dividing the numerator and denominator by 3 produces the result

$$\frac{4}{7}$$

Division of fractions can be thought of as the inverse of multiplication, so the divisor can be inverted and multiplied by the original fraction. Thus:

$$\frac{9}{5} \div \frac{1}{4} = \frac{9}{5} \times \frac{4}{1} = \frac{36}{5}$$

The division of a fraction can also be thought of as a way of converting the fraction to a decimal number. For example, the fraction ⅖ can be converted to a decimal number by dividing its numerator, 2, by its denominator, 5, to produce the decimal number 0.40.

EXPONENTS AND SQUARE ROOTS

Exponentiation (raising a number to a power) provides a shortcut in writing numerous multiplications. For example, $2 \times 2 \times 2 \times 2 \times 2$ can be written as $2^5 = 32$. The 5 represents the exponent (or power) of the number 2, telling you that 2 is to multiplied by itself five times.

Several rules can be applied for multiplying or dividing numbers that contain exponents.

Rule 1. $x^a \cdot x^b = x^{(a + b)}$

If two numbers involving a power of the same number are multiplied, the product is the same number raised to the sum of the powers:

$$4^2 \cdot 4^3 = (4 \cdot 4)(4 \cdot 4 \cdot 4) = 4^5$$

Rule 2. $(x^a)^b = x^{ab}$

If you take the power of a number that is already taken to a power, the result will be a number that is raised to the product of the two powers. For example:

$$(4^2)^3 = (4^2)(4^2)(4^2) = 4^6$$

Rule 3. $\dfrac{x^a}{x^b} = x^{(a-b)}$

If a number raised to a power is divided by the same number raised to a power, the quotient will be the number raised to the difference of the powers. Thus:

$$\frac{3^5}{3^3} = \frac{3 \cdot 3 \cdot 3 \cdot 3 \cdot 3}{3 \cdot 3 \cdot 3} = 3^2$$

If the denominator has a higher power than the numerator, the resulting quotient will be a negative power. Thus:

$$\frac{3^3}{3^5} = \frac{3 \cdot 3 \cdot 3}{3 \cdot 3 \cdot 3 \cdot 3 \cdot 3} = \frac{1}{3^2} = 3^{-2} = \frac{1}{9}$$

If the difference between the powers of the numerator and denominator is 1, the result will be the number itself. In other words, $x^1 = x$. For example:

$$\frac{3^3}{3^2} = \frac{3 \cdot 3 \cdot 3}{3 \cdot 3} = 3^1 = 3$$

If, however, there is no difference in the power of the numbers in the numerator and denominator, the result will be 1. Thus:

$$\frac{x^a}{x^a} = x^{a-a} = x^1 = 1$$

Therefore, any number raised to the zero power equals 1. For example:

$$\frac{3^3}{3^3} = \frac{3 \cdot 3 \cdot 3}{3 \cdot 3 \cdot 3} = 3^0 = 1$$

The square root, represented by the $\sqrt{}$ symbol, is a special power of number, the 1/2 power. It indicates the value that, when multiplied by itself, will produce the original number.

EQUATIONS

In statistics, many formulas are expressed as equations where one unknown value is a function of another value. Thus, it is important to be able to know how to manipulate equations into various forms. The rules of addition, subtraction, multiplication, and division can be used to work with equations. For example, the equation $x - 2 = 5$ can be solved for x by adding 2 to each side of the equation. This results in $x - 2 + 2 = 5 + 2$. Therefore, $x = 7$.

If $x + y = z$, you could solve for x by subtracting y from both sides of the equation, $x + y - y = z - y$. Therefore, $x = z - y$.

If the product of two variables is equal to a third variable, such as $x \cdot y = z$, you can solve for x by dividing both sides of the equation by y. Thus:

$$\frac{x \cdot y}{y} = \frac{z}{y}$$

$$x = \frac{z}{y}$$

Conversely, if:

$$\frac{x}{y} = z$$

you can solve for x by multiplying both sides of the equation by y:

$$\frac{xy}{y} = zy$$

$$x = zy$$

In summary, the various operations of addition, subtraction, multiplication, and division can be applied to equations as long as the same operation is performed on each side of the equation, thereby maintaining the equality.

ANSWERS TO QUIZ

Part 1	Part 2
1. 3/2	**1.** c
2. 0.16	**2.** c
3. 5/3	**3.** a
4. 1/81	**4.** b
5. 0.20	**5.** a
6. 1.30	**6.** b
7. -6.4	**7.** d
8. +1/6	**8.** b
9. 3/200	**9.** a
10. 4	**10.** c

APPENDIX B

Summation Notation

Because the operation of addition occurs so frequently in statistics, the special symbol Σ is used to mean "take the sum of." If there is a set of n values for a variable labeled X, the expression $\sum_{i=1}^{n} X_i$ means that these n values are to be added together from the first value to the last (n^{th}) value. Thus:

$$\sum_{i=1}^{n} X_i = X_1 + X_2 + X_3 + \cdots + X_n$$

To illustrate summation notation, suppose there are five values for a variable X:

$X_1 = 2$, $X_2 = 0$, $X_3 = -1$, $X_4 = 5$, and $X_5 = 7$.

For these data,

$$\sum_{i=1}^{n} X_i = X_1 + X_2 + X_3 + X_4 + X_5$$
$$= 2 + 0 + (-1) + 5 + 7 = 13$$

In statistics, it is also often necessary to sum the squared values of a variable. Using summation notation, the sum of the squared Xs is written as:

$$\sum_{i=1}^{n} X_i^2 = X_1^2 + X_2^2 + X_3^2 + \cdots + X_n^2$$

and using the preceding data:

$$\sum_{i=1}^{n} X_i^2 = X_1^2 + X_2^2 + X_3^2 + X_4^2 + X_5^2$$
$$= 2^2 + 0^2 + (-1)^2 + 5^2 + 7^2$$
$$= 4 + 0 + 1 + 25 + 49$$
$$= 79$$

It is important to understand that, $\sum_{i=1}^{n} X_i^2$, the sum of the squares, is not the same as, $\left(\sum_{i=1}^{n} X_i\right)^2$, the square of the sum.

$$\sum_{i=1}^{n} X_i^2 \neq \left(\sum_{i=1}^{n} X_i\right)^2$$

In the preceding example, the sum of the squares, $\sum_{i=1}^{n} X_i^2$ equals 79. That is not equal to the square of the sum $\left(\sum_{i=1}^{n} X_i\right)^2$, which is $(13)^2 = 169$.

Another frequently used operation involves summing the product of two variables, called the *cross product*. This operation involves two variables, X and Y, each having n values. Then:

$$\sum_{i=1}^{n} X_i Y_i = X_1 Y_1 + X_2 Y_2 + X_3 Y_3 + \cdots + X_5 Y_5$$

Continuing with the preceding data, suppose that a second variable, Y, has the following five values: $Y_1 = 1, Y_2 = 3, Y_3 = -2, X_4 = 4$, and $X_5 = 3$. Then:

$$\begin{aligned}
\sum_{i=1}^{n} X_i Y_i &= X_1 Y_1 + X_2 Y_2 + X_3 Y_3 + X_4 Y_4 + X_5 Y_5 \\
&= (2)(1) + (0)(3) + (-1)(-2) + (5)(4) + (7)(3) \\
&= 2 + 0 + 2 + 20 + 21 \\
&= 45
\end{aligned}$$

In computing $\sum_{i=1}^{n} X_i Y_i$, the first value of X is multiplied by the first value of Y, the second value of X is multiplied by the second value of Y, and so on. These cross products are then summed. Observe that the sum of the cross products is *not* equal to the product of the individual sums; that is:

$$\sum_{i=1}^{n} X_i Y_i \neq \left(\sum_{i=1}^{n} X_i\right)\left(\sum_{i=1}^{n} Y_i\right)$$

Using the preceding data,

$$\sum_{i=1}^{n} X_i = 13$$

and

$$\sum_{i=1}^{n} Y_i = 1 + 3 + (-2) + 4 + 3 = 9$$

so that

$$\left(\sum_{i=1}^{n} X_i\right)\left(\sum_{i=1}^{n} Y_i\right) = (13)(9) = 117$$

This is not the same as, $\sum_{i=1}^{n} X_i Y_i$ which equals 45.

The four basic rules of summation notation are as follows:

Rule 1: The sum of the values of two different variables is equal to the sum of the values of each variable.

$$\sum_{i=1}^{n}(X_i + Y_i) = \sum_{i=1}^{n} X_i + \sum_{i=1}^{n} Y_i$$

Thus, for the preceding data:

$$\sum_{i=1}^{n}(X_i + Y_i) = (2+1) + (0+3) + (-1+(-2)) + (5+4) + (7+3)$$

$$= 3 + 3 + (-3) + 9 + 10$$

$$= 22 = \sum_{i=1}^{5} X_i + \sum_{i=1}^{5} Y_i = 13 + 9 = 22$$

Rule 2: The sum of the difference between the values of two variables is equal to the difference between the sum of the two variables.

$$\sum_{i=1}^{n}(X_i - Y_i) = \sum_{i=1}^{n} X_i - \sum_{i=1}^{n} Y_i$$

Using the preceding data:

$$\sum_{i=1}^{n}(X_i - Y_i) = (2-1) + (0-3) + (-1-(-2)) + (5-4) + (7-3)$$

$$= 1 + (-3) + 1 + 1 + 4$$

$$= 4 = \sum_{i=1}^{5} X_i - \sum_{i=1}^{5} Y_i = 13 - 9 = 4$$

Rule 3: The sum of a constant multiplied by a variable is equal to the constant multiplied by the sum of the values of the variable:

$$\sum_{i=1}^{n} cX_i = c\sum_{i=1}^{n} X_i$$

where c is a constant.

Thus, if $c = 2$:

$$\sum_{i=1}^{5} cX_i = 2\sum_{i=1}^{5} X_i = (2)(2) + 2(0) + (2)(-1) + (2)(5) + (2)(7)$$

$$= 4 + 0 + (-2) + 10 + 14$$

$$= 26 = 2\sum_{i=1}^{5} X_i = (2)(13) = 26$$

Rule 4: A constant summed n times is equal to n multiplied by the value of the constant.

$$\sum_{i=1}^{n} c = nc$$

where c is a constant. Thus, if the constant $c = 2$ is summed five times:

$$\sum_{i=1}^{n} c = 2 + 2 + 2 + 2 + 2$$

$$= 10 = (5)(2) = 10$$

REFERENCES

1. Bashaw, W. L. *Mathematics for Statistics* (New York: Wiley, 1969).

2. Lanzer, P. *Video Review of Arithmetic* (Hickville, NY: Video Aided Instruction, 1999).

3. Levine, D. *The MBA Primer: Business Statistics* (Cincinnati, OH: Southwestern Publishing, 2000).

4. Levine, D. *Video Review of Statistics* (Hickville, NY: Video Aided Instruction, 1989).

5. Shane, H. *Video Review of Elementary Algebra* (Hickville, NY: Video Aided Instruction, 1996).

APPENDIX C

Statistical Tables

TABLE C.1 The Cumulative Standardized Normal Distribution

Each entry represents an area under the cumulative standardized normal distribution from $-\infty$ to Z.

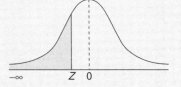

Z	0.00	0.01	0.02	0.03	0.04	0.05	0.06	0.07	0.08	0.09
−3.9	0.00005	0.00005	0.00004	0.00004	0.00004	0.00004	0.00004	0.00004	0.00003	0.00003
−3.8	0.00007	0.00007	0.00007	0.00006	0.00006	0.00006	0.00006	0.00005	0.00005	0.00005
−3.7	0.00011	0.00010	0.00010	0.00010	0.00009	0.00009	0.00008	0.00008	0.00008	0.00008
−3.6	0.00016	0.00015	0.00015	0.00014	0.00014	0.00013	0.00013	0.00012	0.00012	0.00011
−3.5	0.00023	0.00022	0.00022	0.00021	0.00020	0.00019	0.00019	0.00018	0.00017	0.00017
−3.4	0.00034	0.00032	0.00031	0.00030	0.00029	0.00028	0.00027	0.00026	0.00025	0.00024
−3.3	0.00048	0.00047	0.00045	0.00043	0.00042	0.00040	0.00039	0.00038	0.00036	0.00035
−3.2	0.00069	0.00066	0.00064	0.00062	0.00060	0.00058	0.00056	0.00054	0.00052	0.00050
−3.1	0.00097	0.00094	0.00090	0.00087	0.00084	0.00082	0.00079	0.00076	0.00074	0.00071
−3.0	0.00135	0.00131	0.00126	0.00122	0.00118	0.00114	0.00111	0.00107	0.00103	0.00100
−2.9	0.0019	0.0018	0.0018	0.0017	0.0016	0.0016	0.0015	0.0015	0.0014	0.0014
−2.8	0.0026	0.0025	0.0024	0.0023	0.0023	0.0022	0.0021	0.0021	0.0020	0.0019
−2.7	0.0035	0.0034	0.0033	0.0032	0.0031	0.0030	0.0029	0.0028	0.0027	0.0026
−2.6	0.0047	0.0045	0.0044	0.0043	0.0041	0.0040	0.0039	0.0038	0.0037	0.0036
−2.5	0.0062	0.0060	0.0059	0.0057	0.0055	0.0054	0.0052	0.0051	0.0049	0.0048
−2.4	0.0082	0.0080	0.0078	0.0075	0.0073	0.0071	0.0069	0.0068	0.0066	0.0064
−2.3	0.0107	0.0104	0.0102	0.0099	0.0096	0.0094	0.0091	0.0089	0.0087	0.0084
−2.2	0.0139	0.0136	0.0132	0.0129	0.0125	0.0122	0.0119	0.0116	0.0113	0.0110
−2.1	0.0179	0.0174	0.0170	0.0166	0.0162	0.0158	0.0154	0.0150	0.0146	0.0143
−2.0	0.0228	0.0222	0.0217	0.0212	0.0207	0.0202	0.0197	0.0192	0.0188	0.0183
−1.9	0.0287	0.0281	0.0274	0.0268	0.0262	0.0256	0.0250	0.0244	0.0239	0.0233
−1.8	0.0359	0.0351	0.0344	0.0336	0.0329	0.0322	0.0314	0.0307	0.0301	0.0294
−1.7	0.0446	0.0436	0.0427	0.0418	0.0409	0.0401	0.0392	0.0384	0.0375	0.0367
−1.6	0.0548	0.0537	0.0526	0.0516	0.0505	0.0495	0.0485	0.0475	0.0465	0.0455
−1.5	0.0668	0.0655	0.0643	0.0630	0.0618	0.0606	0.0594	0.0582	0.0571	0.0559
−1.4	0.0808	0.0793	0.0778	0.0764	0.0749	0.0735	0.0721	0.0708	0.0694	0.0681
−1.3	0.0968	0.0951	0.0934	0.0918	0.0901	0.0885	0.0869	0.0853	0.0838	0.0823
−1.2	0.1151	0.1131	0.1112	0.1093	0.1075	0.1056	0.1038	0.1020	0.1003	0.0985
−1.1	0.1357	0.1335	0.1314	0.1292	0.1271	0.1251	0.1230	0.1210	0.1190	0.1170
−1.0	0.1587	0.1562	0.1539	0.1515	0.1492	0.1469	0.1446	0.1423	0.1401	0.1379
−0.9	0.1841	0.1814	0.1788	0.1762	0.1736	0.1711	0.1685	0.1660	0.1635	0.1611
−0.8	0.2119	0.2090	0.2061	0.2033	0.2005	0.1977	0.1949	0.1922	0.1894	0.1867
−0.7	0.2420	0.2388	0.2358	0.2327	0.2296	0.2266	0.2236	0.2206	0.2177	0.2148
−0.6	0.2743	0.2709	0.2676	0.2643	0.2611	0.2578	0.2546	0.2514	0.2482	0.2451
−0.5	0.3085	0.3050	0.3015	0.2981	0.2946	0.2912	0.2877	0.2843	0.2810	0.2776
−0.4	0.3446	0.3409	0.3372	0.3336	0.3300	0.3264	0.3228	0.3192	0.3156	0.3121
−0.3	0.3821	0.3783	0.3745	0.3707	0.3669	0.3632	0.3594	0.3557	0.3520	0.3483
−0.2	0.4207	0.4168	0.4129	0.4090	0.4052	0.4013	0.3974	0.3936	0.3897	0.3859
−0.1	0.4602	0.4562	0.4522	0.4483	0.4443	0.4404	0.4364	0.4325	0.4286	0.4247
−0.0	0.5000	0.4960	0.4920	0.4880	0.4840	0.4801	0.4761	0.4721	0.4681	0.4641

Continues

TABLE C.1　The Cumulative Standardized Normal Distribution (Continued)

Z	0.00	0.01	0.02	0.03	0.04	0.05	0.06	0.07	0.08	0.09
0.0	0.5000	0.5040	0.5080	0.5120	0.5160	0.5199	0.5239	0.5279	0.5319	0.5359
0.1	0.5398	0.5438	0.5478	0.5517	0.5557	0.5596	0.5636	0.5675	0.5714	0.5753
0.2	0.5793	0.5832	0.5871	0.5910	0.5948	0.5987	0.6026	0.6064	0.6103	0.6141
0.3	0.6179	0.6217	0.6255	0.6293	0.6331	0.6368	0.6406	0.6443	0.6480	0.6517
0.4	0.6554	0.6591	0.6628	0.6664	0.6700	0.6736	0.6772	0.6808	0.6844	0.6879
0.5	0.6915	0.6950	0.6985	0.7019	0.7054	0.7088	0.7123	0.7157	0.7190	0.7224
0.6	0.7257	0.7291	0.7324	0.7357	0.7389	0.7422	0.7454	0.7486	0.7518	0.7549
0.7	0.7580	0.7612	0.7642	0.7673	0.7704	0.7734	0.7764	0.7794	0.7823	0.7852
0.8	0.7881	0.7910	0.7939	0.7967	0.7995	0.8023	0.8051	0.8078	0.8106	0.8133
0.9	0.8159	0.8186	0.8212	0.8238	0.8264	0.8289	0.8315	0.8340	0.8365	0.8389
1.0	0.8413	0.8438	0.8461	0.8485	0.8508	0.8531	0.8554	0.8577	0.8599	0.8621
1.1	0.8643	0.8665	0.8686	0.8708	0.8729	0.8749	0.8770	0.8790	0.8810	0.8830
1.2	0.8849	0.8869	0.8888	0.8907	0.8925	0.8944	0.8962	0.8980	0.8997	0.9015
1.3	0.9032	0.9049	0.9066	0.9082	0.9099	0.9115	0.9131	0.9147	0.9162	0.9177
1.4	0.9192	0.9207	0.9222	0.9236	0.9251	0.9265	0.9279	0.9292	0.9306	0.9319
1.5	0.9332	0.9345	0.9357	0.9370	0.9382	0.9394	0.9406	0.9418	0.9429	0.9441
1.6	0.9452	0.9463	0.9474	0.9484	0.9495	0.9505	0.9515	0.9525	0.9535	0.9545
1.7	0.9554	0.9564	0.9573	0.9582	0.9591	0.9599	0.9608	0.9616	0.9625	0.9633
1.8	0.9641	0.9649	0.9656	0.9664	0.9671	0.9678	0.9686	0.9693	0.9699	0.9706
1.9	0.9713	0.9719	0.9726	0.9732	0.9738	0.9744	0.9750	0.9756	0.9761	0.9767
2.0	0.9772	0.9778	0.9783	0.9788	0.9793	0.9798	0.9803	0.9808	0.9812	0.9817
2.1	0.9821	0.9826	0.9830	0.9834	0.9838	0.9842	0.9846	0.9850	0.9854	0.9857
2.2	0.9861	0.9864	0.9868	0.9871	0.9875	0.9878	0.9881	0.9884	0.9887	0.9890
2.3	0.9893	0.9896	0.9898	0.9901	0.9904	0.9906	0.9909	0.9911	0.9913	0.9916
2.4	0.9918	0.9920	0.9922	0.9925	0.9927	0.9929	0.9931	0.9932	0.9934	0.9936
2.5	0.9938	0.9940	0.9941	0.9943	0.9945	0.9946	0.9948	0.9949	0.9951	0.9952
2.6	0.9953	0.9955	0.9956	0.9957	0.9959	0.9960	0.9961	0.9962	0.9963	0.9964
2.7	0.9965	0.9966	0.9967	0.9968	0.9969	0.9970	0.9971	0.9972	0.9973	0.9974
2.8	0.9974	0.9975	0.9976	0.9977	0.9977	0.9978	0.9979	0.9979	0.9980	0.9981
2.9	0.9981	0.9982	0.9982	0.9983	0.9984	0.9984	0.9985	0.9985	0.9986	0.9986
3.0	0.99865	0.99869	0.99874	0.99878	0.99882	0.99886	0.99889	0.99893	0.99897	0.99900
3.1	0.99903	0.99906	0.99910	0.99913	0.99916	0.99918	0.99921	0.99924	0.99926	0.99929
3.2	0.99931	0.99934	0.99936	0.99938	0.99940	0.99942	0.99944	0.99946	0.99948	0.99950
3.3	0.99952	0.99953	0.99955	0.99957	0.99958	0.99960	0.99961	0.99962	0.99964	0.99965
3.4	0.99966	0.99968	0.99969	0.99970	0.99971	0.99972	0.99973	0.99974	0.99975	0.99976
3.5	0.99977	0.99978	0.99978	0.99979	0.99980	0.99981	0.99981	0.99982	0.99983	0.99983
3.6	0.99984	0.99985	0.99985	0.99986	0.99986	0.99987	0.99987	0.99988	0.99988	0.99989
3.7	0.99989	0.99990	0.99990	0.99990	0.99991	0.99991	0.99992	0.99992	0.99992	0.99992
3.8	0.99993	0.99993	0.99993	0.99994	0.99994	0.99994	0.99994	0.99995	0.99995	0.99995
3.9	0.99995	0.99995	0.99996	0.99996	0.99996	0.99996	0.99996	0.99996	0.99997	0.99997
4.0	0.99996832									
4.5	0.99999660									
5.0	0.99999971									
5.5	0.99999998									
6.0	0.99999999									

Table C.2   Critical Values of *t*   335

TABLE C.2   Critical Values of *t*

For a particular number of degree of freedom, each entry represents the
critical value of *t* corresponding to a specified upper-tail area (α).

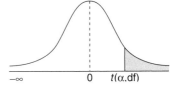

Degrees of Freedom	Upper-Tail Areas					
	0.25	0.10	0.05	0.025	0.01	0.005
1	1.0000	3.0777	6.3138	12.7062	31.8207	63.6574
2	0.8165	1.8856	2.9200	4.3027	6.9646	9.9248
3	0.7649	1.6377	2.3534	3.1824	4.5407	5.8409
4	0.7407	1.5332	2.1318	2.7764	3.7469	4.6041
5	0.7267	1.4759	2.0150	2.5706	3.3649	4.0322
6	0.7176	1.4398	1.9432	2.4469	3.1427	3.7074
7	0.7111	1.4149	1.8946	2.3646	2.9980	3.4995
8	0.7064	1.3968	1.8595	2.3060	2.8965	3.3554
9	0.7027	1.3830	1.8331	2.2622	2.8214	3.2498
10	0.6998	1.3722	1.8125	2.2281	2.7638	3.1693
11	0.6974	1.3634	1.7959	2.2010	2.7181	3.1058
12	0.6955	1.3562	1.7823	2.1788	2.6810	3.0545
13	0.6938	1.3502	1.7709	2.1604	2.6503	3.0123
14	0.6924	1.3450	1.7613	2.1448	2.6245	2.9768
15	0.6912	1.3406	1.7531	2.1315	2.6025	2.9467
16	0.6901	1.3368	1.7459	2.1199	2.5835	2.9208
17	0.6892	1.3334	1.7396	2.1098	2.5669	2.8982
18	0.6884	1.3304	1.7341	2.1009	2.5524	2.8784
19	0.6876	1.3277	1.7291	2.0930	2.5395	2.8609
20	0.6870	1.3253	1.7247	2.0860	2.5280	2.8453
21	0.6864	1.3232	1.7207	2.0796	2.5177	2.8314
22	0.6858	1.3212	1.7171	2.0739	2.5083	2.8188
23	0.6853	1.3195	1.7139	2.0687	2.4999	2.8073
24	0.6848	1.3178	1.7109	2.0639	2.4922	2.7969
25	0.6844	1.3163	1.7081	2.0595	2.4851	2.7874
26	0.6840	1.3150	1.7056	2.0555	2.4786	2.7787
27	0.6837	1.3137	1.7033	2.0518	2.4727	2.7707
28	0.6834	1.3125	1.7011	2.0484	2.4671	2.7633
29	0.6830	1.3114	1.6991	2.0452	2.4620	2.7564
30	0.6828	1.3104	1.6973	2.0423	2.4573	2.7500
31	0.6825	1.3095	1.6955	2.0395	2.4528	2.7440
32	0.6822	1.3086	1.6939	2.0369	2.4487	2.7385
33	0.6820	1.3077	1.6924	2.0345	2.4448	2.7333
34	0.6818	1.3070	1.6909	2.0322	2.4411	2.7284

Continues

TABLE C.2   Critical Values of t (Continued)

Degrees of Freedom	Upper-Tail Areas					
	0.25	0.10	0.05	0.025	0.01	0.005
35	0.6816	1.3062	1.6896	2.0301	2.4377	2.7238
36	0.6814	1.3055	1.6883	2.0281	2.4345	2.7195
37	0.6812	1.3049	1.6871	2.0262	2.4314	2.7154
38	0.6810	1.3042	1.6860	2.0244	2.4286	2.7116
39	0.6808	1.3036	1.6849	2.0227	2.4258	2.7079
40	0.6807	1.3031	1.6839	2.0211	2.4233	2.7045
41	0.6805	1.3025	1.6829	2.0195	2.4208	2.7012
42	0.6804	1.3020	1.6820	2.0181	2.4185	2.6981
43	0.6802	1.3016	1.6811	2.0167	2.4163	2.6951
44	0.6801	1.3011	1.6802	2.0154	2.4141	2.6923
45	0.6800	1.3006	1.6794	2.0141	2.4121	2.6896
46	0.6799	1.3022	1.6787	2.0129	2.4102	2.6870
47	0.6797	1.2998	1.6779	2.0117	2.4083	2.6846
48	0.6796	1.2994	1.6772	2.0106	2.4066	2.6822
49	0.6795	1.2991	1.6766	2.0096	2.4049	2.6800
50	0.6794	1.2987	1.6759	2.0086	2.4033	2.6778
51	0.6793	1.2984	1.6753	2.0076	2.4017	2.6757
52	0.6792	1.2980	1.6747	2.0066	2.4002	2.6737
53	0.6791	1.2977	1.6741	2.0057	2.3988	2.6718
54	0.6791	1.2974	1.6736	2.0049	2.3974	2.6700
55	0.6790	1.2971	1.6730	2.0040	2.3961	2.6682
56	0.6789	1.2969	1.6725	2.0032	2.3948	2.6665
57	0.6788	1.2966	1.6720	2.0025	2.3936	2.6649
58	0.6787	1.2963	1.6716	2.0017	2.3924	2.6633
59	0.6787	1.2961	1.6711	2.0010	2.3912	2.6618
60	0.6786	1.2958	1.6706	2.0003	2.3901	2.6603
61	0.6785	1.2956	1.6702	1.9996	2.3890	2.6589
62	0.6785	1.2954	1.6698	1.9990	2.3880	2.6575
63	0.6784	1.2951	1.6694	1.9983	2.3870	2.6561
64	0.6783	1.2949	1.6690	1.9977	2.3860	2.6549
65	0.6783	1.2947	1.6686	1.9971	2.3851	2.6536
66	0.6782	1.2945	1.6683	1.9966	2.3842	2.6524
67	0.6782	1.2943	1.6679	1.9960	2.3833	2.6512
68	0.6781	1.2941	1.6676	1.9955	2.3824	2.6501
69	0.6781	1.2939	1.6672	1.9949	2.3816	2.6490

Table C.2   Critical Values of *t*   337

Degrees of Freedom	Upper-Tail Areas					
	0.25	0.10	0.05	0.025	0.01	0.005
70	0.6780	1.2938	1.6669	1.9944	2.3808	2.6479
71	0.6780	1.2936	1.6666	1.9939	2.3800	2.6469
72	0.6779	1.2934	1.6663	1.9935	2.3793	2.6459
73	0.6779	1.2933	1.6660	1.9930	2.3785	2.6449
74	0.6778	1.2931	1.6657	1.9925	2.3778	2.6439
75	0.6778	1.2929	1.6654	1.9921	2.3771	2.6430
76	0.6777	1.2928	1.6652	1.9917	2.3764	2.6421
77	0.6777	1.2926	1.6649	1.9913	2.3758	2.6412
78	0.6776	1.2925	1.6646	1.9908	2.3751	2.6403
79	0.6776	1.2924	1.6644	1.9905	2.3745	2.6395
80	0.6776	1.2922	1.6641	1.9901	2.3739	2.6387
81	0.6775	1.2921	1.6639	1.9897	2.3733	2.6379
82	0.6775	1.2920	1.6636	1.9893	2.3727	2.6371
83	0.6775	1.2918	1.6634	1.9890	2.3721	2.6364
84	0.6774	1.2917	1.6632	1.9886	2.3716	2.6356
85	0.6774	1.2916	1.6630	1.9883	2.3710	2.6349
86	0.6774	1.2915	1.6628	1.9879	2.3705	2.6342
87	0.6773	1.2914	1.6626	1.9876	2.3700	2.6335
88	0.6773	1.2912	1.6624	1.9873	2.3695	2.6329
89	0.6773	1.2911	1.6622	1.9870	2.3690	2.6322
90	0.6772	1.2910	1.6620	1.9867	2.3685	2.6316
91	0.6772	1.2909	1.6618	1.9864	2.3680	2.6309
92	0.6772	1.2908	1.6616	1.9861	2.3676	2.6303
93	0.6771	1.2907	1.6614	1.9858	2.3671	2.6297
94	0.6771	1.2906	1.6612	1.9855	2.3667	2.6291
95	0.6771	1.2905	1.6611	1.9853	2.3662	2.6286
96	0.6771	1.2904	1.6609	1.9850	2.3658	2.6280
97	0.6770	1.2903	1.6607	1.9847	2.3654	2.6275
98	0.6770	1.2902	1.6606	1.9845	2.3650	2.6269
99	0.6770	1.2902	1.6604	1.9842	2.3646	2.6264
100	0.6770	1.2901	1.6602	1.9840	2.3642	2.6259
110	0.6767	1.2893	1.6588	1.9818	2.3607	2.6213
120	0.6765	1.2886	1.6577	1.9799	2.3578	2.6174
∞	0.6745	1.2816	1.6449	1.9600	2.3263	2.5758

TABLE C.3   Critical Values of *F*

For a particular combination of numerator and denominator degrees of freedom, each entry represents the critical values of *F* corresponding to a specified upper-tail area (α).

Denominator df_2	Numerator, df_1								
	1	2	3	4	5	6	7	8	9
1	161.40	199.50	215.70	224.60	230.20	234.00	236.80	238.90	240.50
2	18.51	19.00	19.16	19.25	19.30	19.33	19.35	19.37	19.38
3	10.13	9.55	9.28	9.12	9.01	8.94	8.89	8.85	8.81
4	7.71	6.94	6.59	6.39	6.26	6.16	6.09	6.04	6.00
5	6.61	5.79	5.41	5.19	5.05	4.95	4.88	4.82	4.77
6	5.99	5.14	4.76	4.53	4.39	4.28	4.21	4.15	4.10
7	5.59	4.74	4.35	4.12	3.97	3.87	3.79	3.73	3.68
8	5.32	4.46	4.07	3.84	3.69	3.58	3.50	3.44	3.39
9	5.12	4.26	3.86	3.63	3.48	3.37	3.29	3.23	3.18
10	4.96	4.10	3.71	3.48	3.33	3.22	3.14	3.07	3.02
11	4.84	3.98	3.59	3.36	3.20	3.09	3.01	2.95	2.90
12	4.75	3.89	3.49	3.26	3.11	3.00	2.91	2.85	2.80
13	4.67	3.81	3.41	3.18	3.03	2.92	2.83	2.77	2.71
14	4.60	3.74	3.34	3.11	2.96	2.85	2.76	2.70	2.65
15	4.54	3.68	3.29	3.06	2.90	2.79	2.71	2.64	2.59
16	4.49	3.63	3.24	3.01	2.85	2.74	2.66	2.59	2.54
17	4.45	3.59	3.20	2.96	2.81	2.70	2.61	2.55	2.49
18	4.41	3.55	3.16	2.93	2.77	2.66	2.58	2.51	2.46
19	4.38	3.52	3.13	2.90	2.74	2.63	2.54	2.48	2.42
20	4.35	3.49	3.10	2.87	2.71	2.60	2.51	2.45	2.39
21	4.32	3.47	3.07	2.84	2.68	2.57	2.49	2.42	2.37
22	4.30	3.44	3.05	2.82	2.66	2.55	2.46	2.40	2.34
23	4.28	3.42	3.03	2.80	2.64	2.53	2.44	2.37	2.32
24	4.26	3.40	3.01	2.78	2.62	2.51	2.42	2.36	2.30
25	4.24	3.39	2.99	2.76	2.60	2.49	2.40	2.34	2.28
26	4.23	3.37	2.98	2.74	2.59	2.47	2.39	2.32	2.27
27	4.21	3.35	2.96	2.73	2.57	2.46	2.37	2.31	2.25
28	4.20	3.34	2.95	2.71	2.56	2.45	2.36	2.29	2.24
29	4.18	3.33	2.93	2.70	2.55	2.43	2.35	2.28	2.22
30	4.17	3.32	2.92	2.69	2.53	2.42	2.33	2.27	2.21
40	4.08	3.23	2.84	2.61	2.45	2.34	2.25	2.18	2.12
60	4.00	3.15	2.76	2.53	2.37	2.25	2.17	2.10	2.04
120	3.92	3.07	2.68	2.45	2.29	2.17	2.09	2.02	1.96
∞	3.84	3.00	2.60	2.37	2.21	2.10	2.01	1.94	1.88

Table C.3   Critical Values of F 339

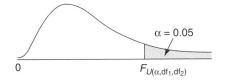

$\alpha = 0.05$

0 $F_{U(\alpha,df_1,df_2)}$

				Numerator, df_1					
10	**12**	**15**	**20**	**24**	**30**	**40**	**60**	**120**	**∞**
241.90	243.90	245.90	248.00	249.10	250.10	251.10	252.20	253.30	254.30
19.40	19.41	19.43	19.45	19.45	19.46	19.47	19.48	19.49	19.50
8.79	8.74	8.70	8.66	8.64	8.62	8.59	8.57	8.55	8.53
5.96	5.91	5.86	5.80	5.77	5.75	5.72	5.69	5.66	5.63
4.74	4.68	4.62	4.56	4.53	4.50	4.46	4.43	4.40	4.36
4.06	4.00	3.94	3.87	3.84	3.81	3.77	3.74	3.70	3.67
3.64	3.57	3.51	3.44	3.41	3.38	3.34	3.30	3.27	3.23
3.35	3.28	3.22	3.15	3.12	3.08	3.04	3.01	2.97	2.93
3.14	3.07	3.01	2.94	2.90	2.86	2.83	2.79	2.75	2.71
2.98	2.91	2.85	2.77	2.74	2.70	2.66	2.62	2.58	2.54
2.85	2.79	2.72	2.65	2.61	2.57	2.53	2.49	2.45	2.40
2.75	2.69	2.62	2.54	2.51	2.47	2.43	2.38	2.34	2.30
2.67	2.60	2.53	2.46	2.42	2.38	2.34	2.30	2.25	2.21
2.60	2.53	2.46	2.39	2.35	2.31	2.27	2.22	2.18	2.13
2.54	2.48	2.40	2.33	2.29	2.25	2.20	2.16	2.11	2.07
2.49	2.42	2.35	2.28	2.24	2.19	2.15	2.11	2.06	2.01
2.45	2.38	2.31	2.23	2.19	2.15	2.10	2.06	2.01	1.96
2.41	2.34	2.27	2.19	2.15	2.11	2.06	2.02	1.97	1.92
2.38	2.31	2.23	2.16	2.11	2.07	2.03	1.98	1.93	1.88
2.35	2.28	2.20	2.12	2.08	2.04	1.99	1.95	1.90	1.84
2.32	2.25	2.18	2.10	2.05	2.01	1.96	1.92	1.87	1.81
2.30	2.23	2.15	2.07	2.03	1.98	1.91	1.89	1.84	1.78
2.27	2.20	2.13	2.05	2.01	1.96	1.91	1.86	1.81	1.76
2.25	2.18	2.11	2.03	1.98	1.94	1.89	1.84	1.79	1.73
2.24	2.16	2.09	2.01	1.96	1.92	1.87	1.82	1.77	1.71
2.22	2.15	2.07	1.99	1.95	1.90	1.85	1.80	1.75	1.69
2.20	2.13	2.06	1.97	1.93	1.88	1.84	1.79	1.73	1.67
2.19	2.12	2.04	1.96	1.91	1.87	1.82	1.77	1.71	1.65
2.18	2.10	2.03	1.94	1.90	1.85	1.81	1.75	1.70	1.64
2.16	2.09	2.01	1.93	1.89	1.84	1.79	1.74	1.68	1.62
2.08	2.00	1.92	1.84	1.79	1.74	1.69	1.64	1.58	1.51
1.99	1.92	1.84	1.75	1.70	1.65	1.59	1.53	1.47	1.39
1.91	1.83	1.75	1.66	1.61	1.55	1.50	1.43	1.35	1.25
1.83	1.75	1.67	1.57	1.52	1.46	1.39	1.32	1.22	1.00

TABLE C.3   Critical Values of *F* (Continued)

Denominator df_2	Numerator, df_1								
	1	2	3	4	5	6	7	8	9
1	647.80	799.50	864.20	899.60	921.80	937.10	948.20	956.70	963.30
2	38.51	39.00	39.17	39.25	39.30	39.33	39.36	39.39	39.39
3	17.44	16.04	15.44	15.10	14.88	14.73	14.62	14.54	14.47
4	12.22	10.65	9.98	9.60	9.36	9.20	9.07	8.98	8.90
5	10.01	8.43	7.76	7.39	7.15	6.98	6.85	6.76	6.68
6	8.81	7.26	6.60	6.23	5.99	5.82	5.70	5.60	5.52
7	8.07	6.54	5.89	5.52	5.29	5.12	4.99	4.90	4.82
8	7.57	6.06	5.42	5.05	4.82	4.65	4.53	4.43	4.36
9	7.21	5.71	5.08	4.72	4.48	4.32	4.20	4.10	4.03
10	6.94	5.46	4.83	4.47	4.24	4.07	3.95	3.85	3.78
11	6.72	5.26	4.63	4.28	4.04	3.88	3.76	3.66	3.59
12	6.55	5.10	4.47	4.12	3.89	3.73	3.61	3.51	3.44
13	6.41	4.97	4.35	4.00	3.77	3.60	3.48	3.39	3.31
14	6.30	4.86	4.24	3.89	3.66	3.50	3.38	3.29	3.21
15	6.20	4.77	4.15	3.80	3.58	3.41	3.29	3.20	3.12
16	6.12	4.69	4.08	3.73	3.50	3.34	3.22	3.12	3.05
17	6.04	4.62	4.01	3.66	3.44	3.28	3.16	3.06	2.98
18	5.98	4.56	3.95	3.61	3.38	3.22	3.10	3.01	2.93
19	5.92	4.51	3.90	3.56	3.33	3.17	3.05	2.96	2.88
20	5.87	4.46	3.86	3.51	3.29	3.13	3.01	2.91	2.84
21	5.83	4.42	3.82	3.48	3.25	3.09	2.97	2.87	2.80
22	5.79	4.38	3.78	3.44	3.22	3.05	2.93	2.84	2.76
23	5.75	4.35	3.75	3.41	3.18	3.02	2.90	2.81	2.73
24	5.72	4.32	3.72	3.38	3.15	2.99	2.87	2.78	2.70
25	5.69	4.29	3.69	3.35	3.13	2.97	2.85	2.75	2.68
26	5.66	4.27	3.67	3.33	3.10	2.94	2.82	2.73	2.65
27	5.63	4.24	3.65	3.31	3.08	2.92	2.80	2.71	2.63
28	5.61	4.22	3.63	3.29	3.06	2.90	2.78	2.69	2.61
29	5.59	4.20	3.61	3.27	3.04	2.88	2.76	2.67	2.59
30	5.57	4.18	3.59	3.25	3.03	2.87	2.75	2.65	2.57
40	5.42	4.05	3.46	3.13	2.90	2.74	2.62	2.53	2.45
60	5.29	3.93	3.34	3.01	2.79	2.63	2.51	2.41	2.33
120	5.15	3.80	3.23	2.89	2.67	2.52	2.39	2.30	2.22
∞	5.02	3.69	3.12	2.79	2.57	2.41	2.29	2.19	2.11

Table C.3   Critical Values of F 341

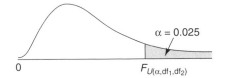

$\alpha = 0.025$

$F_{U(\alpha,df_1,df_2)}$

				Numerator, df_1					
10	**12**	**15**	**20**	**24**	**30**	**40**	**60**	**120**	**∞**
968.60	976.70	984.90	993.10	997.20	1,001.00	1,006.00	1,010.00	1,014.00	1,018.00
39.40	39.41	39.43	39.45	39.46	39.46	39.47	39.48	39.49	39.50
14.42	14.34	14.25	14.17	14.12	14.08	14.04	13.99	13.95	13.90
8.84	8.75	8.66	8.56	8.51	8.46	8.41	8.36	8.31	8.26
6.62	6.52	6.43	6.33	6.28	6.23	6.18	6.12	6.07	6.02
5.46	5.37	5.27	5.17	5.12	5.07	5.01	4.96	4.90	4.85
4.76	4.67	4.57	4.47	4.42	4.36	4.31	4.25	4.20	4.14
4.30	4.20	4.10	4.00	3.95	3.89	3.84	3.78	3.73	3.67
3.96	3.87	3.77	3.67	3.61	3.56	3.51	3.45	3.39	3.33
3.72	3.62	3.52	3.42	3.37	3.31	3.26	3.20	3.14	3.08
3.53	3.43	3.33	3.23	3.17	3.12	3.06	3.00	2.94	2.88
3.37	3.28	3.18	3.07	3.02	2.96	2.91	2.85	2.79	2.72
3.25	3.15	3.05	2.95	2.89	2.84	2.78	2.72	2.66	2.60
3.15	3.05	2.95	2.84	2.79	2.73	2.67	2.61	2.55	2.49
3.06	2.96	2.86	2.76	2.70	2.64	2.59	2.52	2.46	2.40
2.99	2.89	2.79	2.68	2.63	2.57	2.51	2.45	2.38	2.32
2.92	2.82	2.72	2.62	2.56	2.50	2.44	2.38	2.32	2.25
2.87	2.77	2.67	2.56	2.50	2.44	2.38	2.32	2.26	2.19
2.82	2.72	2.62	2.51	2.45	2.39	2.33	2.27	2.20	2.13
2.77	2.68	2.57	2.46	2.41	2.35	2.29	2.22	2.16	2.09
2.73	2.64	2.53	2.42	2.37	2.31	2.25	2.18	2.11	2.04
2.70	2.60	2.50	2.39	2.33	2.27	2.21	2.14	2.08	2.00
2.67	2.57	2.47	2.36	2.30	2.24	2.18	2.11	2.04	1.97
2.64	2.54	2.44	2.33	2.27	2.21	2.15	2.08	2.01	1.94
2.61	2.51	2.41	2.30	2.24	2.18	2.12	2.05	1.98	1.91
2.59	2.49	2.39	2.28	2.22	2.16	2.09	2.03	1.95	1.88
2.57	2.47	2.36	2.25	2.19	2.13	2.07	2.00	1.93	1.85
2.55	2.45	2.34	2.23	2.17	2.11	2.05	1.98	1.91	1.83
2.53	2.43	2.32	2.21	2.15	2.09	2.03	1.96	1.89	1.81
2.51	2.41	2.31	2.20	2.14	2.07	2.01	1.94	1.87	1.79
2.39	2.29	2.18	2.07	2.01	1.94	1.88	1.80	1.72	1.64
2.27	2.17	2.06	1.94	1.88	1.82	1.74	1.67	1.58	1.48
2.16	2.05	1.94	1.82	1.76	1.69	1.61	1.53	1.43	1.31
2.05	1.94	1.83	1.71	1.64	1.57	1.48	1.39	1.27	1.00

Continues

TABLE C.3   Critical Values of F (Continued)

Denominator df_2	Numerator, df_1								
	1	**2**	**3**	**4**	**5**	**6**	**7**	**8**	**9**
1	4,052.00	4,999.50	5,403.00	5,625.00	5,764.00	5,859.00	5,928.00	5,982.00	6,022.00
2	98.50	99.00	99.17	99.25	99.30	99.33	99.36	99.37	99.39
3	34.12	30.82	29.46	28.71	28.24	27.91	27.67	27.49	27.35
4	21.20	18.00	16.69	15.98	15.52	15.21	14.98	14.80	14.66
5	16.26	13.27	12.06	11.39	10.97	10.67	10.46	10.29	10.16
6	13.75	10.92	9.78	9.15	8.75	8.47	8.26	8.10	7.98
7	12.25	9.55	8.45	7.85	7.46	7.19	6.99	6.84	6.72
8	11.26	8.65	7.59	7.01	6.63	6.37	6.18	6.03	5.91
9	10.56	8.02	6.99	6.42	6.06	5.80	5.61	5.47	5.35
10	10.04	7.56	6.55	5.99	5.64	5.39	5.20	5.06	4.94
11	9.65	7.21	6.22	5.67	5.32	5.07	4.89	4.74	4.63
12	9.33	6.93	5.95	5.41	5.06	4.82	4.64	4.50	4.39
13	9.07	6.70	5.74	5.21	4.86	4.62	4.44	4.30	4.19
14	8.86	6.51	5.56	5.04	4.69	4.46	4.28	4.14	4.03
15	8.68	6.36	5.42	4.89	4.56	4.32	4.14	4.00	3.89
16	8.53	6.23	5.29	4.77	4.44	4.20	4.03	3.89	3.78
17	8.40	6.11	5.18	4.67	4.34	4.10	3.93	3.79	3.68
18	8.29	6.01	5.09	4.58	4.25	4.01	3.84	3.71	3.60
19	8.18	5.93	5.01	4.50	4.17	3.94	3.77	3.63	3.52
20	8.10	5.85	4.94	4.43	4.10	3.87	3.70	3.56	3.46
21	8.02	5.78	4.87	4.37	4.04	3.81	3.64	3.51	3.40
22	7.95	5.72	4.82	4.31	3.99	3.76	3.59	3.45	3.35
23	7.88	5.66	4.76	4.26	3.94	3.71	3.54	3.41	3.30
24	7.82	5.61	4.72	4.22	3.90	3.67	3.50	3.36	3.26
25	7.77	5.57	4.68	4.18	3.85	3.63	3.46	3.32	3.22
26	7.72	5.53	4.64	4.14	3.82	3.59	3.42	3.29	3.18
27	7.68	5.49	4.60	4.11	3.78	3.56	3.39	3.26	3.15
28	7.64	5.45	4.57	4.07	3.75	3.53	3.36	3.23	3.12
29	7.60	5.42	4.54	4.04	3.73	3.50	3.33	3.20	3.09
30	7.56	5.39	4.51	4.02	3.70	3.47	3.30	3.17	3.07
40	7.31	5.18	4.31	3.83	3.51	3.29	3.12	2.99	2.89
60	7.08	4.98	4.13	3.65	3.34	3.12	2.95	2.82	2.72
120	6.85	4.79	3.95	3.48	3.17	2.96	2.79	2.66	2.56
∞	6.63	4.61	3.78	3.32	3.02	2.80	2.64	2.51	2.41

Table C.3   Critical Values of F 343

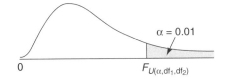

α = 0.01

$F_{U(\alpha, df_1, df_2)}$

					Numerator, df_1				
10	12	15	20	24	30	40	60	120	∞
6,056.00	6,106.00	6,157.00	6,209.00	6,235.00	6,261.00	6,287.00	6,313.00	6,339.00	6,366.00
99.40	99.42	99.43	94.45	99.46	99.47	99.47	99.48	99.49	99.50
27.23	27.05	26.87	26.69	26.60	26.50	26.41	26.32	26.22	26.13
14.55	14.37	14.20	14.02	13.93	13.84	13.75	13.65	13.56	13.46
10.05	9.89	9.72	9.55	9.47	9.38	9.29	9.20	9.11	9.02
7.87	7.72	7.56	7.40	7.31	7.23	7.14	7.06	6.97	6.88
6.62	6.47	6.31	6.16	6.07	5.99	5.91	5.82	5.74	5.65
5.81	5.67	5.52	5.36	5.28	5.20	5.12	5.03	4.95	4.86
5.26	5.11	4.96	4.81	4.73	4.65	4.57	4.48	4.40	4.31
4.85	4.71	4.56	4.41	4.33	4.25	4.17	4.08	4.00	3.91
4.54	4.40	4.25	4.10	4.02	3.94	3.86	3.78	3.69	3.60
4.30	4.16	4.01	3.86	3.78	3.70	3.62	3.54	3.45	3.36
4.10	3.96	3.82	3.66	3.59	3.51	3.43	3.34	3.25	3.17
3.94	3.80	3.66	3.51	3.43	3.35	3.27	3.18	3.09	3.00
3.80	3.67	3.52	3.37	3.29	3.21	3.13	3.05	2.96	2.87
3.69	3.55	3.41	3.26	3.18	3.10	3.02	2.93	2.81	2.75
3.59	3.46	3.31	3.16	3.08	3.00	2.92	2.83	2.75	2.65
3.51	3.37	3.23	3.08	3.00	2.92	2.84	2.75	2.66	2.57
3.43	3.30	3.15	3.00	2.92	2.84	2.76	2.67	2.58	2.49
3.37	3.23	3.09	2.94	2.86	2.78	2.69	2.61	2.52	2.42
3.31	3.17	3.03	2.88	2.80	2.72	2.64	2.55	2.46	2.36
3.26	3.12	2.98	2.83	2.75	2.67	2.58	2.50	2.40	2.31
3.21	3.07	2.93	2.78	2.70	2.62	2.54	2.45	2.35	2.26
3.17	3.03	2.89	2.74	2.66	2.58	2.49	2.40	2.31	2.21
3.13	2.99	2.85	2.70	2.62	2.54	2.45	2.36	2.27	2.17
3.09	2.96	2.81	2.66	2.58	2.50	2.42	2.33	2.23	2.13
3.06	2.93	2.78	2.63	2.55	2.47	2.38	2.29	2.20	2.10
3.03	2.90	2.75	2.60	2.52	2.44	2.35	2.26	2.17	2.06
3.00	2.87	2.73	2.57	2.49	2.41	2.33	2.23	2.14	2.03
2.98	2.84	2.70	2.55	2.47	2.39	2.30	2.21	2.11	2.01
2.80	2.66	2.52	2.37	2.29	2.20	2.11	2.02	1.92	1.80
2.63	2.50	2.35	2.20	2.12	2.03	1.94	1.84	1.73	1.60
2.47	2.34	2.19	2.03	1.95	1.86	1.76	1.66	1.53	1.38
2.32	2.18	2.04	1.88	1.79	1.70	1.59	1.47	1.32	1.00

Continues

TABLE C.3   Critical Values of F (Continued)

Denominator df_2	Numerator, df_1								
	1	2	3	4	5	6	7	8	9
1	16,211.00	20,000.000	21,615.00	22,500.00	23,056.00	23,437.00	23,715.00	23,925.00	24,091.00
2	198.50	199.00	199.20	199.20	199.30	199.30	199.40	199.40	199.40
3	55.55	49.80	47.47	46.19	45.39	44.84	44.43	44.13	43.88
4	31.33	26.28	24.26	23.15	22.46	21.97	21.62	21.35	21.14
5	22.78	18.31	16.53	15.56	14.94	14.51	14.20	13.96	13.77
6	18.63	14.54	12.92	12.03	11.46	11.07	10.79	10.57	10.39
7	16.24	12.40	10.88	10.05	9.52	9.16	8.89	8.68	8.51
8	14.69	11.04	9.60	8.81	8.30	7.95	7.69	7.50	7.34
9	13.61	10.11	8.72	7.96	7.47	7.13	6.88	6.69	6.54
10	12.83	9.43	8.08	7.34	6.87	6.54	6.30	6.12	5.97
11	12.23	8.91	7.60	6.88	6.42	6.10	5.86	5.68	5.54
12	11.75	8.51	7.23	6.52	6.07	5.76	5.52	5.35	5.20
13	11.37	8.19	6.93	6.23	5.79	5.48	5.25	5.08	4.94
14	11.06	7.92	6.68	6.00	5.56	5.26	5.03	4.86	4.72
15	10.80	7.70	6.48	5.80	5.37	5.07	4.85	4.67	4.54
16	10.58	7.51	6.30	5.64	5.21	4.91	4.69	4.52	4.38
17	10.38	7.35	6.16	5.50	5.07	4.78	4.56	4.39	4.25
18	10.22	7.21	6.03	5.37	4.96	4.66	4.44	4.28	4.14
19	10.07	7.09	5.92	5.27	4.85	4.56	4.34	4.18	4.04
20	9.94	6.99	5.82	5.17	4.76	4.47	4.26	4.09	3.96
21	9.83	6.89	5.73	5.09	4.68	4.39	4.18	4.02	3.88
22	9.73	6.81	5.65	5.02	4.61	4.32	4.11	3.94	3.81
23	9.63	6.73	5.58	4.95	4.54	4.26	4.05	3.88	3.75
24	9.55	6.66	5.52	4.89	4.49	4.20	3.99	3.83	3.69
25	9.48	6.60	5.46	4.84	4.43	4.15	3.94	3.78	3.64
26	9.41	6.54	5.41	4.79	4.38	4.10	3.89	3.73	3.60
27	9.34	6.49	5.36	4.74	4.34	4.06	3.85	3.69	3.56
28	9.28	6.44	5.32	4.70	4.30	4.02	3.81	3.65	3.52
29	9.23	6.40	5.28	4.66	4.26	3.98	3.77	3.61	3.48
30	9.18	6.35	5.24	4.62	4.23	3.95	3.74	3.58	3.45
40	8.83	6.07	4.98	4.37	3.99	3.71	3.51	3.35	3.22
60	8.49	5.79	4.73	4.14	3.76	3.49	3.29	3.13	3.01
120	8.18	5.54	4.50	3.92	3.55	3.28	3.09	2.93	2.81
∞	7.88	5.30	4.28	3.72	3.35	3.09	2.90	2.74	2.62

Table C.3   Critical Values of F 345

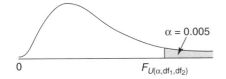

$\alpha = 0.005$

$F_{U(\alpha,df_1,df_2)}$

				Numerator, df_1					
10	12	15	20	24	30	40	60	120	∞
24,224.00	24,426.00	24,630.00	24,836.00	24,910.00	25,044.00	25,148.00	25,253.00	25,359.00	25,465.00
199.40	199.40	199.40	199.40	199.50	199.50	199.50	199.50	199.50	199.50
43.69	43.39	43.08	42.78	42.62	42.47	42.31	42.15	41.99	41.83
20.97	20.70	20.44	20.17	20.03	19.89	19.75	19.61	19.47	19.32
13.62	13.38	13.15	12.90	12.78	12.66	12.53	12.40	12.27	12.11
10.25	10.03	9.81	9.59	9.47	9.36	9.24	9.12	9.00	8.88
8.38	8.18	7.97	7.75	7.65	7.53	7.42	7.31	7.19	7.08
7.21	7.01	6.81	6.61	6.50	6.40	6.29	6.18	6.06	5.95
6.42	6.23	6.03	5.83	5.73	5.62	5.52	5.41	5.30	5.19
5.85	5.66	5.47	5.27	5.17	5.07	4.97	4.86	4.75	1.61
5.42	5.24	5.05	4.86	4.75	4.65	4.55	4.44	4.34	4.23
5.09	4.91	4.72	4.53	4.43	4.33	4.23	4.12	4.01	3.90
4.82	4.64	4.46	4.27	4.17	4.07	3.97	3.87	3.76	3.65
4.60	4.43	4.25	4.06	3.96	3.86	3.76	3.66	3.55	3.41
4.42	4.25	4.07	3.88	3.79	3.69	3.58	3.48	3.37	3.26
4.27	4.10	3.92	3.73	3.64	3.54	3.44	3.33	3.22	3.11
4.14	3.97	3.79	3.61	3.51	3.41	3.31	3.21	3.10	2.98
4.03	3.86	3.68	3.50	3.40	3.30	3.20	3.10	2.89	2.87
3.93	3.76	3.59	3.40	3.31	3.21	3.11	3.00	2.89	2.78
3.85	3.68	3.50	3.32	3.22	3.12	3.02	2.92	2.81	2.69
3.77	3.60	3.43	3.24	3.15	3.05	2.95	2.84	2.73	2.61
3.70	3.54	3.36	3.18	3.08	2.98	2.88	2.77	2.66	2.55
3.64	3.47	3.30	3.12	3.02	2.92	2.82	2.71	2.60	2.48
3.59	3.42	3.25	3.06	2.97	2.87	2.77	2.66	2.55	2.43
3.54	3.37	3.20	3.01	2.92	2.82	2.72	2.61	2.50	2.38
3.49	3.33	3.15	2.97	2.87	2.77	2.67	2.56	2.45	2.33
3.45	3.28	3.11	2.93	2.83	2.73	2.63	2.52	2.41	2.29
3.41	3.25	3.07	2.89	2.79	2.69	2.59	2.48	2.37	2.25
3.38	3.21	3.04	2.86	2.76	2.66	2.56	2.45	2.33	2.21
3.34	3.18	3.01	2.82	2.73	2.63	2.52	2.42	2.30	2.18
3.12	2.95	2.78	2.60	2.50	2.40	2.30	2.18	2.06	1.93
2.90	2.74	2.57	2.39	2.29	2.19	2.08	1.96	1.83	1.69
2.71	2.54	2.37	2.19	2.09	1.98	1.87	1.75	1.61	1.43
2.52	2.36	2.19	2.00	1.90	1.79	1.67	1.53	1.36	1.00

TABLE C.4   Control Chart Constants

Number of Observations in Subgroup, n	A_2	A_3	B_3	B_4	c_4	d_2	d_3	D_3	D_4	E_2
2	1.880	2.659	0.000	3.267	0.7979	1.128	0.853	0.000	3.267	2.660
3	1.023	1.954	0.000	2.568	0.8862	1.693	0.888	0.000	2.574	1.772
4	0.729	1.628	0.000	2.266	0.9213	2.059	0.880	0.000	2.282	1.457
5	0.577	1.427	0.000	2.089	0.9400	2.326	0.864	0.000	2.114	1.290
6	0.483	1.287	0.030	1.970	0.9515	2.534	0.848	0.000	2.004	1.184
7	0.419	1.182	0.118	1.882	0.9594	2.704	0.833	0.076	1.924	1.109
8	0.373	1.099	0.185	1.815	0.9650	2.847	0.820	0.136	1.864	1.054
9	0.337	1.032	0.239	1.761	0.9693	2.970	0.808	0.184	1.816	1.010
10	0.308	0.975	0.284	1.716	0.9727	3.078	0.797	0.223	1.777	0.975
11	0.285	0.927	0.321	1.679	0.9754	3.173	0.787	0.256	1.744	
12	0.266	0.886	0.354	1.646	0.9776	3.258	0.778	0.283	1.717	
13	0.249	0.850	0.382	1.618	0.9794	3.336	0.770	0.307	1.693	
14	0.235	0.817	0.406	1.594	0.9810	3.407	0.762	0.328	1.672	
15	0.223	0.789	0.428	1.572	0.9823	3.472	0.755	0.347	1.653	
16	0.212	0.763	0.448	1.552	0.9835	3.532	0.749	0.363	1.637	
17	0.203	0.739	0.466	1.534	0.9845	3.588	0.743	0.378	1.622	
18	0.194	0.718	0.482	1.518	0.9854	3.640	0.738	0.391	1.608	
19	0.187	0.698	0.497	1.503	0.9862	3.689	0.733	0.403	1.597	
20	0.180	0.680	0.510	1.490	0.9869	3.735	0.729	0.415	1.585	
21	0.173	0.663	0.523	1.477	0.9876	3.778	0.724	0.425	1.575	
22	0.167	0.647	0.534	1.466	0.9882	3.819	0.720	0.434	1.566	
23	0.162	0.633	0.545	1.455	0.9887	3.858	0.716	0.443	1.557	
24	0.157	0.619	0.555	1.445	0.9892	3.895	0.712	0.451	1.548	
25	0.153	0.606	0.565	1.435	0.9896	3.931	0.709	0.459	1.541	
More than 25		$3/\sqrt{n}$	$1-3/\sqrt{2n}$	$1+3/\sqrt{2n}$						

Source: $A_2, A_3, B_3, B_4, c_4, d_2, d_3, D_4, E_2$ reprinted with permission from *ASTM Manual on the Presentation of Data and Control Chart Analysis* (Philadelphia, PA: ASTM, 1976), pp. 134–36. Copyright ASTM.

APPENDIX D

Documentation of Data Files

The following is an alphabetical listing and description of all the Minitab and JMP files found on the text web site located at http://www.prenhall.com/statisticsforsixsigma. The icons that appear throughout the text identify these files.

ANSCOMBE — Data sets A, B, C, and D — each with 11 pairs of X and Y values.

BANKTIME — Waiting times of four bank customers per day for 20 days.

BREAKFAST — Delivery time difference, menu choice, and desired time.

BREAKFAST2 — Delivery time difference, menu choice, and desired time.

CAKE — Flour, shortening, egg powder, oven temperature, baking time, and rating score.

COMPLAINTS — Week and number of complaints.

CONFINTERVAL — Times for a sample of 200 and 20 samples of 10 items.

CYCLETIME2 — Time, transaction, and cycle time.

DEFECTIVES — Number of defective entries.

DINNER — Delivery time, complexity, elevator, and order volume.

ERRORCODE — Number of lines and number of code errors.

ERWAITING — Emergency room waiting time (in minutes) at the main facility, satellite 1, satellite 2, and satellite 3.

GAGER&R1—Random order, standard order, patient, psychologist, and score.

INSURANCE-TIME—Time to process.

LABTESTS—Causes and frequency of lab test errors.

LUGGAGE—Delivery time in minutes for luggage in Wing A and Wing B of a hotel.

MEDREC—Day, number of discharged patients, and number of records not processed.

MOVING—Labor hours, cubic feet, number of large pieces of furniture, and availability of an elevator.

ORDER—Time to receive order.

PREPARATION—Preparation time, dessert, side dishes, potato, and entrée.

PREPARATION2—Preparation time, entrée, beverage, order volume, dessert, and complexity.

REVENUE—Month, revenue in millions of dollars.

ROOMSREADY—Day, rooms, and rooms not ready.

SATISFACTION—Satisfaction, delivery time difference, and previous stay at hotel.

STANDBY—Standby hours, staff, remote hours, Dubner hours, and labor hours.

TIMES—Times to get ready.

GLOSSARY

α **risk** — The probability of committing a Type I error or the probability of rejecting the null hypothesis when it is true.

Alternative hypothesis (H_1) — The opposite of the null hypothesis (H_0).

Analysis of variance (ANOVA) — A statistical method that tests the significance of different factors on a variable of interest.

Analytic study — Leads to actions on the cause-and-effect system of a process.

Arithmetic mean — The balance point in a set of data that is calculated by summing the observed numerical values in a set of data and then dividing by the number of values involved.

β **risk** — The probability of committing a Type II error or the probability of failing to reject the null hypothesis when it is false.

Bar chart — A chart containing rectangles ("bars") in which the length of each bar represents the count, amount, or percentage of responses of one category.

Best-subsets approach — Evaluates either all possible regression models for a given set of independent variables or the best subsets of models for a given number of independent variables.

Bimodal distribution — A distribution with two concentrations of data.

Binomial distribution — A distribution that finds the probability of a given number of successes for a given probability of success and sample size.

Black Belt — A full-time change agent and improvement leader who may not be an expert in the process under study. A Black Belt is an individual who possesses a deep understanding of statistical methods and has successfully led two or more Six Sigma projects that have led to dramatic quality improvements and cost reductions.

Box-and-whisker plot — A graphical representation of the five-number summary that consists of the smallest value, the first quartile (or 25th percentile), the median, the third quartile (or 75th percentile), and the largest value.

Categorical variable—A variable whose results consist of a tally of the number of items in each category.

Champion—Takes a very active sponsorship and leadership role in conducting and implementing Six Sigma projects. A Champion is an individual who is aware of the theory and practice of Six Sigma project teams while able to adequately review projects, remove impediments, and secure adequate resources and support.

Cluster sample—A probability sample in which the N individuals or items in the frame are divided into many clusters.

Coefficient of correlation—Measures the strength of the linear relationship between two numerical variables.

Coefficient of determination—Measures the proportion of variation in the dependent variable Y that is explained by the independent variable X in the regression model.

Coefficient of multiple determination—Represents the proportion of the variation in the dependent variable Y that is explained by the set of independent variables selected.

Collectively exhaustive events—A set of events such that one of the events in the set must occur.

Collinearity of the independent variables—Refers to situations in which one or more of the independent variables are highly correlated with each other.

Common causes of variation—Represent the inherent variability that exists in the system.

Completely randomized design—An experimental design in which there is only a single factor.

Confidence interval estimate—An estimate of the population parameter given by an interval with a lower and upper limit.

Confounding—Occurs when the effect of one factor or interaction is mixed up with the effect of another factor or interaction.

Continuous numerical variables—Values of these variables are measurements.

Control chart—A tool for distinguishing between the common and special causes of variation.

Critical value—Divides the nonrejection region from the rejection region.

CTP—Acronym for a critical-to-process characteristic in the design of a product or service.

CTQ—Acronym for critical-to-quality characteristic for a product, service, or process. It is a measure of what is important to customers. Six Sigma projects are designed to improve one or more CTQs.

Data—Information collected about a product, service, process, individual person, item, or thing.

Data mining—A research method where huge data sets are explored to discover significant statistical relationships among a large number of variables.

Degrees of freedom—The actual number of values that are free to vary.

Dependent variable—The variable to be predicted in a regression analysis.

Descriptive statistics—The branch of statistics that focuses on collecting, summarizing, and presenting a set of data.

Design of experiments (DOE)—A collection of statistical methods for studying the relationships between independent variables or factors, the Xs (also called *input variables* or *process variables*), and their interactions on a dependent variable, the CTQ, or Y (also called the *outcome variable* or *response variable*).

Discrete numeric variables—The values of these variables are counts of the number of occurrences.

DMAIC model—Has five phases: Define, Measure, Analyze, Improve, and Control. It is the model utilized in Six Sigma management to move from the existing system to the revised system.

Dot plot—A graph of measurement data in which dots that represent data values are stacked vertically on the horizontal axis for each value of the variable of interest.

Dummy variable—A categorical independent variable that has been coded into categories such as 0 and 1 or -1, 0, and +1.

Enumerative studies—Statistical investigations that have the purpose of drawing conclusions about a population.

Error sum of squares (*SSE*)—In regression, consists of variation that is due to factors other than the relationship between X and Y. In design of experiments, it consists of variation that is not due to factors or their interactions.

Event—Each possible type of occurrence.

Expected value—The mean of a probability distribution.

F distribution—A distribution used for testing the ratio of two variances. Also used in design of experiments and regression to test the significance of different sources of variation.

Factorial designs—An experimental design in which more than one factor (X) is examined simultaneously to determine the effect on a CTQ.

First quartile (Q_1)—The value such that 25.0% of the values are smaller and 75.0% are larger.

Five-number summary—Consists of smallest value, Q_1, median, Q_3, and largest value.

Fractional factorial designs—An experimental design that is most often used when the number of Xs to be studied is large or when there is a moderate level of knowledge about the interactions between the key Xs needed to optimize the CTQ. Fractional factorial designs are used to decrease the number of trials, hence the cost, of an experiment by taking advantage of knowledge about interactions. They are a design in which only a subset of all possible treatment combinations is used.

Frame—The list of all items in the population from which samples will be selected.

Frequency distribution—A table of grouped numerical data in which the names of each group are listed in the first column and the percentages of each group of numerical data are listed in the second column.

Full-factorial designs—An experimental design used when researchers want to understand all of the interactions between the high-risk Xs necessary to optimizing the CTQ or when there are only a few Xs to be studied in the experiment.

Green Belt—An individual who works on projects part time (25%), either as a team member for complex projects or as a project leader for simpler projects.

Histogram—A special bar chart for grouped numerical data in which the frequencies or percentages of each group of numerical data are represented as individual bars.

Hypothesis testing—Methods used to make inferences about the hypothesized values of population parameters using sample statistics.

Independent events—Events in which the occurrence of one event in no way affects the probability of the second event.

Independent variable—The variable used to predict the dependent variable in a regression analysis.

Inferential statistics—The branch of statistics that analyzes sample data to draw conclusions about a population.

Interaction effects—Interaction effects are the effects on a CTQ caused by one X variable depending on the level(s) or value(s) of other X variables.

Interaction plot—Used to identify interaction effects among a set of Xs on a CTQ. All combinations of levels of X variables are studied to produce an interaction plot.

Level of significance—Probability of committing a Type I error.

Levene test—A hypothesis test for the difference between variances.

Logistic regression—A type of regression that enables you to use regression models to predict the probability of a particular categorical response for a given set of independent variables (CTPs or Xs).

Lurking variable—See *noise variable*.

Master Black Belt—A Six Sigma professional who takes on a leadership role of keeper of the Six Sigma process and advisor to executives or business unit managers, and mentor to projects led by Black Belts and Green Belts. A Master Black Belt is an individual who has successfully supervised two or more Black Belts while leading at least two Six Sigma projects that led to dramatic revenue enhancements or cost reductions in their organizations.

Mean—The balance point in a set of data that is calculated by summing the observed numerical values in a set of data and then dividing by the number of values involved.

Mean squares—The variances in an analysis-of-variance table.

Measurement data—Continuous data representing a characteristic of a product, process, or service. Results from a measurement taken on an item or person of interest.

Median—The middle value in a set of data that has been ordered from the lowest to highest value.

Mode—The value in a set of data that appears most frequently.

Multiple comparisons—A procedure used to determine which of the means are statistically significantly different from each other.

Multiple regression models—Use two or more independent variables (Xs) to predict the value of a dependent variable (Y).

Mutually exclusive events—Events are mutually exclusive if both events cannot occur at the same time.

Net regression coefficient—In a multiple regression model, a net regression coefficient represents the change in the mean of the dependent variable Y per unit change in each independent variable X, taking into account the effect of all the other Xs.

Noise variable (also called a *lurking variable*)—A factor (X) that is not included in an experiment and can affect the central tendency, variation, and shape of a CTQ.

Nonprobability sample—A nonrandom sample in which the items or individuals included are chosen without the benefit of a frame; hence, the individual units have an unknown probability of selection into the sample.

Normal distribution—Defined by its mean (μ) and standard deviation (σ) and is bell-shaped.

Normal probability plot—A graphical device for helping to evaluate whether a set of data follows a normal distribution.

Null hypothesis—A statement about a parameter equal to a specific value, or the statement that there is no difference between the parameters for two or more populations.

Numerical variables—The values of these variables involve measurements.

Odds ratio—Represents the probability of a success compared with the probability of failure.

Operational definition—Promotes understanding between people by putting communicable meaning into words. An operational definition contains three parts: a criterion to be applied to an object or group, a test of the object or group, and a decision as to whether the object or group met the criterion.

Outliers—Extreme values in a data set.

***p*-value**—The probability of getting a test statistic equal to or more extreme than the result obtained from the sample data, given that the null hypothesis H_0 is true.

Parameter—A numerical measure that describes a characteristic of a population.

Pareto diagram—A special type of bar chart in which the count, amount, or percentage of responses of each category are presented in descending order from left to right, along with a superimposed plotted line that represents a running cumulative percentage.

Poisson distribution—A distribution to find the probability of the number of occurrences in an area of opportunity.

Population—All the members of a group about which you want to draw a conclusion.

Power of a statistical test—The probability of rejecting the null hypothesis when it is false and should be rejected.

Prediction interval—An interval estimate of the outcome of a future individual value.

Probability—The numeric value representing the chance, likelihood, or possibility a particular event will occur.

Probability distribution for a discrete random variable—A listing of all possible distinct outcomes and their probabilities of occurring.

Probability sampling—A sampling process that takes into consideration the chance of occurrence of each item being selected.

Range—The difference between the largest and smallest values in a set of data.

Region of rejection—Consists of the values of the test statistic that are unlikely to occur if the null hypothesis is true.

Regression sum of squares (*SSR*)—Consists of variation that is due to the relationship between the independent variable X and the dependent variable Y.

Replicate—The sample size for a given combination of the factors (Xs) in an experiment on a CTQ.

Residual—The difference between the observed and predicted values of the dependent variable for a given value of X.

Resolution III designs—An experiment in which main effects are confounded with two-way interactions (such as A being confounded with BC).

Resolution IV designs—An experiment in which a two-way interaction is confounded with another two-way interaction and/or a main effect is confounded with a three-way interaction.

Resolution V designs—An experiment in which main effects are confounded with four-way interactions and/or two-factor interactions are confounded with three-way interactions.

Robust test — A test that is not sensitive to departures from its assumptions.

Sample — The part of the population selected for analysis.

Sampling — The process by which members of a population are selected for a sample.

Sampling distribution — The distribution of a sample statistic (such as the arithmetic mean) for all possible samples of a given size n.

Sampling error — Variation of the sample statistic from sample to sample.

Scatter plot — A chart that plots the values of two variables for each response. In a scatter plot, the X-axis (the horizontal axis) always represents units of one variable, and the Y-axis (the vertical axis) always represents units of the second variable.

Shape — The shape of a distribution of data indicates how the data are distributed between its lowest value and its highest value.

Simple linear regression — A statistical technique that uses a single numerical independent variable X to predict the numerical dependent variable Y.

Simple random sampling — The probability sampling process in which every individual or item from a population has the same chance of selection as every other individual or item.

Six Sigma management — The relentless and rigorous pursuit of the reduction of variation in all critical processes to achieve continuous and breakthrough improvements that impact the bottom and/or top line of the organization and increase customer satisfaction.

Skewness — A skewed distribution is not symmetric. There are extreme values either in the lower portion of the distribution or in the upper portion of the distribution.

Slope — The change in Y per unit change in X.

Special causes of variation — Represent large fluctuations or patterns in the data that are not inherent to a process.

Standard deviation — Measure of variation around the mean of a set of data.

Standard error of the estimate — The standard deviation around the line of regression.

Standard order — The standard order for the trials in an experiment is a listing of the trials such that the first factor alternates between – and +, the second factor alternates between –,– and +,+, the third factor alternates between –,–,–,– and +,+,+,+, and so on.

Statistic — A numerical measure that describes a characteristic of a sample.

Statistics — The branch of mathematics that consists of methods of processing and analyzing data to better support rational decision-making processes.

Stepwise regression — A model-building approach that attempts to find the "best" regression model without examining all possible models.

Stratified sample — A probability sample in which the N items in the frame are divided into subpopulations, or *strata*, according to some common characteristic.

Sum of squares among groups (SSA) — The sum of the squared differences between the sample mean of each group and the mean of all the values, weighted by the sample size in each group.

Sum of squares due to factor A (SSA) — The sum of squares of the deviations of the mean levels of factor A with the grand mean of the CTQ.

Sum of squares due to factor B (SSB) — The sum of squares of the deviations of the mean levels of factor B with the grand mean of the CTQ.

Sum of squares due to the interaction effect of A and B (SSAB) — The effect of the joint combination of factor A and factor B on the CTQ.

Sum of squares error (SSE) — The sum of squares of deviations of the individual values of the CTQ within each cell (i.e., each specific combination of one level of X_A and one level of X_B) with the corresponding cell mean.

Sum of squares total (SST) — Represents the sum of the squared differences between each individual value and the mean of all the values.

Sum of squares within groups (SSW) — Measures the difference between each value and the mean of its own group and sums the squares of these differences over all groups.

Summary table — A two-column table in which the names of the categories are listed in the first column, and the count, amount, or percentage of responses are listed in a second column.

Symmetry — Distribution in which each half of a distribution is a mirror image of the other half of the distribution.

Systematic sample — A probability sample in which the N individuals or items in the frame are placed into k groups by dividing the size of the frame N by the desired sample size n.

t **distribution** — A distribution used to estimate the mean of a population and to test hypotheses about means. Also used in regression analysis to test the significance of the slope.

Test statistic — The statistic used to determine whether to reject the null hypothesis.

Third quartile (Q_3) — The value such that 75.0% of the values are smaller and 25.0% are larger.

Type I error — Occurs if the null hypothesis H_0 is rejected when it is true and should not be rejected. The probability of a Type I error occurring is α.

Type II error — Occurs if the null hypothesis H_1 is not rejected when it is false and should be rejected. The probability of a Type II error occurring is β.

Variable — A characteristic of an item or an individual that will be analyzed using statistics.

Variance — The square of the standard deviation.

Variation — The amount of dispersion in the data.

Y **intercept** — The value of Y when $X = 0$.

INDEX

A

α risk, 118, 349

Alias, 191

Alternative hypothesis, 115, 349

Among-group variation, 135

Analysis of variance (ANOVA), 349

Analytical studies, 9, 349

Area of opportunity, 76, 290

Arithmetic mean, 40–42, 349

Arithmetic and algebra review, 321–327

Assignable causes of variation. *See* Special causes of variation

Assumptions
of ANOVA, 140–141
of the confidence interval estimate
for the proportion, 108
of the mean (σ unknown), 104
of the *F*-test for the difference between two variances, 132
of the pooled-variance *t* test, 128
of regression, 226

Attribute control chart, 280

Attribute data, 13

B

β risk, 119, 349

Background variable, 158

Bar chart, 24–25, 349

Best subsets approach to model building, 261–265, 349

Bimodal, 51, 349

Binomial distribution, 72–74, 349
Characteristics, 75
Properties, 72

Black belt, 4, 349

Box-and-whisker plot, 53–55, 349

C

c-chart, 290–292

Categorical variable, 13, 350

Central limit theorem, 97

Certain event, 63

Champions, 3, 350

Chance causes of variation. *See* Common causes of variation

Classical approach to probability, 60–61

Cluster sample, 12, 350

Coefficient of correlation (*r*), 224–225, 350

Coefficient of determination (*r*²), 224, 350

Coefficient of multiple determination, 246, 350

Collectively exhaustive, 63, 350

Collinearity, 255, 350

Common causes of variation, 283, 350

Completely randomized design. *See* One-way analysis of variance

Confidence coefficient, 118

Confidence interval estimate, 99–102, 350
for the proportion, 106–107
of the mean (σ unknown), 102–105
of the slope, 231, 249–250

Confounding, 189, 350

Continuous numerical variable, 13, 350

Control chart, 280, 350

   c-chart, 290–292

   Factors table, 346

   Individual value and moving range, 306–309

   Limits, 282

   Mean and range, 296–301

   p-chart, 285–290

   Patterns, 282

   Rules for out-of-control points, 283–285

   Standard deviation and mean, 301–305

   u-chart, 293–296

Control chart factors

   A_2, 300

   A_3, 305

   B_3, 304

   B_4, 304

   c_4, 304

   d_2, 299

   d_3, 299

   D_3, 299

   D_4, 299

   E_2, 309

Convenience sample, 10

C_p statistic, 262, 264

Critical region, 117

Critical-to-Process (CTP), 13, 351

Critical-to-Quality (CTQ), 2, 351

Critical value of the test statistic, 116–117, 350

Cross product term. *See* Interaction term

D

Data, 13, 351

Data file documentation, 347–348

Data mining, 261, 351

Defining contrast, 191

Degrees of freedom, 130, 135, 351

Dependent variable, 158, 212, 351

Descriptive statistics, 8, 351

Design of experiments, 158, 351

Deviance statistic, 271

Discrete variable, 67, 351

DMAIC model, 2, 351

   Phases, 5

Dot plot, 28, 351

Dummy variables, 250, 351

E

Elementary event, 60

Empirical approach to probability, 61–62

Enumerative studies, 8, 351

Equal variance, 226, 228

Equations, 326–327

   Arithmetic mean, 42

   Binomial distribution, 74

   c-chart, 292

   Coefficient of determination (r^2), 224

   Confidence interval estimate

      for the proportion, 107

      of the mean (σ unknown), 104–105

   Control limits, 282

   C_p statistic, 264

   Estimated effects, 170–171, 178–180

   F test for the difference between two variances, 133

   F Test for the Slope, 230–231

Individual value and moving range, 308–309

Median, 42

Mean of a binomial distribution, 75

Mean of a probability distribution, 69

Multiple regression model, 243

Odds ratio, 266

p-chart, 287

Poisson distribution, 77–78

Pooled-variance *t* test, 129

Prediction interval estimate for a future individual value, 105

Probability of event (classical approach), 61

Probability of event (empirical approach), 61

Q_1, 44

Q_3, 44

Range, 46

Range and mean control charts, 299–301

Regression line, 214

Slope, 219

SSE, 222–224

SSR, 222–223

SST, 221–223

Standard deviation, 49

Standard deviation and mean control charts, 304–305

Standard deviation of a binomial distribution, 75

Standard deviation of a probability distribution, 70

Standard error of the estimate, 225

t Test for the Slope, 229–230

u-chart, 295–296

Variance, 49

Variance inflationary factor (*VIF*), 256

Y-intercept, 219

Z test for the difference between two proportions, 125

Event, 60, 351

Executive committee, 3

Expected value of a probability distribution, 68, 352

Exponentiation, 325

F

F distribution, 352

F Test for the slope, 230–231

Factorial designs, 159, 171–188, 352

First quartile, 44, 352

Five-number summary, 52–53, 352

Fractional factorial designs, 189–203, 352

Frame, 9, 352

G

Gap, 9

Graphics, 24

Green belt, 4, 352

H

Half-normal plot, 176

Histogram, 27–28, 352

Homoscedasticity, 226

Hypothesis testing, 114, 352

I

Independence, 140

Independent, 65, 352

Independent variable, 158, 212, 352

Individual value and moving range control chart, 306–309

Inferential statistics, 8, 96, 352

Interaction, 165, 254, 352

Interaction term, 254

Interval estimate, 99

Interval scale, 13

J

JMP

Bar chart, 25, 35

Best subsets approach to regression, 261, 278

Binomial distribution, 91–92

Box-and-whisker plot, 55, 58, 129, 142

c-chart, 292, 318–319

Confidence interval estimate

for the proportion, 111

of the mean (σ unknown), 103, 111

Data tables, 20

Descriptive statistics, 45–46, 58

Difference between variances, 133, 155–156

Dummy variable model, 253, 255, 277

Estimated coefficients, 182, 193, 198

Factorial design, 174, 184, 201, 210

Fractional factorial design, 200, 210

Half-normal plot, 177, 183, 194, 199, 210

Histogram, 27, 36

Individual value and moving range, 307, 320

Interaction plot, 166, 168, 175, 186–187, 195, 202, 209

Interaction terms, 277–278

Kruskal-Wallis test, 147, 156

Levene test, 143, 155–156

Logistic regression, 270, 278

Main effects plot, 165, 174, 185, 194, 201, 209

Mean and range control charts, 298, 319–320

Mean and standard deviation control charts, 303, 320

Multiple regression, 244, 276

Normal probabilities, 92–93

Normal probability plot, 86, 93

One-way ANOVA, 138, 156

p-chart, 289, 318

Pareto diagram, 26, 35–36

Poisson distribution, 92

Pooled-variance t test, 128, 155–156

Regression, 217, 239

Residual plot, 227, 248

Run chart, 29, 36–37

Scatter plot, 216, 239

Selecting a random sample, 21

Separate-variance t test, 131, 155–156

Stacking data, 155

Stepwise regression, 260, 278

Tukey multiple comparisons, 140, 156

Two-way ANOVA, 163, 209

u-chart, 295, 319

Wilcoxon rank sum test, 145, 155–156

JMP dialog boxes

Binomial probability, 92

Chart

for run chart, 37

Control chart

c-chart, 319

Mean and range, 320

Mean and standard deviation, 320

p-chart, 318

u-chart, 319

Zone selection, 318

Distribution

for bar chart, 35

for histogram, 36

Dummy variable creation, 277

Fit model

for two-way ANOVA, 209

Formula, 91

Half-normal plot, 210

Individual value and moving range, 320

Interaction effects plot, 209

Main effects plot, 209

Menu bar and starter window, 20

Pareto plot, 36

Report: Fit Y by X–Contextual, 156, 239

Save residuals, 276

Stack, 155

Stepwise fit, 278

Subset, 21

Joint probability, 64

Judgment sample, 10

K

Kruskal-Wallis test, 145–147

L

Least-squares method, 214

Left skewed, 50

Level of significance, 118, 353

Levene test for the difference between variances, 134, 142–143, 353

Linearity, 226, 227

Logarithms, 267–268

Logistic regression, 266–272, 353

Lurking variable, 158, 353

M

Master black belt, 3, 353

Mean and range control charts, 296–301

Mean squares, 135

Measurement data, 13, 353

Measures of central tendency

Arithmetic mean, 40–42, 353

Median, 42–43, 353

Mode, 43, 353

Measures of variation

Range, 46–47

Standard deviation, 47–49

Variance, 47–49

Median, 42–43, 353

Minitab

Bar chart, 25, 31–32

Best subsets approach to regression, 261, 274–275

Binomial distribution, 74, 88

Box-and-whisker plot, 54–55, 57–58, 129, 141

c-chart, 291, 313

Confidence interval estimate

for the proportion, 106, 110

of the mean (σ unknown), 103, 109

Descriptive statistics, 45–46, 57

Difference between two proportions, 123, 150

Difference between variances, 133, 152

Dot plot, 28, 33–34, 52

Dummy variable model, 252, 254, 274

Estimated effects, 182, 193, 198

Factorial design, 173, 184, 206–208

Fractional factorial design, 200, 208

Histogram, 27, 32–33, 51, 228

Individual value and moving range, 307, 316–317

Interaction plot, 166, 168, 175, 186, 195, 202, 205–206

Kruskal-Wallis test, 147, 154

Levene test, 143, 153

Logistic regression, 269, 275

Main effects plot, 165, 174, 185, 194, 201, 205

Mean and range control charts, 298, 314–315

Mean and standard deviation control charts, 303, 315–316

Multiple regression, 244, 273

Normal probabilities, 83, 84, 89

Normal probability plot, 86, 89–90, 176, 183, 193, 199

One-way ANOVA, 137, 152–153

Opening worksheets, 17

p-chart, 289, 312–313

Pareto diagram, 26, 32

Poisson distribution, 77, 88

Pooled-variance t test, 128, 150–151

Printing, 18

Projects, 16

Regression, 217, 237–238

Residual plot, 227, 248, 263

Run chart, 29, 34

Saving worksheets, 17

Scatter plot, 216–217, 237

Selecting a random sample, 19

Separate-variance t test, 131, 150–151

Stepwise regression, 260, 274

Tukey multiple comparisons, 140

Two-way ANOVA, 163, 205

u-chart, 295, 313–314

Wilcoxon rank sum test, 145, 154

Worksheets, 16

Zone limits, 312

Minitab dialog boxes

1 – Proportion (Options), 110

1 – Proportion (Test and Confidence Interval), 110

1 – Sample t (Options), 109

1 – Sample t (Test and Confidence Interval), 109

2 – Proportion (Options), 150

2 – Proportions (Test and Confidence Interval), 150

2 – Sample t (Test and Confidence Interval), 151

2 – Sample t–Graphs, 151

2 – Sample t–Options, 151

2 Variances, 152

3D Scatterplot–Simple, 274

Analyze factorial design, 207

Analyze factorial design–Graphs, 207

Analyze factorial design–Terms, 207, 208

Application window, 16

Bar charts, 31

Bar chart–Values from a table, 31

Best subsets, 275

Binary regression, 276

Binomial distribution, 88

Boxplots, 58

Boxplots–One Y, Simple, 58

C chart, 313

Creating a factorial design, 206

Data window print options, 19

Define custom factorial design, 206

Define custom factorial
    design–Low/High, 207

Descriptive statistics–Statistics, 57

Display descriptive statistics, 57

Dotplots, 34

Dotplot–One Y, Simple, 34

Edit bars, 32

Edit bars Binning tab, 33

Histograms, 33

Histogram–Simple, 33

Individuals–Moving Range, 317

Interaction plot, 206

Kruskal-Wallis, 154

Main effects plot, 205

Mann-Whitney, 154

Normal distribution, 89

One-Way Analysis of Variance, 152

One-Way Analysis of Variance–
    Graphs, 153

One-Way multiple comparisons, 153

Open worksheet, 17

P-chart, 312

Pareto chart, 32

Poisson distribution, 88

Probability plot–Distribution, 90

Probability plot–Single, 90

Regression, 238

Regression–Graphs, 238

Regression–Options, 238

Regression–Results, 238

Run chart, 34

Sample from columns, 19

Save worksheet, 18

Scatterplot–Simple, 237

Scatterplots, 237

Stepwise regression, 274

Stepwise–Methods, 275

Test for equal variances, 153

Two-way ANOVA, 205

U chart, 314

XBar-R chart, 315

XBar-R chart–Options, Estimate tab, 315

XBar-R chart–Options, Tests tab, 315

XBar-S chart, 316

Mode, 43

Model building in regression, 257–266

Model validation in regression, 266

Multiple comparisons, 138, 353

Multiple regression models, 242, 353

Mutually exclusive, 63, 354

N

Net regression coefficient, 243, 354

Nominal scale, 13

Nonprobability sample, 10, 354

Normal distribution, 78–79, 354

    Properties, 79

    Table, 333–334

Normal probability plot, 85–86, 354
Normality, 141
Null event, 62
Null hypothesis, 114, 354
Numerical variable, 354

O

Odds ratio, 266, 354
One-way analysis of variance, 134–143
Operational definition, 14, 354
Ordinal scale, 13
Outliers, 354
Overall F test, 246

P

p-chart, 285–290
p-value, 121, 354
Parameter, 354
Pareto diagram, 25–26, 354
Parsimony, 258
Point estimate, 99
Poisson distribution, 76–77, 355
    Characteristics, 78
    Properties, 76
Population, 8, 9, 355
Post hoc, 138
Power of a statistical test, 119, 355
Prediction interval, 232
Prediction interval estimate for a future
    individual value, 105, 355
Probability, 60, 62, 355
Probability distribution, 66–68, 355
Probability sample, 11, 355
Process owner, 3

Q

Quota sample, 10
Quartiles, 44–46

R

Randomness, 140
Range, 46–47, 355
Ratio scale, 13
Region of nonrejection, 117
Region of rejection, 117, 355
Regression coefficients, 214
Regression model prediction, 218
Relevant range, 218
Replicates, 159, 355
Residual analysis, 226–228, 247–248, 355
Resolution III designs, 189, 355
Resolution IV designs, 189, 355
Resolution V designs, 189, 355
Right skewed, 50
Robust test, 356
Run chart, 28–29

S

Sample, 8, 9, 356
Sampling distribution, 96, 356
    of the mean, 97–98
    of the proportion, 99
Sampling error, 100, 356
Scatter plot, 212, 356
Senior executive, 3
Shape, 50, 356
Simple linear regression, 212, 356

Simple random sample, 11, 356

Six Sigma, 2, 356

Skewed, 50, 356

Slope, 212, 356

Special causes of variation, 281, 356

Standard deviation, 47–49, 356

Standard deviation and mean control charts, 301–305

Standard deviation of a probability distribution, 69–70

Standard error of the estimate, 225, 356

Standard order, 171, 356

Standardized normal distribution, 83

Standardized normal units, 79

Statistics, 357

Stepwise regression, 259–261, 357

Stratified sample, 11, 357

Subjective approach to probability, 62

Summary table, 357

Summation notation, 41–42, 329–332

Sum of squares (SS), 47

    Among groups (SSA), 135, 357

    Due to factor A (SSA), 159, 357

    Due to factor B (SSB), 159, 357

    Due to the interaction of A and B ($SSAB$), 159, 357

    Error (SSE), 222–224, 357

    Regression (SSR), 222–223, 355

    Total (SST), 135, 159, 221–223, 357

    Within-groups (SSW), 135

Symmetrical, 50, 357

Systematic sample, 12, 357

T

t distribution, 358

t test for the slope, 229–230, 249

Tables

    Control chart factors, 346

    F-distribution, 338–345

    Normal distribution, 333–334

    t distribution, 335–337

Testing for the difference between the means of two independent groups

    Pooled-variance t test, 126–130

    Separate-variance t test, 131

Testing for the difference between two proportions, 122–126

Testing for the difference between two variances

    F test, 132–133

    Levene test, 134

Tests of statistical significance, 114

Test statistic, 117, 358

Third quartile, 44, 358

Treatment combinations, 168, 190

Treatment effects, 135

Tukey procedure, 138

Two factor ANOVA, 159–171

Type I error, 118, 358

Type II error, 118, 358

U

u-chart, 293–296

V

Variable, 13, 358

Variables control chart, 280

Variance, 47–49, 358

Variation, 46, 358

Variance inflationary factor (*VIF*), 255–256

W

Wald statistic, 272

Wilcoxon rank sum test, 143–145

Within-group variation, 135

Y

Y-intercept, 212, 358

Z

Z test for the difference between two
    proportions, 125

Zone boundaries, 283